RAND McNALLY

W9-CEO-731

2024 Easy to Read

Road Atlas

Contents

Travel Information

Celebrating 100 Years on the Open Road 2–6

Take a trip down memory lane with a nostalgic look back at 100 years of roadside culture, cars, and the highway system that shaped the open road with this 2024 Collector's Edition of the Rand McNally *Road Atlas*.

Mileage Chart 7

Driving distances between 77 North American cities.

Mileage and Driving Times Map inside back cover

Distances and driving times between over a hundred North American cities.

Maps

Map legend **inside front cover**

United States overview map **8–9**

U.S. states **10–109**

Canada overview map **110–111**

Canadian provinces **112–127**

Mexico overview map and Puerto Rico **160**

U.S. and Canadian cities **128–159**

Photo Credits: p. 2 (clockwise from top) ©Jupiter Images / Getty, ©pidjoe / Getty, ©Rand McNally, ©Stockbyte / Getty; p. 3 (from top) (l) ©Charles Phelps Cushing / Alamy, (r) ©Oliver Strewe / Image Bank / Getty, ©Kurt Hutton / Stringer / Getty, ©Rand McNally; p. 4 (t to b) ©tomekbudujedomek / Getty, ©miroslav_1 / istockphoto / Getty, ©Circa Images / Alamy; p. 5 (t to b) ©H. Armstrong Roberts / Alamy, ©Matthew Richardson / Alamy, ©Anjar Suwarno / Getty (2), ©Baxternator / Getty.

For licensing information and copyright permissions, contact us at permissions@randmcnally.com

If you have a comment, suggestion, or even a compliment, please visit us at randmcnally.com/tellrand.

RAND McNALLY PUBLISHING

State & Province Maps

United States

Alabama 10 - 11
Alaska 12 - 13
Arizona 14 - 15
Arkansas 16 - 17
California 18 - 21
Colorado 22 - 23
Connecticut 24 - 27
Delaware 28 - 29
Florida 30 - 31
Georgia 32 - 33
Hawaii 13
Idaho 34 - 35
Illinois 36 - 37
Indiana 38 - 39
Iowa 40 - 41
Kansas 42 - 43
Kentucky 44 - 47
Louisiana 48 - 49
Maine 50 - 51
Maryland 28 - 29
Massachusetts 24 - 27
Michigan 52 - 53
Minnesota 54 - 55
Mississippi 56 - 57
Missouri 58 - 59
Montana 60 - 61
Nebraska 62 - 63
Nevada 18 - 21
New Hampshire 64 - 65
New Jersey 66 - 67
New Mexico 68 - 69
New York 70 - 73
North Carolina 74 - 77
North Dakota 78 - 79
Ohio 80 - 83
Oklahoma 84 - 85
Oregon 86 - 87
Pennsylvania 88 - 91
Rhode Island 24 - 27
South Carolina 74 - 77
South Dakota 92 - 93
Tennessee 45 - 47
Texas 94 - 97
Utah 98 - 99
Vermont 64 - 65
Virginia 100 - 103
Washington 104 - 105
West Virginia 100 - 103
Wisconsin 106 - 107
Wyoming 108 - 109

Canada

Alberta 112 - 115
British Columbia 112 - 115
Manitoba 116 - 119
New Brunswick 126 - 127
Newfoundland and Labrador 126 - 127
Nova Scotia 126 - 127
Ontario 120 - 123
Prince Edward Island 126 - 127
Québec 124 - 125
Saskatchewan 116 - 119

City Maps

Albuquerque 129
Atlanta 128
Austin 130
Baltimore 129
Birmingham 129
Boston 130 - 131
Buffalo 132
Charlotte 130
Chicago 132 - 133
Cincinnati 134
Cleveland 137
Columbus 135
Dallas 134 & 136
Denver 135
Detroit 138 - 139
Fort Lauderdale 142 - 143
Fort Worth 134 & 136
Greensboro 138 - 139
Hartford 137
Houston 140
Indianapolis 139
Jacksonville 137
Kansas City 142 - 143
Las Vegas 143
Los Angeles 144 - 145
Louisville 139
Memphis 146
Mexico City 160
Miami 142 - 143
Milwaukee 146 - 147
Minneapolis 141
Nashville 144
New Orleans 146
New York 148 - 149
Newark 148 - 149
Norfolk 146 - 147
Orlando 153
Ottawa 111
Philadelphia 150 - 151
Phoenix 147
Pittsburgh 152 - 153
Portland 151
Raleigh 154
St. Louis 150 - 151
St. Paul 141
St. Petersburg 154 - 155
Sacramento 154 - 155
Salt Lake City 157
San Antonio 155
San Diego 154
San Francisco 156 - 157
Seattle 152 - 153
Tampa 154 - 155
Toronto 158
Vancouver 158
Washington D.C. 158 - 159
Winston-Salem 138 - 139

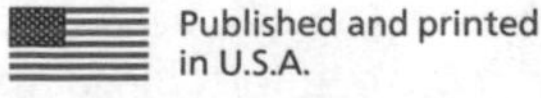

Published and printed in U.S.A.

3 WR 24 23

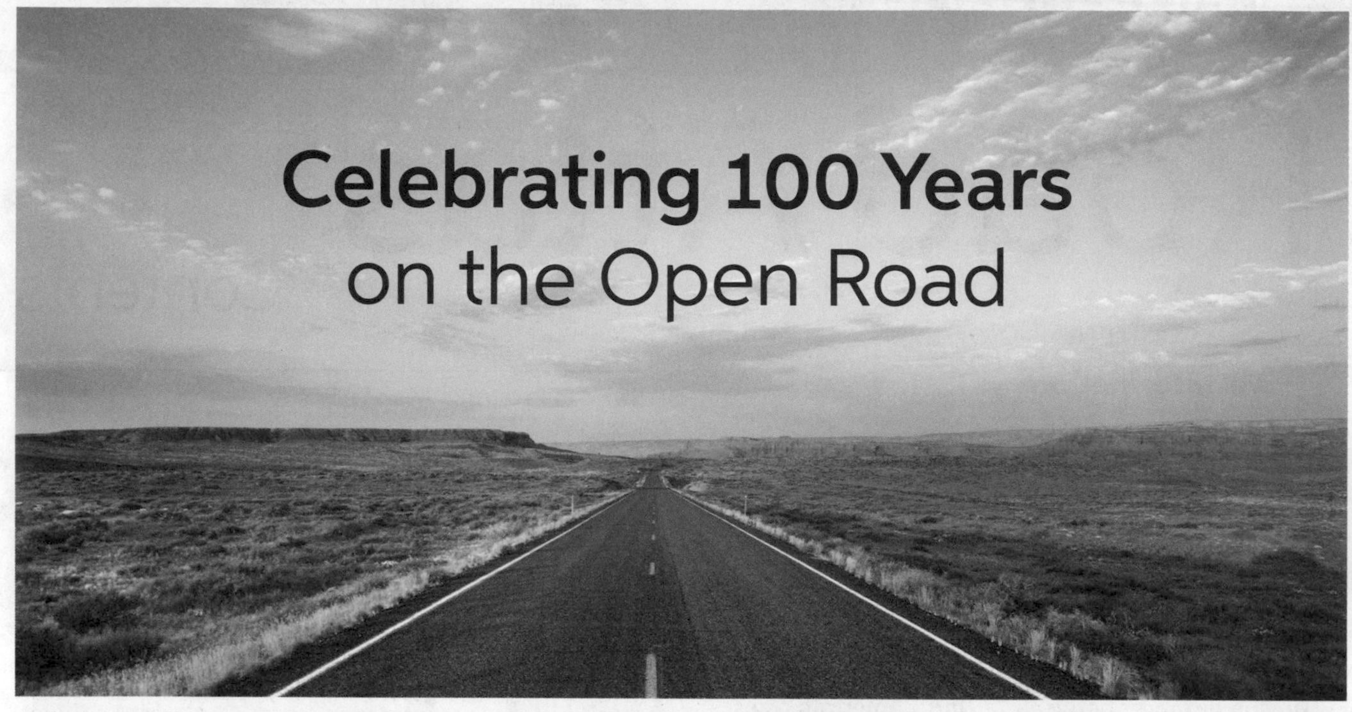

Celebrating 100 Years on the Open Road

Back in 1924, long-distance road trips required not only a true sense of adventure, but also lots of time (sometimes weeks, rather than days!), determination, and a packing list geared toward self-sufficiency.

Roadside amenities were rare; breakdowns and punctured tires were not. Travel was slow along a hodgepodge of routes—some marked, others not; some paved, others gravel or hard-packed dirt that was dusty in dry weather and muddy after rain. You might not encounter another person for days, and you were bound to get lost. Unless, of course, you had the Rand McNally *Auto Chum*.

The predecessor of Rand McNally's iconic atlas revolutionized road-travel navigation, and the company continues this tradition 100 years later. Although today's road trips are faster and more comfortable, a good one still requires a true sense of adventure—and a thoughtful packing list that includes a Rand McNally *Road Atlas*.

To help celebrate the atlas centennial, following are some highlights of the open road and Rand McNally through the decades.

1920s: Modernity for the Masses

From music to motion pictures to motor cars, the 1920s roared with excitement and adventure, all fueled by a booming economy. Vehicles became more drivable—and affordable—paving the way for new jobs in the oil fields, auto service shops, and roadside amenities.

The End is Just the Beginning. In May of 1927, Ford ceased production (begun in 1908) of the beloved Model T. The company's moving assembly line and other innovations enabled more than 15 million customers to afford the so-called Tin Lizzie and, essentially, launched the automotive and road-travel industries.

New Roads to Adventure. Many of the routes that were funded and developed during the previous decade's grassroots Good Roads Movement were well-established by the 1920s. Among them was the Lincoln Highway, America's first transcontinental route (from New York City to San Francisco) dedicated to auto travel.

It was the 1926 adoption of the U.S. Highway System that really made inroads, though, by setting uniform naming conventions and construction standards, with asphalt and cement becoming more common paving materials. Though some of the earlier auto routes became obsolete, others served as the basis for U.S. Highways. Portions of the Lincoln Highway, for instance, became U.S. Route 30.

RMC **MILE • MARKER**

May of 1927 was also when Charles Lindbergh successfully completed a solo, nonstop flight across the Atlantic Ocean, marking a first in aviation history. He used Rand McNally maps to navigate over land.

1930s Shell gas station at night.

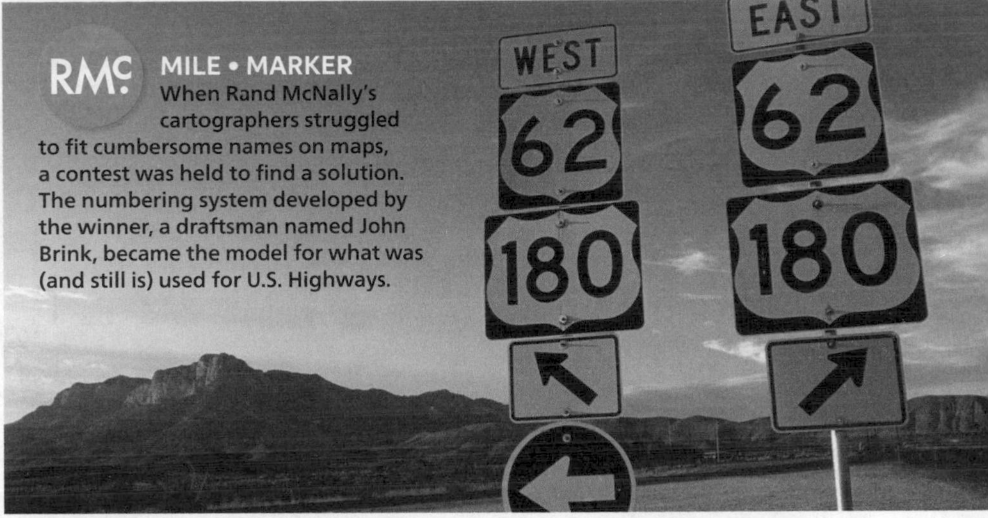

RMC MILE • MARKER When Rand McNally's cartographers struggled to fit cumbersome names on maps, a contest was held to find a solution. The numbering system developed by the winner, a draftsman named John Brink, became the model for what was (and still is) used for U.S. Highways.

Fueling Cars and Culture. Prior to 1905, when the first self-measuring gasoline-storage pump was invented, the chances to "fill 'er up" were few and far between. In the 1920s, though, rough-and-ready refuel and repair shops and curb-side pumps were being replaced by more-sophisticated filling stations. Some featured English Cottage, Tudor, Colonial, and other residential architectural styles. Others took the form of whimsical shapes, from teapots to windmills—the earliest examples of the loveable kitsch adopted by many roadside businesses.

1930s: Great Depression Recovery Efforts Pave the Way

American life went from boom to bust with the 1929 stock market crash. Building more roads became part of the federal Works Progress Administration (WPA) plan for boosting the economy during the Great Depression. By 1939, the country had nearly 1.4 million miles of paved roads—and more amenities catering to the needs of drivers.

Good Grub on the Go. In the 1920s, with iconic chains like KFC (1952) and McDonald's (1954) still decades in the future, finding a good roadside eatery was hard. That changed in 1929, when word first got out about Howard Johnson's—a down-home restaurant in Quincy, MA, that served 28 flavors of ice cream, hot dogs, chicken pot pies, baked beans, and soft drinks. In the 1930s, as its popularity grew, "HoJos" added locations and introduced its hallmark orange roofs with cupolas and weathervanes. By the 1960s and '70s, it was America's largest restaurant chain, with more than 1,000 company owned and franchised outlets.

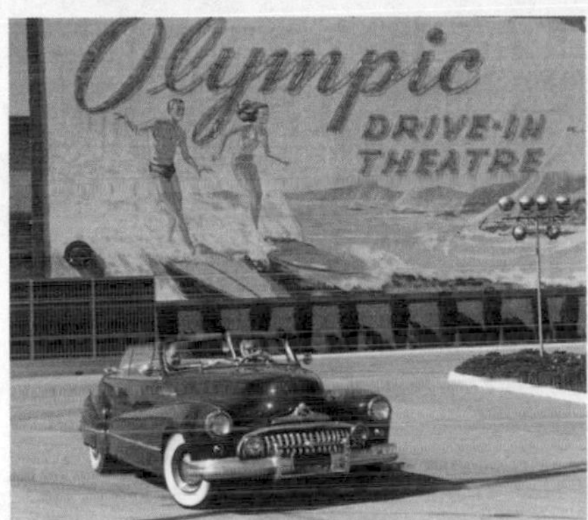

A Hollywood, CA, drive-in circa 1951.

Road Shows. In 1932, Richard Hollingshead, Jr. was awarded U.S. Patent 01909537, leading to the development of drive-in movie theaters. By 1958, America had an estimated 5,000 of them. Rising land values and changing tastes and technology have since reduced that number to about 300, including the oldest one in continuous operation: Shankweiler's (1934) in Orefield, PA.

RMC MILE • MARKER In 1937, the first Rand McNally Map & Travel Store opened in New York City. The chain would grow to 29 outlets. Within 24 hours of Germany's invasion of Poland in 1939, stores across the U.S. sold out of Rand McNally's Europe maps. Throughout WW II, company presses operated around the clock to keep up with demand for maps of the theaters of battle.

Airstream Blows In. Wally Byam had been designing and building camping trailers in his backyard and selling his plans to thousands of do-it-yourselfers, when, in 1931 his wife, Marion, insisted that he incorporate a working kitchen. Until then, he hadn't thought beyond his original teardrop-shape, two-tone-painted, Masonite camper.

Inspired by an airplane fuselage, Byam created the skinned, riveted-aluminum, aerodynamic Clipper—the original Airstream Trailer Company design. Early standard features included not only that storied kitchen but also a side door, pressurized water, a toilet, and holding tanks for water and waste. Airstreams were also the first fully contained trailers inside which an adult could stand fully upright.

1940s–1950s: War-Time Austerity, Post-War Prosperity

Within months of the December 7, 1941, attack on Pearl Harbor, road construction and automobile production all but stopped. During WW II, gasoline was rationed, and more people used public transit. The postwar years, however, saw an economic recovery, and the Greatest Generation began to hit the road with their Baby Boomers in tow. In addition, a prewar plan to connect American cities became a reality—so did the suburbs.

The Highway That's the Best. Built atop earlier auto trails, one of the first U.S. Highways, the beloved Route 66, was initially used by migrants fleeing the Dust Bowl for California during the Depression and by military trucks transporting troops and materiel during WW II.

Bob's Gasoline Alley on historic Route 66 in Missouri.

In postwar America, however, it was favored by vacationers, who followed it, as the famous song says, "from Chicago to LA / More than 2,000 miles all the way." It was soon lined with myriad roadside amenities, more and more of which adopted the colorful, kitschy twists—an unusual shape structure, a giant statue, a flashing sign—that we associate with the Golden Days of American road travel.

A Bad Trip Leads to Inn-Sight. By the 1930s, you could pull off the road into a mom-and-pop motor court and, for a few dollars, step into a cabin with electricity, plumbing, and (hopefully) a clean bed. Over time, amenities—maybe a filling station, a restaurant, and a store—were added.

In 1951, Memphis contractor Kemmons Wilson—irked by the hit-and-miss quality of motor courts during a family vacation to Washington, DC—sketched out a concept for a better hotel experience. Draftsman Eddie Bluestone cleaned up Wilson's sketches, and, having just watched the 1942 Bing Crosby film *Holiday Inn*, wrote the name on his plans. It stuck. Wilson then hired a theater-marquee company to create an illuminated sign. Done in green, gold, and red and shaped (roughly) like America, it caught the attention of drivers and the nation.

The first Holiday Inn's success led to three more—each a day's drive from the other. As it grew, the chain over-delivered with now-standard touches like free ice, vending machines, TVs, phones, pools, and a kids-stay-free policy. By 1958, Wilson had opened 50. That number reached 500 by 1964 and surpassed 1,000 by 1968.

Iconic Holiday Inn sign.

Paving the Nation. Just as the U.S. Highway System made earlier routes like the Lincoln Highway obsolete, so, too, did interstates make some highways, like Route 66, obsolete. The origin of what would become the Dwight D. Eisenhower National System of Interstate and Defense Highways, named for the president who spearheaded it, was the Federal Highway Act of 1956, which earmarked $30 billion for a comprehensive network of roads with 12-foot-wide lanes, 10-foot-wide paved right shoulders, 4-foot-wide paved left shoulders, and curves—all allowing for speeds of 50–70 mph.

"See the USA / in Your Chevrolet . . . ." It was 1952 when Dinah Shore first belted out her sponsor's zippy tune to end her weekly NBC variety show. Chevy continued its small-screen prominence when, in 1960, CBS launched the popular Friday night show, *Route 66*, featuring the adventures of two guys traveling in a Corvette convertible. The 116-episode series ran until 1964—doing a lot to promote road travel and Chevy!

Fast forward to 2005. The show? CW Network's cult-classic *Supernatural* (which ended in 2020). The travelers? Two brothers who traverse rural America battling supernatural forces along the way. What do they drive? A vintage (1967), black, Chevy Impala, of course.

MILE • MARKER
In some episodes of the TV series, *Supernatural*, the protagonists use Rand McNally maps! It's just one of many TV shows and movies in which the company's maps and atlases have cameos. Keep an eye out.

1960s–1970s: From Cheap Fuel and Big Cars to Gas Shortages and Economy Cars

By 1960, 61 million cars were registered in the U.S., and interstate construction was booming. Gas was 31 cents per gallon, and a luxury car cost about $2,600. Young people were buying new cars; more than 600,000 Ford Mustangs were sold in 1966 alone.

In the 1970s, OPEC's oil embargo led to gas shortages and price increases. Americans turned to smaller, more fuel-efficient Japanese cars. Throughout both decades, people also began to question the aesthetic and environmental effects of the "superhighway."

Greener and Cleaner. Toll ways and freeways built in the '50s and '60s meant cars could go faster than ever on bigger, straighter roads. However, interstates were also monotonous; separated drivers from their surroundings; and infamous for their smog, noise pollution, and roadside trash.

In 1965, First Lady "Ladybird" Johnson was instrumental in rallying support for the Highway Beautification Act. Five years later, the Federal-Aid Highway Act addressed environmental concerns, including noise and air quality. In 1974, an international oil embargo led to the need for fuel conservation. This, in turn, resulted in a new maximum national speed limit of 55 mph (where it stayed until 1995)—not to mention Sammy Hagar's hit song, "I Can't Drive 55."

MILE • MARKER
The company's first full-color *Road Atlas* premieres in 1960.

That's a Big 10-4, Good Buddy: In the 1970s, two-way CB (citizens band) radios became a popular (though not very private) way to keep in touch with others out on the road. The craze began with truckers, who shared information on gas stations with good supplies of fuel (not always a given during the oil crisis), alerted each other to speed traps, and organized convoys and blockades protesting things like the 55-mph national speed limit.

OPEC's oil embargo led to gas shortages during the 1970s.

Fuel's Gold

Gas prices always seem to be on rise, sometimes increasing between the time you head to work and the time you drive home! Was fuel always so expensive? Relatively speaking, yes.

Year	Estimated Average Cost per Gallon*	Cost Adjusted for Inflation
1920	0.30	$4.47
1930	0.20	$3.57
1940	0.18	$3.83
1950	0.27	$3.44
1960	0.31	$3.12
1970	0.36	$2.77
1980	$1.19	$4.30
1990	$1.15	$2.62
2000	$1.51	$2.61
2010	$2.79	$3.81
2020	$2.17	$2.50

*Source: the U.S. Department of Energy.

Songs like C.W. McCall's 1975 hit "Convoy" and movies such as 1977's *Smokey and the Bandit* introduced a mainstream audience to the life of the long-distance trucker. Noncommercial drivers began using CBs, adopting creative call signs, or "handles," and learning the equally creative lingo. Celebrities also got in on the act: First Lady Betty Ford's handle was "Big Mama." James Earl Jones reportedly signed on as "Darth" and Mel Blanc as "Daffy" or "Bugs," with both men using character voices to match their handles.

1980s–1990s: The Future Looks Brighter as Technology Blooms

In the 1980s, a stronger economy and renewed national pride made exploring the United States popular, and the introduction of minivans made road travel more comfortable. By the 1990s, most major interstates were complete, and 80% of U.S. travel was by car.

The decade also saw auto technology make giant strides, with things like airbags, onboard diagnostics, LED headlamps, and smart keys. The world wide web arrived, and telecommunications, Geographic Information Systems (GIS), and navigation technology accelerated.

Greetings From . . . . In the early days, most road trippers kept in touch with home using postcards, telegrams, or payphones. That began to change in 1983, when Motorola introduced the first of its commercially produced, hand-held mobile phones. Before complaining about any aspect of today's smartphones, consider this: the DynaTAC 8000X, nicknamed "the brick," weighed just under 2 pounds, was 13 inches long, took about 10 hours to fully charge, and allowed roughly 30 minutes of talk time—for a cost of 24 cents (off peak) or 40 cents (peak) per minute.

Such rates were comparable to those for long-distance land-line calls, but the DynaTAC 8000X also came with a price tag befitting the ostentatious 1980s: around $4,000. At that time, it cost 10 cents to make a local payphone call and 13 cents to mail a postcard.

Although clunky versions of the car phone had been available to an elite few since the 1940s, in the late 1980s, they became sleeker and more reliable. Again, Motorola led the way, but, by 1987 (when postcard postage had risen to 15 cents), you could also pick one up at Radio Shack for about $1,400.

Classic Car Colors

Thanks to traditional sensibilities (holdovers from the days of carriages and stage coaches) and practicality (oh, those muddy roads), most early automobiles came in black or very dark colors, like burgundy or hunter green. The palette became increasingly varied after WW II. Here's a rundown on the most popular colors from the 1950s onward.

1950s

Blue (with chrome trim) is popular, as are two-tone schemes, with one part of the body painted a dark color, and the roof or other areas painted a lighter color, usually white.

1960s

Blue and green are tied, though some sports cars stand out in red. Bright yellow and violet also debut.

1970s

Brown, beige, and cream rise to the top as increasingly environmentally aware Americans begin a love affair with earth tones. Olive green also makes the scene, as does that classic VW chartreuse.

1980s

Black and red lead this slick decade, though blue continues as a favorite, too.

1990s

The color of choice is green in all hues. Aqua adds still more depth to the palette.

The New Millennium

Silver earned the top spot in the first decade, when high-tech went into overdrive. It has since been overtaken by white with gray, black, and blue toward the top of the list as well. Thanks to the environmental-movement reboot, though, earth tones like burnt orange and olive green are on the uptick.

1958 Pontiac Laurentian Safari Wagon

Motorola leads the mobile-phone way—first with a "brick" and then with a "flip."

Before there were minivans, families piled into station wagons. Above: Chevrolet's Caprice faux "woodie."

Nine years later, telecom advancements (and the arrival of cellular-service plans) enabled Motorola to release its revolutionary, wallet-size, 3-ounce, hand-held StarTAC "clamshell" or "flip" phone. It cost about $1,000, and roughly 60 million were sold. By then, it cost 20 cents to mail a postcard and 25 cents to make a local payphone call. But who needed either when sending greetings from the road was easier than ever?

From the Station Wagon to the SUV: Until the 1980s, the station wagon was the darling of family travel. As early as 1909, innovative car jockeys had modified Henry Ford's Model T, giving it a larger body, often using wood, to accommodate more people or cargo. These vehicles, popular for transporting passengers to and from railroad stations, were dubbed "depot hacks," "woodies" and, of course, "station wagons." Car manufacturers took note, including Ford (Model A, 1929); Chevrolet (Suburban, 1935); and Chrysler (Town and Country, 1941).

After WW II, wagons hit the road in a big way. Though Ford's Country Squires, known for their faux-wood steel-panel siding, were popular, all the major manufacturers had models that made trips to the grocery store, Sunday drives, and camping getaways easy thanks to colossal rear cargo areas. Anything that didn't fit in the back was simply tied to the roof rack.

Volkswagen's 1950 Microbus and Chevy's 1961 Corvan (part Corvair, part cargo van) were early forerunners of the family minivan, though the first such vehicles as we know them (sliding side doors, higher seats and more of them) didn't roll off assembly lines till 1983. Soccer moms everywhere took note; Chrysler alone sold more than 12 million minivans. By the 1990s, the minivan was on its way out, and the smaller but more fuel-efficient and agile sport utility vehicle (SUV) was on its way in, led by models from Jeep, Ford, and Chevrolet.

The New Millennium: Technology Booms and Road Travel Zooms

Technological advances continue to drive the auto industry. Smartphones, in-car Wi-Fi and Bluetooth technology, and electric and hybrid vehicles have given road travelers more options to navigate, stay connected, and save on fuel costs (while helping to save the planet).

The country has also turned its attention back to a few road-travel basics. The 2021 Bipartisan Infrastructure Law has allocated billions of dollars to upgrades and improvements, including much-needed road and bridge repairs and the installation of electric-vehicle charging stations across the nation. The timing is perfect: because of the COVID-19 pandemic, more Americans have discovered the joys of road trips.

Road Travel Renaissance. After months of lockdown, Americans found that road trips were the best way to break free while maintaining social distance. Bookings on RVshare, a leading rental marketplace, rose by 650% in 2020, and the Recreational Vehicle Industry Association reported that 2021 manufacturer shipments of RVs for sale increased by 40%. National Park visitation also skyrocketed, with several parks setting or breaking annual records.

The demographics have shifted, too. Prior to the pandemic, lack of time prevented Gen Xers and Millennials from taking road trips. Remote work, however, has enabled them to join their retiree counterparts out on the open road—often more than once a year for journeys that last longer and go farther than was previously possible. The road travel Renaissance continues.

Because of the pandemic, RV sales and rentals skyrocketed, as did national park visitation. Above, Arches National Park, UT.

RMC **MILE • MARKER** **Sure, GPS is nice, but what if you lose your signal? Or you want more geographic context than what's shown on a small screen? Or you're feeling nostalgic and want your kids to learn about maps and atlases? You wouldn't be alone. Throughout the pandemic, the 2021 and 2022 editions of the Rand McNally *Large Scale Road Atlas* were on the *Publisher's Weekly* Top 25 List, reaching #9 in August of 2021. After 100 years and more than 200 million copies sold, the Rand McNally *Road Atlas* is still going strong!**

Mileage Chart

This handy chart offers more than 2,400 mileages covering 77 North American cities. Want more mileages? Visit **randmcnally.com/MC** and type in any two cities or addresses.

	Albuquerque, NM	Atlanta, GA	Billings, MT	Boston, MA	Charlotte, NC	Chicago, IL	Cincinnati, OH	Dallas, TX	Denver, CO	Detroit, MI	Houston, TX	Indianapolis, IN	Kansas City, MO	Los Angeles, CA	Memphis, TN	Miami, FL	Milwaukee, WI	Minneapolis, MN	New Orleans, LA	New York, NY	Omaha, NE	Orlando, FL	Philadelphia, PA	Phoenix, AZ	Pittsburgh, PA	Portland, OR	St. Louis, MO	Salt Lake City, UT	San Francisco, CA	Seattle, WA	Washington, DC	Wichita, KS
Albuquerque, NM		1386	998	2219	1626	1333	1387	647	446	1570	884	1279	784	786	1008	1952	1354	1225	1165	2001	863	1730	1924	425	1641	1363	1037	599	1086	1438	1885	591
Amarillo, TX	288	1102	965	1935	1342	1049	1103	363	424	1286	589	995	570	1072	720	1668	1132	1009	881	1716	647	1446	1640	746	1357	1669	752	883	1370	1743	1600	418
Atlanta, GA	1386		1831	1095	244	715	461	780	1404	722	794	533	800	2174	379	661	809	1127	468	882	992	440	780	1844	684	2603	555	1878	2472	2649	637	955
Atlantic City, NJ	1985	831	2072	338	590	818	632	1518	1792	644	1598	703	1187	2774	1063	1248	910	1232	1273	126	1272	1038	60	2447	365	2922	948	2201	2934	2889	188	1379
Austin, TX	705	920	1495	1959	1164	1121	1128	196	950	1358	163	1067	702	1381	643	1341	1204	1136	503	1737	839	1124	1658	1010	1411	2068	825	1304	1760	2143	1524	542
Baltimore, MD	1887	683	1953	400	442	699	513	1368	1673	524	1448	584	1068	2670	914	1082	792	1112	1124	192	1153	889	97	2349	246	2804	829	2081	2816	2771	39	1260
Billings, MT	998	1831		2236	1990	1246	1546	1425	551	1535	1652	1435	1026	1240	1477	2497	1173	838	1868	2041	845	2275	2011	1210	1713	891	1278	552	1173	818	1951	1064
Birmingham, AL	1241	146	1780	1177	390	660	466	636	1329	724	668	478	749	2030	233	746	754	1072	343	960	939	534	880	1700	748	2551	502	1826	2327	2598	745	810
Boise, ID	938	2177	621	2660	2336	1693	1943	1702	830	1960	1930	1835	1372	842	1825	2844	1732	1461	2216	2465	1225	2622	2435	914	2137	431	1622	340	639	503	2375	1338
Boston, MA	2219	1095	2236		841	983	870	1764	1970	724	1844	937	1421	2983	1312	1482	1074	1396	1520	216	1436	1288	306	2681	570	3086	1182	2365	3098	3054	439	1613
Branson, MO	864	652	1241	1433	868	545	601	435	806	784	602	493	209	1651	274	1284	630	643	597	1201	402	1062	1138	1326	851	2013	249	1288	1950	2060	1081	292
Calgary, AB	1542	2357	541	2615	2400	1627	1925	1967	1096	1916	2209	1814	1567	1557	2028	3018	1555	1221	2419	2439	1387	2797	2391	1524	2093	787	1820	869	1500	678	2334	1606
Charleston, SC	1703	319	2133	970	209	908	620	1099	1706	826	1105	726	1103	2491	696	583	1002	1324	742	768	1294	380	668	2165	654	2904	857	2180	2789	2951	532	1272
Charlotte, NC	1626	244	1990	841		769	477	1023	1566	616	1038	583	961	2414	619	728	867	1180	712	641	1151	526	539	2088	446	2761	714	2037	2712	2808	398	1092
Chicago, IL	1333	715	1246	983	769		289	926	1002	282	1085	181	526	2015	531	1381	90	408	923	787	470	1153	757	1795	459	2118	295	1398	2130	2063	697	724
Cincinnati, OH	1387	461	1546	870	477	289		934	1187	259	1055	109	584	2172	482	1127	381	703	804	637	722	905	571	1849	288	2369	348	1647	2380	2363	512	779
Cleveland, OH	1598	714	1597	638	514	344	248	1194	1330	169	1315	315	799	2342	729	1240	434	756	1057	460	797	1043	428	2060	134	2446	560	1725	2458	2414	370	992
Columbus, OH	1457	567	1606	763	426	354	107	1039	1261	212	1174	189	657	2244	587	1164	445	766	910	533	792	954	468	1920	174	2439	421	1718	2451	2425	411	851
Corpus Christi, TX	855	1001	1622	2051	1244	1338	1262	410	1077	1542	207	1228	919	1494	782	1394	1421	1353	554	1844	1056	1172	1754	1122	1561	2218	1042	1454	1873	2292	1619	758
Dallas, TX	647	780	1425	1764	1023	926	934		880	1163	239	873	489	1437	453	1307	1010	928	519	1548	656	1086	1467	1066	1221	2128	630	1403	1734	2193	1332	361
Denver, CO	446	1404	551	1970	1566	1002	1187	880		1270	1035	1083	603	1015	1097	2069	1042	913	1398	1775	534	1851	1732	908	1447	1256	854	533	1268	1320	1671	519
Des Moines, IA	983	902	946	1299	1057	335	580	683	670	599	938	474	194	1682	617	1567	375	244	1008	1105	135	1339	1074	1445	777	1786	350	1065	1798	1764	1015	391
Detroit, MI	1570	722	1535	724	616	282	259	1163	1270		1319	277	764	2281	742	1354	374	696	1066	613	736	1144	583	2032	285	2385	533	1664	2397	2353	522	964
Duluth, MN	1375	1187	860	1370	1239	466	760	1092	1063	754	1331	651	586	2076	963	1852	394	152	1354	1264	530	1632	1230	1838	932	1749	679	1458	2033	1677	1171	785
Edmonton, AB	1724	2391	722	2549	2443	1670	1968	2149	1278	1958	2391	1857	1626	1755	2147	3058	1598	1264	2538	2482	1445	2836	2434	1721	2136	966	1878	1069	1695	793	2377	1787
El Paso, TX	266	1418	1257	2373	1662	1455	1569	635	707	1702	744	1398	929	796	1089	1934	1497	1377	1095	2202	1004	1712	2102	424	1774	1630	1157	866	1175	1705	1967	730
Fargo, ND	1318	1361	607	1629	1414	641	937	1079	873	930	1321	825	600	1848	1054	2025	569	234	1445	1438	420	1807	1405	1780	1107	1497	841	1160	1781	1424	1348	685
Gatlinburg, TN	1439	196	1803	922	202	578	290	884	1376	552	964	396	773	2226	431	865	677	994	640	707	964	640	625	1901	493	2574	527	1850	2525	2621	490	905
Guadalajara, JA	1194	1739	2194	2789	1982	1954	1962	1028	1639	2191	948	1901	1535	1501	1482	2131	2037	1969	1292	2592	1672	1910	2492	1212	2261	2545	1658	1792	1963	2631	2356	1377
Gulfport, MS	1221	399	1912	1482	643	896	767	562	1386	1025	403	780	883	1949	365	792	988	1196	78	1266	1073	572	1180	1577	1052	2633	647	1909	2307	2730	1036	867
Houston, TX	884	794	1652	1844	1038	1085	1055	239	1035	1319		1021	732	1550	575	1186	1163	1171	348	1632	898	965	1547	1178	1354	2356	784	1634	1929	2431	1411	595
Indianapolis, IN	1279	533	1435	937	583	181	109	873	1083	277	1021		482	2068	464	1198	272	591	818	707	613	968	643	1742	359	2260	243	1541	2273	2253	582	674
Jacksonville, FL	1636	346	2183	1146	379	1068	796	992	1756	1002	871	874	1152	2421	677	349	1163	1474	547	939	1344	141	844	2050	825	2954	907	2230	2723	3001	706	1272
Kansas City, MO	784	800	1026	1421	961	526	584	489	603	764	732	482		1616	451	1466	565	436	844	1196	184	1246	1127	1246	840	1797	248	1073	1808	1844	1066	198
Key West, FL	2099	809	2646	1659	886	1534	1275	1455	2222	1515	1334	1348	1617	2884	1159	160	1632	1944	1010	1446	1807	387	1357	2514	1332	3417	1370	2693	3186	3464	1213	1735
Las Vegas, NV	572	1959	973	2714	2199	1746	1932	1220	747	2013	1457	1828	1349	270	1581	2525	1786	1656	1739	2518	1278	2303	2480	285	2190	1023	1600	419	569	1128	2428	1164
Lexington, KY	1371	369	1610	917	400	370	83	076	1106	344	996	184	581	2158	423	1030	464	782	745	701	771	817	638	1833	370	2381	334	1657	2392	2428	533	773
Little Rock, AR	877	515	1407	1447	754	650	617	319	965	885	439	583	381	1666	136	1147	724	815	425	1230	574	925	1150	1340	905	2211	345	1488	1963	2275	1015	446
Los Angeles, CA	786	2174	1240	2983	2414	2015	2172	1437	1015	2281	1550	2068	1616		1794	2735	2055	1925	1894	2787	1546	2515	2713	370	2428	963	1821	688	380	1134	2670	1377
Memphis, TN	1008	379	1477	1312	619	531	482	453	1097	742	575	464	451	1794		1012	622	831	394	1094	641	778	1014	1471	768	2245	283	1524	2095	2299	079	577
Mexico City, DF	1404	1718	2301	2768	1962	2017	1979	1090	1756	2254	924	1963	1598	1839	1500	2111	2100	2032	1272	2571	1735	1889	2471	1469	2279	2768	1721	2003	2218	2842	2336	1440
Miami, FL	1952	661	2497	1482	728	1381	1127	1307	2069	1354	1186	1198	1466	2735	1012		1475	1791	861	1288	1658	235	1180	2362	1173	3260	1221	2544	3038	3315	1044	1587
Milwaukee, WI	1354	809	1173	1074	867	90	381	1010	1042	374	1163	272	565	2055	622	1475		337	1015	879	509	1258	849	1817	551	2062	379	1437	2170	1990	788	763
Minneapolis, MN	1225	1127	838	1396	1180	408	703	928	913	696	1171	591	436	1925	831	1791	337		1223	1204	372	1573	1171	1687	874	1727	563	1308	2040	1655	1110	634
Mobile, AL	1234	328	1874	1427	571	917	721	589	1414	978	468	733	850	2014	382	719	1011	1224	144	1202	1038	497	1101	1643	1000	2661	645	1936	2320	2727	965	894
Montréal, QC	2129	1218	2099	310	980	847	824	1722	1832	560	1884	847	1330	2845	1314	1647	938	1262	1640	382	1302	1437	454	2591	603	2948	1092	2228	2960	2916	587	1529
Nashville, TN	1219	248	1586	1099	408	469	273	664	1158	534	786	287	555	2006	209	913	564	881	532	884	747	692	802	1682	560	2357	307	1633	2306	2404	667	688
New Orleans, LA	1165	468	1868	1520	712	923	804	519	1398	1066	348	818	844	1894	394	861	1015	1223		1304	1032	641	1222	1523	1090	2642	675	1920	2252	2716	1087	880
New York, NY	2001	882	2041	216	641	787	637	1548	1775	613	1632	707	1196	2787	1094	1288	879	1204	1304		1245	1089	95	2463	369	2891	954	2170	2902	2858	228	1391
Norfolk, VA	1910	558	2132	569	328	878	605	1350	1758	704	1362	720	1155	2707	898	950	969	1295	1026	370	1335	755	271	2373	425	2962	911	2238	2973	2949	193	1349
Oklahoma City, OK	542	844	1203	1678	1084	792	846	206	631	1029	437	739	348	1326	466	1476	876	788	722	1460	452	1254	1384	1005	1101	1922	496	1200	1627	1948	1344	160
Omaha, NE	863	992	845	1436	1151	470	722	656	534	736	898	613	184	1546	641	1658	509	372	1032	1245		1436	1212	1325	914	1650	439	930	1662	1663	1151	298
Orlando, FL	1730	440	2275	1288	526	1153	905	1086	1851	1144	965	968	1246	2515	778	235	1258	1573	641	1089	1436		986	2145	975	3048	999	2323	2816	3093	849	1365
Ottawa, ON	2039	1158	1768	428	920	760	732	1632	1748	471	1804	757	1240	2763	1230	1618	859	1032	1582	440	1213	1408	447	2501	546	2660	1002	2142	2877	2586	566	1439
Philadelphia, PA	1924	780	2011	306	539	757	571	1467	1732	583	1547	643	1127	2713	1014	1180	849	1171	1222	95	1212	986		2387	305	2861	888	2140	2873	2828	137	1319
Phoenix, AZ	425	1844	1210	2681	2088	1795	1849	1066	908	2032	1178	1742	1246	373	1471	2362	1817	1687	1523	2463	1325	2145	2387		2104	1332	1499	653	749	1414	2348	1053
Pittsburgh, PA	1641	684	1713	570	446	459	288	1221	1447	285	1354	359	840	2428	768	1173	551	874	1090	369	914	975	305	2104		2563	604	1842	2574	2530	243	1035
Portland, ME	2315	1192	2333	107	938	1079	967	1861	2067	825	1940	1034	1518	3082	1408	1585	1176	1492	1616	304	1533	1385	402	2778	666	3186	1279	2461	3196	3151	535	1710
Portland, OR	1363	2603	891	3086	2761	2118	2369	2128	1256	2385	2356	2260	1797	963	2245	3260	2062	1727	2642	2891	1650	3048	2861	1332	2563		2050	765	635	174	2800	1764
Rapid City, SD	843	1508	323	1900	1670	912	1208	1061	397	1200	1291	1100	704	1312	1160	2173	840	575	1551	1708	525	1956	1675	1305	1378	1215	959	649	1384	1142	1618	699
Reno, NV	1019	2396	958	2881	2555	1913	2163	1668	1051	2180	1904	2056	1591	470	2029	3063	1953	1818	2186	2685	1445	2841	2656	733	2357	578	1844	518	218	720	2595	1558
Richmond, VA	1832	532	2051	547	293	797	512	1278	1671	622	1329	627	1069	2620	824	944	888	1210	1002	334	1259	742	245	2294	344	2869	822	2145	2880	2868	108	1261
St. Louis, MO	1037	555	1278	1182	714	295	348	630	854	533	784	243	248	1821	284	1221	379	563	675	954	439	999	888	1499	604	2050		1326	2061	2096	827	442
Salt Lake City, UT	599	1878	552	2365	2037	1398	1647	1403	533	1664	1634	1541	1073	688	1524	2544	1437	1308	1920	2170	930	2323	2140	653	1842	765	1326		735	839	2079	1042
San Antonio, TX	712	986	1480	2039	1230	1202	1210	276	935	1439	195	1149	766	1357	727	1379	1285	1205	541	1822	920	1160	1742	985	1495	2076	906	1311	1736	2150	1607	625
San Diego, CA	810	2138	1302	3046	2381	2080	2196	1359	1077	2346	1472	2089	1597	120	1819	2656	2118	1986	1816	2809	1613	2436	2738	355	2452	1083	1845	750	501	1256	2693	1401
San Francisco, CA	1086	2472	1173	3098	2712	2130	2380	1734	1268	2397	1929	2273	1808	382	2095	3038	2170	2040	2252	2902	1662	2816	2873	749	2574	635	2061	735		807	2812	1775
Santa Fe, NM	58	1379	943	2212	1618	1313	1379	640	391	1562	877	1272	766	846	998	1944	1336	1207	1158	1994	891	1723	1917	520	1634	1388	1029	625	1144	1463	1879	572
Sault Ste. Marie, ON	1777	1040	1273	923	947	483	577	1370	1428	348	1527	540	951	2465	972	1685	400	545	1355	921	850	1475	911	2240	614	2166	740	1848	2581	2090	854	1150
Seattle, WA	1438	2649	818	3054	2808	2063	2363	2193	1320	2353	2431	2253	1844	1134	2299	3315	1990	1655	2716	2858	1663	3093	2828	1414	2530	174	2096	839	807		2768	1828
Spokane, WA	1320	2369	541	2774	2528	1785	2084	1964	1091	2075	2192	1973	1564	1216	2018	3035	1712	1377	2409	2580	1383	2814	2550	1381	2252	352	1817	720	874	279	2490	1600
Tampa, FL	1746	451	2293	1342	578	1166	916	1102	1860	1178	980	984	1252	2525	779	280	1260	1578	651	1138	1445	85	1040	2153	1023	3064	1008	2340	2832	3111	904	1381
Toronto, ON	1800	963	1771	548	756	519	493	1393	1504	231	1551	518	1001	2517	983	1483	609	933	1306	489	974	1284	497	2262	316	2620	763	1899	2632	2588	486	1188
Tulsa, OK	645	782	1234	1576	1022	687	738	258	692	927	487	635	263	1433	402	1414	773	704	671	1350	380	1192	1282	1107	994	1938	392	1215	1731	2012	1234	175
Vancouver, BC	1575	2785	953	3188	2944	2198	2499	2338	1465	2487	2565	2389	1980	1275	2437	3451	2125	1790	2851	2993	1799	3229	2963	1550	2665	313	2232	973	947	141	2903	1973
Washington, DC	1885	637	1951	439	398	697	512	1332	1671	522	1411	582	1066	2670	879	1044	788	1110	1087	228	1151	849	137	2348	244	2800	827	2079	2812	2768		1258
Wichita, KS	591	955	1064	1613	1092	724	779	361	519	964	595	674	198	1377	577	1587	763	634	880	1391	298	1365	1319	1053	1035	1764	442	1042	1775	1828	1258	

Mileages in this chart are based upon the routes usually followed by motorists. Highway systems include interstate, U.S., and state highways.

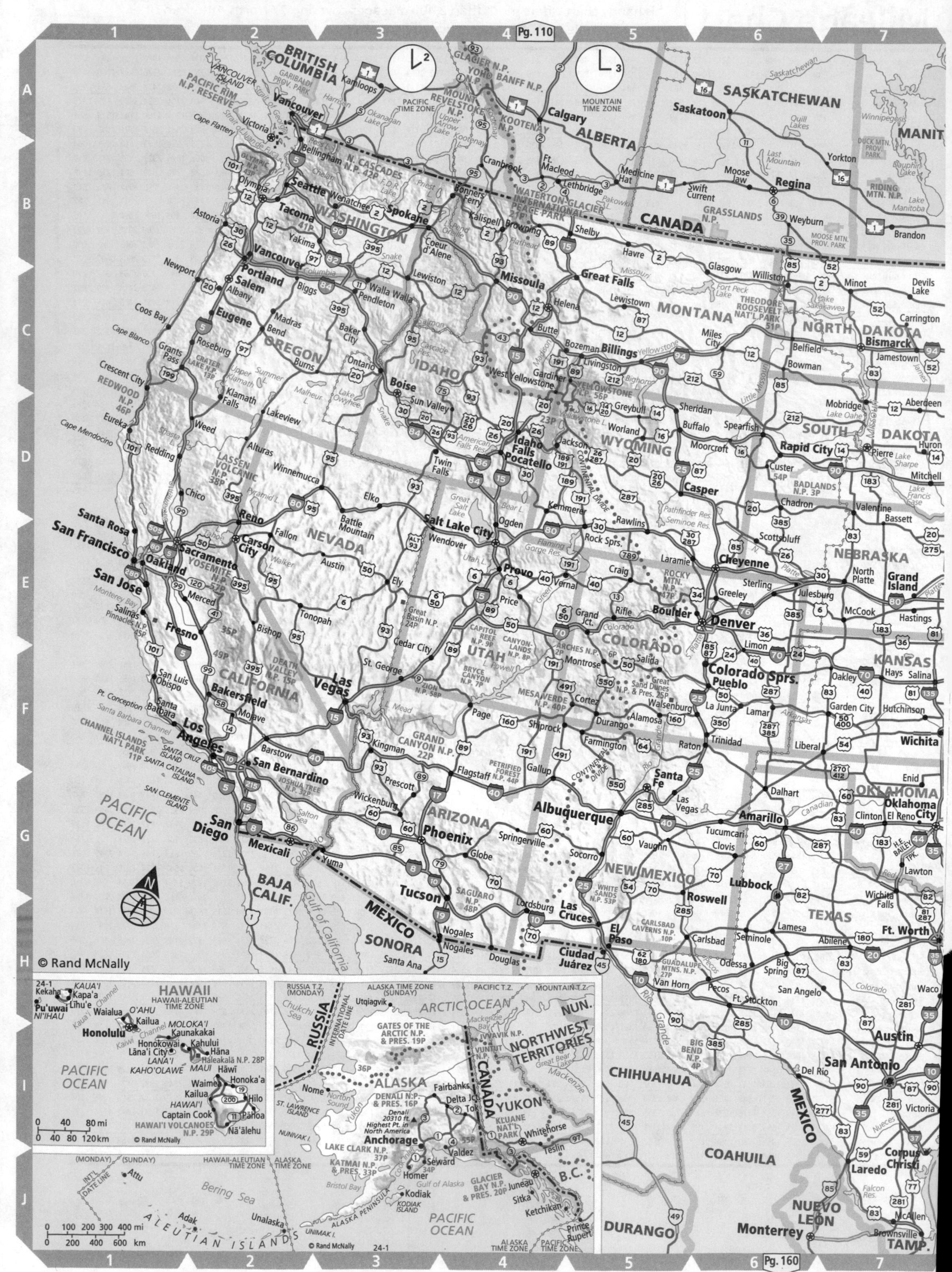

Pg. 110
Pg. 160
© Rand McNally
PACIFIC TIME ZONE
MOUNTAIN TIME ZONE
BRITISH COLUMBIA
ALBERTA
SASKATCHEWAN
CANADA
WASHINGTON
OREGON
IDAHO
MONTANA
WYOMING
NORTH DAKOTA
SOUTH DAKOTA
NEBRASKA
KANSAS
OKLAHOMA
TEXAS
NEW MEXICO
COLORADO
UTAH
NEVADA
CALIFORNIA
ARIZONA
MEXICO
BAJA CALIF.
SONORA
CHIHUAHUA
COAHUILA
DURANGO
NUEVO LEON
TAMP.
PACIFIC OCEAN
Gulf of California
Vancouver
Victoria
Kamloops
Calgary
Saskatoon
Regina
Brandon
Seattle
Tacoma
Olympia
Spokane
Portland
Salem
Eugene
Boise
Missoula
Great Falls
Helena
Billings
Bismarck
Pierre
Rapid City
Casper
Cheyenne
Denver
Boulder
Colorado Sprs.
Pueblo
Salt Lake City
Provo
Reno
Carson City
Sacramento
San Francisco
Oakland
San Jose
Fresno
Bakersfield
Los Angeles
San Bernardino
San Diego
Las Vegas
Phoenix
Tucson
Flagstaff
Albuquerque
Santa Fe
El Paso
Ciudad Juárez
Amarillo
Lubbock
Wichita
Oklahoma City
Ft. Worth
Austin
San Antonio
Laredo
Corpus Christi
Monterrey
HAWAII
HAWAII-ALEUTIAN TIME ZONE
Honolulu
Hilo
ALASKA
Anchorage
Fairbanks
Juneau
Nome
YUKON
NORTHWEST TERRITORIES
RUSSIA
ARCTIC OCEAN
Bering Sea
ALEUTIAN ISLANDS

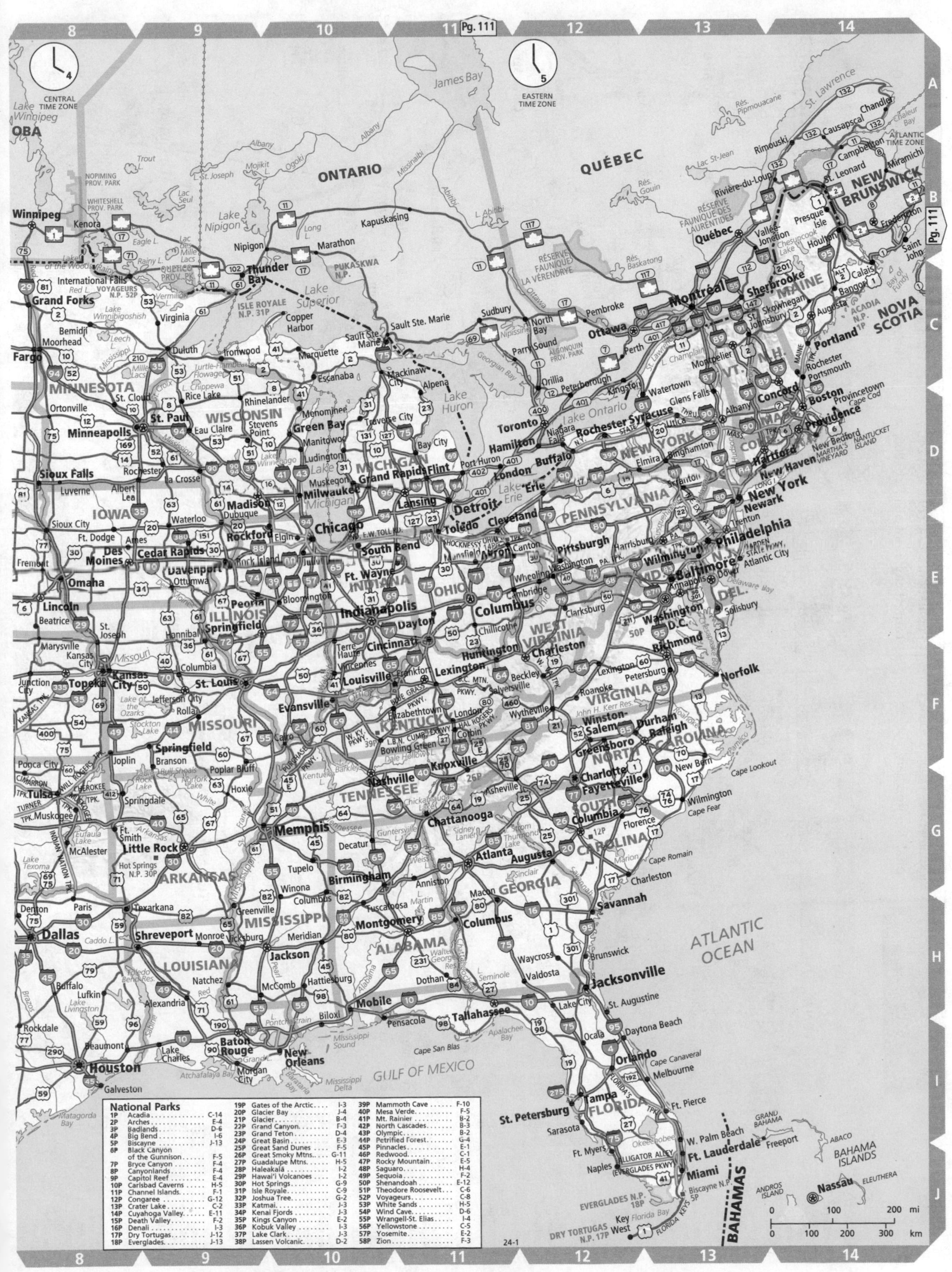

National Parks

1P	Acadia	C-14
2P	Arches	E-4
3P	Badlands	D-6
4P	Big Bend	I-6
5P	Biscayne	J-13
6P	Black Canyon of the Gunnison	F-5
7P	Bryce Canyon	F-4
8P	Canyonlands	F-4
9P	Capitol Reef	E-4
10P	Carlsbad Caverns	H-5
11P	Channel Islands	F-1
12P	Congaree	G-12
13P	Crater Lake	C-2
14P	Cuyahoga Valley	E-11
15P	Death Valley	F-2
16P	Denali	I-3
17P	Dry Tortugas	J-12
18P	Everglades	J-13
19P	Gates of the Arctic	I-3
20P	Glacier Bay	J-4
21P	Glacier	B-4
22P	Grand Canyon	F-3
23P	Grand Teton	D-4
24P	Great Basin	E-3
25P	Great Sand Dunes	F-5
26P	Great Smoky Mtns.	G-11
27P	Guadalupe Mtns.	H-5
28P	Haleakalā	I-2
29P	Hawai'i Volcanoes	I-2
30P	Hot Springs	G-9
31P	Isle Royale	C-9
32P	Joshua Tree	G-2
33P	Katmai	J-3
34P	Kenai Fjords	J-3
35P	Kings Canyon	E-2
36P	Kobuk Valley	I-3
37P	Lake Clark	J-3
38P	Lassen Volcanic	D-2
39P	Mammoth Cave	F-10
40P	Mesa Verde	F-5
41P	Mt. Rainier	B-2
42P	North Cascades	B-3
43P	Olympic	B-2
44P	Petrified Forest	G-4
45P	Pinnacles	E-1
46P	Redwood	C-1
47P	Rocky Mountain	E-5
48P	Saguaro	H-4
49P	Sequoia	F-2
50P	Shenandoah	E-12
51P	Theodore Roosevelt	C-6
52P	Voyageurs	C-8
53P	White Sands	H-5
54P	Wind Cave	D-6
55P	Wrangell-St. Elias	I-4
56P	Yellowstone	C-5
57P	Yosemite	E-2
58P	Zion	F-3

Alabama state facts

Nickname: The Heart of Dixie
Capital: Montgomery, F-4

Population: 5,024,279 (rank: 24th)
Largest city: Huntsville, 215,006, A-4

Land area: 50,633 sq. mi. (rank: 28th)
Highest point: Cheaha Mountain, 2,407 ft., D-5

Pg. 45
Pg. 56
Pg. 32

Alabama

Cities and Towns

Abbeville H-6
Alabaster D-3
Albertville B-4
Alexander City E-5
Aliceville E-1
Andalusia H-4
Anniston C-5
Arab B-4
Ashland D-5
Ashville C-4
Athens A-3
Atmore I-2
Attalla C-4
Auburn F-5
Bay Minette I-2
Bessemer D-3
Birmingham D-3
Boaz B-4
Brent E-3
Brewton H-3
Bridgeport A-5
Butler G-1
Calera E-3
Camden G-3
Carrollton D-1
Centre C-5
Centreville E-3
Chatom H-1
Childersburg D-4
Citronelle H-1
Clanton E-4
Clayton G-6
Columbiana D-4
Cullman B-3
Dadeville E-5
Daleville H-5
Daphne I-1
Decatur B-3
Demopolis F-2
Dothan H-6
Double Springs C-2
East Brewton H-3
Elba H-5
Enterprise H-5
Eufaula G-6
Eutaw E-2
Evergreen H-3
Fairhope J-1
Fayette C-2
Florence A-2
Foley J-2
Fort Payne B-5
Fultondale D-3
Gadsden C-5
Geneva I-5
Greensboro E-2
Greenville G-4
Grove Hill G-2
Guin C-2
Gulf Shores J-2
Guntersville B-4
Haleyville B-2
Hamilton C-1
Hanceville C-3
Hartford H-5
Hartselle B-3
Hayneville F-4
Hazel Green A-4
Headland H-6
Heflin C-5

Henagar B-5
Homewood D-3
Hoover D-3
Huntsville A-4
Irondale D-3
Jackson H-2
Jacksonville C-5
Jasper C-3
LaFayette E-6
Lanett E-6
Leeds D-4
Lincoln D-4
Linden F-2
Lineville D-5
Livingston F-1
Luverne G-4
Madison A-3
Marion E-2
Midfield D-3
Mobile I-1
Monroeville H-2
Montevallo E-3
Montgomery F-4
Moulton B-3
Muscle Shoals A-2
Northport D-2
Oneonta C-4
Opelika E-6
Opp H-4
Orange Beach J-2
Oxford D-5
Ozark H-5
Pelham D-3
Pell City D-4
Phenix City F-6
Piedmont C-5
Pinson C-4
Prattville F-4
Prichard I-1
Rainbow City C-5
Rainsville B-5
Red Bay B-1
Roanoke D-5
Robertsdale J-2
Rockford E-4
Russellville B-2
Saraland I-1
Scottsboro B-5
Selma F-3
Sheffield A-2
Spanish Fort I-1
Springville C-4
Sumiton C-3
Sylacauga D-4
Talladega D-4
Tallassee F-5
Theodore J-1
Thomasville G-2
Troy G-5
Trussville D-4
Tuscaloosa D-2
Tuscumbia A-2
Tuskegee F-5
Union Springs F-5
Valley E-6
Vernon C-1
Warrior C-3
Wedowee D-5
Wetumpka F-4
Winfield C-2
York F-1

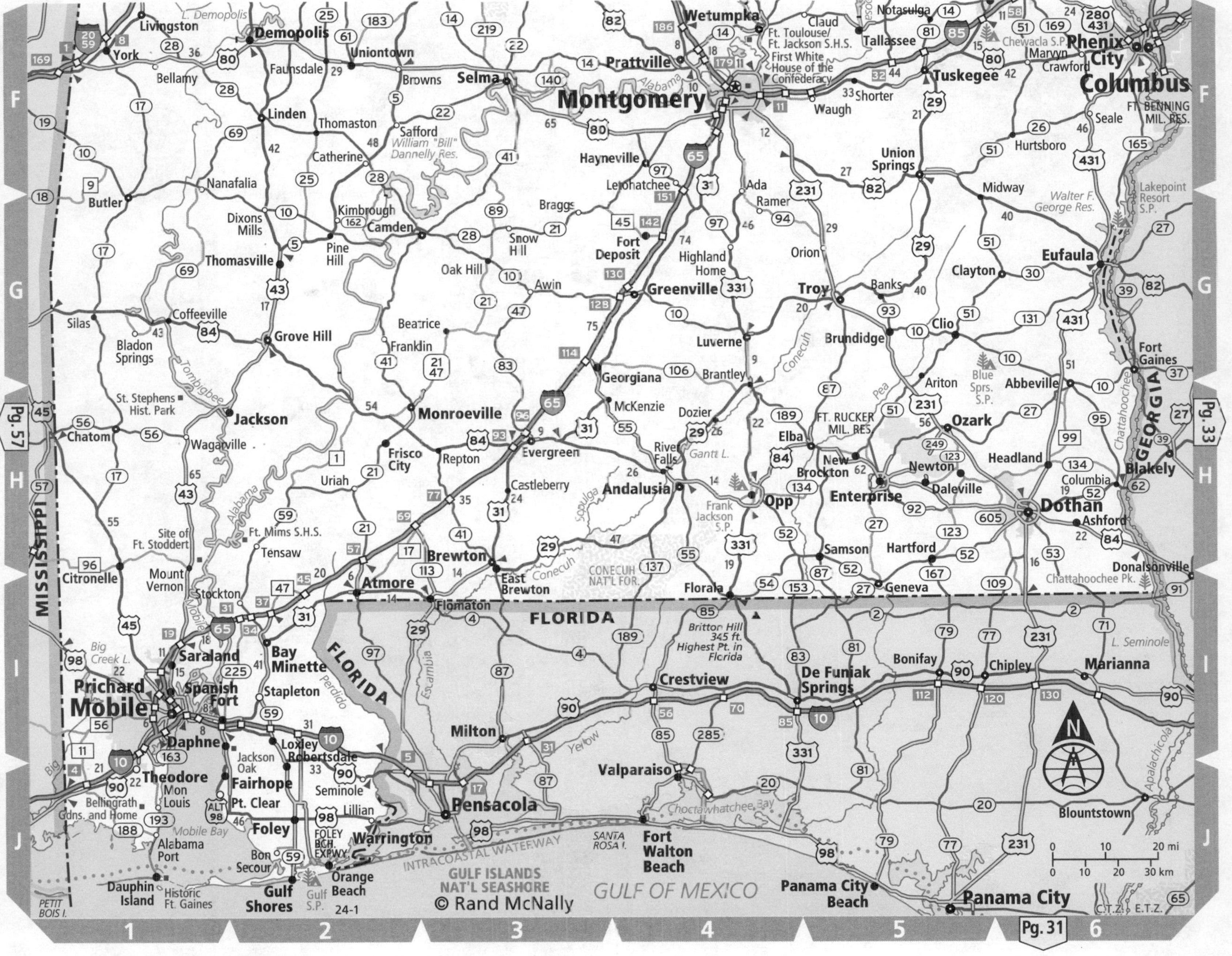

Travel planning & on-the-road resources

Tourism Information
Alabama Tourism Department:
(800) 252-2262, (334) 242-4169
alabama.travel

Road Conditions & Construction
(888) 588-2848
algotraffic.com, www.dot.state.al.us

Alaska state facts

Nickname: The Last Frontier
Capital: Juneau, E-6
Population: 733,391 (rank: 48th)
Largest city: Anchorage, 291,247, D-4
Land area: 570,866 sq. mi. (rank: 1st)
Highest point: Denali, 20,310 ft., D-3

Travel planning & on-the-road resources

Tourism Information	Alaska Travel Indus. Assoc.: www.travelalaska.com	**Road Conditions & Construction**	511, (866) 282-7577 dot.state.ak.us

Alaska

Cities and Towns

City	Grid
Alakanuk	C-2
Allakaket	C-3
Anchorage	D-3
Aniak	D-2
Bethel	D-2
Big Delta	C-4
Cantwell	C-4
Chignik	E-2
Circle	C-4
Circle Hot Springs	C-4
Cold Bay	E-1
Cordova	D-4
Delta Junction	C-4
Dillingham	E-2
Eagle	C-5
Eek	D-2
Fairbanks	C-4
Fort Yukon	C-4
Glenallen	D-4
Haines	D-5
Homer	D-3
Hoonah	E-6
Hooper Bay	D-1
Iditarod	D-2
Juneau	E-6
Kaltag	C-2
Karluk	E-3
Kenai	D-3
Ketchikan	E-6
Kodiak	E-3
Kotlik	C-2
Kotzebue	B-2
Kwethluk	D-2
Kwigillingok	D-2
Livengood	C-4
McGrath	D-3
Nenana	C-4
Ninilchik	D-3
Noatak	B-2
Nome	C-2
Palmer	D-4
Perryville	E-2
Petersburg	E-6
Port Graham	E-3
Point Hope	B-2
Prudhoe Bay	B-4
Ruby	C-3
Sand Point	F-2
Savoonga	C-1
Scammon Bay	D-1
Seward	D-4
Shungnak	B-3
Sitka	E-6
Skagway	D-5
Soldotna	D-3
Tanana	C-3
Taylor	C-2
Tok	D-4
Umiat	B-3
Unalaska	F-1
Utqiagvik	A-3
Valdez	D-4
Wainwright	A-3
Wasilla	D-4
Willow	D-3
Wrangell	E-6
Yakutat	D-5

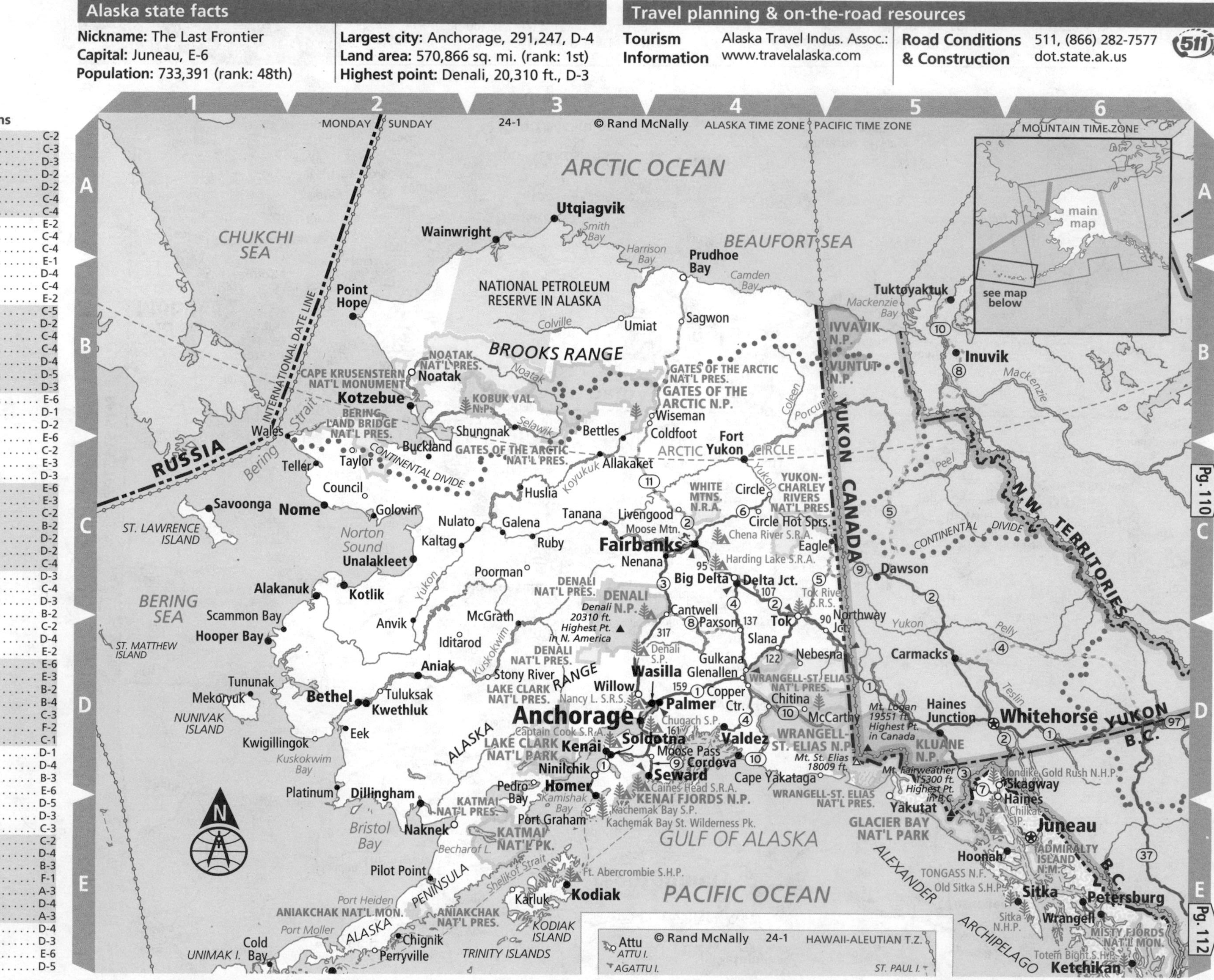

NOTE: Maps are not always in alphabetical order.
See Page 1 for map location in this atlas.

Hawaii

Cities and Towns

'Aiea J-2
'Ewa Beach J-2
'Ewa Villages J-2
Hala'ula I-5
Hale'iwa H-2
Hāna H-5
Hau'ula H-3
Hilo I-6
Hōlualoa J-5
Hōnaunau J-5
Honoka'a I-6
Honolulu J-3
Honomū I-6
Ho'olehua H-4
Kahalu'u I-3
Kahana I-3
Kahuku H-2
Kahului G-5
Kailua I-3
Kailua Kona I-5
Kainaliu J-5
Kalāheo G-1
Kalaupapa H-4
Kāne'ohe I-3
Kapa'a G-2
Kaunakakai H-4
Kea'au I-6
Kekaha G-1
Kīhei G-5
Kīlauea G-2
Kīpahulu G-6
Kōloa G-1
Kukuihaele I-6
Kurtistown J-6
Lahaina G-5
Lā'ie H-2
Lāna'i City H-4
Līhu'e G-2
Mā'alaea G-5
Mā'ili I-1
Makakilo City J-2
Mākaha I-1
Makawao G-6
Maunaloa H-4
Nā'ālehu J-6
Nānākuli J-1
Ō'ōkala I-6
Pāhala J-6
Pāhoa J-6
Pāpa'ikou I-6
Pa'uwela G-6
Pearl City I-2
Pukalani G-5
Volcano J-6
Wahiawā I-2
Waialua H-1
Wai'anae I-1
Wailuku G-5
Waimānalo J-4
Waimānalo Beach J-4
Waimea H-2
Waipahu I-2
Whitmore Village I-2

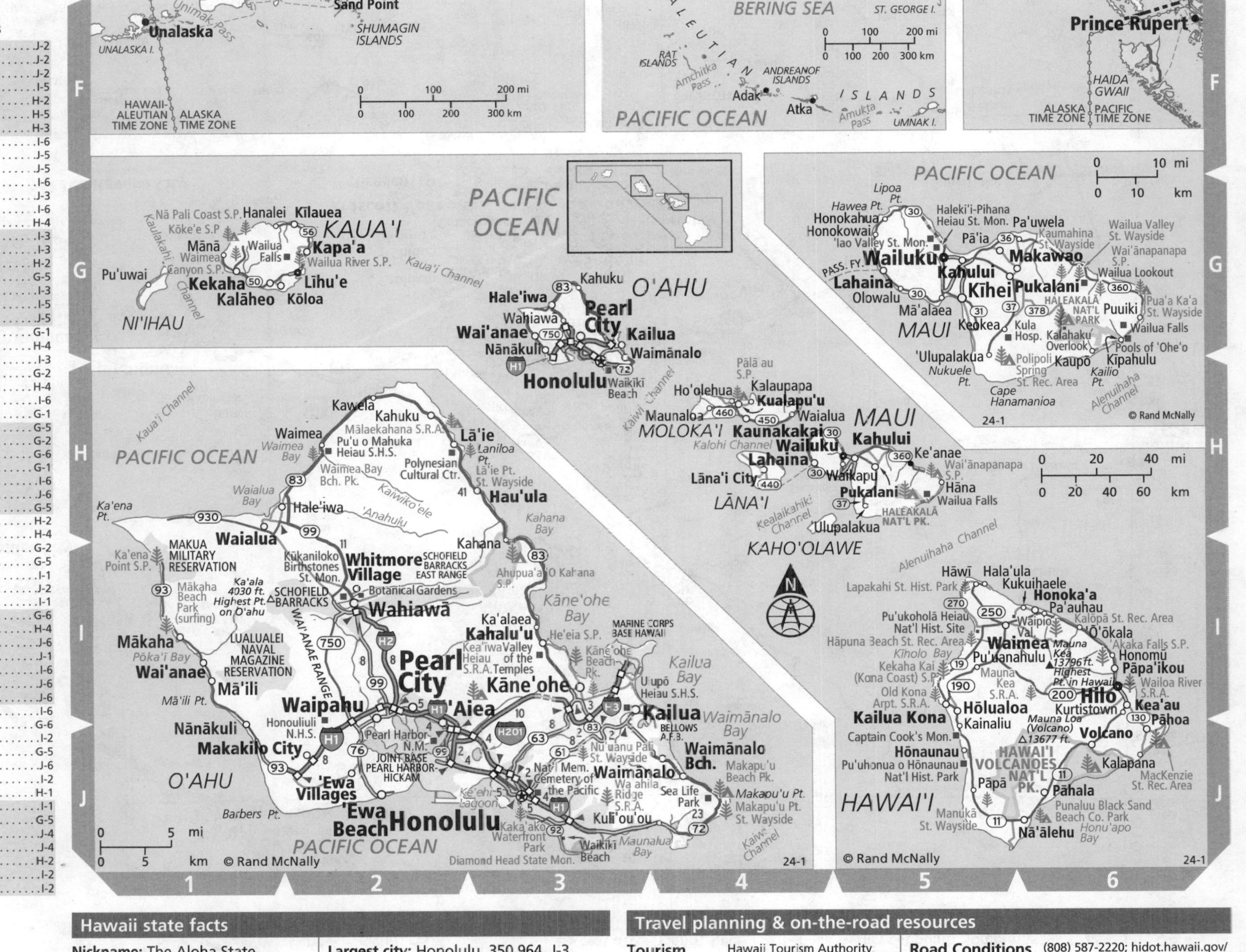

Hawaii state facts

Nickname: The Aloha State
Capital: Honolulu, J-3
Population: 1,455,271 (rank: 40th)
Largest city: Honolulu, 350,964, J-3
Land area: 6,421 sq. mi. (rank: 47th)
Highest point: Mauna Kea, 13,796 ft., I-6

Travel planning & on-the-road resources

Tourism Information Hawaii Tourism Authority (800) 464-2924 www.gohawaii.com

Road Conditions & Construction (808) 587-2220; hidot.hawaii.gov/highways/roadwork
O'ahu only: 511; goakamai.org

Arizona state facts

Nickname: The Grand Canyon State
Capital: Phoenix; F-4
Population: 7,151,502 (rank: 14th)
Largest city: Phoenix, 1,608,139, F-4
Land area: 113,623 sq. mi. (rank: 6th)
Highest point: Humphreys Peak, 12,633 ft., C-4

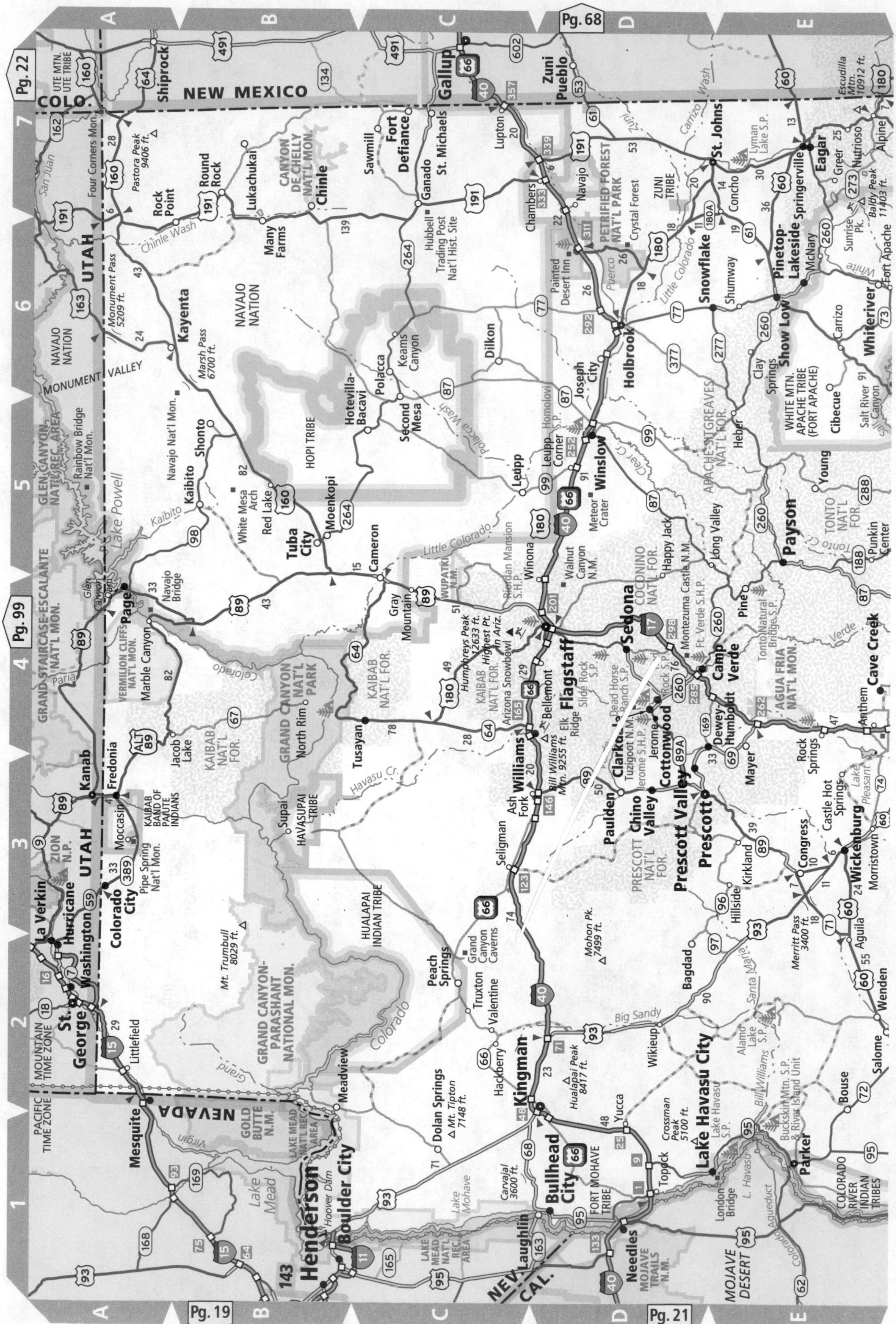

NOTE: Maps are not always in alphabetical order.
See Page 1 for map location in this atlas.

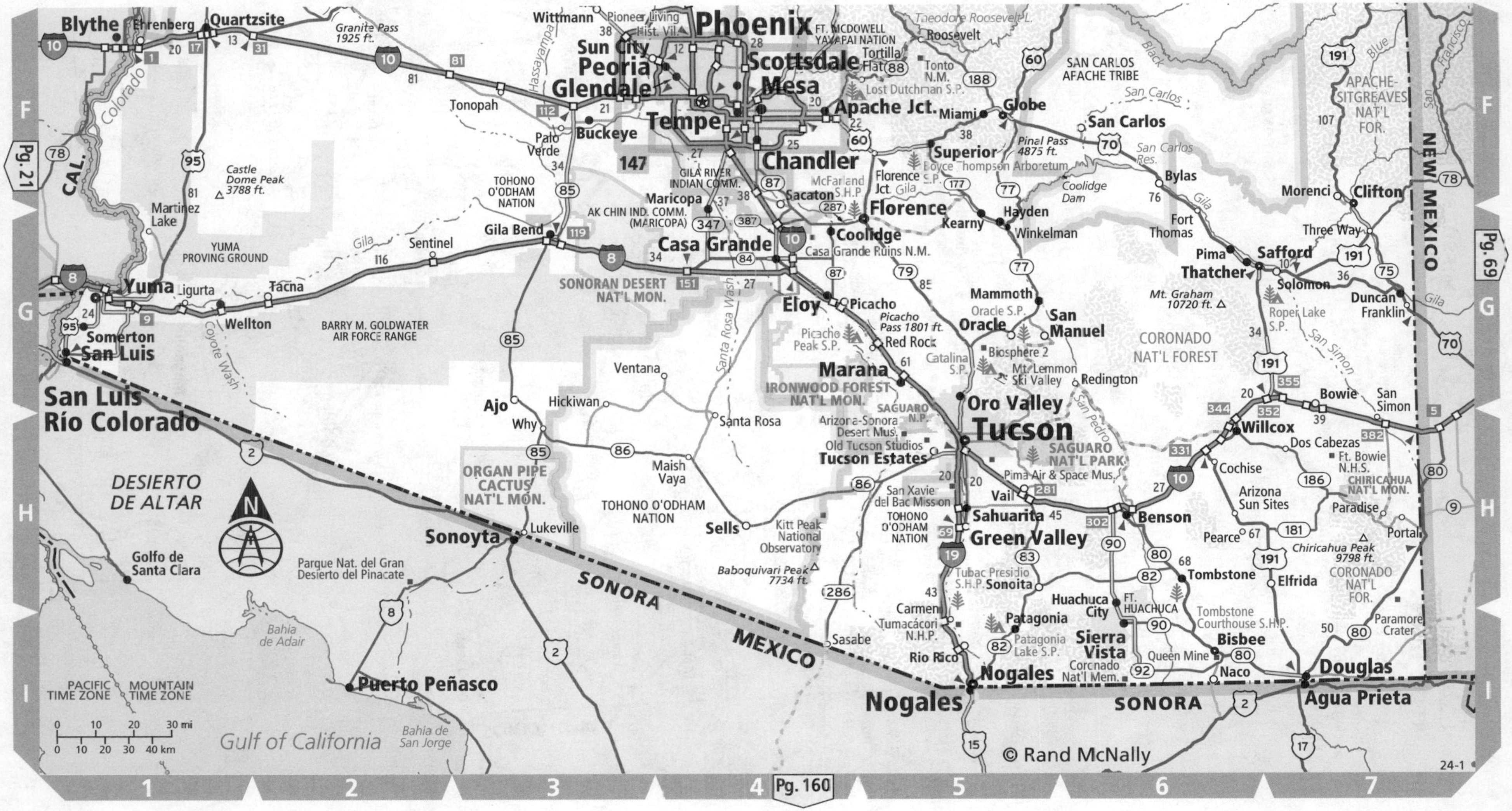

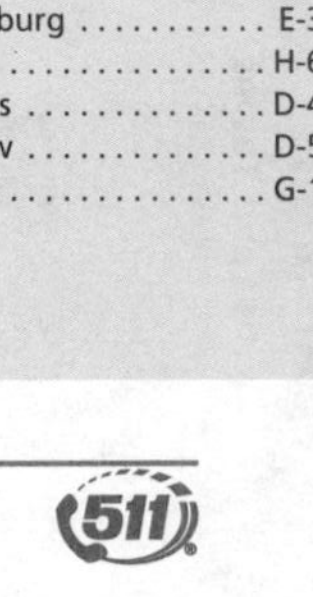

Arizona

Cities and Towns

Anthem E-4
Apache Junction F-4
Bagdad D-2
Bellemont D-4
Benson H-6
Bisbee I-6
Buckeye F-3
Bullhead City D-1
Camp Verde D-4
Casa Grande G-4
Cave Creek E-4
Chandler F-4
Chinle B-7
Chino Valley D-3
Clarkdale D-4
Clifton F-7
Colorado City A-3
Congress E-3
Coolidge G-4
Cottonwood D-4
Dolan Springs C-1
Douglas I-7
Eagar E-7
Eloy G-4
Flagstaff D-4
Florence G-5
Fort Defiance C-7
Ganado C-7
Gila Bend G-3
Glendale F-4
Globe F-5
Green Valley H-5
Holbrook D-6
Huachuca City H-6
Kaibito B-5
Kayenta A-6
Kearny G-5
Kingman D-2
Lake Havasu City E-1
Lukachukai B-7
Mammoth G-5
Many Farms B-6
Marana G-5
Mayer E-4
Mesa F-4
Miami F-5
Morenci F-7
Nogales I-5
Oracle G-5
Oro Valley G-5
Page A-4
Parker E-1
Paulden D-3
Payson E-5
Peoria F-4
Phoenix F-4
Pima G-6
Pine E-4
Pinetop-Lakeside E-6
Prescott D-3
Prescott Valley D-3
Quartzsite F-1
Sacaton F-4
Safford G-6
Sahuarita H-5
St. Johns D-7
Salome E-2
San Carlos F-6
San Luis G-1
San Manuel G-5
Scottsdale F-4
Sedona D-4
Sells H-4
Show Low E-6
Sierra Vista I-6
Snowflake D-6
Somerton G-1
Springerville E-7
Sun City F-3
Superior F-5
Tempe F-4
Thatcher G-6
Tombstone H-6
Tuba City B-5
Tucson H-5
Tucson Estates H-5
Vail H-5
Wellton G-1
Whiteriver E-6
Wickenburg E-3
Willcox H-6
Williams D-4
Winslow D-5
Yuma G-1

Travel planning & on-the-road resources

Tourism Information
Arizona Office of Tourism:
(866) 275-5816, (602) 364-3700
www.visitarizona.com

Road Conditions & Construction
511, (888) 411-7623
www.az511.com
azdot.gov

Arkansas state facts

Nickname: The Natural State

Capital: Little Rock, D-4

Population: 3,011,524 (rank: 33rd)

Largest city: Little Rock, 202,591, D-4

Land area: 52,024 sq. mi. (rank: 27th)

Highest point: Magazine Mtn., 2753 ft., C-2

Arkansas

Cities and Towns

City	Grid
Arkadelphia	E-3
Arkansas City	F-6
Ash Flat	A-6
Ashdown	F-2
Augusta	C-6
Batesville	B-6
Bella Vista	A-1
Benton	D-4
Bentonville	A-2
Berryville	A-3
Blytheville	B-8
Booneville	C-2
Cabot	D-5
Camden	F-4
Charleston	C-2
Clarendon	D-6
Clarksville	C-3
Clinton	B-4
Conway	C-4
Corning	A-7
Crossett	G-5
Danville	C-3
Dardanelle	C-3
De Queen	E-1
De Valls Bluff	D-6
Des Arc	D-6
DeWitt	E-6
Dumas	F-6
El Dorado	G-4
Eureka Springs	A-2
Fayetteville	A-2
Fordyce	F-4
Forrest City	D-7
Fort Smith	C-1
Greenwood	C-1
Hamburg	G-5
Hampton	F-4
Harrisburg	B-7
Harrison	A-3
Heber Springs	C-5
Helena-W. Helena	D-7
Hope	F-2
Hot Springs	E-3
Hot Springs Village	D-3
Huntsville	A-2
Jacksonville	D-5
Jasper	B-3
Jonesboro	B-7
Lake City	B-7
Lake Village	G-6
Lewisville	G-2
Little Rock	D-4
Lonoke	D-5
Magnolia	G-3
Malvern	E-4
Marianna	D-7
Marion	C-8
Marshall	B-4
McGehee	F-6
Melbourne	B-5
Mena	D-1
Monticello	F-5
Morrilton	C-4
Mount Ida	D-2
Mountain Home	A-4
Mountain View	B-5
Murfreesboro	E-2
Nashville	F-2
Newport	B-6
North Little Rock	D-5
Osceola	B-8
Ozark	C-2
Paragould	B-7
Paris	C-2
Perryville	D-4
Piggott	A-8
Pine Bluff	E-5
Pocahontas	A-7
Prescott	F-3
Rison	F-5
Rogers	A-2
Russellville	C-3
Salem	A-5
Searcy	C-5
Sheridan	E-4
Siloam Springs	A-1
Springdale	A-2
Star City	F-5
Stuttgart	E-6
Texarkana	G-2
Trumann	B-7
Van Buren	C-1
Waldron	D-2
Walnut Ridge	A-7
Warren	F-5
West Memphis	C-8
Wynne	C-7
Yellville	A-4

Pg. 58

Pg. 85

Pg. 96

Pg. 48

NOTE: Maps are not always in alphabetical order.
See Page 1 for map location in this atlas.

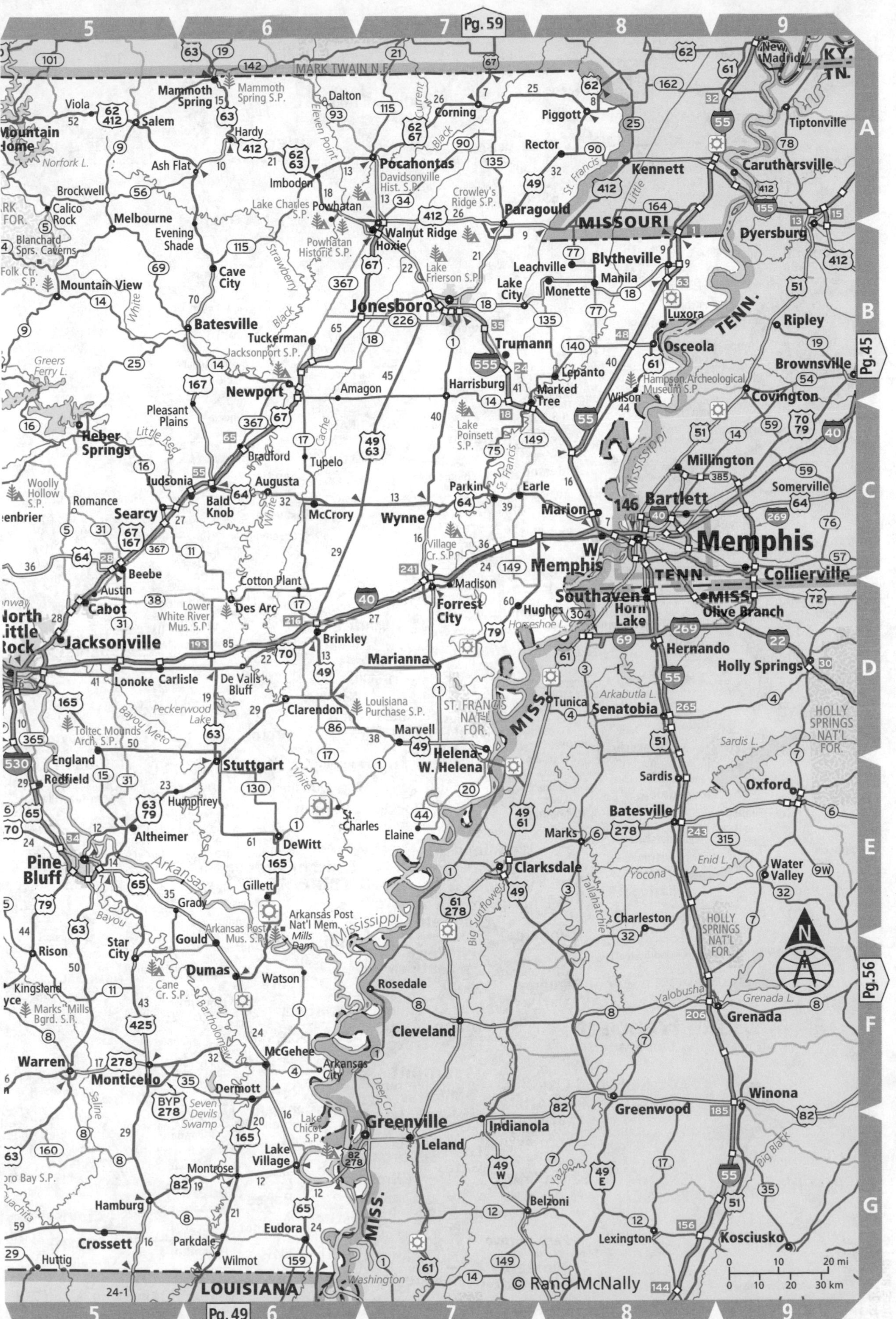

Road Conditions & Construction
(501) 569-2374
www.idrivearkansas.com
www.ardot.gov

Tourism Information
Arkansas State Tourism:
(800) 628-8725; www.arkansas.com

Travel planning & on-the-road resources

California state facts

Nickname: The Golden State
Capital: Sacramento, E-3
Population: 39,538,223 (rank: 1st)
Largest city: Los Angeles, 3,898,747, J-6
Land area: 155,813 sq. mi. (rank: 3rd)
Highest point: Mt. Whitney, 14,494 ft., G-6

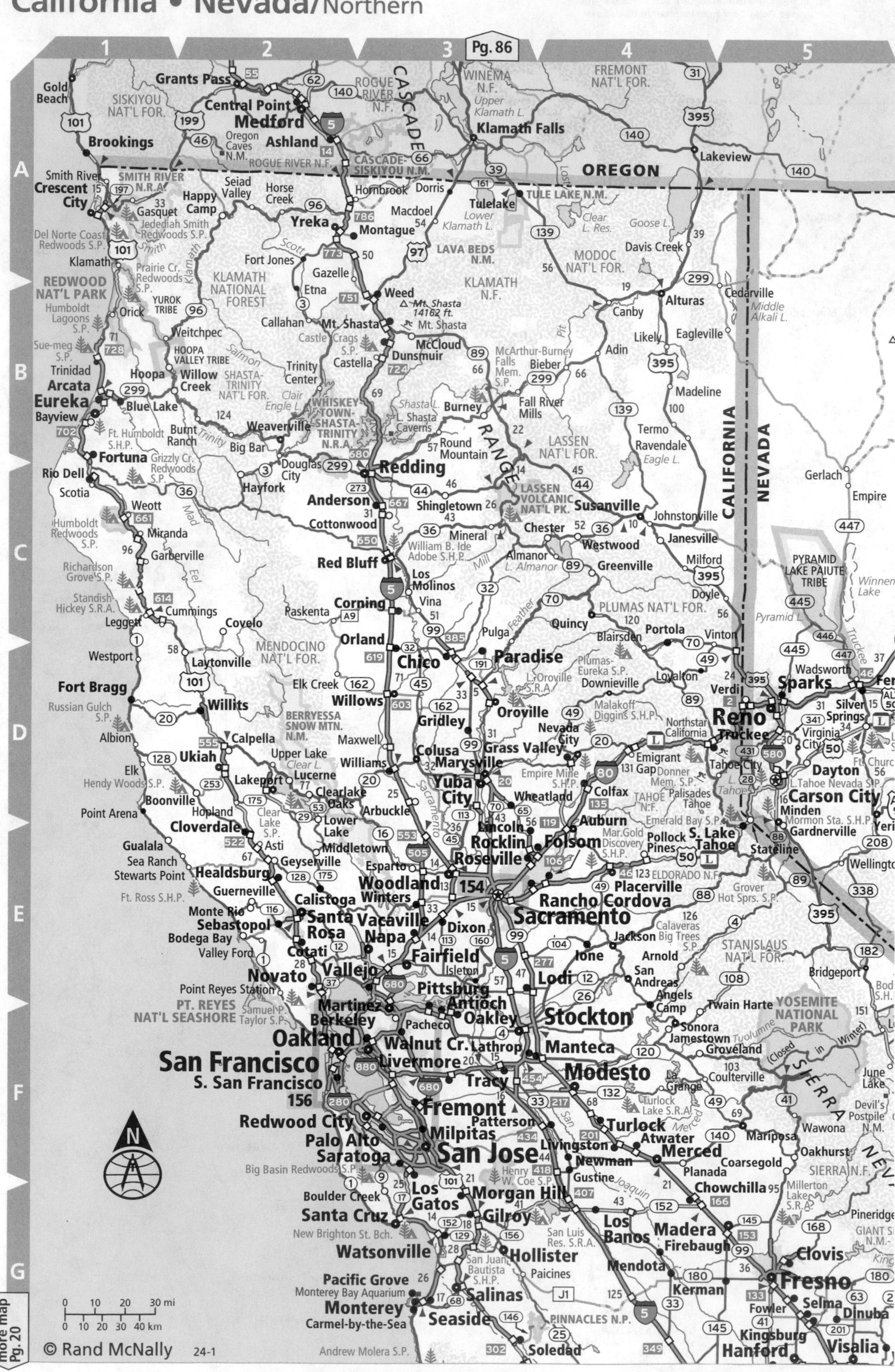

more map Pg. 20

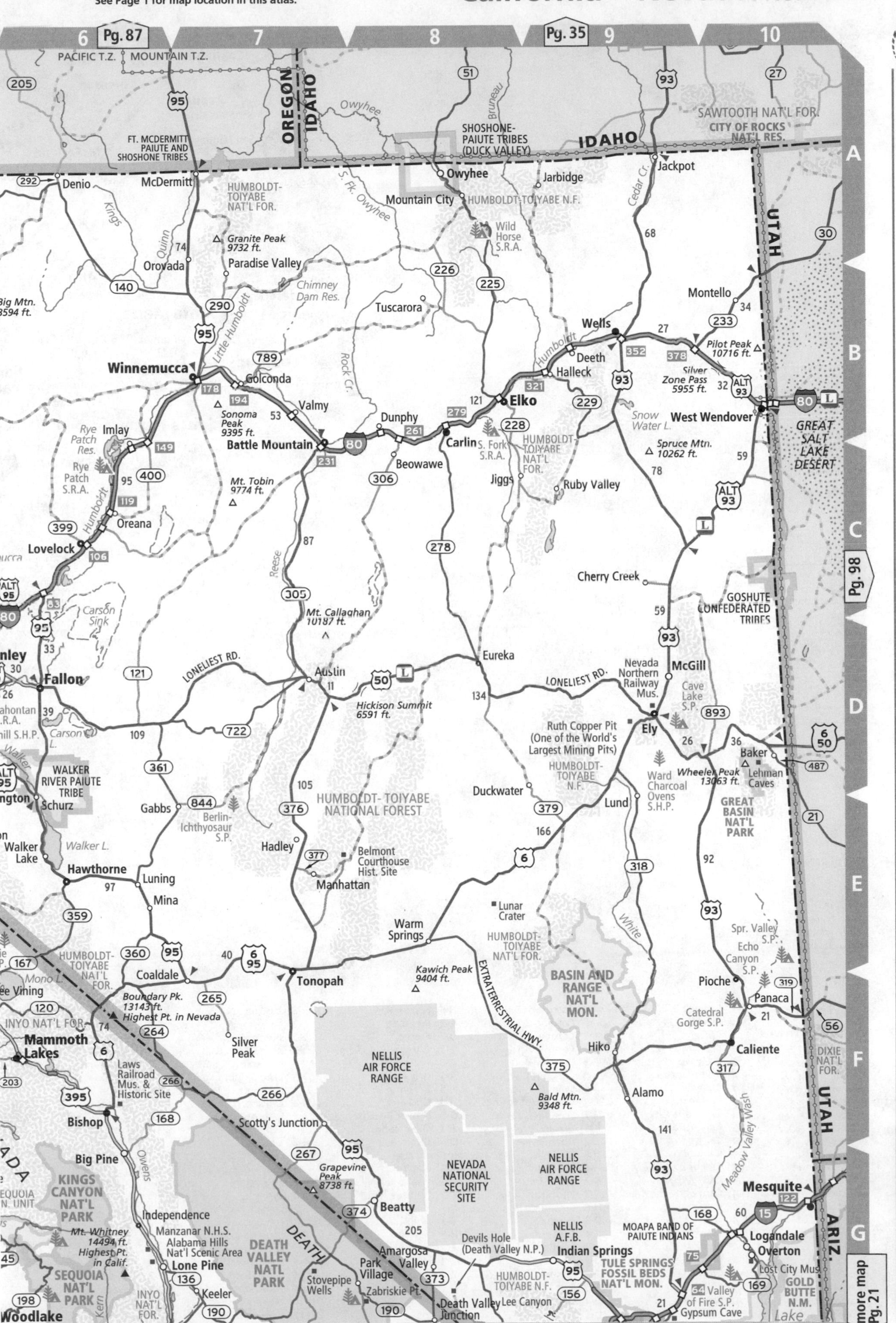

Travel planning & on-the-road resources

Tourism Information

Visit California:
(916) 444-4429, (877) 225-4367
www.visitcalifornia.com

Road Conditions & Construction

(800) 427-7623, (916) 654-2852; roads.dot.ca.gov, dot.ca.gov
Eastern Sierras/Bishop area: 511
Inland Empire region: 511, (877) 694-3511; gc511.com
Los Angeles metro area: 511, (877) 224-6511; go511.com
Sacramento area: 511, sacregion511.org

San Diego area: 511, (855) 467-3511; www.511sd.com
San Francisco Bay area: 511, (888) 500-4636; 511.org
San Luis Obispo area: 511, (866) 928-8923

Nevada state facts

Nickname: The Silver State
Capital: Carson City, D-5
Population: 3,104,614 (rank: 32nd)
Largest city: Las Vegas, 641,903, H-9
Land area: 109,831 sq. mi. (rank: 7th)
Highest point: Boundary Pk., 13,143 ft., F-6

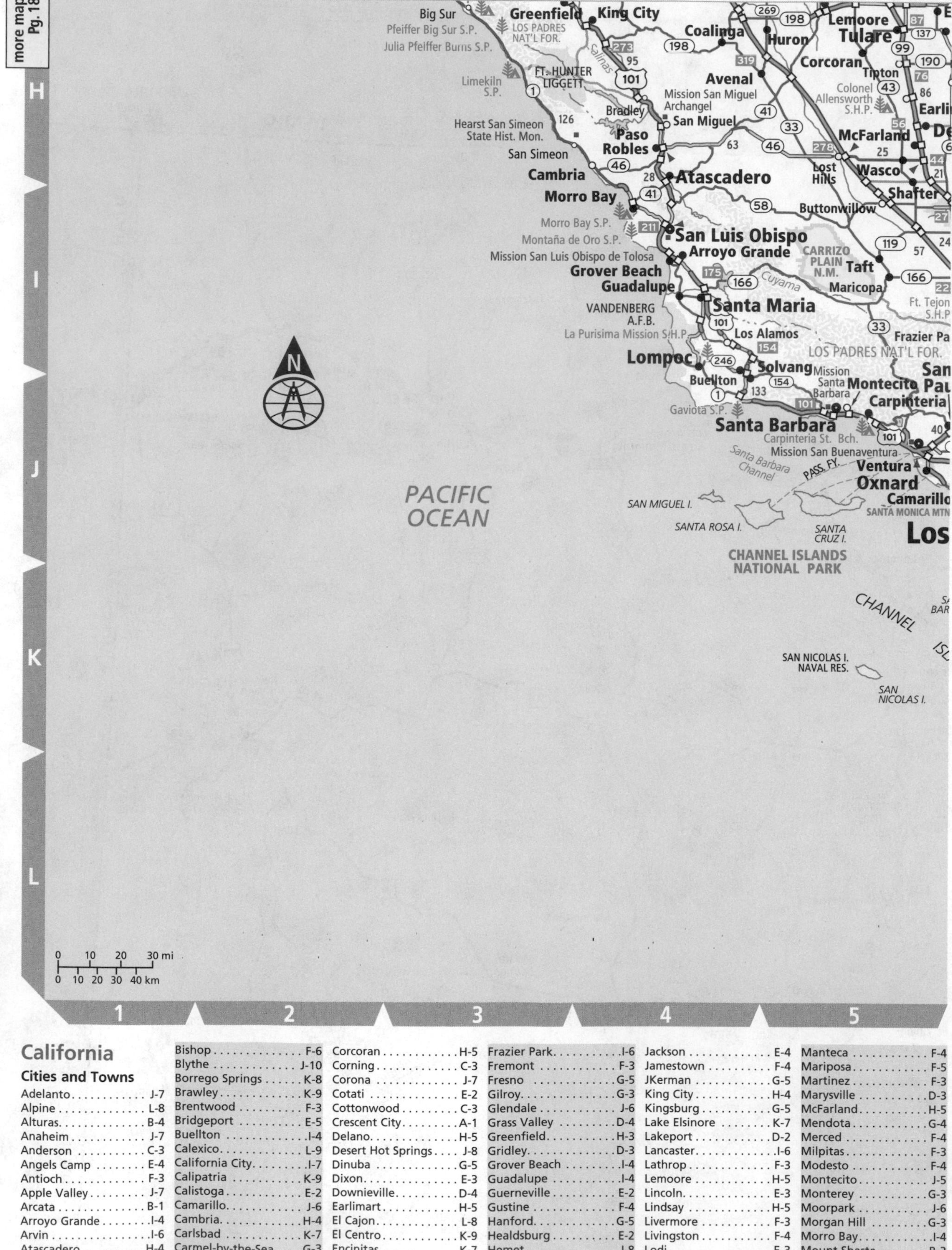

California

Cities and Towns

Adelanto J-7
Alpine L-8
Alturas B-4
Anaheim J-7
Anderson C-3
Angels Camp E-4
Antioch F-3
Apple Valley J-7
Arcata B-1
Arroyo Grande I-4
Arvin I-6
Atascadero H-4
Atwater F-4
Auburn E-4
Avalon K-6
Avenal H-4
Bakersfield I-6
Barstow I-7
Bayview B-1
Beaumont J-8
Berkeley F-3
Bishop F-6
Blythe J-10
Borrego Springs K-8
Brawley K-9
Brentwood F-3
Bridgeport E-5
Buellton I-4
Calexico L-9
California City I-7
Calipatria K-9
Calistoga E-2
Camarillo J-6
Cambria H-4
Carlsbad K-7
Carmel-by-the-Sea G-3
Carpinteria J-5
Chico D-3
Chowchilla G-4
Chula Vista L-7
Clearlake Oaks D-2
Cloverdale E-2
Clovis G-5
Coalinga H-4
Colusa D-3
Corcoran H-5
Corning C-3
Corona J-7
Cotati E-2
Cottonwood C-3
Crescent City A-1
Delano H-5
Desert Hot Springs J-8
Dinuba G-5
Dixon E-3
Downieville D-4
Earlimart H-5
El Cajon L-8
El Centro K-9
Encinitas K-7
Escondido K-7
Eureka B-1
Exeter H-5
Fairfield E-3
Firebaugh G-4
Folsom E-4
Fort Bragg D-1
Fortuna B-1
Fowler G-5
Frazier Park I-6
Fremont F-3
Fresno G-5
Gilroy G-3
Glendale J-6
Grass Valley D-4
Greenfield H-3
Gridley D-3
Grover Beach I-4
Guadalupe I-4
Guerneville E-2
Gustine F-4
Hanford G-5
Healdsburg E-2
Hemet J-8
Hesperia J-7
Hollister G-3
Holtville K-9
Huron H-5
Imperial K-9
Independence G-6
Indio J-8
Ione E-4
Irvine K-7
Jackson E-4
Jamestown F-4
JKerman G-5
King City H-4
Kingsburg G-5
Lake Elsinore K-7
Lakeport D-2
Lancaster I-6
Lathrop F-3
Lemoore H-5
Lincoln E-3
Lindsay H-5
Livermore F-3
Livingston F-4
Lodi E-3
Loma Linda J-7
Lompoc I-4
Long Beach J-6
Los Angeles J-6
Los Banos G-4
Los Gatos F-3
Lucerne D-2
Madera G-5
Mammoth Lakes F-6
Manteca F-4
Mariposa F-5
Martinez F-3
Marysville D-3
McFarland H-5
Mendota G-4
Merced F-4
Milpitas F-3
Modesto F-4
Montecito J-5
Monterey G-3
Moorpark J-6
Morgan Hill G-3
Morro Bay I-4
Mount Shasta B-3
Napa E-3
National City L-7
Needles I-10
Nevada City D-4
Newman F-4
Newport Beach K-7
Novato E-2
Oakhurst F-5
Oakland F-3

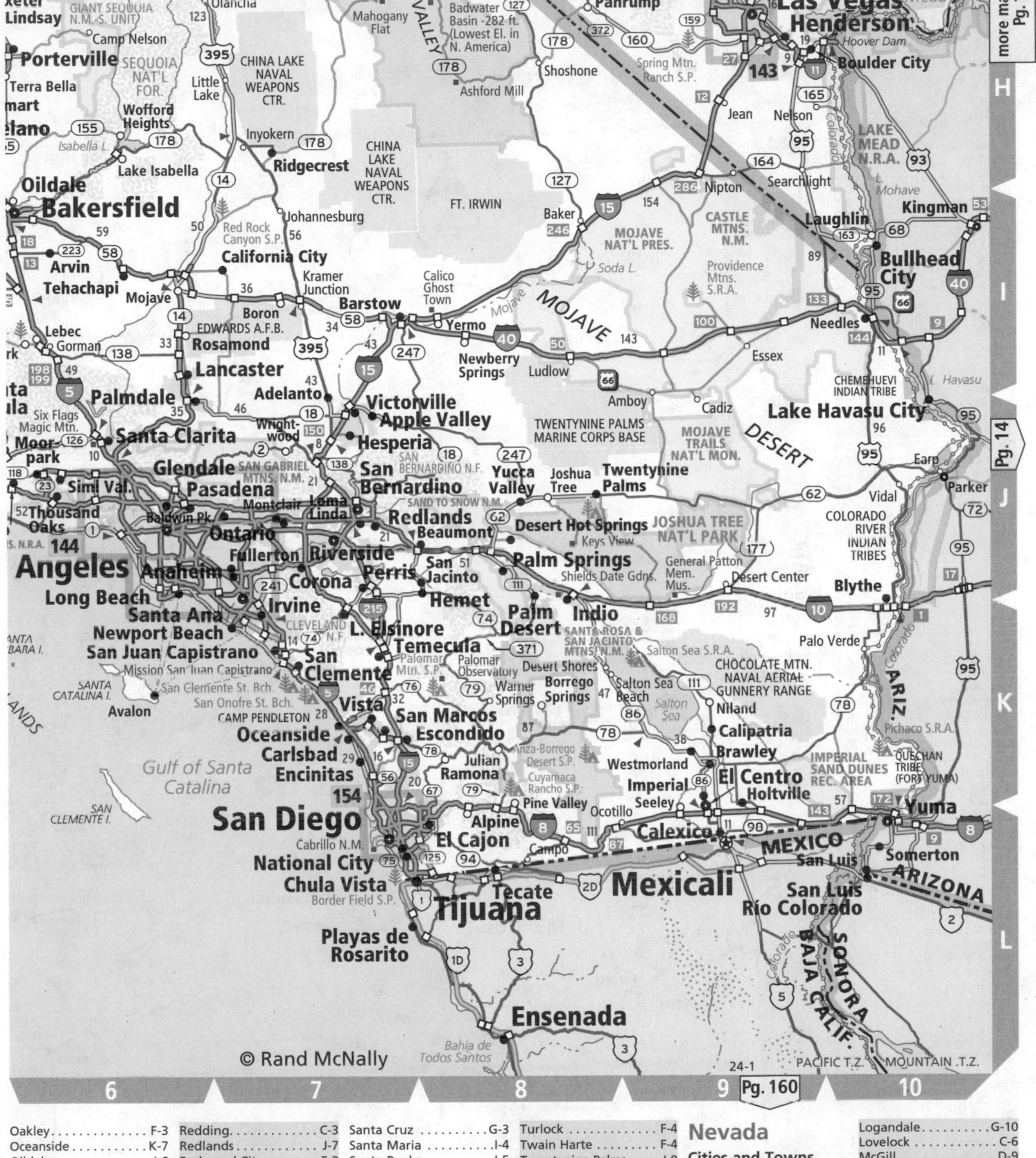

Road Conditions & Construction
511, (877) 687-6237, (775) 888-7000
www.nvroads.com
www.dot.nv.gov

Tourism Information
Travel Nevada:
(775) 687-4322
travelnevada.com

Travel planning & on-the-road resources

Oakley F-3
Oceanside K-7
Oildale I-6
Ontario J-7
Orland D-3
Oroville D-3
Oxnard J-5
Pacific Grove G-3
Palm Desert J-8
Palm Springs J-8
Palmdale J-6
Palo Alto F-3
Paradise D-3
Pasadena J-6
Paso Robles H-4
Patterson F-4
Perris J-7
Pittsburg F-3
Placerville E-4
Porterville H-6
Quincy C-4
Ramona K-8
Rancho Cordova E-3
Red Bluff C-3
Redding C-3
Redlands J-7
Redwood City F-3
Ridgecrest H-7
Rio Dell C-1
Riverside J-7
Rocklin E-4
Rosamond I-6
Roseville E-3
Sacramento E-3
Salinas G-3
San Andreas E-4
San Bernardino J-7
San Clemente K-7
San Diego L-7
San Francisco F-2
San Jacinto J-8
San Jose F-3
San Juan Capistrano K-7
San Luis Obispo I-4
San Marcos K-7
Santa Ana J-7
Santa Barbara J-5
Santa Clarita J-6
Santa Cruz G-3
Santa Maria I-4
Santa Paula J-5
Santa Rosa E-2
Saratoga F-3
Seaside G-3
Sebastopol E-2
Selma G-5
Shafter H-5
Simi Valley J-6
Soledad G-3
Solvang I-4
Sonora F-4
South Lake Tahoe E-5
South San Francisco F-2
Stockton F-3
Susanville C-4
Taft I-5
Tehachapi I-6
Temecula K-7
Thousand Oaks J-6
Tracy F-3
Truckee D-4
Tulare H-5
Turlock F-4
Twain Harte F-4
Twentynine Palms J-8
Ukiah D-2
Vacaville E-3
Vallejo E-3
Ventura J-5
Victorville J-7
Visalia G-5
Vista K-7
Wasco H-5
Watsonville G-3
Weaverville B-2
Williams D-3
Willits D-2
Willows D-3
Winters E-3
Woodlake G-5
Woodland E-3
Yreka A-2
Yuba City D-3
Yucca Valley J-8

Nevada

Cities and Towns

Alamo F-9
Amargosa Valley G-8
Battle Mountain B-7
Beatty G-8
Boulder City H-9
Caliente F-10
Carlin B-8
Carson City D-5
Dayton D-5
Elko B-8
Ely D-9
Eureka D-8
Fallon D-6
Fernley D-5
Gardnerville E-5
Hawthorne E-6
Henderson H-9
Indian Springs G-9
Jackpot A-9
Las Vegas H-9
Laughlin I-10
Logandale G-10
Lovelock C-6
McGill D-9
Mesquite G-10
Minden D-5
Overton G-10
Owyhee A-8
Pahrump H-8
Panaca F-10
Pioche F-10
Reno D-5
Schurz D-6
Searchlight H-9
Silver Springs D-5
Sparks D-5
Stateline D-5
Tonopah E-7
Verdi D-5
Virginia City D-5
Wadsworth D-5
Walker Lake E-6
Wells B-9
West Wendover B-10
Winnemucca B-7
Yerington D-5

Colorado

Cities and Towns

Akron . . . B-8
Alamosa . . . F-5
Arvada . . . C-6
Aspen . . . D-3
Aurora . . . C-6
Basalt . . . D-3
Bennett . . . C-6
Boulder . . . C-5
Breckenridge . . . C-4
Brighton . . . C-6
Brush . . . B-7
Buena Vista . . . D-4
Burlington . . . D-9
Cañon City . . . E-5
Carbondale . . . D-3
Castle Rock . . . D-6
Center . . . F-4
Central City . . . C-5
Cheyenne Wells . . . D-9
Clifton . . . D-2
Colorado City . . . F-6
Colorado Springs . . . D-6
Conejos . . . G-4
Cortez . . . G-1
Craig . . . B-3
Creede . . . F-3
Cripple Creek . . . E-5
Del Norte . . . F-4
Delta . . . D-2
Denver . . . C-6
Dove Creek . . . F-1
Durango . . . G-2
Eads . . . E-8
Eagle . . . C-4
Eaton . . . B-6
Englewood . . . C-6
Estes Park . . . B-5
Evans . . . B-6
Fairplay . . . D-4
Florence . . . E-6
Fort Collins . . . B-6
Fort Lupton . . . C-6
Fort Morgan . . . B-7
Fountain . . . E-6
Frederick . . . B-6
Fruita . . . D-1
Fruitvale . . . D-2
Georgetown . . . C-5
Glenwood Springs . . . C-3
Golden . . . C-5
Grand Junction . . . D-1
Greeley . . . B-6
Gunnison . . . E-3
Gypsum . . . C-3
Holyoke . . . B-9
Hot Sulphur Springs . . . C-4
Hugo . . . D-7
Julesburg . . . A-9
Kiowa . . . D-6
Lake City . . . F-3
Lakewood . . . C-6
Lamar . . . E-8
Las Animas . . . F-8
Leadville . . . D-4
Limon . . . D-7
Lincoln Park . . . E-5
Littleton . . . C-6
Longmont . . . B-6
Loveland . . . B-6
Manitou Springs . . . D-6
Meeker . . . C-2
Monte Vista . . . F-4
Montrose . . . E-2
Ordway . . . E-7
Ouray . . . F-2
Pagosa Springs . . . G-3
Palisade . . . D-2
Parker . . . C-6
Penrose . . . E-6
Platteville . . . B-6
Pueblo . . . E-6
Rangely . . . B-1
Rifle . . . C-2
Rocky Ford . . . F-7
Saguache . . . F-4
Salida . . . E-4
San Luis . . . G-5
Silverton . . . F-2
Springfield . . . G-9
Steamboat Springs . . . B-4
Sterling . . . B-8
Telluride . . . F-2
Thornton . . . C-6
Trinidad . . . G-6
Vail . . . C-4
Walden . . . B-4
Walsenburg . . . F-6
Wellington . . . B-6
Westcliffe . . . E-5
Windsor . . . B-6
Woodland Park . . . D-6
Wray . . . B-9
Yuma . . . B-8

Colorado state facts

Nickname: The Centennial State
Capital: Denver, C-6

Population: 5,773,714 (rank: 21st)
Largest city: Denver, 715,522, C-6

Land area: 103,610 sq. mi. (rank: 8th)
Highest point: Mt. Elbert, 14,433 ft., D-4

© Rand McNally

Pg. 109
Pg. 98
Pg. 68

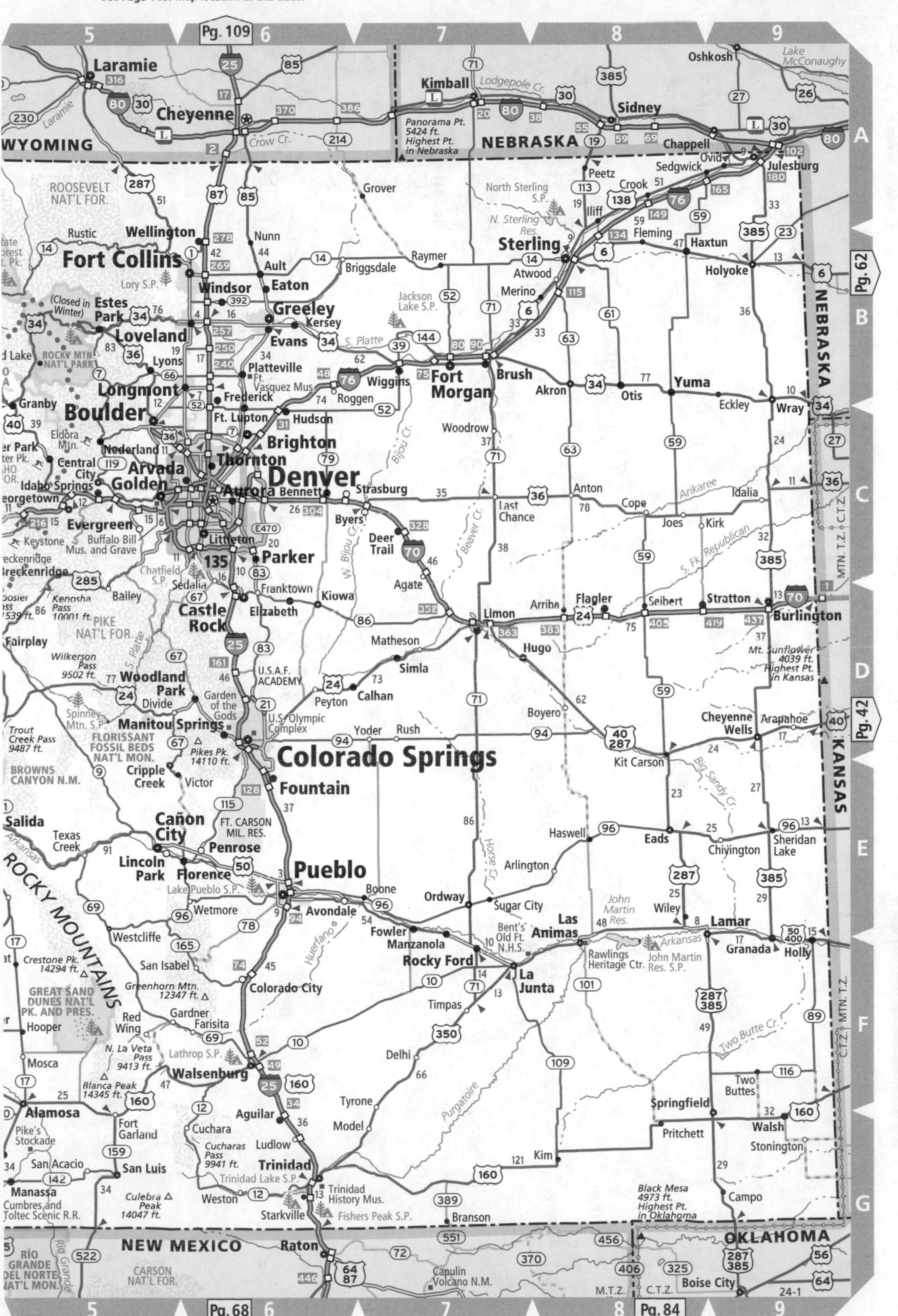

Road Conditions & Construction
511, (800) 288-1047
www.cotrip.org, www.codot.gov

Tourism Information
Colorado Tourism Office:
(800) 265-6723, (303) 892-3540
www.colorado.com

Travel planning & on-the-road resources

Connecticut state facts

Nickname: The Constitution State
Capital: Hartford, F-4
Population: 3,605,944 (rank: 29th)
Largest city: Bridgeport, 148,654, I-2
Land area: 4,841 sq. mi. (rank: 48th)
Highest point: Mt. Frissell, 2,380 ft., E-1

Travel planning & on-the-road resources

Tourism Information
Connecticut Tourism Office:
(888) 288-4748, (860) 500-2300
www.ctvisit.com

Road Conditions & Construction
(860) 594-2560
cttravelsmart.org
portal.ct.gov/dot
www.i-84waterbury.com

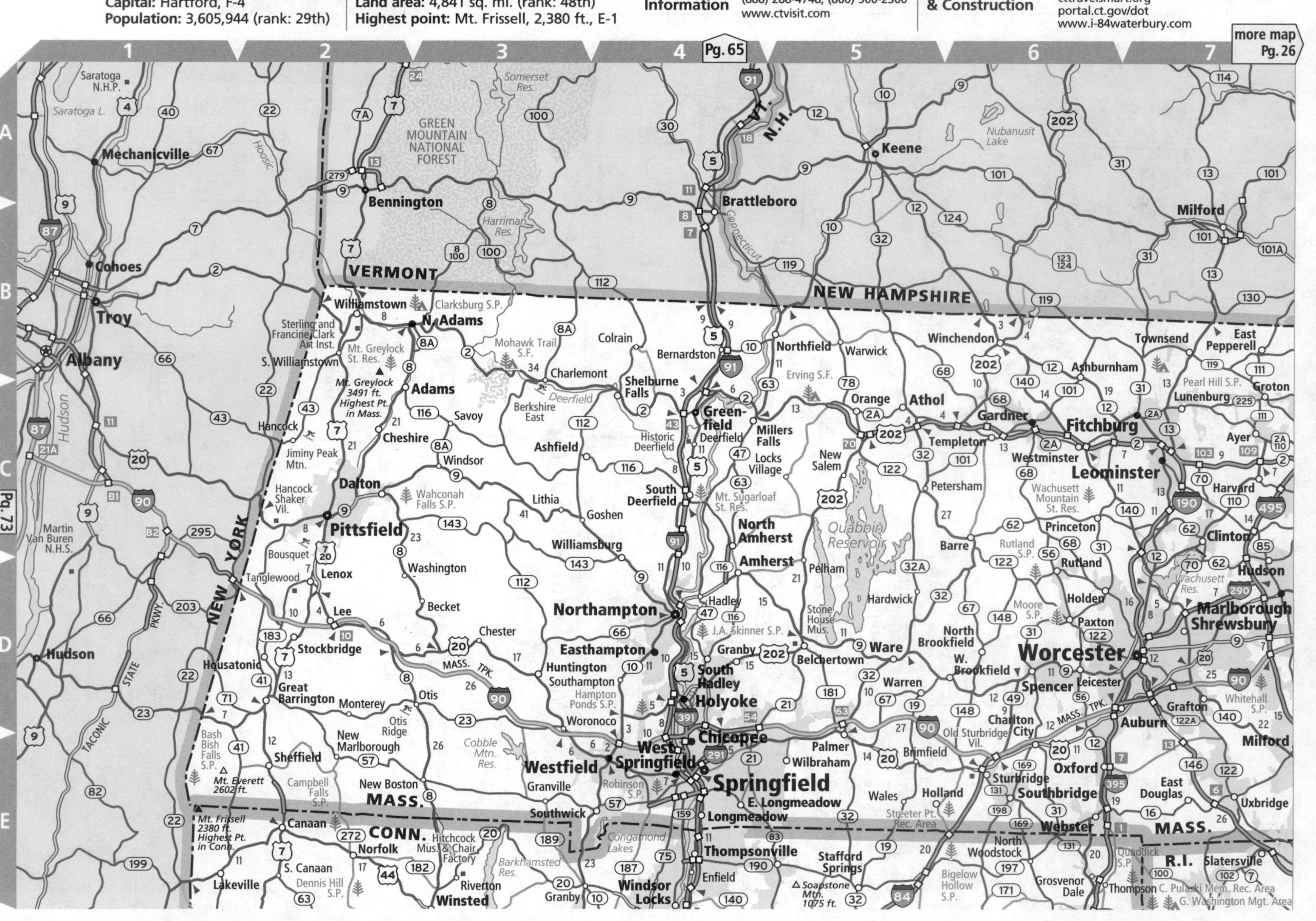

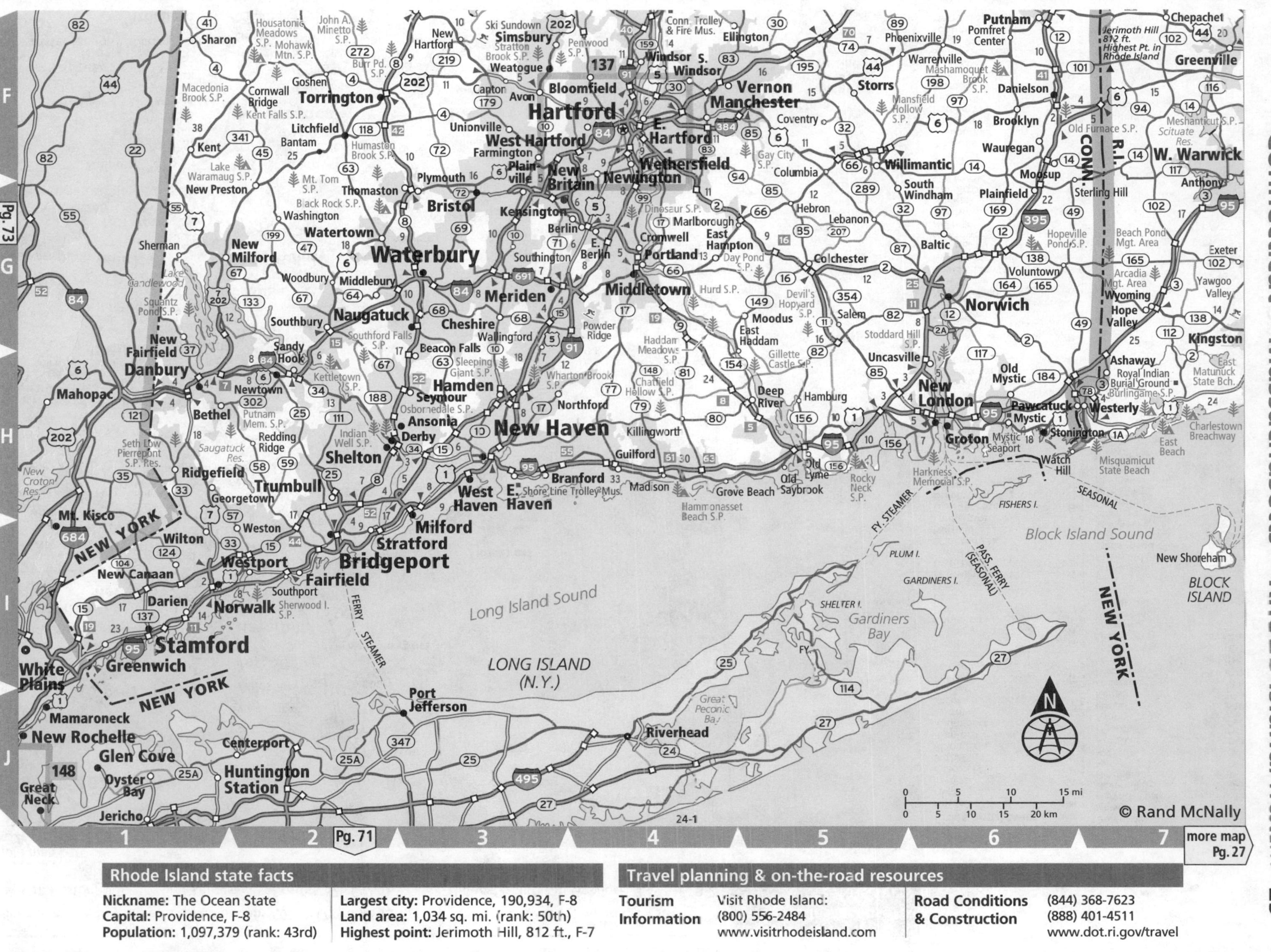

Rhode Island state facts

Nickname: The Ocean State
Capital: Providence, F-8
Population: 1,097,379 (rank: 43rd)
Largest city: Providence, 190,934, F-8
Land area: 1,034 sq. mi. (rank: 50th)
Highest point: Jerimoth Hill, 812 ft., F-7

Travel planning & on-the-road resources

Tourism Information	Visit Rhode Island: (800) 556-2484 www.visitrhodeisland.com
Road Conditions & Construction	(844) 368-7623 (888) 401-4511 www.dot.ri.gov/travel

Massachusetts state facts

Nickname: The Bay State
Capital: Boston, D-9
Population: 7,029,917 (rank: 15th)
Largest city: Boston, 675,647, D-9
Land area: 7,799 sq. mi. (rank: 45th)
Highest point: Mt. Greylock, 3,491 ft., B-2

more map Pg. 24
Pg. 65

Gloucester . . . C-10
Great Barrington . . . D-2
Greenfield . . . C-4
Harwich . . . F-12
Harwich Port . . . G-12
Haverhill . . . B-9
Hingham . . . D-9
Holden . . . D-6
Holliston . . . D-8
Holyoke . . . D-4
Hudson . . . D-7
Hyannis . . . G-11
Ipswich . . . B-10
Kingston . . . E-10
Lawrence . . . B-9
Lee . . . D-2
Leicester . . . D-6
Leominster . . . C-7
Lexington . . . C-8
Lincoln . . . C-8
Longmeadow . . . E-4
Lowell . . . B-8
Lunenburg . . . C-7
Lynn . . . C-9
Lynnfield . . . C-9
Mansfield . . . E-8
Marblehead . . . C-10
Marlborough . . . D-7
Marshfield . . . E-10
Maynard . . . C-8
Medfield . . . D-8
Methuen . . . B-9
Middleborough . . . F-9
Middleton . . . C-9
Milford . . . E-8
Millis . . . D-8
Nantucket . . . H-12
Natick . . . D-8
New Bedford . . . G-9
Newburyport . . . B-10
Newton . . . D-9
North Adams . . . B-3
North Amherst . . . C-4
North Andover . . . B-9
North Attleboro . . . E-8
North Billerica . . . C-8
North Brookfield . . . D-6
Northampton . . . D-4
Norton . . . E-9
Norwood . . . D-9
Oak Bluffs . . . G-11
Orange . . . C-5
Orleans . . . F-12
Oxford . . . E-6
Palmer . . . E-5
Peabody . . . C-9
Pittsfield . . . C-2
Plymouth . . . E-10
Pocasset . . . F-10
Provincetown . . . E-12
Quincy . . . D-9
Randolph . . . D-9
Revere . . . C-9
Rockland . . . E-9
Rockport . . . B-10
Rutland . . . D-6
Salem . . . C-9
Salisbury . . . B-10
Sandwich . . . F-11
Saugus . . . C-9
Scituate . . . D-10
Sharon . . . E-9
Shelburne Falls . . . C-4
Shrewsbury . . . D-7

Connecticut

Cities and Towns

Ansonia . . . H-3
Avon . . . F-3
Baltic . . . G-6
Beacon Falls . . . H-3
Bethel . . . H-1
Bloomfield . . . F-4
Branford . . . H-3
Bridgeport . . . I-2
Bristol . . . G-3
Brooklyn . . . F-6
Canaan . . . E-2
Cheshire . . . G-3
Colchester . . . G-5
Columbia . . . F-5
Cromwell . . . G-4
Danbury . . . H-1
Danielson . . . F-6
Darien . . . I-1
Deep River . . . H-5
Derby . . . H-2
East Hampton . . . G-4
East Hartford . . . F-4
East Haven . . . H-3
Ellington . . . F-4
Fairfield . . . I-2
Farmington . . . F-3
Georgetown . . . H-1
Greenwich . . . I-1
Groton . . . H-6
Guilford . . . H-4
Hamden . . . H-3
Hartford . . . F-4
Kensington . . . G-4
Lakeville . . . E-1
Litchfield . . . F-2
Manchester . . . F-4
Meriden . . . G-3
Middlebury . . . G-2
Middletown . . . G-4
Milford . . . H-3
Moosup . . . F-6
Mystic . . . H-6
Naugatuck . . . G-3
New Britain . . . G-3
New Canaan . . . I-1
New Fairfield . . . G-1
New Haven . . . H-3
New London . . . H-6
New Milford . . . G-1
Newington . . . F-4
Newtown . . . H-2
Norfolk . . . E-2
Northford . . . H-3
Norwalk . . . I-1
Norwich . . . G-6
Old Mystic . . . H-6
Pawcatuck . . . H-6
Plainfield . . . G-6
Plainville . . . G-3
Plymouth . . . G-3
Portland . . . G-4
Putnam . . . F-6
Ridgefield . . . H-1
Seymour . . . H-3
Shelton . . . H-2
Simsbury . . . F-3
South Windham . . . G-5
South Windsor . . . F-4
Southbury . . . G-2
Stafford Springs . . . E-5

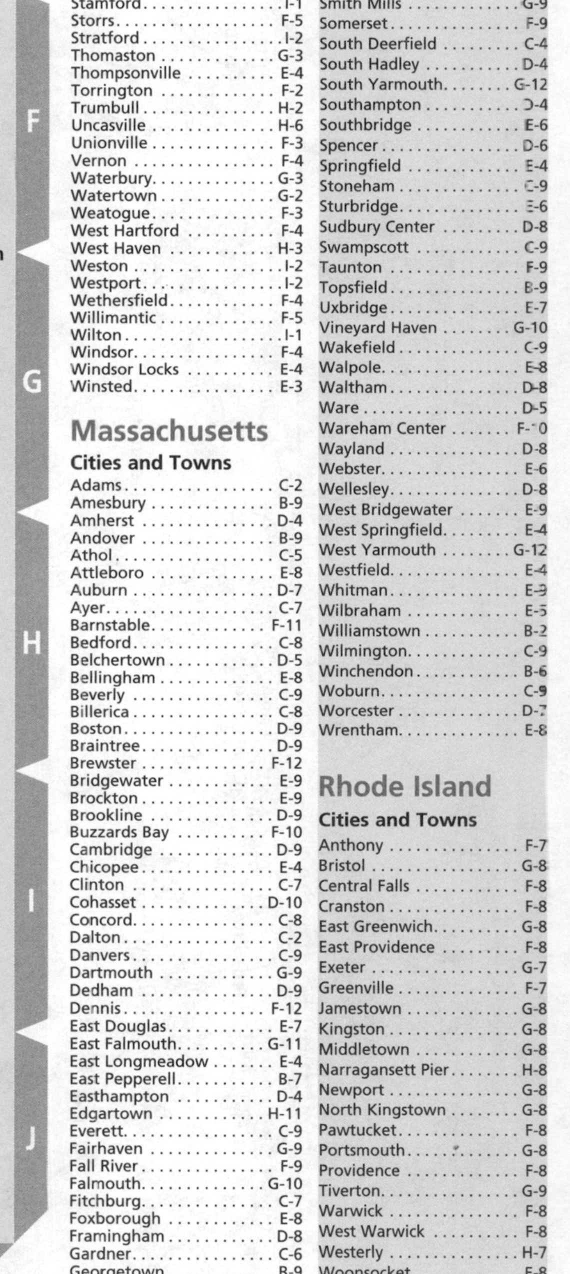

more map Pg. 25

Stamford I-1
Storrs F-5
Stratford I-2
Thomaston G-3
Thompsonville E-4
Torrington F-2
Trumbull H-2
Uncasville H-6
Unionville F-3
Vernon F-4
Waterbury G-3
Watertown G-2
Weatogue F-3
West Hartford F-4
West Haven H-3
Weston I-2
Westport I-2
Wethersfield F-4
Willimantic F-5
Wilton I-1
Windsor F-4
Windsor Locks E-4
Winsted E-3

Massachusetts

Cities and Towns

Adams C-2
Amesbury B-9
Amherst D-4
Andover B-9
Athol C-5
Attleboro E-8
Auburn D-7
Ayer C-7
Barnstable F-11
Bedford C-8
Belchertown D-5
Bellingham E-8
Beverly C-9
Billerica C-8
Boston D-9
Braintree D-9
Brewster F-12
Bridgewater E-9
Brockton E-9
Brookline D-9
Buzzards Bay F-10
Cambridge D-9
Chicopee E-4
Clinton C-7
Cohasset D-10
Concord C-8
Dalton C-2
Danvers C-9
Dartmouth G-9
Dedham D-9
Dennis F-12
East Douglas E-7
East Falmouth G-11
East Longmeadow E-4
East Pepperell B-7
Easthampton D-4
Edgartown H-11
Everett C-9
Fairhaven G-9
Fall River F-9
Falmouth G-10
Fitchburg C-7
Foxborough E-8
Framingham D-8
Gardner C-6
Georgetown B-9
Smith Mills G-9
Somerset F-9
South Deerfield C-4
South Hadley D-4
South Yarmouth G-12
Southampton D-4
Southbridge E-6
Spencer D-6
Springfield E-4
Stoneham C-9
Sturbridge E-6
Sudbury Center D-8
Swampscott C-9
Taunton F-9
Topsfield B-9
Uxbridge E-7
Vineyard Haven G-10
Wakefield C-9
Walpole E-8
Waltham D-8
Ware D-5
Wareham Center F-10
Wayland D-8
Webster E-6
Wellesley D-8
West Bridgewater E-9
West Springfield E-4
West Yarmouth G-12
Westfield E-4
Whitman E-9
Wilbraham E-5
Williamstown B-2
Wilmington C-9
Winchendon B-6
Woburn C-9
Worcester D-7
Wrentham E-8

Rhode Island

Cities and Towns

Anthony F-7
Bristol G-8
Central Falls F-8
Cranston F-8
East Greenwich G-8
East Providence F-8
Exeter G-7
Greenville F-7
Jamestown G-8
Kingston G-8
Middletown G-8
Narragansett Pier H-8
Newport G-8
North Kingstown G-8
Pawtucket F-8
Portsmouth G-8
Providence F-8
Tiverton G-9
Warwick F-8
West Warwick F-8
Westerly H-7
Woonsocket E-8

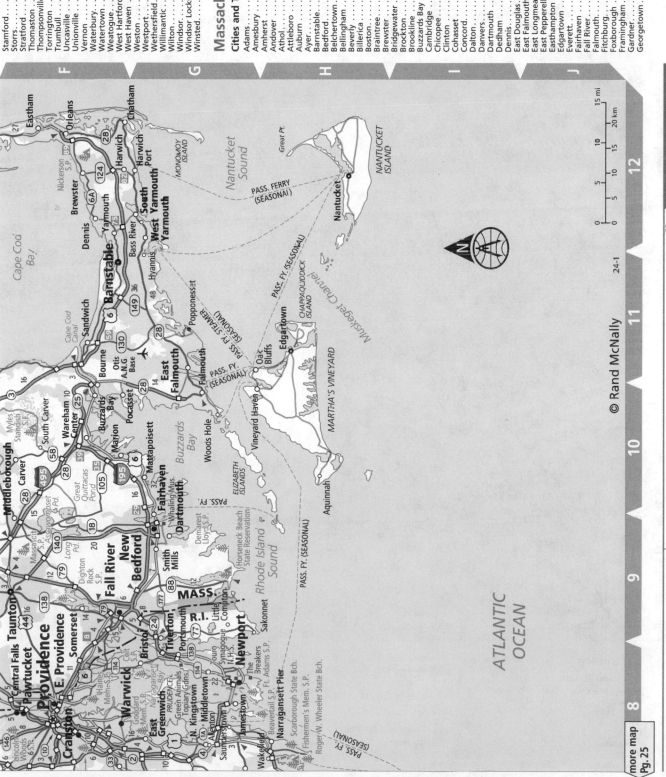

Tourism Information Mass. Office of Travel & Tourism: (800) 227-6277, (617) 973-8500 www.visitma.com

Road Conditions & Construction 511, Metro Boston: (617) 986-5511 Central: (508) 499-5511, Western: (413) 754-5511 www.mass511.com

Travel planning & on-the-road resources

Delaware state facts

Nickname: The First State
Capital: Dover, C-9
Population: 989,948 (rank: 45th)
Largest city: Wilmington, 70,898, A-9
Land area: 1,948 sq. mi. (rank: 49th)
Highest point: Ebright Azimuth, 448 ft., A-9

Travel planning & on-the-road resources

Tourism Information
Delaware Tourism Office:
(866) 284-7483
www.visitdelaware.com

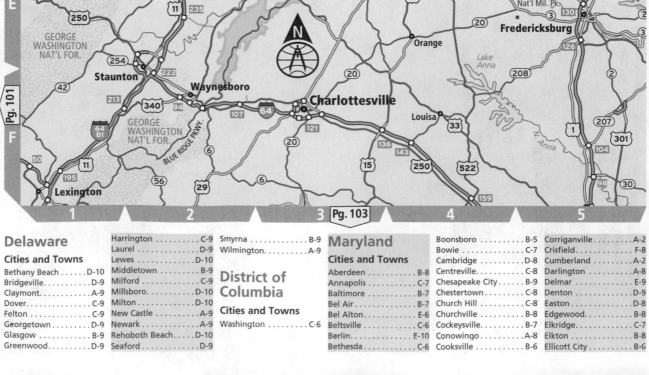

Road Conditions & Construction
(800) 652-5600
(302) 760-2080
www.deldot.gov

Pg. 89
Pg. 100
Pg. 101
Pg. 103

Delaware

Cities and Towns

Bethany Beach D-10
Bridgeville. D-9
Claymont. A-9
Dover. C-9
Felton C-9
Georgetown D-9
Glasgow B-9
Greenwood. D-9
Harrington C-9
Laurel D-9
Lewes D-10
Middletown B-9
Milford C-9
Millsboro. D-10
Milton D-10
New Castle A-9
Newark A-9
Rehoboth Beach. D-10
Seaford D-9
Smyrna B-9
Wilmington. A-9

District of Columbia

Cities and Towns

Washington C-6

Maryland

Cities and Towns

Aberdeen B-8
Annapolis C-7
Baltimore B-7
Bel Air. B-7
Bel Alton. E-6
Beltsville C-6
Berlin. E-10
Bethesda C-6
Boonsboro B-5
Bowie C-7
Cambridge D-8
Centreville. C-8
Chesapeake City. B-9
Chestertown C-8
Church Hill C-8
Churchville B-8
Cockeysville. B-7
Conowingo A-8
Cooksville B-6
Corriganville A-2
Crisfield. F-8
Cumberland A-2
Darlington A-8
Delmar E-9
Denton D-9
Easton D-8
Edgewood. B-8
Elkridge. C-7
Elkton B-8
Ellicott City B-6

NOTE: Maps are not always in alphabetical order.
See Page 1 for map location in this atlas.

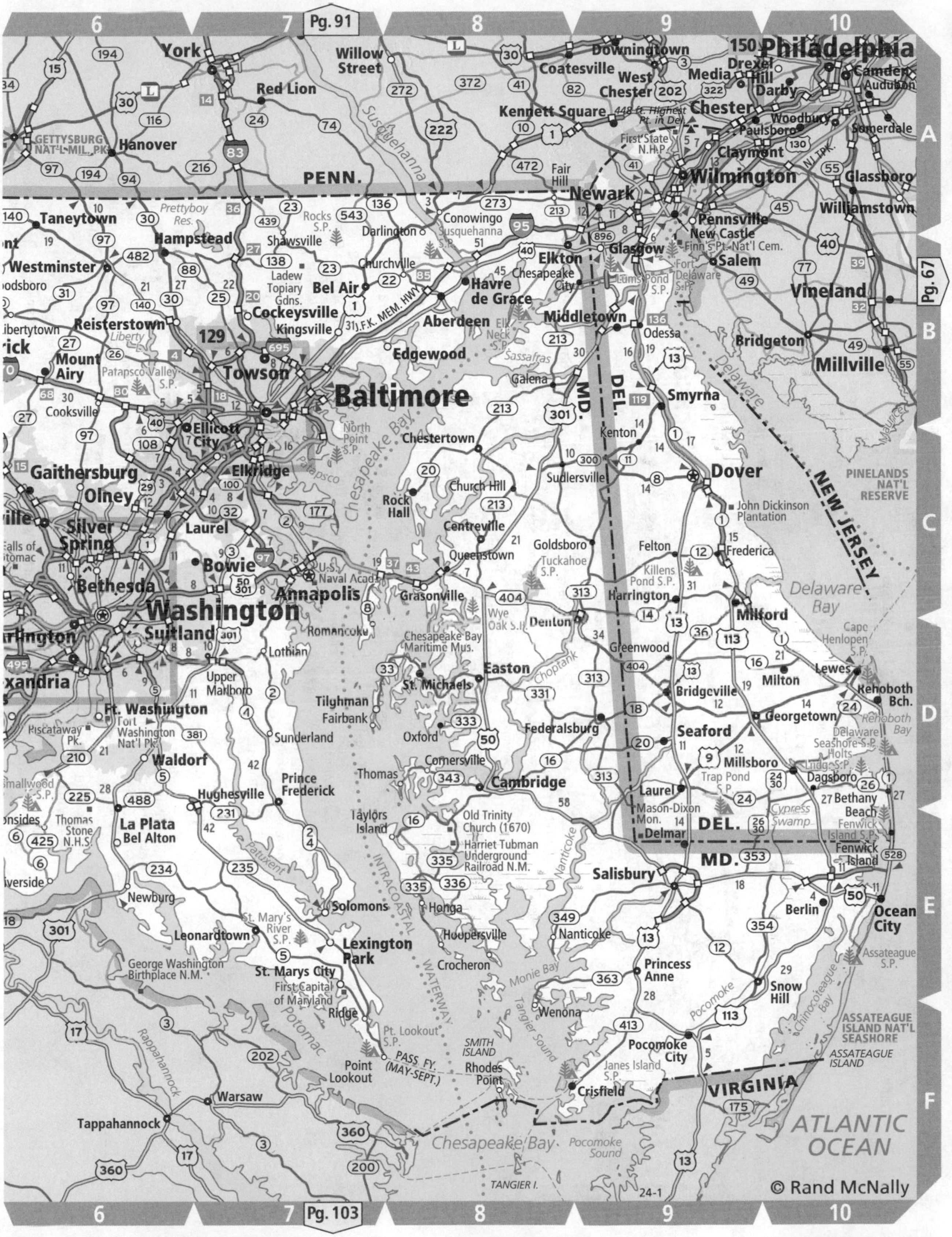

Pg. 91
Pg. 67
Pg. 103

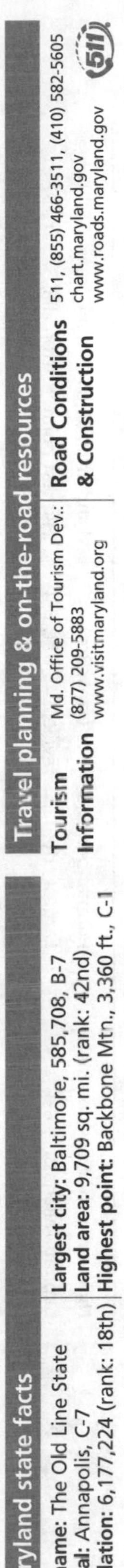

Place	Grid	Place	Grid	Place	Grid	Place	Grid	Place	Grid	Place	Grid
Emmitsburg	A-5	Grasonville	C-8	Laurel	C-6	Oxford	D-8	St. Marys City	E-7	Thurmont	B-5
Federalsburg	D-9	Hagerstown	A-5	Leonardtown	E-7	Pocomoke City	F-9	St. Michaels	D-8	Tilghman	D-7
Flintstone	A-3	Hampstead	B-6	Lexington Park	E-7	Prince Frederick	D-7	Salisbury	E-9	Towson	B-7
Fort Washington	D-6	Hancock	A-4	Libertytown	B-6	Princess Anne	E-9	Silver Spring	C-6	Tuscarora	C-5
Frederick	B-5	Havre de Grace	B-8	Lothian	D-7	Queenstown	C-8	Snow Hill	E-9	Upper Marlboro	D-7
Frostburg	A-2	Hoopersville	E-8	Mount Airy	B-6	Reisterstown	B-6	Solomons	E-7	Waldorf	D-6
Gaithersburg	C-6	Hughesville	D-6	Nanticoke	E-8	Rhodes Point	F-8	Sudlersville	C-8	Wenona	F-8
Galena	B-8	Ironsides	E-6	Newburg	E-6	Ridge	F-7	Suitland	D-6	Westernport	B-2
Germantown	C-5	Kingsville	B-7	Oakland	B-1	Rock Hall	C-8	Sunderland	D-7	Westminster	B-6
Goldsboro	C-9	La Plata	D-6	Ocean City	E-10	Rockville	C-6	Taneytown	A-6	Williamsport	B-4
Grantsville	A-2	La Vale	A-2	Olney	C-6	Romancoke	D-7	Taylors Island	E-8	Woodsboro	B-5

Florida state facts

Nickname: The Sunshine State
Capital: Tallahassee, B-1

Population: 18,801,310 (rank: 3rd)
Largest city: Jacksonville, 949,611, B-4

Land area: 53,634 sq. mi. (rank: 26th)
Highest point: Britton Hill, 345 ft., I-2

Pg. 33

For continuation see inset below

Florida

Cities and Towns

Altamonte Springs . . . D-4
Apalachicola . . . I-3
Arcadia . . . F-4
Atlantic Beach . . . B-4
Bartow . . . E-4
Belle Glade . . . G-5
Blountstown . . . H-3
Boca Raton . . . G-6
Bonifay . . . H-3
Bradenton . . . F-3
Brandon . . . E-3
Brooksville . . . D-3
Bunnell . . . C-4
Bushnell . . . D-4
Cape Canaveral . . . E-5
Cape Coral . . . G-4
Chipley . . . H-3
Clearwater . . . E-3
Clermont . . . D-4
Cocoa Beach . . . E-5
Coral Gables . . . H-6
Crawfordville . . . B-1
Crestview . . . H-2
Cross City . . . C-2
Dade City . . . E-3
Dania Beach . . . H-6
Daytona Beach . . . D-5
De Funiak Springs . . . H-2
DeBary . . . D-4
Deerfield Beach . . . G-6
DeLand . . . D-4
Delray Beach . . . G-6
Dunedin . . . E-3
Edgewater . . . D-5
Englewood . . . F-3
Eustis . . . D-4
Fernandina Beach . . . B-4
Fort Lauderdale . . . H-6
Fort Myers . . . G-4
Fort Pierce . . . F-6
Fort Walton Beach . . . H-2
Gainesville . . . C-3
Green Cove Springs . . . C-4
Haines City . . . E-4
Hallandale Beach . . . H-6
Hialeah . . . H-6
Holly Hill . . . C-5
Hollywood . . . H-6
Homestead . . . H-6
Homosassa . . . D-3
Homosassa Springs . . . D-3
Hudson . . . E-3
Immokalee . . . G-4
Inverness . . . D-3
Jacksonville . . . B-4
Jacksonville Beach . . . B-4
Jasper . . . B-3
Jensen Beach . . . F-6
Jupiter . . . F-6
Kendall . . . H-6
Key Largo . . . I-6
Key West . . . J-4
Kissimmee . . . E-4
La Belle . . . G-4
Lady Lake . . . D-4
Lake Buena Vista . . . E-4
Lake Butler . . . B-3
Lake City . . . B-3
Lake Wales . . . E-4
Lake Worth Beach . . . G-6

NOTE: Maps are not always in alphabetical order. See Page 1 for map location in this atlas.

Lakeland	E-4
Largo	E-3
Leesburg	D-4
Lehigh Acres	G-4
Live Oak	B-3
Lutz	E-3
Macclenny	B-3
Madeira Beach	E-3
Madison	B-2
Marathon	I-5
Marco Island	H-4
Marianna	H-3
Melbourne	E-5
Miami	H-6
Miami Beach	H-6
Middleburg	B-4
Milton	H-1
Monticello	B-2
Moore Haven	G-5
Naples	H-4
New Port Richey	E-3
New Smyrna Beach	D-5
North Palm Beach	G-6
Ocala	D-3
Okeechobee	F-5
Orange Park	B-4
Orlando	D-4
Ormond Beach	C-5
Palatka	C-4
Palm Bay	E-5
Palm Beach	G-6
Palm Coast	C-5
Palmetto	F-3
Panama City	I-3
Pensacola	H-1
Perry	B-2
Plant City	E-4
Pompano Beach	G-6
Port Charlotte	F-4
Port Orange	D-5
Port St. Joe	I-3
Port St. Lucie	F-6
Punta Gorda	G-4
Quincy	B-1
St. Augustine	C-4
St. Cloud	E-4
St. Pete Beach	E-3
St. Petersburg	E-3
Sanford	D-4
Sarasota	F-3
Sebastian	E-5
Sebring	F-4
Starke	C-4
Stuart	F-6
Sunrise	G-6
Tallahassee	B-1
Tampa	E-3
Tarpon Springs	E-3
Tavares	D-4
Titusville	D-5
Trenton	C-3
Venice	F-3
Vero Beach	F-6
Warrington	H-1
Wauchula	F-4
West Palm Beach	G-6
Weston	H-6
Winter Garden	D-4
Winter Haven	E-4
Yeehaw Junction	E-5
Zephyrhills	E-3

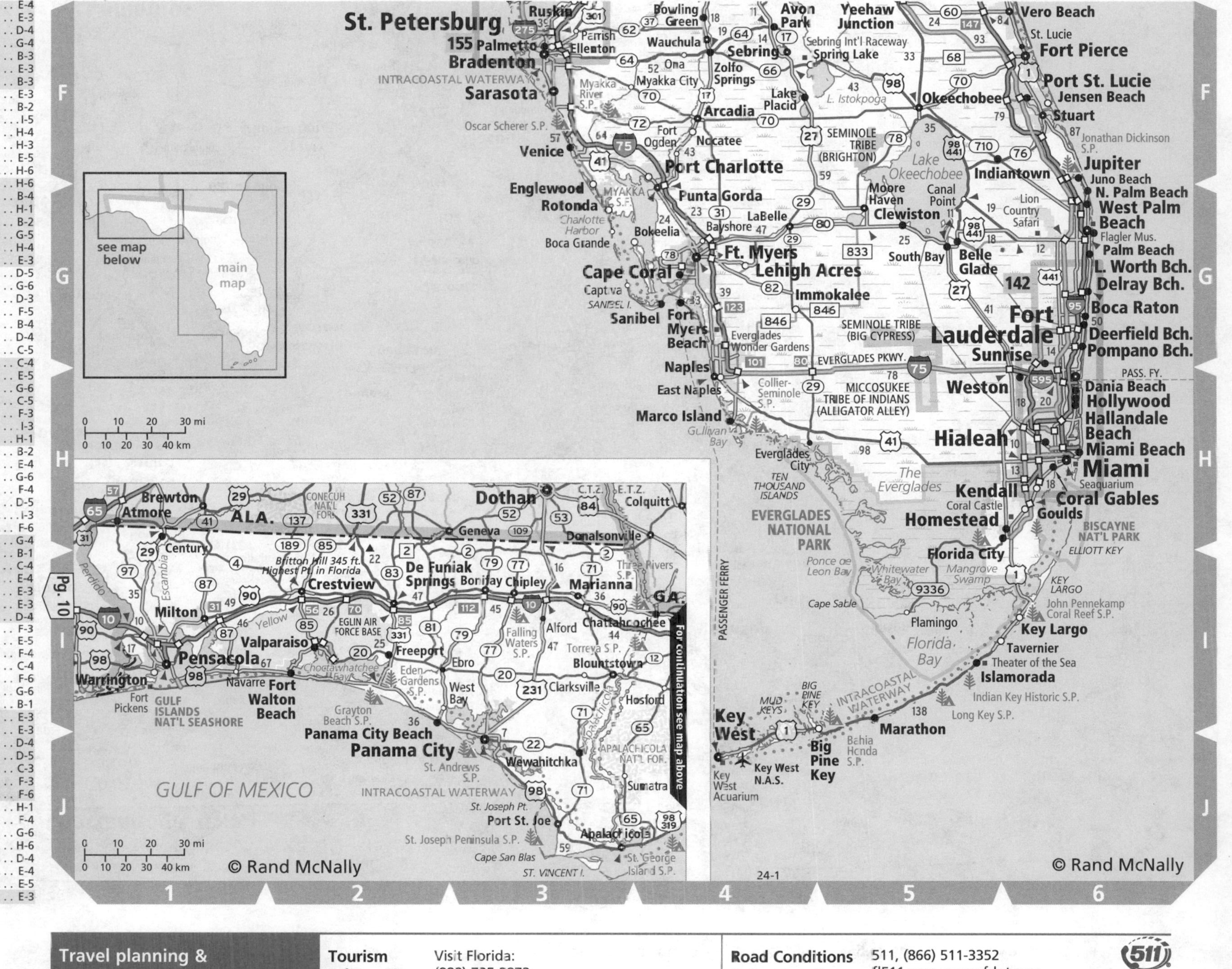

Travel planning & on-the-road resources

Tourism Information — Visit Florida: (888) 735-2872 www.visitflorida.com

Road Conditions & Construction — 511, (866) 511-3352 fl511.com, www.fdot.gov

Georgia state facts

Nickname: The Peach State
Capital: Atlanta, C-2

Population: 10,711,908 (rank: 8th)
Largest city: Atlanta, 498,715, C-2

Land area: 57,701 sq. mi. (rank: 21st)
Highest point: Brasstown Bald, 4,784 ft., A-3

Pg. 47 Pg. 74 Pg. 75 Pg. 10

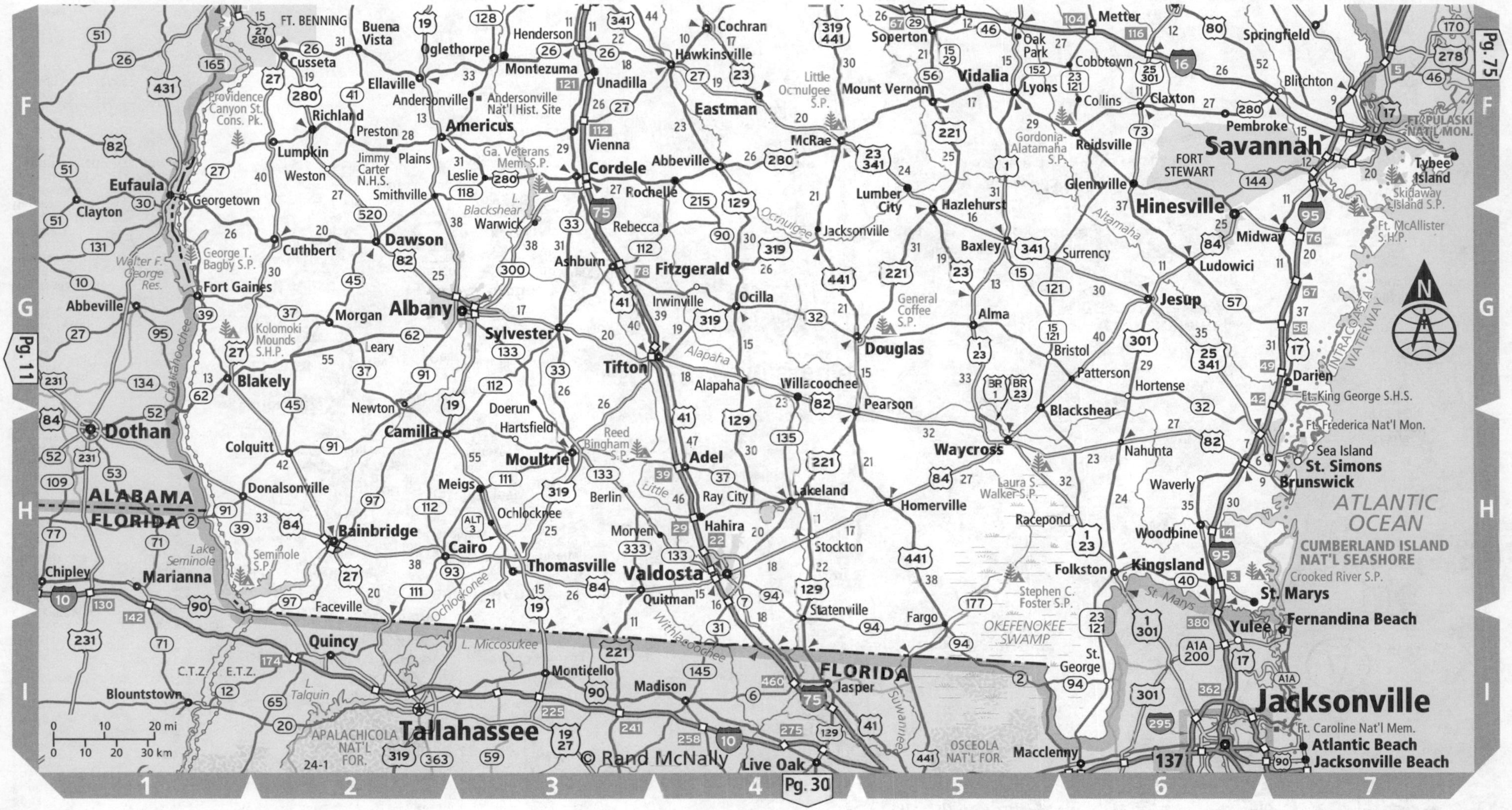

Pg. 75
Pg. 11
Pg. 30

Georgia

Cities and Towns

City	Grid
Adel	H-4
Albany	G-3
Alpharetta	C-2
Americus	F-2
Ashburn	G-3
Athens	C-4
Atlanta	C-2
Augusta	D-6
Austell	C-2
Bainbridge	H-2
Barnesville	D-3
Blakely	G-1
Bremen	C-1
Brunswick	H-7
Buford	C-3
Cairo	H-2
Calhoun	B-1
Camilla	H-2
Canton	B-2
Carrollton	D-1
Cartersville	C-2
Cedartown	C-1
Cochran	F-4
College Park	C-2
Columbus	E-1
Commerce	B-4
Conyers	C-3
Cordele	F-3
Covington	D-3
Cumming	B-3
Dallas	C-2
Dalton	A-1
Dawson	G-2
Decatur	C-2
Douglas	G-4
Douglasville	C-2
Dublin	E-4
Duluth	C-3
East Point	C-2
Eastman	F-4
Eatonton	D-4
Elberton	C-4
Fairburn	D-2
Fayetteville	D-2
Fitzgerald	G-4
Fort Oglethorpe	A-1
Fort Valley	E-3
Gainesville	B-3
Glennville	F-6
Griffin	D-2
Hawkinsville	F-4
Hinesville	G-6
Jesup	G-6
Kingsland	H-6
LaGrange	D-1
LaFayette	B-1
Lawrenceville	C-3
Lilburn	C-3
Lithia Springs	C-2
Macon	E-3
Marietta	C-2
McDonough	D-3
Milledgeville	D-4
Monroe	C-3
Morrow	D-2
Moultrie	H-3
Newnan	D-2
Norcross	C-3
Perry	E-3
Quitman	H-3
Rome	B-1
Roswell	C-2
St. Marys	H-6
Sandersville	E-5
Savannah	F-7
Smyrna	C-2
St. Simons	H-7
Statesboro	E-6
Stockbridge	D-2
Stone Mountain	C-3
Summerville	B-1
Swainsboro	E-5
Sylvester	G-3
Thomaston	E-2
Thomasville	H-3
Thomson	D-5
Tifton	G-4
Toccoa	B-4
Valdosta	H-4
Vidalia	F-5
Warner Robins	E-3
Washington	C-5
Waycross	H-5
Waynesboro	D-6
Winder	C-3

Travel planning & on-the-road resources

Tourism Information
Explore Georgia:
(800) 847-4842
www.exploregeorgia.org

Road Conditions & Construction
511, (877) 694-2511
511ga.org

Idaho state facts

Nickname: The Gem State
Capital: Boise, H-2
Population: 1,839,106 (rank: 38th)
Largest city: Boise, 235,684, H-2
Land area: 82,623 sq. mi. (rank: 11th)
Highest point: Borah Peak, 12,662 ft., G-4

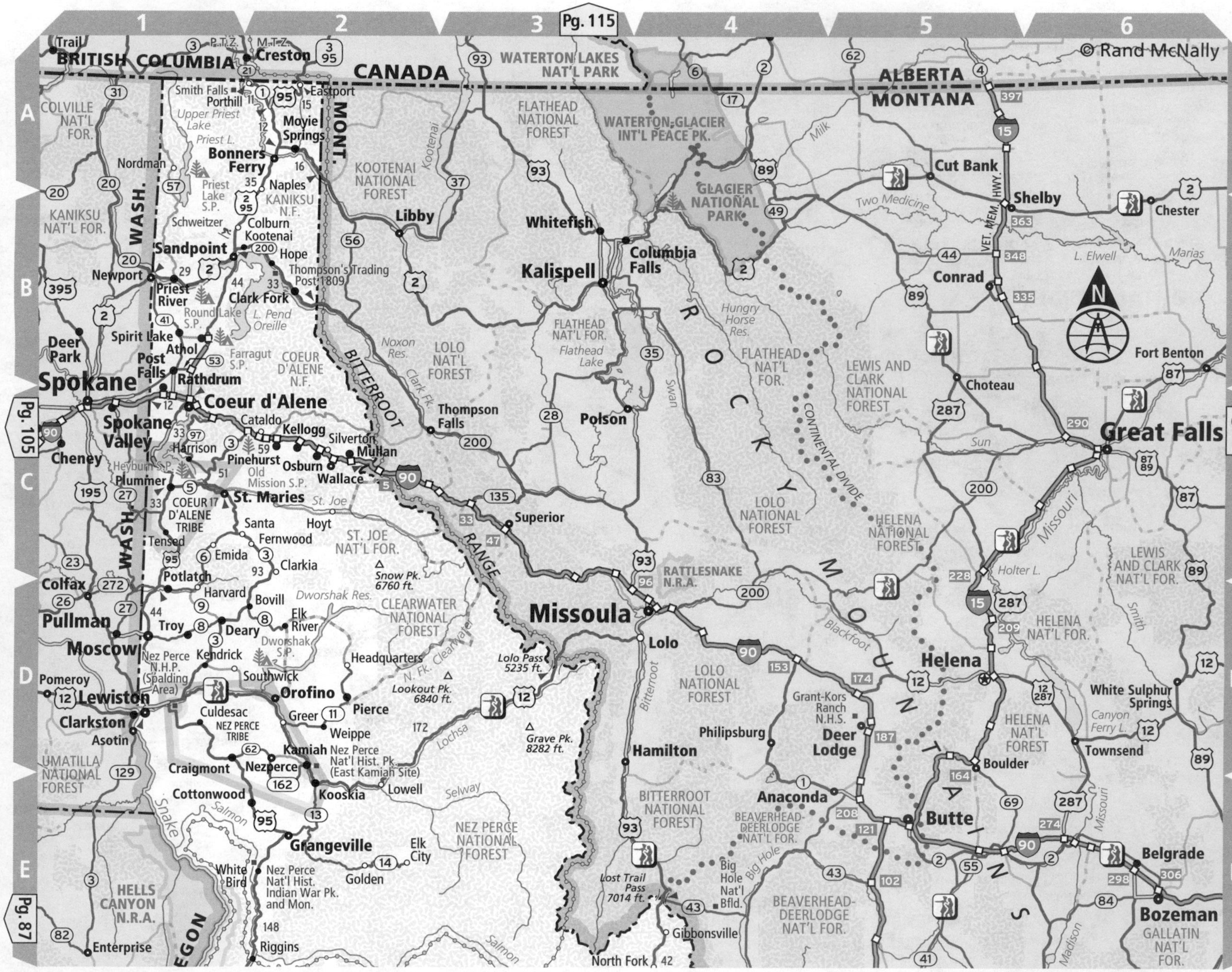

Idaho

Cities and Towns

Aberdeen	I-5
Albion	I-4
American Falls	I-5
Arco	H-4
Ashton	G-6
Athol	B-1
Bancroft	I-6
Bellevue	H-3
Blackfoot	H-5
Bliss	I-3
Bloomington	I-6
Boise	H-2
Bonners Ferry	A-2
Bovill	D-2
Buhl	I-3
Burley	I-4
Caldwell	H-1
Cambridge	G-1
Carey	H-4
Cascade	G-2
Castleford	I-3
Cataldo	C-2
Challis	G-3
Chester	G-6
Clark Fork	B-2
Coeur d'Alene	C-1
Cottonwood	E-2
Council	F-1
Craigmont	D-1
Culdesac	D-1
Dayton	J-5
Deary	D-1
Declo	I-4
Downey	I-5
Driggs	H-6
Dubois	G-5
Eden	I-3
Elk City	E-2
Emmett	G-1
Fairfield	H-3
Fernwood	C-2
Filer	I-3
Firth	H-5
Franklin	J-6
Fruitland	G-1
Georgetown	I-6
Glenns Ferry	I-2
Gooding	I-3
Grace	I-6
Grand View	I-2
Grangeville	E-2
Hagerman	I-3
Hailey	H-3
Hammett	I-2
Hansen	I-3
Harrison	C-1
Hollister	I-3
Homedale	H-1
Horseshoe Bend	G-2
Idaho City	G-2
Idaho Falls	H-5
Inkom	I-5
Jerome	I-3
Kamiah	D-2
Kellogg	C-2
Kendrick	D-1
Ketchum	H-3
Kimberly	I-3
Kooskia	E-2
Kootenai	B-2

Lava Hot Springs I-5
Letha G-1
Lewiston D-1
Mackay G-4
Malad City J-5
Marsing H-1
McCall F-2
McCammon I-5
Melba H-1
Meridian H-1
Montpelier I-6
Moreland H-5
Moscow D-1
Mountain Home H-2
Moyie Springs A-2
Mud Lake G-5
Mullan C-2
Murphy H-1
Nampa H-1
Naples A-2
New Meadows F-2
New Plymouth G-1
Newdale G-6
Nezperce D-2
Oakley I-4
Orofino D-2
Osburn C-2
Paris I-6
Paul I-4
Payette G-1
Pierce D-2
Pinehurst C-2
Pleasantview J-5
Plummer C-1
Pocatello I-5
Post Falls C-1
Potlatch D-1
Preston J-6
Priest River B-1
Rathdrum B-1
Rexburg G-6
Richfield H-3
Rigby H-5
Riggins E-2
Ririe H-6
Roberts H-5
Rockland I-5
Rupert I-4
St. Anthony G-6
St. Maries C-1
Salmon F-4
Sandpoint B-1
Shelley H-5
Shoshone I-3
Silverton C-2
Soda Springs I-6
Spirit Lake B-1
Star H-1
Sugar City G-6
Sun Valley H-3
Swan Valley H-6
Sweet G-2
Tetonia G-6
Troy D-1
Twin Falls I-3
Victor H-6
Wallace C-2
Weippe D-2
Weiser G-1
Wendell I-3
Weston J-5

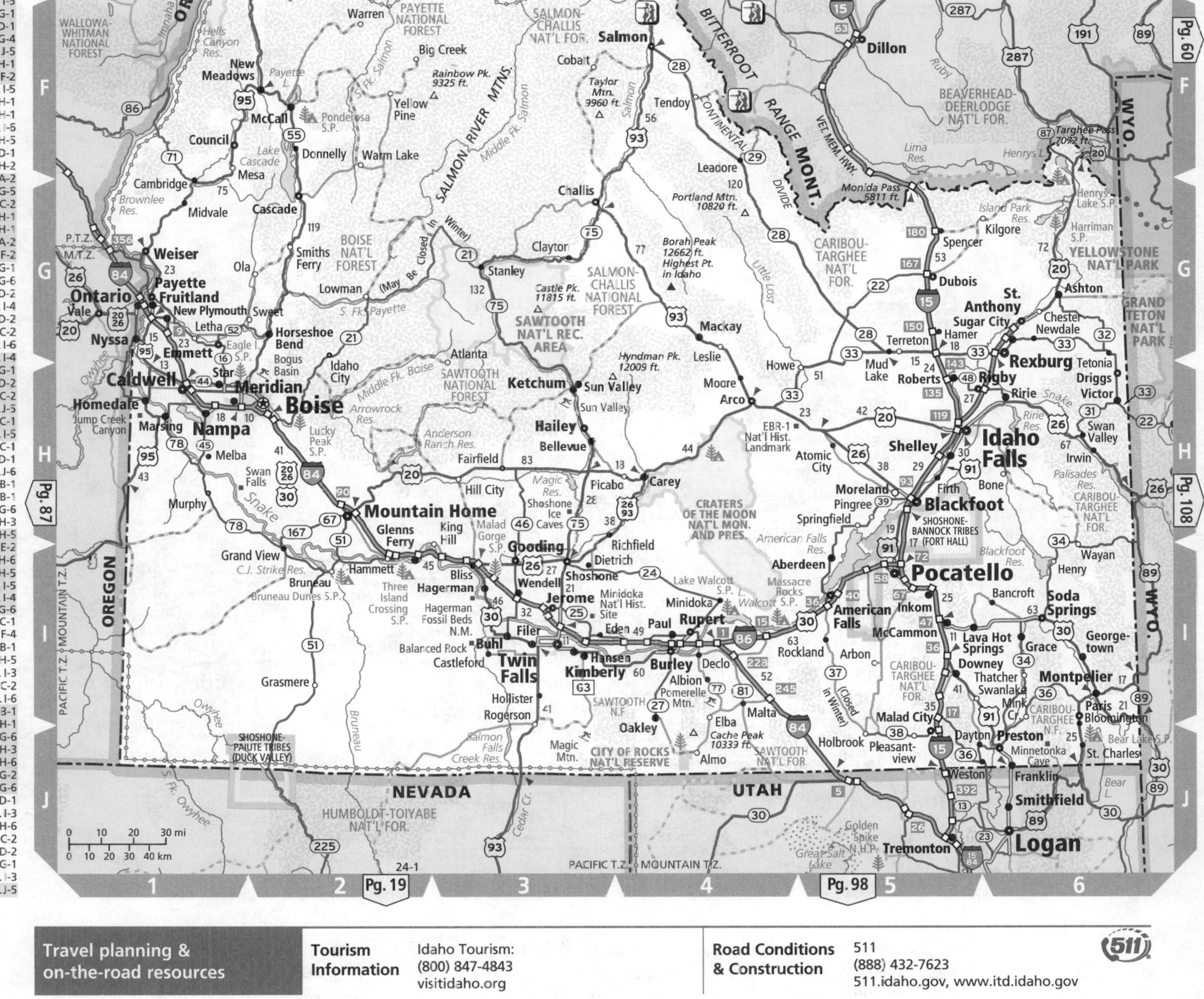

Travel planning & on-the-road resources

Tourism Information	Idaho Tourism: (800) 847-4843 visitidaho.org	**Road Conditions & Construction**	511 (888) 432-7623 511.idaho.gov, www.itd.idaho.gov

Illinois state facts

Nickname: Land of Lincoln
Capital: Springfield, E-3
Population: 12,812,508 (rank: 6th)
Largest city: Chicago, 2,746,388, B-6
Land area: 55,499 sq. mi. (rank: 24th)
Highest point: Charles Mound, 1,235 ft., A-2

Illinois

Cities and Towns

Albion H-5
Aledo C-2
Alton G-2
Arlington Heights B-5
Aurora B-5
Belleville H-3
Belvidere A-4
Benton I-4
Bloomington D-4
Cairo J-4
Cambridge C-3
Canton D-3
Carbondale I-4
Carlinville F-3
Carlyle G-4
Carmi H-5
Carrollton F-2
Carthage D-1
Centralia H-4
Champaign E-5
Charleston F-5
Chester I-3
Chicago B-6
Chicago Heights C-6
Clinton E-4
Collinsville G-3
Crete C-6
Crystal Lake A-5
Danville E-6
Decatur E-4
DeKalb B-4
Des Plaines B-5
Dixon B-3
East Moline C-2
East St. Louis G-3
Edwardsville G-3
Effingham G-5
Elgin B-5
Eureka D-4
Evanston B-6
Fairfield H-5
Forsyth E-4
Freeport A-3
Galena A-2
Galesburg C-2
Granite City G-3
Greenville G-3
Harrisburg I-5
Havana E-3
Herrin I-4
Highland Park A-6
Hillsboro G-3
Jacksonville F-2
Jerseyville G-2
Joliet B-5
Jonesboro I-4
Kankakee C-5
Kewanee C-3
La Salle C-4
Lacon C-3
Lake Forest A-5
Lawrenceville G-6
Lewistown D-3
Libertyville A-5
Lincoln E-4
Lisle B-5
Louisville G-5
Macomb D-2
Manteno C-6
Marion I-4

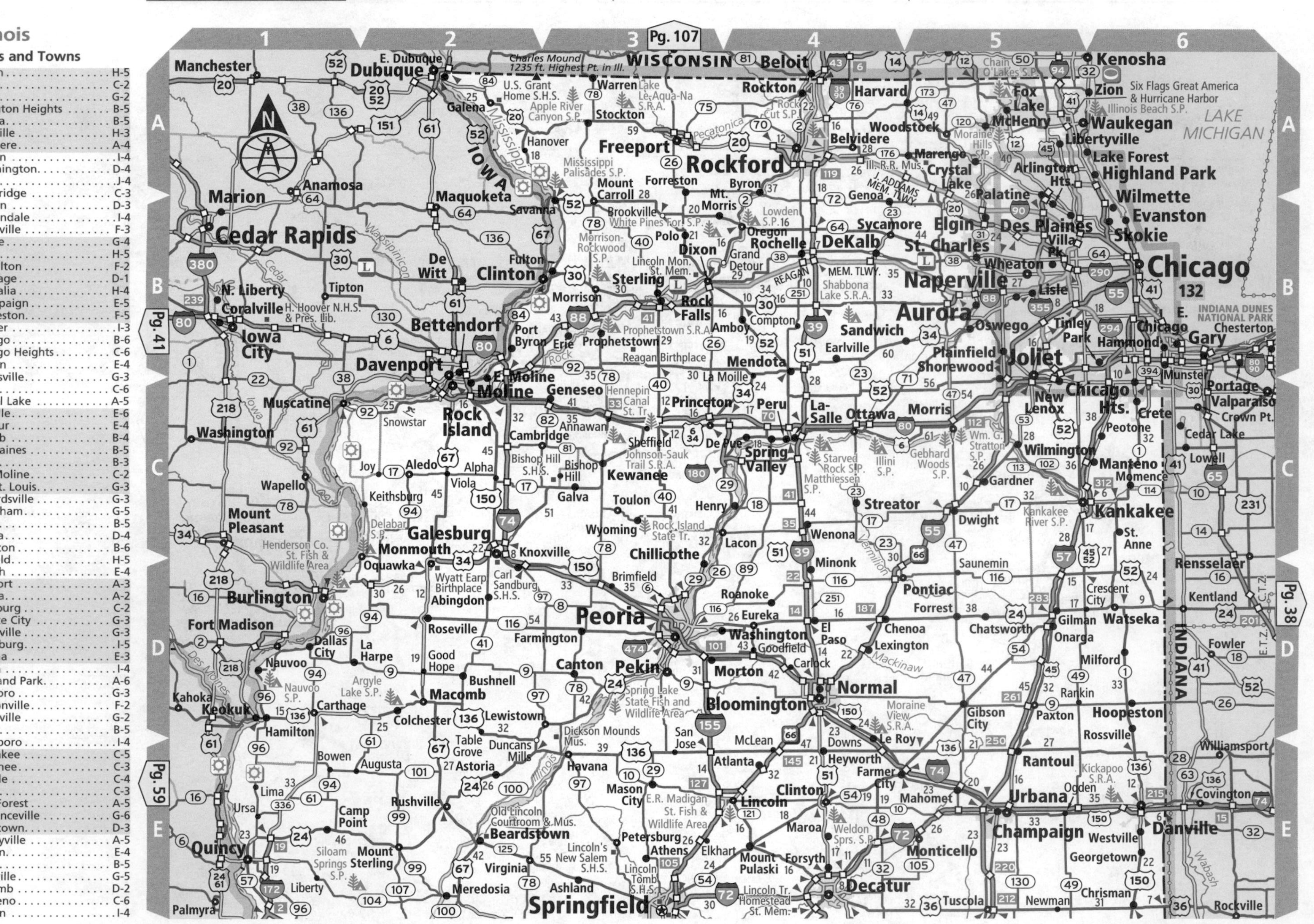

NOTE: Maps are not always in alphabetical order.
See Page 1 for map location in this atlas.

Marshall F-6
Mattoon F-5
McHenry A-5
McLeansboro H-5
Metropolis J-4
Moline C-2
Monmouth D-2
Monticello E-5
Morris C-5
Morrison B-3
Morton D-3
Mount Carmel H-6
Mount Carroll B-3
Mount Sterling E-2
Mount Vernon H-4
Murphysboro I-4
Naperville B-5
Nashville H-4
New Lenox C-5
Newton G-5
Normal D-4
O'Fallon G-3
Olney G-5
Oquawka C-2
Oregon B-4
Oswego B-5
Ottawa C-4
Paris F-6
Paxton D-5
Pekin D-3
Peoria D-3
Peru C-4
Petersburg E-3
Pinckneyville H-4
Pittsfield F-2
Plainfield B-5
Pontiac D-4
Princeton C-3
Quincy E-1
Rantoul E-5
Robinson G-6
Rock Falls B-3
Rock Island C-2
Rockford A-4
Rushville E-2
St. Charles B-5
Salem G-4
Shawneetown I-5
Shelbyville F-4
Shorewood C-5
Skokie B-6
Springfield E-3
Sterling B-3
Streator C-4
Sycamore B-4
Taylorville F-4
Toulon C-3
Tuscola E-5
Urbana E-5
Vandalia G-4
Virginia E-2
Washington D-3
Waterloo H-2
Watseka D-6
Waukegan A-5
Wheaton B-5
Wilmette B-6
Winchester F-2
Winnetka B-6
Woodstock A-5
Zion A-6

Travel planning & on-the-road resources

Tourism Information
Illinois Bureau of Tourism:
(312) 814-4732
www.enjoyillinois.com

Road Conditions & Construction
(800) 452-4368
www.gettingaroundillinois.com
idot.illinois.gov

Indiana state facts

Nickname: The Hoosier State
Capital: Indianapolis, F-4

Population: 6,785,528 (rank: 17th)
Largest city: Indianapolis, 887,642, F-4

Land area: 35,817 sq. mi. (rank: 38th)
Highest point: Hoosier Hill, 1,257 ft., E-6

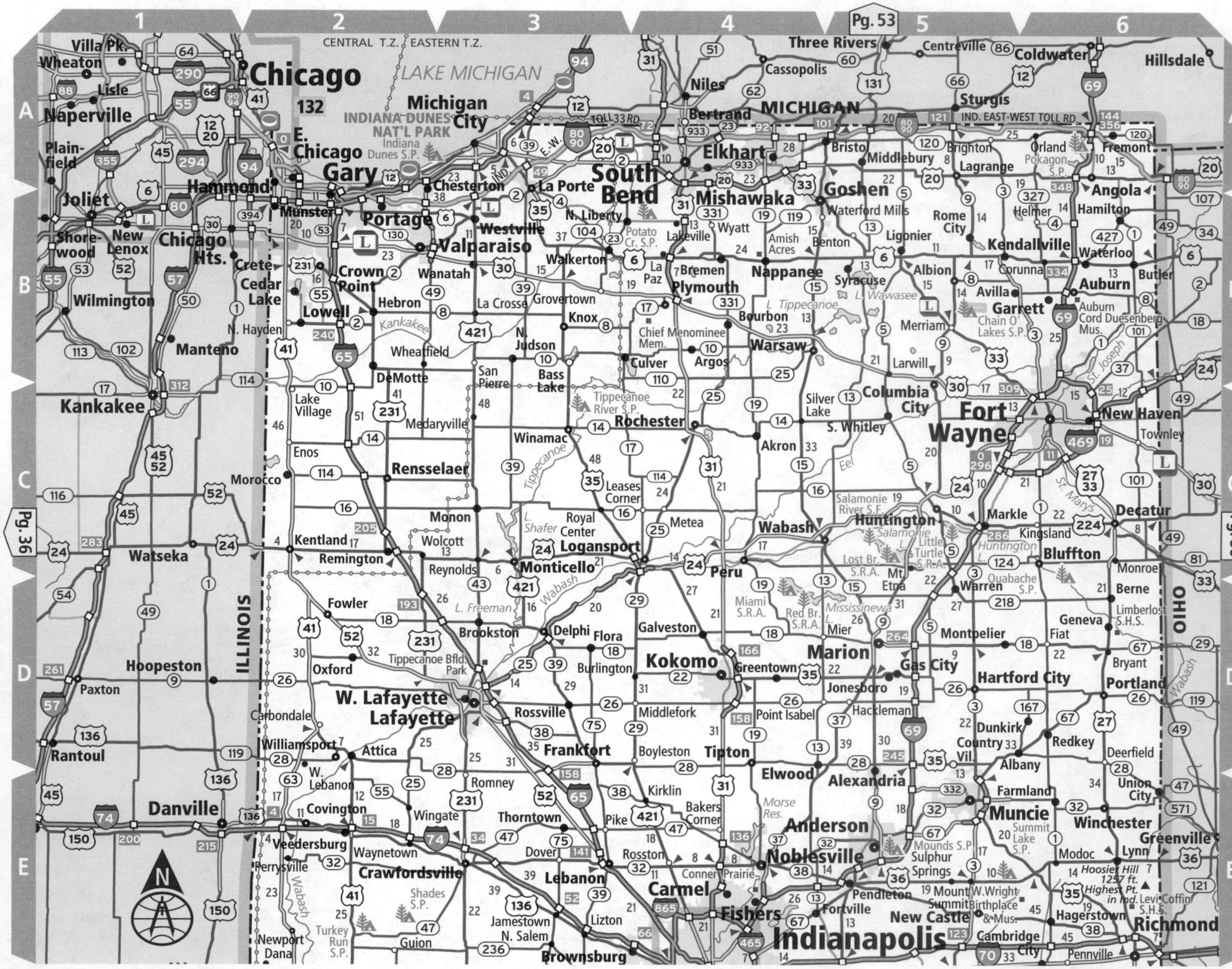

Indiana

Cities and Towns

City	Grid
Albion	B-5
Alexandria	D-5
Anderson	E-5
Angola	A-6
Attica	D-2
Auburn	B-6
Batesville	G-6
Bedford	H-3
Berne	D-6
Bicknell	H-2
Bloomfield	G-3
Bloomington	G-3
Bluffton	C-6
Boonville	I-2
Brazil	F-2
Bremen	B-4
Brookville	F-6
Brownsburg	E-4
Brownstown	H-4
Carmel	E-4
Cedar Lake	B-2
Charlestown	I-5
Chesterton	A-2
Clarksville	I-5
Clinton	F-2
Columbia City	B-5
Columbus	G-4
Connersville	F-6
Corydon	I-4
Covington	E-2
Crawfordsville	E-3
Crown Point	B-2
Danville	F-3
Decatur	C-6
Delphi	D-3
DeMotte	B-2
East Chicago	A-2
Edinburgh	G-4
Elkhart	A-4
Elwood	D-4
English	I-3
Evansville	J-1
Fort Wayne	C-6
Fortville	E-4
Fowler	D-2
Frankfort	D-3
Franklin	F-4
French Lick	H-3
Garrett	B-6
Gary	B-2
Gas City	D-5
Goshen	B-4
Greencastle	F-3
Greenfield	F-5
Greensburg	G-5
Greenwood	F-4
Hammond	A-2
Hartford City	D-5
Hebron	B-2
Huntingburg	I-3
Huntington	C-5
Indianapolis	F-4
Jasper	I-3
Jeffersonville	I-5
Kendallville	B-5
Kentland	C-2
Knox	B-3
Kokomo	D-4
Lafayette	D-3
Lagrange	A-5

Pg. 53

Pg. 36

Pg. 80

NOTE: Maps are not always in alphabetical order.
See Page 1 for map location in this atlas.

La Porte A-3
Lawrenceburg G-6
Lebanon E-3
Liberty F-6
Ligonier B-5
Linton G-2
Logansport C-4
Lowell B-2
Madison H-5
Marion D-5
Martinsville F-3
Michigan City A-3
Mishawaka A-4
Mitchell H-3
Monticello C-3
Mooresville F-4
Mount Vernon J-1
Muncie E-5
Nappanee B-4
Nashville G-4
New Albany I-5
New Castle E-5
New Haven C-6
Newport E-2
Noblesville E-4
North Terre Haute F-2
North Vernon G-5
Paoli H-3
Pendleton E-5
Peru C-4
Petersburg H-2
Plainfield F-4
Plymouth B-4
Portage B-2
Portland D-6
Princeton I-1
Rensselaer C-2
Richmond E-6
Rising Sun G-6
Rochester C-4
Rockport J-2
Rockville F-2
Rushville F-5
Salem H-4
Schererville B-2
Scottsburg H-5
Sellersburg I-5
Seymour G-4
Shelbyville F-5
Shoals H-3
South Bend A-4
Spencer G-3
Sullivan G-2
Syracuse B-5
Tell City J-3
Terre Haute F-2
Tipton D-4
Union City E-6
Valparaiso B-2
Vernon G-5
Versailles G-6
Vevay H-6
Vincennes H-2
Wabash C-5
Warsaw B-4
Washington H-2
West Lafayette D-3
Westville B-3
Williamsport D-2
Winamac C-3
Winchester E-6

Pg. 82

Pg. 37

Pg. 44

Pg. 46

© Rand McNally

Travel planning & on-the-road resources

Tourism Information
Indiana Office of Tourism Development:
(317) 232-8860
visitindiana.com

Road Conditions & Construction
(800) 261-7623
511in.org, pws.trafficwise.org/pws, www.in.gov/indot/travel-conditions/travel-information

Iowa state facts

Nickname: The Hawkeye State
Capital: Des Moines, D-5
Population: 3,190,369 (rank: 31st)
Largest city: Des Moines, 214,133, D-5
Land area: 55,839 sq. mi. (rank: 23rd)
Highest point: Hawkeye Point, 1,670 ft., A-2

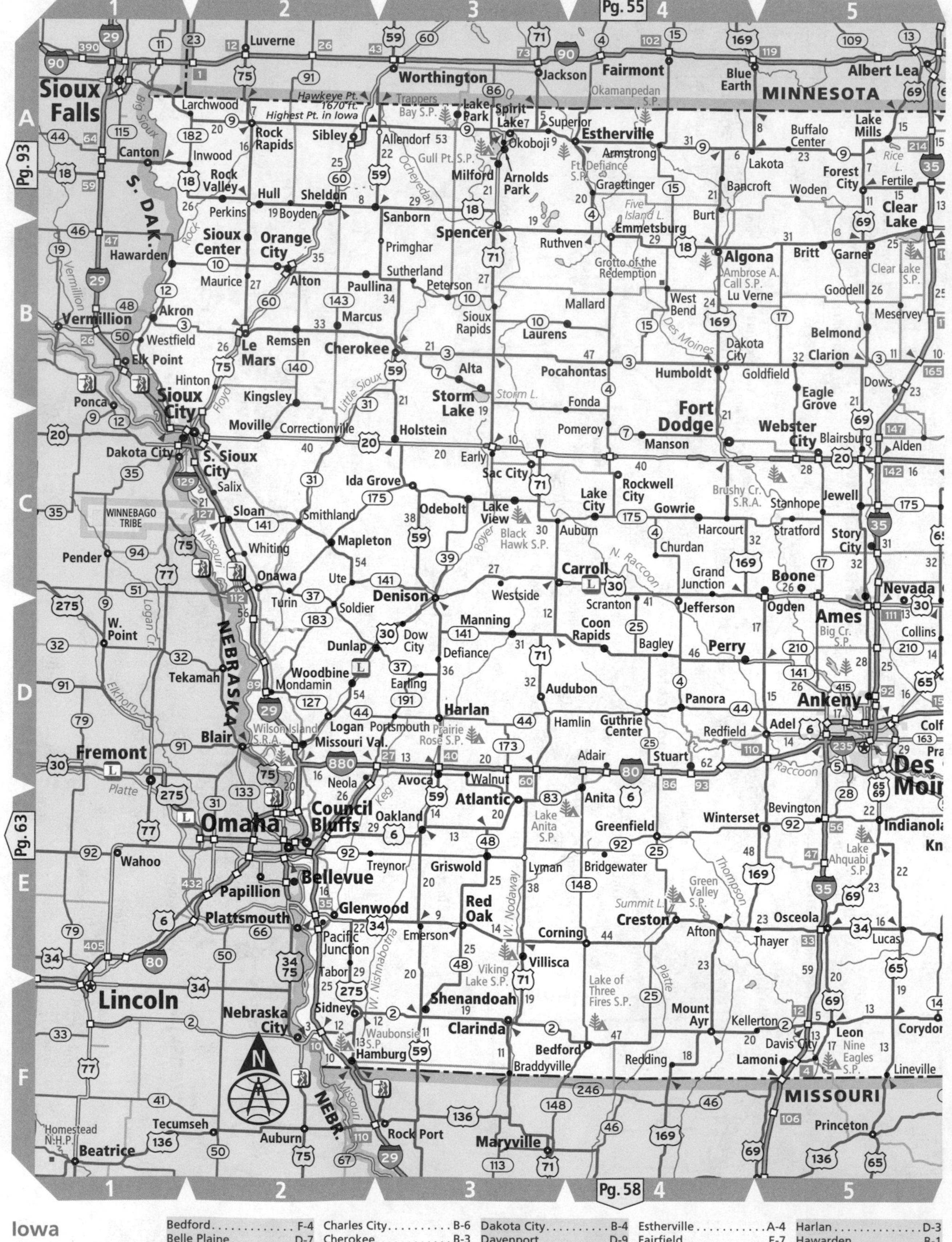

Iowa

Cities and Towns

Adel D-5
Albia E-6
Algona B-4
Allison B-6
Ames C-5
Anamosa C-8
Ankeny D-5
Atlantic E-3
Audubon D-3
Bedford F-4
Belle Plaine D-7
Belmond B-5
Bettendorf D-9
Bloomfield F-7
Boone C-5
Burlington F-8
Carroll C-3
Cedar Falls C-7
Cedar Rapids D-8
Centerville F-6
Chariton E-5
Charles City B-6
Cherokee B-3
Clarinda F-3
Clarion B-5
Clear Lake B-5
Clinton D-10
Coralville D-8
Corning E-4
Corydon F-5
Council Bluffs E-2
Cresco A-7
Creston E-4
Dakota City B-4
Davenport D-9
De Witt D-9
Decorah A-7
Denison C-3
Des Moines D-5
Dubuque C-9
Dyersville C-8
Eagle Grove B-5
Eldora C-6
Elkader B-8
Emmetsburg B-4
Estherville A-4
Fairfield E-7
Forest City A-5
Fort Dodge C-4
Fort Madison F-8
Garner B-5
Glenwood E-2
Greenfield E-4
Grinnell D-6
Grundy Center C-6
Guthrie Center D-4
Hampton B-6
Harlan D-3
Hawarden B-1
Humboldt B-4
Ida Grove C-3
Independence C-7
Indianola E-5
Iowa City D-8
Iowa Falls C-6
Jefferson D-4
Keokuk F-8
Keosauqua F-7
Knoxville E-6

NOTE: Maps are not always in alphabetical order.
See Page 1 for map location in this atlas.

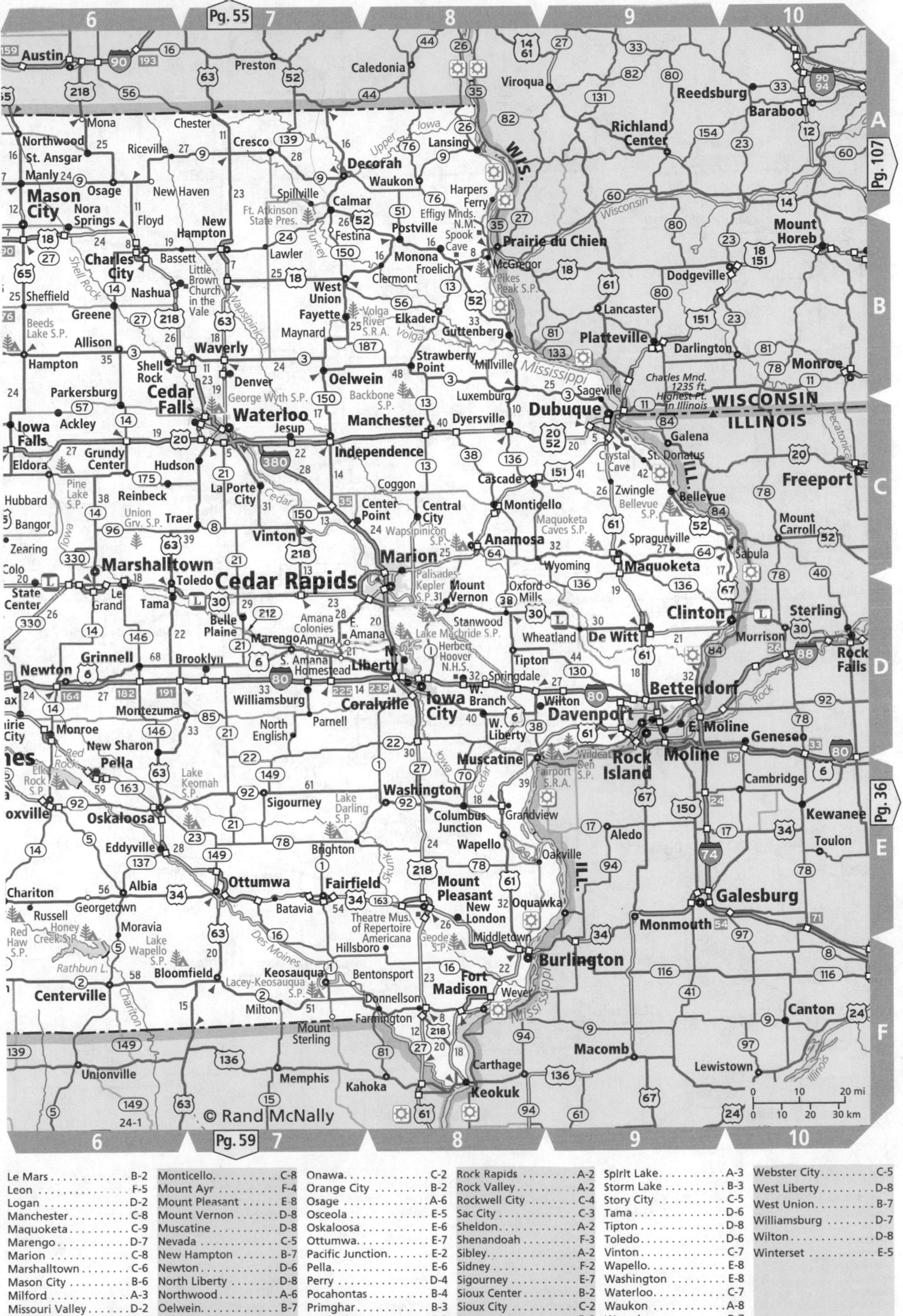

Road Conditions & Construction
511
(800) 288-1047
www.511ia.org, iowadot.gov

Tourism Information
Iowa Tourism Office:
(800) 345-4692
www.traveliowa.com

Travel planning & on-the-road resources

Le Mars B-2
Leon F-5
Logan D-2
Manchester C-8
Maquoketa C-9
Marengo D-7
Marion C-8
Marshalltown C-6
Mason City B-6
Milford A-3
Missouri Valley D-2
Montezuma D-7
Monticello C-8
Mount Ayr F-4
Mount Pleasant E-8
Mount Vernon D-8
Muscatine D-8
Nevada C-5
New Hampton B-7
Newton D-6
North Liberty D-8
Northwood A-6
Oelwein B-7
Okoboji A-3
Onawa C-2
Orange City B-2
Osage A-6
Osceola E-5
Oskaloosa E-6
Ottumwa E-7
Pacific Junction E-2
Pella E-6
Perry D-4
Pocahontas B-4
Primghar B-3
Red Oak E-3
Rock Rapids A-2
Rock Valley A-2
Rockwell City C-4
Sac City C-3
Sheldon A-2
Shenandoah F-3
Sibley A-2
Sidney F-2
Sigourney E-7
Sioux Center B-2
Sioux City C-2
Spencer B-3
Spirit Lake A-3
Storm Lake B-3
Story City C-5
Tama D-6
Tipton D-8
Toledo D-6
Vinton C-7
Wapello E-8
Washington E-8
Waterloo C-7
Waukon A-8
Waverly B-7
Webster City C-5
West Liberty D-8
West Union B-7
Williamsburg D-7
Wilton D-8
Winterset E-5

Kansas state facts

Nickname: The Sunflower State
Capital: Topeka, C-9
Population: 2,937,880 (rank: 35th)
Largest city: Wichita, 397,532, E-7
Land area: 81,737 sq. mi. (rank: 13th)
Highest point: Mount Sunflower, 4,039 ft., C-1

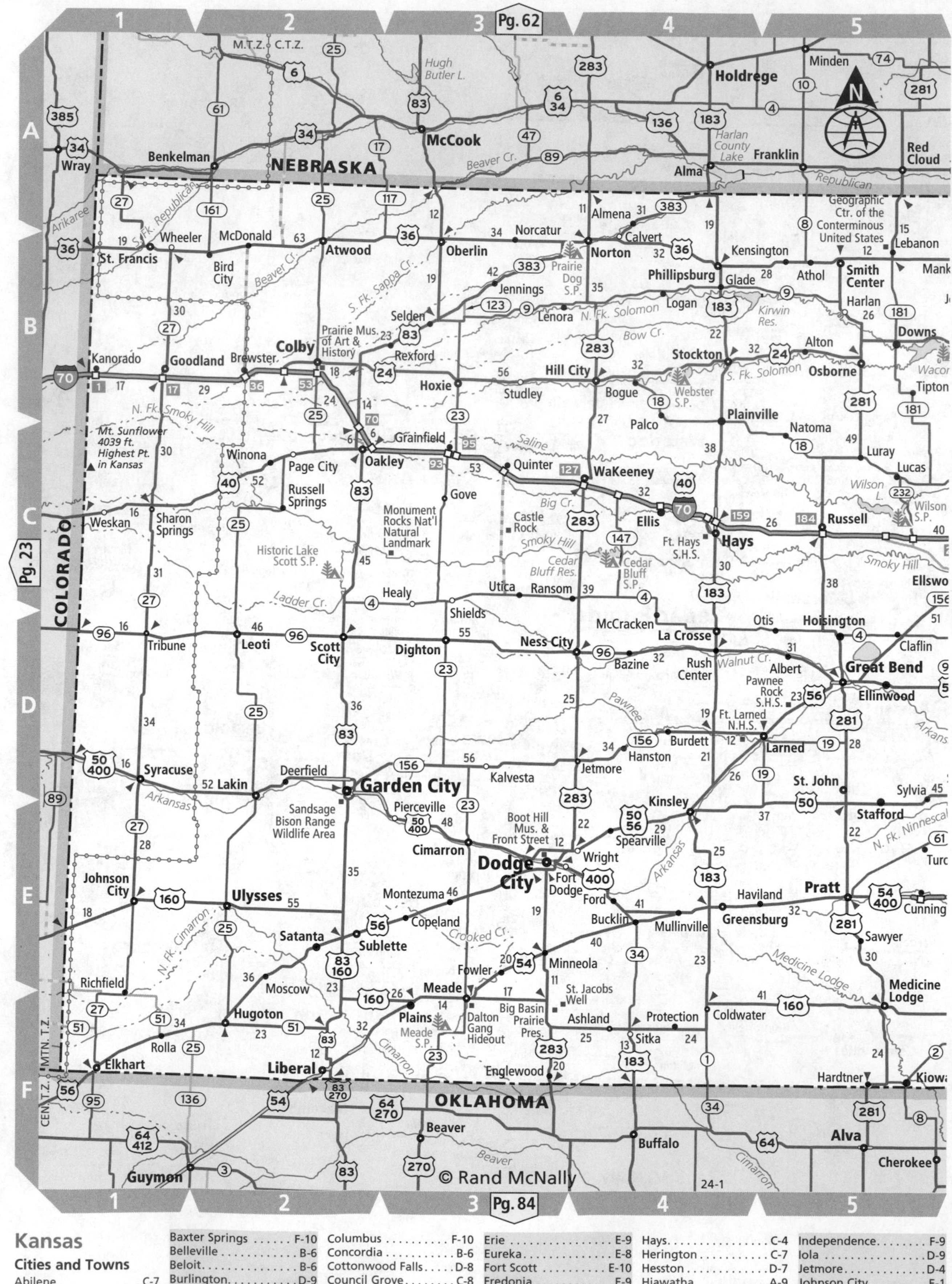

Kansas

Cities and Towns

Abilene C-7
Alma C-8
Anthony F-6
Arkansas City F-7
Ashland F-4
Atchison B-9
Atwood B-2
Augusta E-7
Baldwin City C-9
Baxter Springs F-10
Belleville B-6
Beloit B-6
Burlington D-9
Caney F-8
Chanute E-9
Cherryvale F-9
Cimarron E-3
Clay Center B-7
Coffeyville F-9
Colby B-2
Coldwater F-4
Columbus F-10
Concordia B-6
Cottonwood Falls D-8
Council Grove C-8
Derby E-7
Dighton D-3
Dodge City E-3
El Dorado E-7
Elkhart F-1
Ellinwood D-5
Ellsworth C-6
Emporia D-8
Erie E-9
Eureka E-8
Fort Scott E-10
Fredonia E-9
Frontenac E-10
Garden City D-2
Garnett D-9
Girard E-10
Goodland B-1
Gove C-3
Great Bend D-5
Greensburg E-4
Hays C-4
Herington C-7
Hesston D-7
Hiawatha A-9
Hill City B-4
Hillsboro D-7
Hoisington D-5
Holton B-9
Howard E-8
Hoxie B-3
Hugoton F-2
Hutchinson D-6
Independence F-9
Iola D-9
Jetmore D-4
Johnson City E-1
Junction City C-7
Kansas City C-10
Kingman E-6
Kinsley E-4
La Crosse D-4
Lakin D-2
Larned D-5
Lawrence C-9

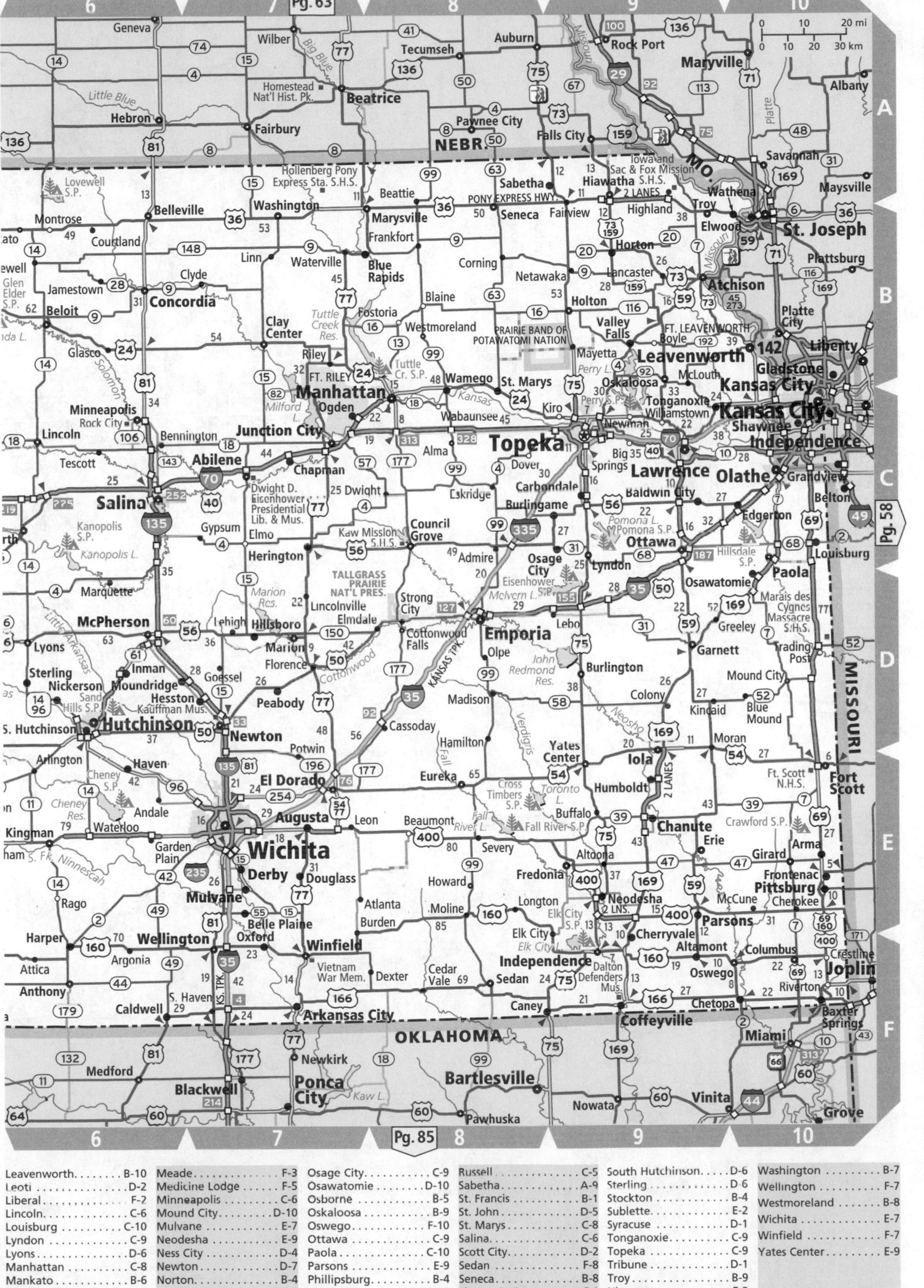

Road Conditions & Construction

511
(866) 511-5368
www.kandrive.org, www.ksdot.org

Tourism Information

Kansas Tourism Office:
(785) 296-2009
www.travelks.com

Travel planning & on-the-road resources

Leavenworth........B-10
Leoti..............D-2
Liberal............F-2
Lincoln............C-6
Louisburg.........C-10
Lyndon.............C-9
Lyons..............D-6
Manhattan..........C-8
Mankato............B-6
Marion.............D-7
Marysville.........B-8
McPherson..........D-6
Meade..............F-3
Medicine Lodge.....F-5
Minneapolis........C-6
Mound City........D-10
Mulvane............E-7
Neodesha...........E-9
Ness City..........D-4
Newton.............D-7
Norton.............B-4
Oakley.............C-2
Oberlin............B-3
Olathe............C-10
Osage City.........C-9
Osawatomie........D-10
Osborne............B-5
Oskaloosa..........B-9
Oswego............F-10
Ottawa.............C-9
Paola.............C-10
Parsons............E-9
Phillipsburg.......B-4
Pittsburg.........E-10
Plainville.........B-4
Pratt..............E-5
Russell............C-5
Sabetha............A-9
St. Francis........B-1
St. John...........D-5
St. Marys..........C-8
Salina.............C-6
Scott City.........D-2
Sedan..............F-8
Seneca.............B-8
Sharon Springs.....C-1
Shawnee...........C-10
Smith Center.......B-5
South Hutchinson...D-6
Sterling...........D-6
Stockton...........B-4
Sublette...........E-2
Syracuse...........D-1
Tonganoxie.........C-9
Topeka.............C-9
Tribune............D-1
Troy...............B-9
Ulysses............E-2
WaKeeney...........C-4
Wamego.............C-8
Washington.........B-7
Wellington.........F-7
Westmoreland.......B-8
Wichita............E-7
Winfield...........F-7
Yates Center.......E-9

Kentucky state facts

Nickname: The Bluegrass State
Capital: Frankfort, C-9

Population: 4,505,836 (rank: 26th)
Largest city: Louisville, 633,045, C-8

Land area: 39,481 sq. mi. (rank: 36th)
Highest point: Black Mountain, 4,145 ft., E-12

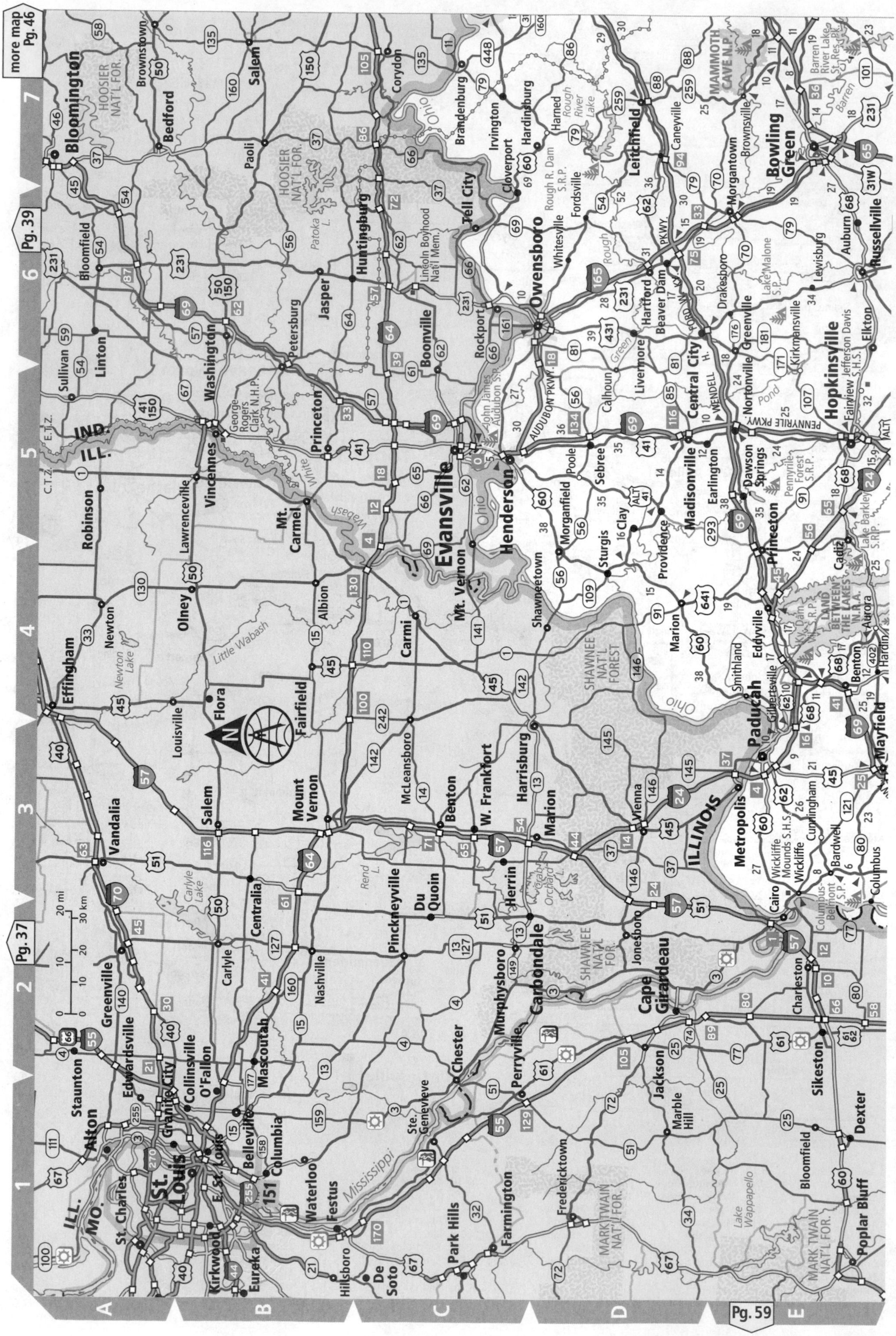

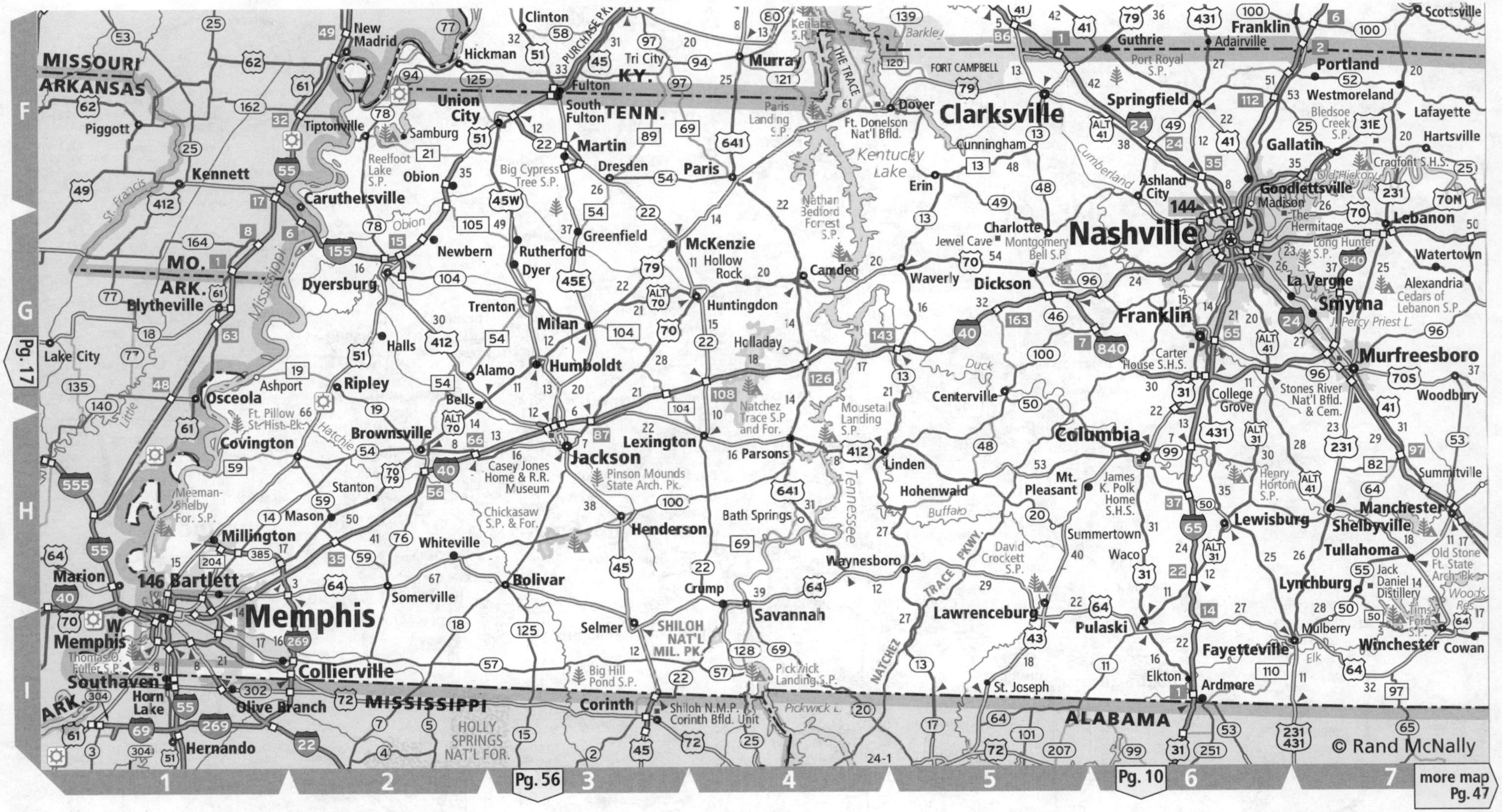

Pg. 17
Pg. 56
Pg. 10
more map Pg. 47

Kentucky

Cities and Towns

Albany . . . F-9
Alexandria . . . A-10
Ashland . . . B-13
Barbourville . . . E-11
Bardstown . . . C-8
Beaver Dam . . . D-6
Benton . . . E-4
Berea . . . D-10
Bowling Green . . . E-7
Cadiz . . . E-5
Campbellsville . . . D-9
Carrollton . . . B-9
Central City . . . D-6
Columbia . . . E-9
Corbin . . . E-10
Cumberland . . . E-12
Cynthiana . . . B-10
Danville . . . D-9
Dawson Springs . . . E-5
Eddyville . . . E-4
Elizabethtown . . . D-8
Eminence . . . B-9
Falmouth . . . B-10
Flemingsburg . . . B-11
Florence . . . A-10
Fort Thomas . . . A-10
Frankfort . . . C-9
Franklin . . . F-7
Fulton . . . F-3
Georgetown . . . C-10
Glasgow . . . E-8
Greensburg . . . E-8
Greenville . . . E-6
Hardinsburg . . . C-7
Harlan . . . E-12
Harrodsburg . . . D-9
Hartford . . . D-6
Hazard . . . E-12
Henderson . . . C-5
Hickman . . . F-2
Hopkinsville . . . E-5
Horse Cave . . . E-8
Irvine . . . D-11
Jackson . . . D-12
Jeffersontown . . . C-8
Jenkins . . . E-13
La Grange . . . B-8
Lancaster . . . D-10
Lawrenceburg . . . C-9
Lebanon . . . D-9
Leitchfield . . . D-7
Lexington . . . C-10
London . . . E-11
Louisville . . . C-8
Madisonville . . . D-5
Marion . . . D-4
Mayfield . . . E-3
Middlesboro . . . F-11
Middletown . . . C-8
Monticello . . . E-9
Morehead . . . C-11
Morganfield . . . D-4
Morgantown . . . E-6
Mount Sterling . . . C-11
Mount Vernon . . . D-10
Mount Washington . . . C-8
Murray . . . F-4
Nicholasville . . . C-10
Owensboro . . . D-6
Paducah . . . E-3
Paintsville . . . C-12
Paris . . . C-10
Pikeville . . . D-13
Pineville . . . E-11
Prestonsburg . . . D-13
Princeton . . . E-4
Providence . . . D-5
Radcliff . . . C-8
Richmond . . . D-10
Russell Springs . . . E-9
Russellville . . . E-6
Scottsville . . . F-7
Shelbyville . . . C-9
Shepherdsville . . . C-8
Shively . . . C-8
Somerset . . . E-10
Springfield . . . D-9
Stanford . . . D-10
Stanton . . . C-11
Tompkinsville . . . F-8
Versailles . . . C-9
West Liberty . . . C-12
Williamsburg . . . F-10
Williamstown . . . B-10
Wilmore . . . C-10
Winchester . . . C-10

Travel planning & on-the-road resources

Tourism Information
Kentucky Department of Tourism:
(800) 225-8747, (502) 564-4930
www.kentuckytourism.com

Road Conditions & Construction
511, (866) 737-3767
transportation.ky.gov/sites/goky
drive.ky.gov

Tennessee state facts

Nickname: The Volunteer State
Capital: Nashville, G-6
Population: 6,910,840 (rank: 16th)
Largest city: Nashville, 689,447, G-6
Land area: 41,227 sq. mi. (rank: 34th)
Highest point: Clingmans Dome, 6,643 ft., H-11

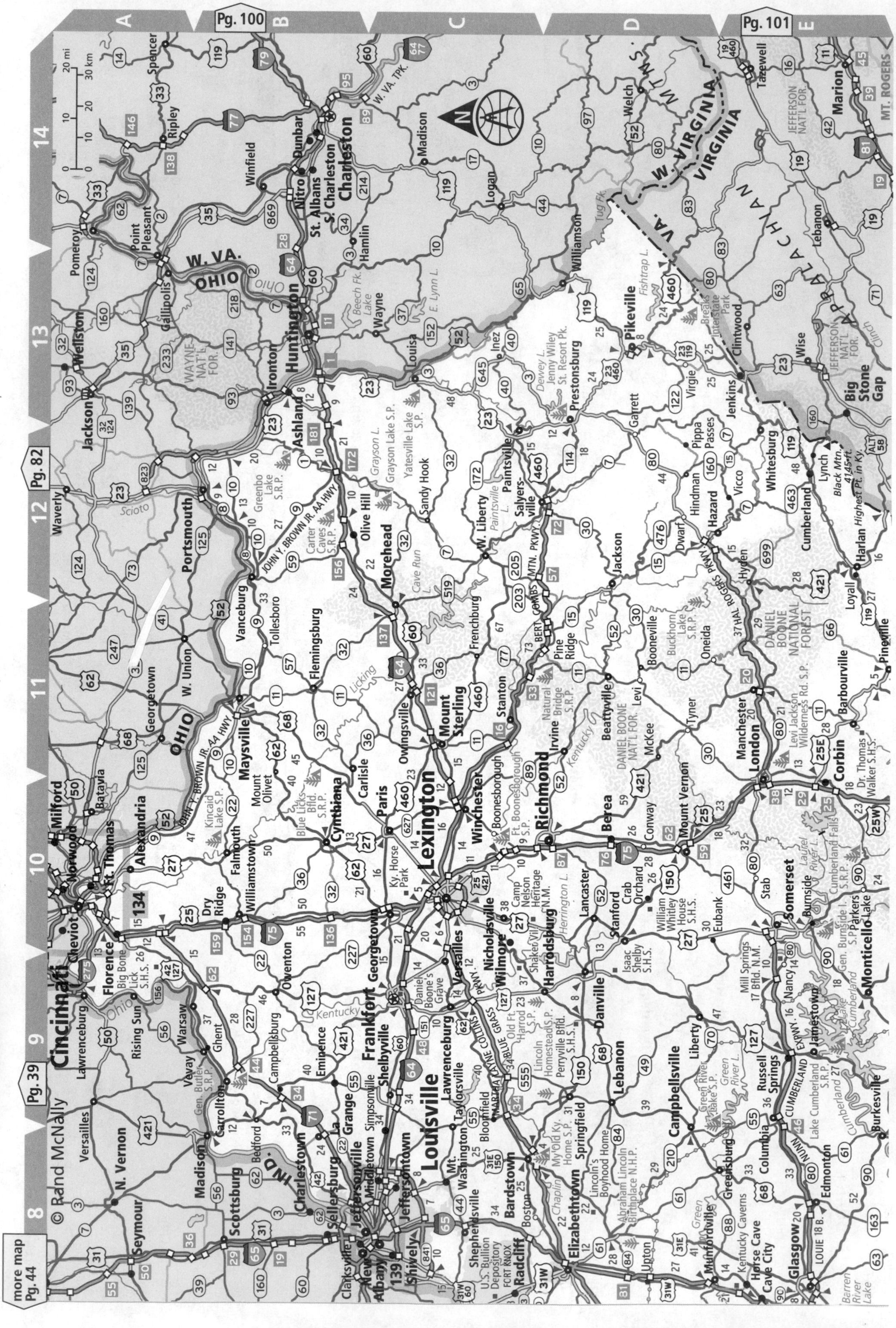

more map Pg. 44
Pg. 39
Pg. 82
Pg. 100
Pg. 101

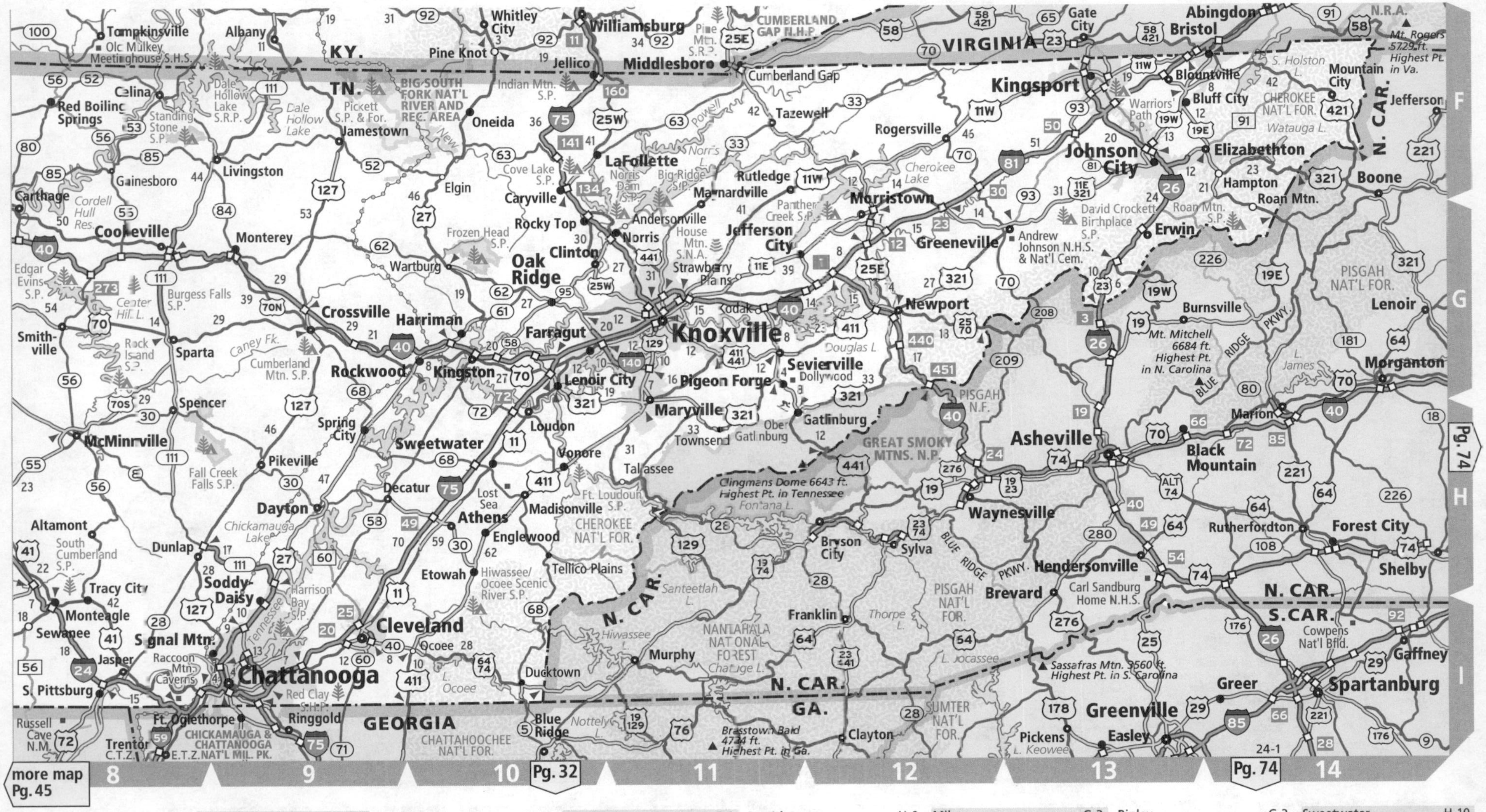

NOTE: Maps are not always in alphabetical order. See Page 1 for map location in this atlas.

more map Pg. 45

Pg. 32

Pg. 74

Tennessee

Cities and Towns

Ashland City	F-6
Athens	H-10
Bartlett	H-1
Bolivar	H-3
Bristol	F-14
Brownsville	H-2
Camden	G-4
Centerville	G-5
Chattanooga	I-9
Clarksville	F-5
Cleveland	I-9
Clinton	G-10
Collierville	I-1
Columbia	H-6
Cookeville	G-8
Covington	H-2
Crossville	G-9
Dayton	H-9
Dickson	G-5
Dunlap	H-8
Dyersburg	G-2
Elizabethton	F-14
Erwin	G-13
Etowah	H-10
Farragut	G-10
Fayetteville	I-7
Franklin	G-6
Gallatin	F-7
Gatlinburg	H-11
Goodlettsville	F-6
Greeneville	G-13
Harriman	G-10
Henderson	H-3
Hohenwald	H-5
Humboldt	G-3
Huntingdon	G-4
Jackson	H-3
Jefferson City	G-11
Johnson City	F-13
Kingsport	F-13
Kingston	G-10
Knoxville	G-11
La Vergne	G-7
Lafayette	F-7
LaFollette	F-10
Lawrenceburg	H-5
Lebanon	G-7
Lenoir City	G-10
Lewisburg	H-6
Lexington	H-4
Livingston	F-9
Loudon	H-10
Lynchburg	H-7
Madison	G-6
Madisonville	H-10
Manchester	H-7
Martin	F-3
Maryville	G-11
McKenzie	G-3
McMinnville	H-8
Memphis	I-1
Milan	G-3
Millington	H-1
Morristown	G-12
Mount Pleasant	H-5
Murfreesboro	G-7
Nashville	G-6
Newport	G-12
Oak Ridge	G-10
Oneida	F-10
Paris	F-4
Pigeon Forge	G-11
Portland	F-7
Pulaski	I-6
Ripley	G-2
Rockwood	G-10
Rogersville	F-12
Savannah	H-4
Selmer	I-3
Sevierville	G-11
Shelbyville	H-7
Signal Mountain	I-9
Smithville	G-8
Smyrna	G-7
Soddy-Daisy	H-9
Sparta	G-8
Springfield	F-6
Sweetwater	H-10
Tallassee	H-11
Tellico Plains	H-10
Trenton	G-3
Tullahoma	H-7
Union City	F-3
Waverly	G-5
Whiteville	H-2
Winchester	I-7

Travel planning & on-the-road resources

Tourism Information — Tennessee Department of Tourist Dev.: (615) 741-2159 www.tnvacation.com

Road Conditions & Construction — 511, (877) 244-0065 smartway.tn.gov, www.tn.gov/tdot/ welcome-to-tennessee-511

Louisiana state facts

Nickname: The Pelican State
Capital: Baton Rouge, E-6
Population: 4,657,757 (rank: 25th)
Largest city: New Orleans, 383,997, F-7
Land area: 43,193 sq. mi. (rank: 33rd)
Highest point: Driskill Mountain, 535 ft., B-3

Louisiana

Cities and Towns

Abbeville	F-4
Alexandria	D-4
Amite City	E-7
Arcadia	A-3
Baldwin	F-5
Bastrop	A-5
Baton Rouge	E-6
Benton	A-2
Bogalusa	D-8
Bossier City	A-2
Breaux Bridge	E-5
Broussard	F-4
Bunkie	D-4
Cameron	F-2
Chalmette	F-7
Clinton	D-6
Colfax	C-3
Columbia	B-4
Coushatta	B-2
Covington	E-7
Crowley	E-4
Delhi	B-5
Denham Springs	E-6
DeQuincy	E-2
DeRidder	D-2
Donaldsonville	F-6
Edgard	F-7
Eunice	E-4
Farmerville	A-4
Ferriday	C-5
Franklin	F-5
Franklinton	D-7
Gramercy	F-6
Greensburg	D-6
Greenwood	B-1
Gretna	F-7
Hahnville	F-7
Hammond	E-7
Harrisonburg	C-5
Haynesville	A-3
Homer	A-3
Houma	G-6
Iowa	E-3
Jackson	D-6
Jeanerette	F-5
Jena	C-4
Jennings	E-3
Jonesboro	B-3
Jonesville	C-5
Kaplan	F-4
Lafayette	E-4
Lake Arthur	F-3
Lake Charles	E-3
Lake Providence	A-6
Laplace	F-7
Leesville	D-3
Livingston	E-6
Mamou	E-4
Mandeville	E-7
Mansfield	B-2
Many	C-2
Marksville	D-4
Metairie	F-7
Minden	A-3
Monroe	A-4
Morgan City	F-6
Napoleonville	F-6
Natchitoches	C-3
New Iberia	F-5
New Orleans	F-7
New Roads	E-5
Oak Grove	A-5
Oakdale	D-3
Oberlin	E-3
Opelousas	E-4
Patterson	F-5
Plaquemine	E-6
Ponchatoula	E-7
Port Allen	E-6
Port Sulphur	G-8
Raceland	F-7
Rayne	E-4
Rayville	B-5
Ruston	A-3
St. Francisville	D-5
St. Joseph	C-6
St. Martinville	F-5
Scott	E-4
Shreveport	A-2
Simmesport	D-5
Slidell	E-8
Springhill	A-2
Sulphur	E-2
Tallulah	B-6
Thibodaux	F-6
Vidalia	C-5
Ville Platte	E-4
Vivian	A-2
Walker	E-6
Welsh	E-3
West Monroe	A-4
Winnfield	C-3
Winnsboro	B-5

Pg. 16
Pg. 96

NOTE: Maps are not always in alphabetical order.
See Page 1 for map location in this atlas.

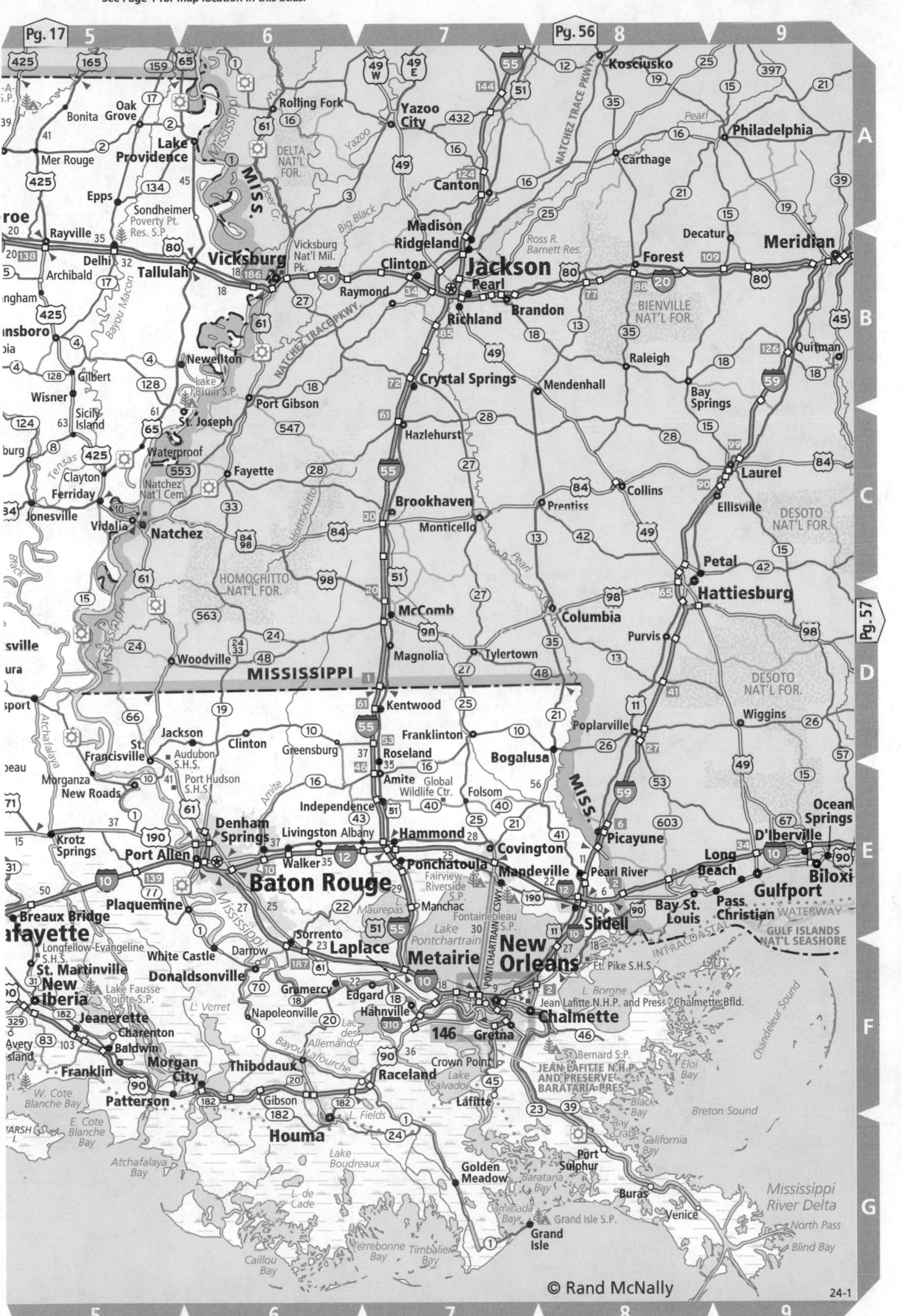

Road Conditions & Construction
511
(888) 762-3511
www.511la.org, www.dotd.la.gov

Tourism Information
Louisiana Office of Tourism:
(225) 342-8100
www.louisianatravel.com

Travel planning & on-the-road resources

Maine state facts

Nickname: The Pine Tree State
Capital: Augusta, G-2
Population: 1,362,359 (rank: 42nd)
Largest city: Portland, 68,408, H-2
Land area: 30,837 sq. mi. (rank: 39th)
Highest point: Mount Katahdin, 5,268 ft., D-4

Maine

Cities and Towns

Andover . . . F-1
Ashland . . . C-4
Auburn . . . H-2
Augusta . . . G-2
Bailey Island . . . H-2
Bangor . . . F-4
Bar Harbor . . . G-5
Bath . . . H-2
Belfast . . . G-3
Bethel . . . G-1
Biddeford . . . I-1
Bingham . . . F-2
Blue Hill . . . G-4
Boothbay Harbor . . . H-3
Brewer . . . F-4
Bridgewater . . . C-5
Bridgton . . . H-1
Brownville Junction . . . E-3
Brunswick . . . H-2
Bucksport . . . G-4
Calais . . . E-6
Camden . . . G-3
Caribou . . . B-5
Castine . . . G-4
Cherryfield . . . G-5
Corinna . . . F-3
Cornish . . . H-1
Damariscotta . . . H-3
Danforth . . . D-5
Deer Isle . . . G-4
Dexter . . . F-3
Dixfield . . . G-1
Dover-Foxcroft . . . E-3
Eagle Lake . . . B-4
East Corinth . . . F-3
East Millinocket . . . E-4
Eastport . . . F-6
Ellsworth . . . G-4
Fairfield . . . G-3
Falmouth . . . H-2
Farmington . . . F-2
Fort Fairfield . . . B-5
Fort Kent . . . A-4
Freeport . . . H-2
Friendship . . . H-3
Fryeburg . . . H-1
Gardiner . . . G-2
Gorham . . . H-1
Gray . . . H-2
Greenville . . . E-3
Guilford . . . E-3
Hampden . . . F-4
Harrington . . . G-5
Harrison . . . H-1
Houlton . . . D-5
Howland . . . E-4
Jackman . . . E-2
Jonesport . . . G-5
Kennebunk . . . I-1
Kennebunkport . . . I-1
Kingfield . . . F-2
Kittery . . . J-1
Lewiston . . . H-2
Limestone . . . B-5
Lincoln . . . E-4
Livermore Falls . . . G-2
Lubec . . . F-6
Machias . . . F-6
Madison . . . F-2
Mars Hill . . . C-5

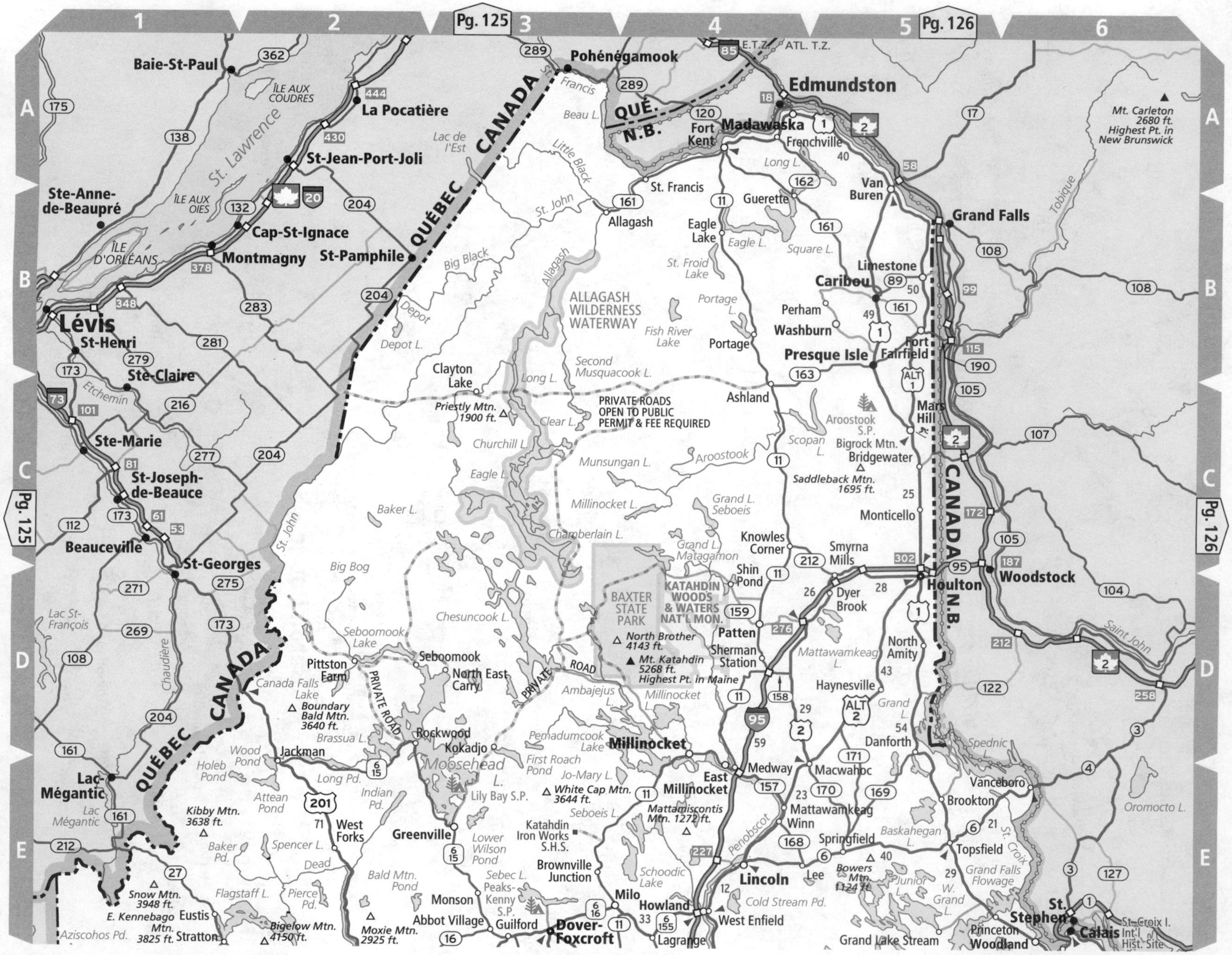

Pg. 125
Pg. 126

NOTE: Maps are not always in alphabetical order.
See Page 1 for map location in this atlas.

Mattawamkeag E-4
Medway E-4
Mexico. G-1
Milbridge G-5
Millinocket D-4
Milo. E-4
Monson. E-3
Monticello. C-5
Naples H-1
Newport F-3
Norridgewock. F-2
North Anson. F-2
North Berwick I-1
North Bridgton. H-1
North Windham H-1
Northeast Harbor G-4
Norway G-1
Ogunquit I-1
Old Orchard Beach. I-1
Old Town F-4
Orono F-4
Patten D-4
Phillips. F-2
Pittsfield F-3
Poland H-1
Port Clyde. H-3
Portage B-4
Portland H-2
Presque Isle. B-5
Princeton. E-6
Rangeley F-1
Rockland H-3
Rockwood D-2
Rumford G-1
Saco. I-1
Sanford I-1
Scarborough I-2
Searsport. G-4
Sebago Lake H-1
Sherman Station. D-4
Skowhegan. F-2
Solon F-2
South China G-3
South Paris G-1
South Portland H-2
Southwest Harbor G-4
Standish H-1
Stonington G-4
Stratton. E-1
Thomaston H-3
Turner G-2
Union G-3
Unity G-3
Van Buren. A-5
Vinalhaven H-4
Waldoboro H-3
Washburn B-5
Waterville. G-3
Wells I-1
West Enfield E-4
West Scarborough I-1
Westbrook H-2
Wilton. G-2
Winslow G-3
Winterport F-4
Winthrop G-2
Woodland. E-6
Yarmouth H-2
York Beach I-1
York Harbor I-1
York Village I-1

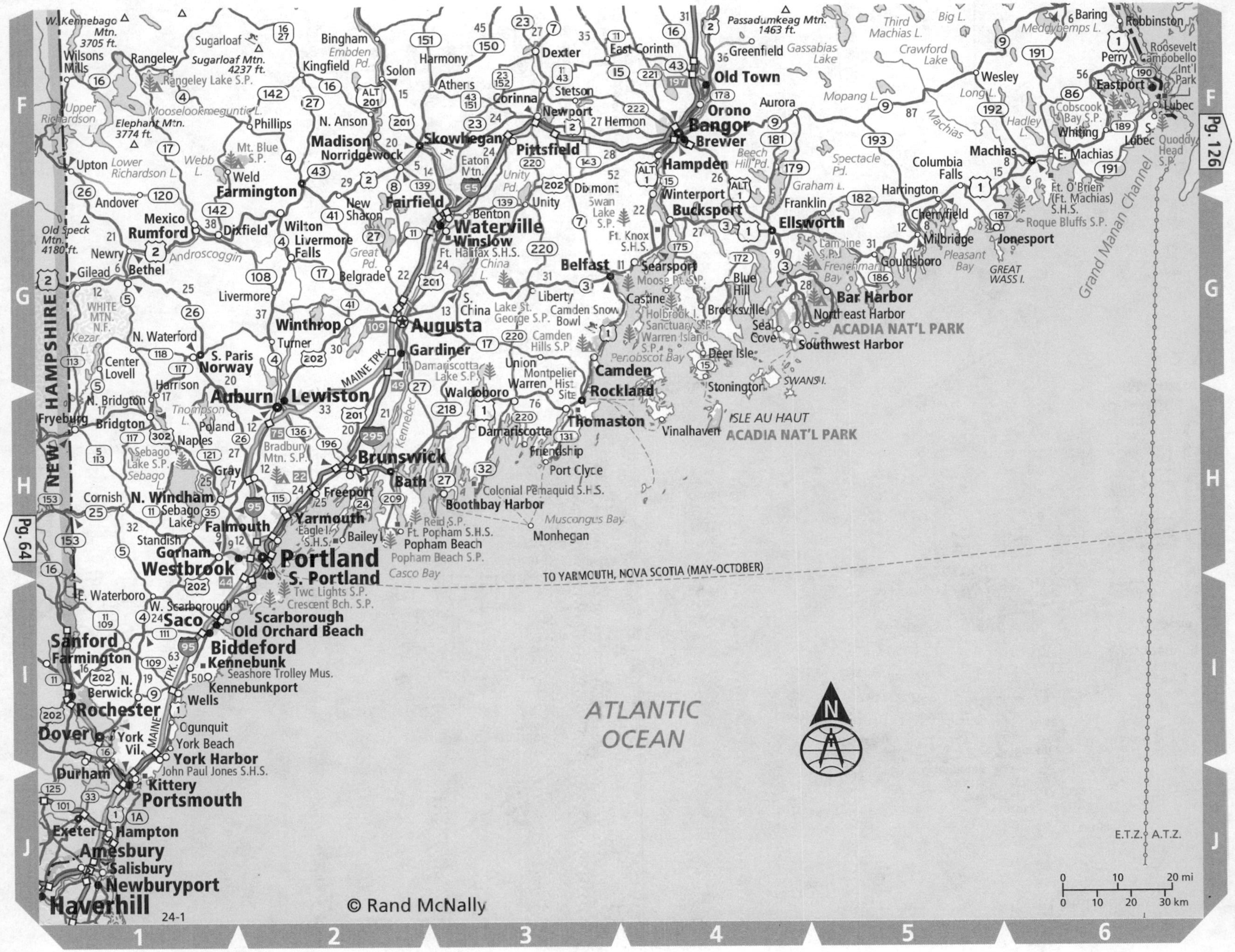

Pg. 126
Pg. 64

F G H I J
1 2 3 4 5 6

NEW HAMPSHIRE
ATLANTIC OCEAN
Grand Manan Channel
TO YARMOUTH, NOVA SCOTIA (MAY-OCTOBER)
ACADIA NAT'L PARK
ISLE AU HAUT
Wilsons Mills
Rangeley
Sugarloaf
Sugarloaf Mtn. 4237 ft.
W. Kennebago Mtn. 3705 ft.
Elephant Mtn. 3774 ft.
Old Speck Mtn. 4180 ft.
Passadumkeag Mtn. 1463 ft.
Bingham
Kingfield
Solon
Harmony
Athens
Phillips
Weld
Farmington
N. Anson
Madison
Norridgewock
Skowhegan
Pittsfield
Newport
Corinna
Dexter
Stetson
Hermon
East Corinth
Old Town
Orono
Bangor
Brewer
Hampden
Greenfield
Aurora
Wesley
Machias
E. Machias
Whiting
Lubec
Eastport
Perry
Robbinston
Baring
Campobello
Roosevelt Campobello Int'l Park
Quoddy Head S.P.
Upton
Andover
Mexico
Rumford
Dixfield
Wilton
Livermore Falls
Newry
Bethel
Gilead
Fairfield
Waterville
Winslow
Benton
Unity
Dixmont
Winterport
Bucksport
Ellsworth
Franklin
Harrington
Columbia Falls
Cherryfield
Milbridge
Jonesport
Gouldsboro
Roque Bluffs S.P.
Ft. O'Brien (Ft. Machias) S.H.S.
Belfast
Searsport
Castine
Blue Hill
Brooksville
Sedgwick
Seal Cove
Deer Isle
Stonington
Bar Harbor
Northeast Harbor
Southwest Harbor
Vinalhaven
Livermore
Belgrade
Augusta
Gardiner
S. China
Liberty
Camden
Rockland
Thomaston
Union
Warren
Waldoboro
Damariscotta
Friendship
Port Clyde
Monhegan
Boothbay Harbor
Winthrop
Turner
N. Waterford
S. Paris
Norway
Auburn
Lewiston
Center Lovell
Fryeburg
N. Bridgton
Bridgton
Harrison
Naples
Poland
Gray
Brunswick
Bath
Freeport
Yarmouth
Cornish
N. Windham
Sebago Lake
Standish
Gorham
Westbrook
Falmouth
Portland
S. Portland
Scarborough
Old Orchard Beach
Saco
Biddeford
Kennebunk
Kennebunkport
Wells
Ogunquit
York Beach
York Harbor
York Vil.
Kittery
Portsmouth
E. Waterboro
W. Scarborough
Sanford
Farmington
N. Berwick
Rochester
Dover
Durham
Exeter
Hampton
Amesbury
Salisbury
Newburyport
Haverhill
Muscongus Bay
Casco Bay
Penobscot Bay
E.T.Z. A.T.Z.
0 10 20 mi
0 10 20 30 km

© Rand McNally

Travel planning & on-the-road resources

Tourism Information Maine Office of Tourism: (888) 624-6345, (207) 624-7483 visitmaine.com

Road Conditions & Construction 511, (207) 624-3000 newengland511.org www.maine.gov/mdot

Michigan state facts

Nickname: The Great Lake State
Capital: Lansing, H-4

Population: 10,077,331 (rank: 10th)
Largest city: Detroit, 639,111, I-6

Land area: 56,591 sq. mi. (rank: 22nd)
Highest point: Mount Arvon, 1,979 ft., B-6

Michigan

Cities and Towns

Adrian J-4
Albion I-4
Allegan I-2
Alma G-4
Alpena D-5
Ann Arbor I-5
Atlanta E-4
Bad Axe F-6
Baldwin F-2
Battle Creek I-3
Bay City G-4
Bellaire E-3
Benton Harbor I-2
Benton Heights I-2
Bertrand J-2
Bessemer B-5
Beulah E-2
Big Rapids G-3
Birch Run G-5
Brighton I-5
Buchanan J-2
Burton H-5
Cadillac F-3
Caro G-5
Cassopolis J-2
Cement City I-4
Centreville J-3
Charlevoix D-3
Charlotte I-3
Cheboygan D-4
Chelsea I-4
Coldwater J-3
Corunna H-4
Crystal Falls B-6
Davison H-5
Dearborn I-5
Detroit I-6
Dimondale H-4
Dowagiac I-2
Eagle River A-6
Eaton Rapids I-4
Escanaba C-1
Fenton H-5
Flint H-5
Frankenmuth G-5
Fremont G-2
Gaylord E-4
Gladstone C-1
Gladwin F-4
Grand Haven H-2
Grand Ledge H-4
Grand Rapids H-2
Grayling E-3
Greenville H-3
Harrison F-3
Harrisville E-5
Hart G-2
Hastings H-3
Hillsdale J-4
Holland H-2
Holly H-5
Houghton A-6
Howell H-5
Hudsonville H-2
Ionia H-3
Iron Mountain C-6
Ironwood B-5
Ishpeming B-6
Ithaca G-4
Jackson I-4

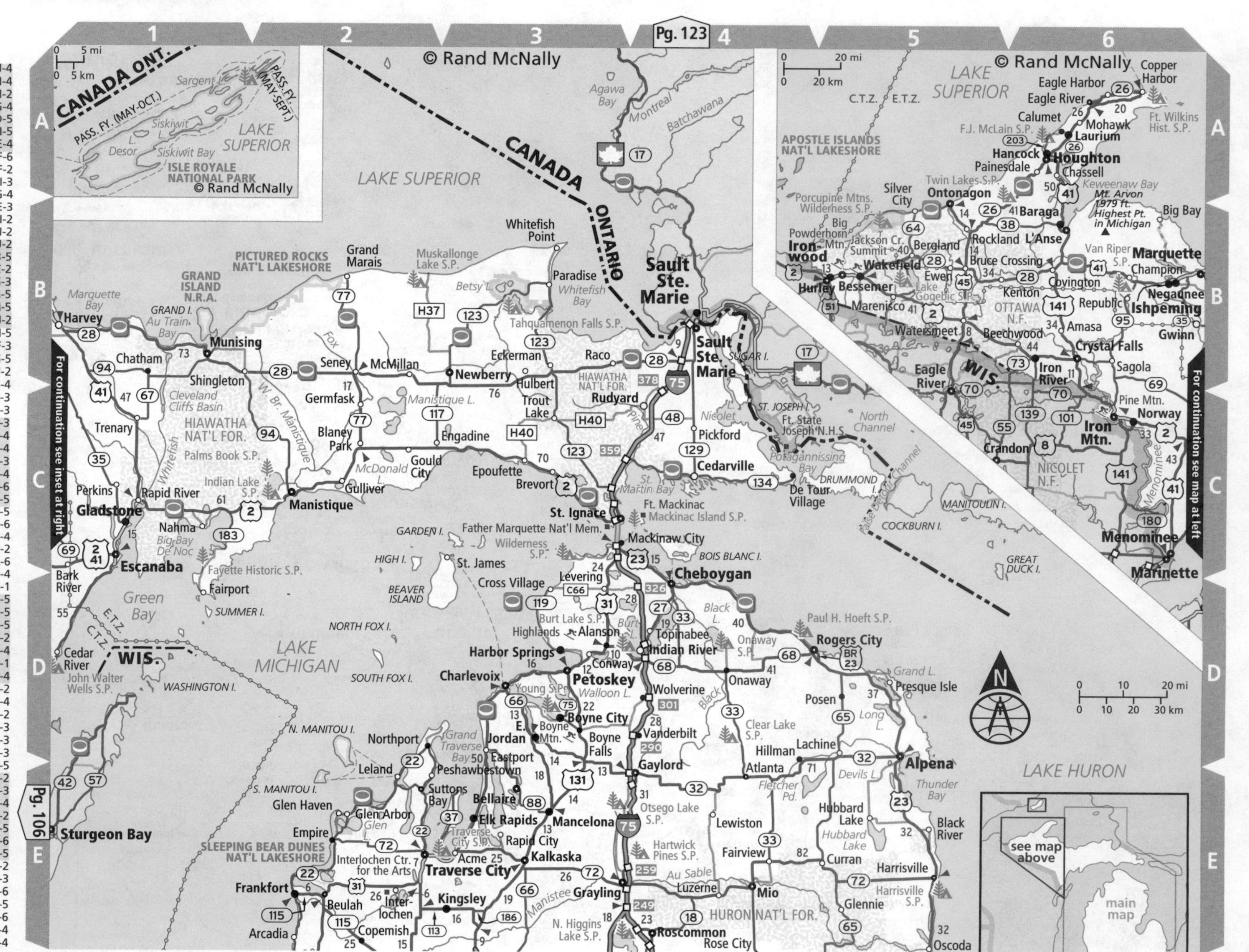

NOTE: Maps are not always in alphabetical order.
See Page 1 for map location in this atlas.

Kalamazoo I-3
Kalkaska E-3
L'Anse B-6
Lake City F-3
Lansing H-4
Lapeer H-5
Leland E-2
Livonia I-5
Ludington F-2
Mackinaw City C-3
Manistee F-2
Manistique C-2
Marine City H-6
Marquette B-6
Marshall I-3
Marysville H-6
Mason H-4
Menominee C-6
Michigan Center I-4
Midland G-4
Milan I-5
Mio E-4
Monroe J-5
Mount Clemens H-6
Mount Pleasant G-3
Munising B-1
Muskegon G-2
Muskegon Heights H-2
Negaunee B-6
New Baltimore H-6
Newberry B-3
Niles J-2
Novi I-5
Ontonagon B-5
Owosso H-4
Paw Paw I-2
Petoskey D-3
Pontiac H-5
Port Huron H-6
Portage I-3
Reed City F-3
Richmond H-6
Rockford H-3
Rogers City D-4
Roscommon E-4
Saginaw G-4
St. Clair H-6
St. Ignace C-3
St. Johns H-4
St. Joseph I-1
St. Louis G-4
Saline I-5
Sandusky G-6
Sault Ste. Marie B-4
South Haven I-2
Standish F-4
Stanton G-3
Sturgis J-3
Tawas City F-5
Tecumseh I-4
Three Rivers J-2
Traverse City E-2
Trenton I-5
Warren I-6
Waterford H-5
West Branch F-4
Westland I-5
Wyandotte I-5
Wyoming H-2
Ypsilanti I-5
Zeeland H-2

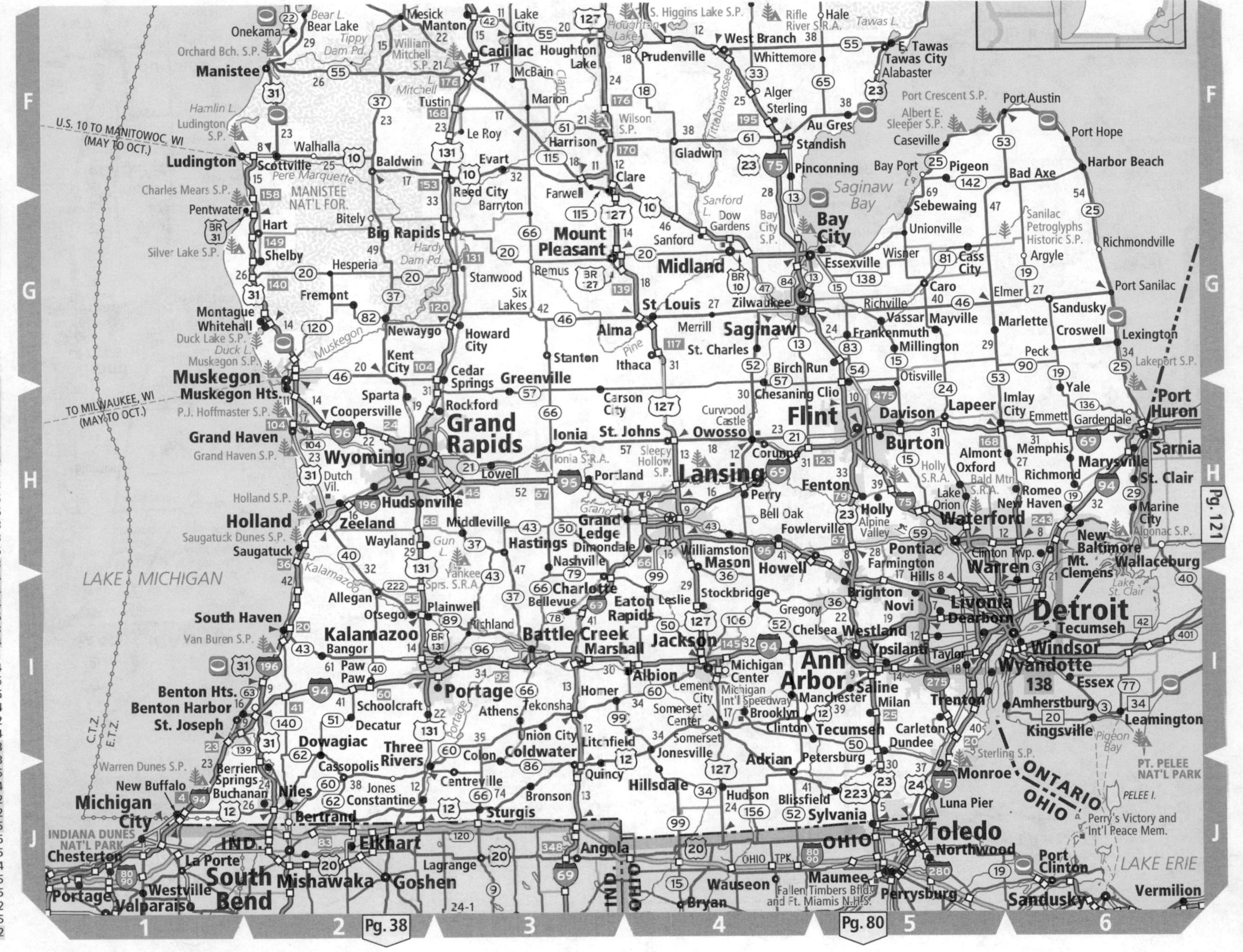

Travel planning & on-the-road resources

Tourism Information
Pure Michigan:
(888) 784-7328
www.michigan.org

Road Conditions & Construction
(517) 241-2400
mdotjboss.state.mi.us/MiDrive/map
www.michigan.gov/mdot

Minnesota state facts

Nickname: The North Star State
Capital: St. Paul, H-5

Population: 5,706,494 (rank: 22nd)
Largest city: Minneapolis, 429,954, H-4

Land area: 79,605 sq. mi. (rank: 14th)
Highest point: Eagle Mountain, 2,301 ft., A-5

Minnesota

Cities and Towns

Ada E-1
Aitkin F-4
Albert Lea J-4
Alexandria G-2
Anoka H-4
Appleton H-2
Austin J-5
Bagley D-2
Baudette C-3
Baxter F-3
Becker G-4
Belle Plaine H-4
Bemidji D-3
Benson G-2
Big Lake G-4
Blaine H-4
Bloomington H-4
Blue Earth J-3
Brainerd F-3
Breckenridge F-1
Buffalo H-4
Caledonia J-6
Cambridge G-4
Cannon Falls I-5
Chaska H-4
Chatfield J-5
Chisholm D-5
Cloquet E-5
Cohasset E-4
Cokato H-3
Crookston D-1
Crosby F-4
Delano H-4
Detroit Lakes E-2
Duluth E-5
East Grand Forks D-1
Eden Prairie H-4
Elbow Lake G-2
Elk River G-4
Ely D-6
Eveleth D-5
Fairmont J-3
Faribault I-4
Farmington H-4
Fergus Falls F-2
Foley G-4
Forest Lake H-5
Gaylord I-3
Glencoe H-3
Glenwood G-2
Grand Marais B-6
Grand Rapids E-4
Granite Falls H-2
Hallock C-1
Hastings H-5
Hibbing D-5
Hutchinson H-3
International Falls C-4
Ivanhoe I-1
Jackson J-3
Jordan H-4
Kasson I-5
La Crescent J-6
Lake City I-5
Lake Crystal I-3
Lakeville H-4
Le Sueur I-4
Litchfield H-3
Little Falls G-3
Long Prairie G-3

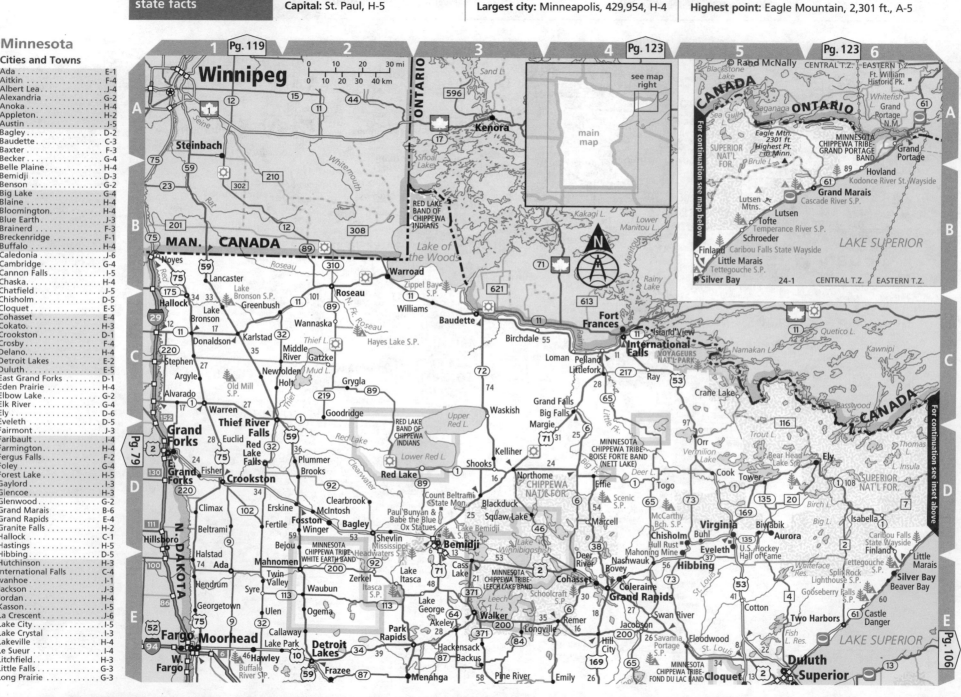

Pg. 119
Pg. 123
Pg. 123
Pg. 79
Pg. 106
For continuation see map below
For continuation see inset above

Luverne . . . J-1
Madelia . . . I-3
Madison . . . H-1
Mahnomen . . . E-2
Mankato . . . I-4
Marshall . . . I-2
Milaca . . . G-4
Minneapolis . . . H-4
Montevideo . . . H-2
Montgomery . . . I-4
Monticello . . . G-4
Moorhead . . . E-1
Moose Lake . . . F-5
Mora . . . G-4
Morris . . . G-2
New Prague . . . I-4
New Ulm . . . I-3
North Branch . . . G-5
Northfield . . . I-4
Olivia . . . H-3
Ortonville . . . G-1
Owatonna . . . I-4
Park Rapids . . . E-3
Paynesville . . . G-3
Pelican Rapids . . . F-2
Perham . . . F-2
Pine City . . . G-5
Pine Island . . . I-5
Pipestone . . . I-1
Plainview . . . I-5
Preston . . . J-6
Princeton . . . G-4
Raymond . . . H-2
Red Lake Falls . . . D-1
Red Wing . . . I-5
Redwood Falls . . . I-2
Rochester . . . I-5
Roseau . . . B-2
St. Cloud . . . G-3
St. James . . . I-3
St. Joseph . . . G-3
St. Paul . . . H-5
St. Peter . . . I-4
Sandstone . . . F-5
Sauk Centre . . . G-3
Sauk Rapids . . . G-3
Shakopee . . . H-4
Slayton . . . I-2
Sleepy Eye . . . I-3
Spring Valley . . . J-5
Staples . . . F-3
Stewartville . . . J-5
Stillwater . . . H-5
Thief River Falls . . . C-1
Tracy . . . I-2
Two Harbors . . . E-6
Virginia . . . D-5
Wabasha . . . I-6
Wadena . . . F-2
Walker . . . E-3
Warren . . . C-1
Waseca . . . I-4
Wells . . . J-4
Wheaton . . . G-1
White Bear Lake . . . H-5
Willmar . . . H-3
Windom . . . J-2
Winona . . . I-6
Worthington . . . J-2
Zimmerman . . . G-4
Zumbrota . . . I-5

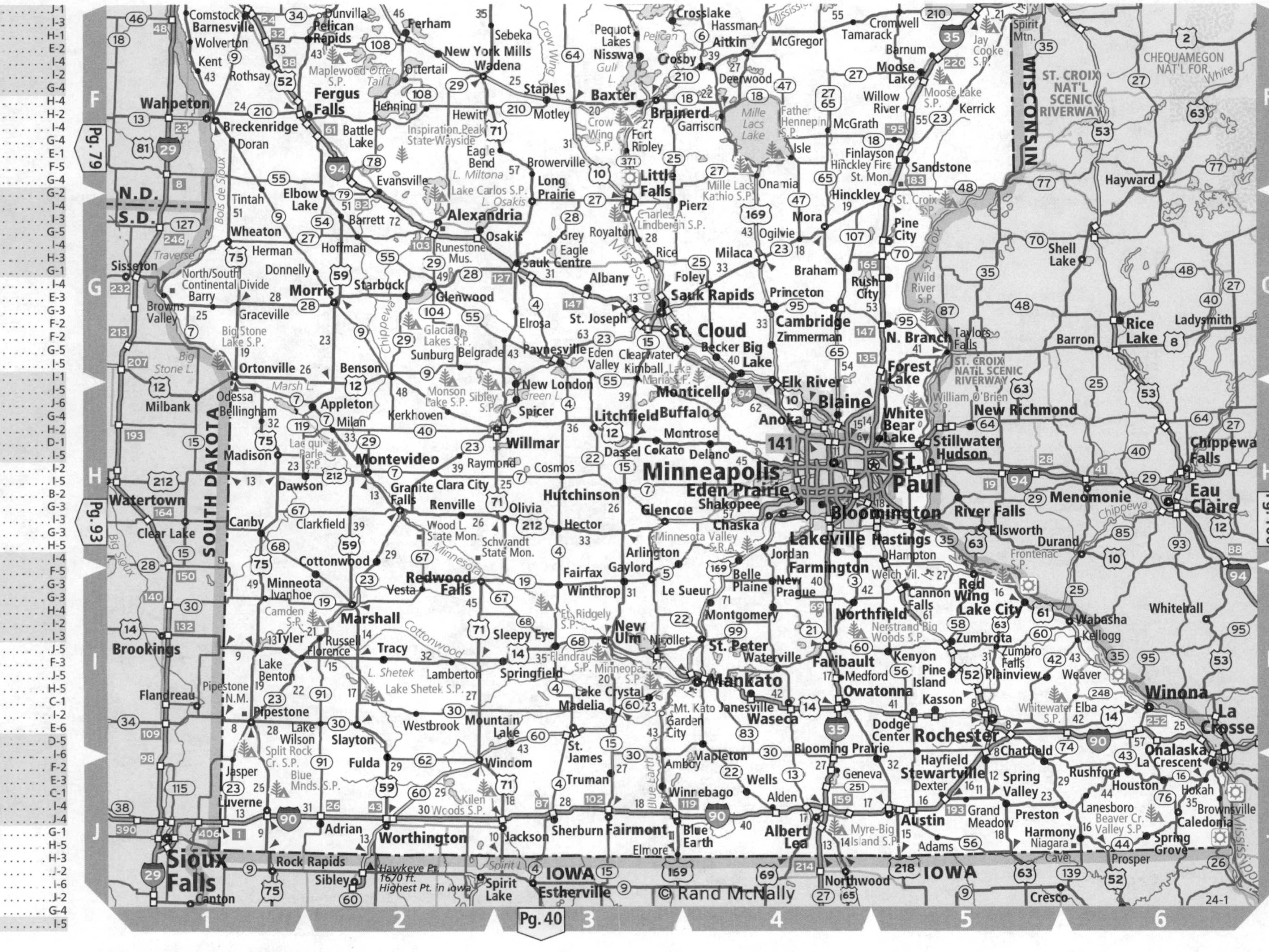

Tourism Information Explore Minnesota: (888) 847-4866, (651) 556-8465 www.exploreminnesota.com

Road Conditions & Construction 511, (800) 542-0220 511mn.org, www.dot.state.mn.us

Mississippi state facts

Nickname: The Magnolia State
Capital: Jackson, F-3
Population: 2,961,279 (rank: 34th)
Largest city: Jackson, 153,701, F-3
Land area: 46,913 sq. mi. (rank: 31st)
Highest point: Woodall Mountain, 806 ft., B-6

Mississippi

Cities and Towns

Aberdeen C-5
Ackerman D-5
Amory C-6
Ashland B-4
Baldwyn B-5
Batesville B-3
Bay St. Louis J-4
Bay Springs G-4
Belmont B-6
Belzoni D-3
Biloxi J-5
Booneville B-5
Brandon F-3
Brookhaven G-3
Brooksville D-5
Bruce C-4
Calhoun City C-4
Canton F-3
Carthage E-4
Centreville H-2
Charleston C-3
Clarksdale C-2
Cleveland C-2
Clinton F-3
Coffeeville C-4
Collins G-4
Columbia H-4
Columbus D-6
Como B-3
Corinth A-5
Crystal Springs G-3
D'Iberville I-5
De Kalb E-5
Decatur F-5
Drew C-2
Durant E-3
Edwards F-2
Ellisville G-5
Eupora D-4
Fayette G-2
Flora F-3
Florence F-3
Forest F-4
Fulton C-6
Gautier J-5
Greenville D-2
Greenwood D-3
Grenada C-4
Gulfport J-5
Hattiesburg H-4
Hazlehurst G-3
Hernando B-3
Hollandale E-2
Holly Springs B-4
Horn Lake A-3
Houston C-5
Indianola D-2
Itta Bena D-3
Iuka B-6
Jackson F-3
Kosciusko E-4
Lambert C-3
Laurel G-5
Leakesville H-6
Leland D-2
Lexington E-3
Liberty H-2
Long Beach J-5
Louisville E-5
Lucedale I-5

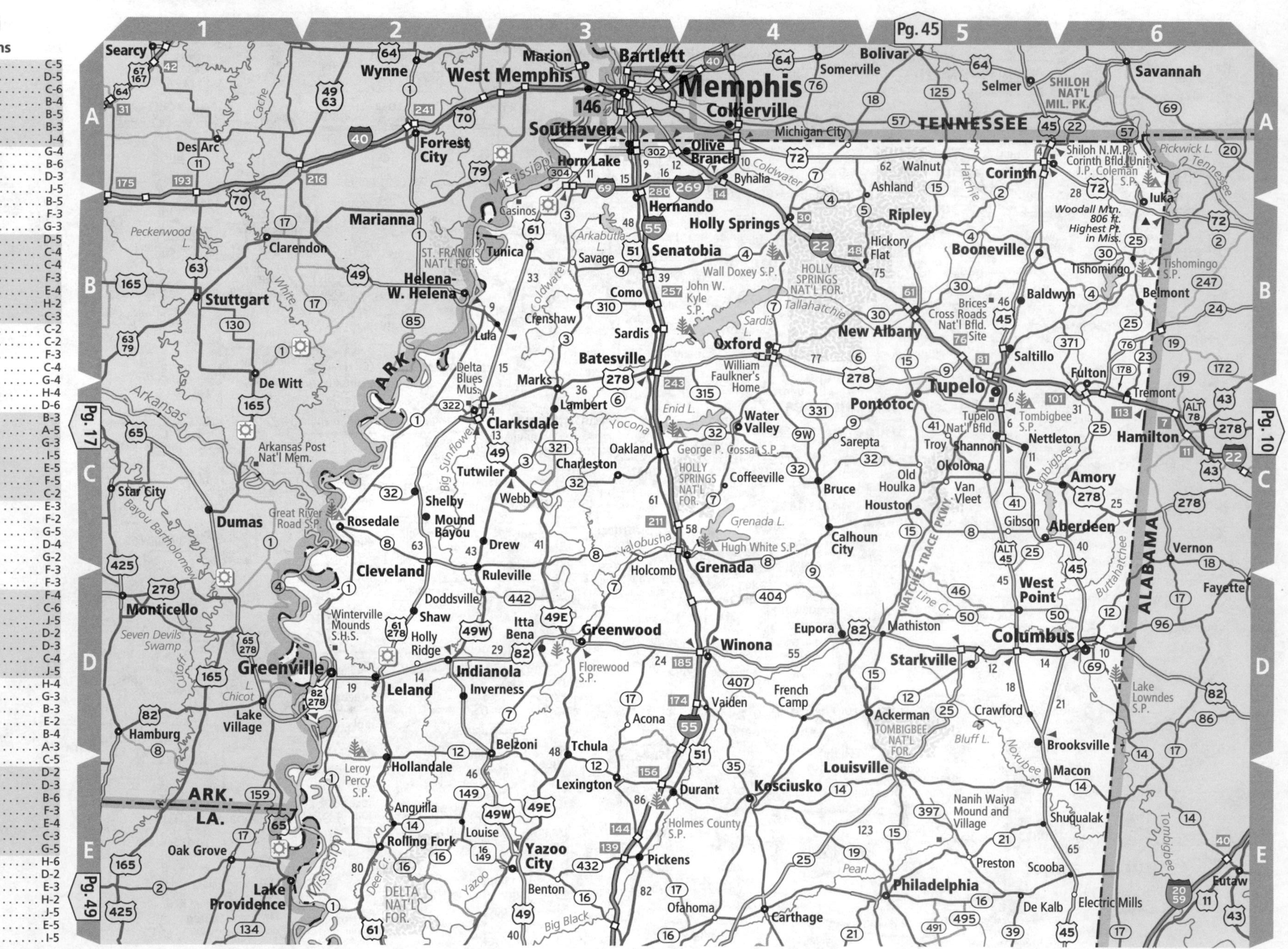

NOTE: Maps are not always in alphabetical order.
See Page 1 for map location in this atlas.

Lumberton H-4
Macon E-5
Madison F-3
Magee G-4
Magnolia H-3
Marks C-3
McComb H-3
Meadville H-2
Mendenhall G-3
Meridian F-5
Monticello G-3
Morton F-4
Moss Point J-6
Mound Bayou C-2
Natchez G-1
Nettleton C-5
New Albany B-5
Newton F-5
Ocean Springs I-5
Okolona C-5
Olive Branch A-4
Oxford B-4
Pascagoula J-6
Pass Christian J-4
Pearl F-3
Petal H-4
Philadelphia E-5
Picayune I-4
Pickens E-3
Pontotoc C-5
Poplarville I-4
Port Gibson G-2
Prentiss G-3
Purvis H-4
Quitman G-5
Raleigh G-4
Raymond F-3
Richland F-3
Ridgeland F-3
Ripley B-5
Rolling Fork E-2
Rosedale C-2
Ruleville C-2
Saltillo B-5
Sardis B-3
Saucier I-5
Senatobia B-3
Shannon C-5
Shaw D-2
Shelby C-2
Southaven A-3
Starkville D-5
Summit H-3
Taylorsville G-4
Tchula D-3
Tunica B-3
Tupelo C-5
Tutwiler C-3
Tylertown H-3
Union F-5
Vaiden D-4
Vancleave I-5
Vicksburg F-2
Water Valley C-4
Waynesboro G-5
Wesson G-3
West Point D-5
Wiggins I-5
Winona D-4
Woodville H-1
Yazoo City E-3

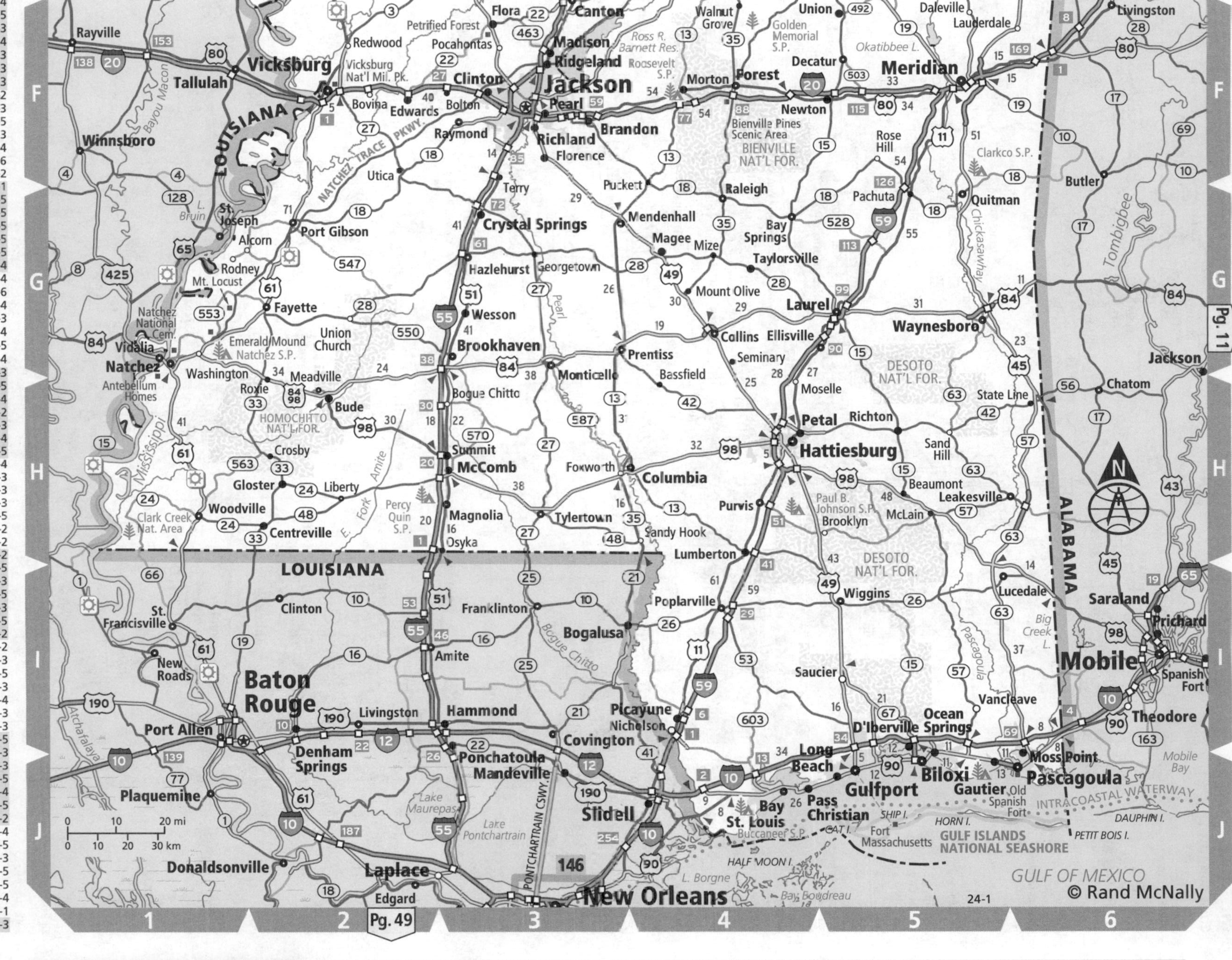

Travel planning & on-the-road resources

Tourism Information Visit Mississippi: (866) 733-6477, (601) 359-3129 visitmississippi.org

Road Conditions & Construction (866) 521-6368 www.mdottraffic.com

Missouri

Cities and Towns

Aurora F-3
Belton C-2
Blue Springs C-3
Bolivar E-4
Bonne Terre E-7
Boonville C-4
Bowling Green B-6
Branson F-4
Brookfield B-4
Butler D-2
California D-4
Cameron B-3
Cape Girardeau E-8
Carrollton B-3
Carthage F-2
Caruthersville G-8
Centralia C-5
Charleston F-8
Chillicothe B-3
Clinton D-3
Columbia C-5
Crystal City D-7
De Soto D-7
Dexter F-8
El Dorado Springs E-3
Eldon D-4
Eureka D-7
Excelsior Springs B-3
Farmington E-7
Festus D-7
Fredericktown E-7
Fulton C-5
Gladstone C-2
Grandview C-2
Hannibal B-6
Harrisonville C-2
Hollister F-4
Independence C-2
Jackson E-8
Jefferson City D-5
Joplin F-2
Kansas City C-2
Kearney B-2
Kennett G-7
Kirksville A-4
Kirkwood D-7
Lamar E-3
Lebanon E-4
Lexington C-3
Liberty C-2
Louisiana B-6
Macon B-5
Malden F-8
Marshall C-4
Marshfield E-4
Maryville A-2
Mexico C-5
Moberly B-5
Monett F-3
Mount Vernon F-3
Mountain Grove F-5
Neosho F-2
Nevada E-2
New Madrid F-8
Nixa F-4
Odessa C-3
Osage Beach D-4
Ozark F-4
Pacific D-7
Park Hills E-7
Perryville E-8
Platte City B-2
Pleasant Hill C-3
Poplar Bluff F-7
Republic F-3
Richmond C-3
Rolla E-5
St. Charles C-7
St. Clair D-6
St. James D-6
St. Joseph B-2
St. Louis C-7
Ste. Genevieve D-7
Salem E-6
Savannah B-2
Scott City F-8
Sedalia C-4
Sikeston F-8
Springfield F-4
Sullivan D-6
Trenton A-3
Troy C-6
Union D-6
Vandalia C-6
Villa Ridge D-6
Warrensburg C-3
Warrenton C-6
Washington D-6
Waynesville E-5
Webb City F-2
Weldon Spring C-7
Wentzville C-6
West Plains F-5

Missouri state facts

Nickname: The Show Me State

Capital: Jefferson City, D-5

Population: 6,154,913 (rank: 19th)

Largest city: Kansas City, 508,090, C-2

Land area: 68,727 sq. mi. (rank: 18th)

Highest point: Taum Sauk Mtn., 1,772 ft., E-7

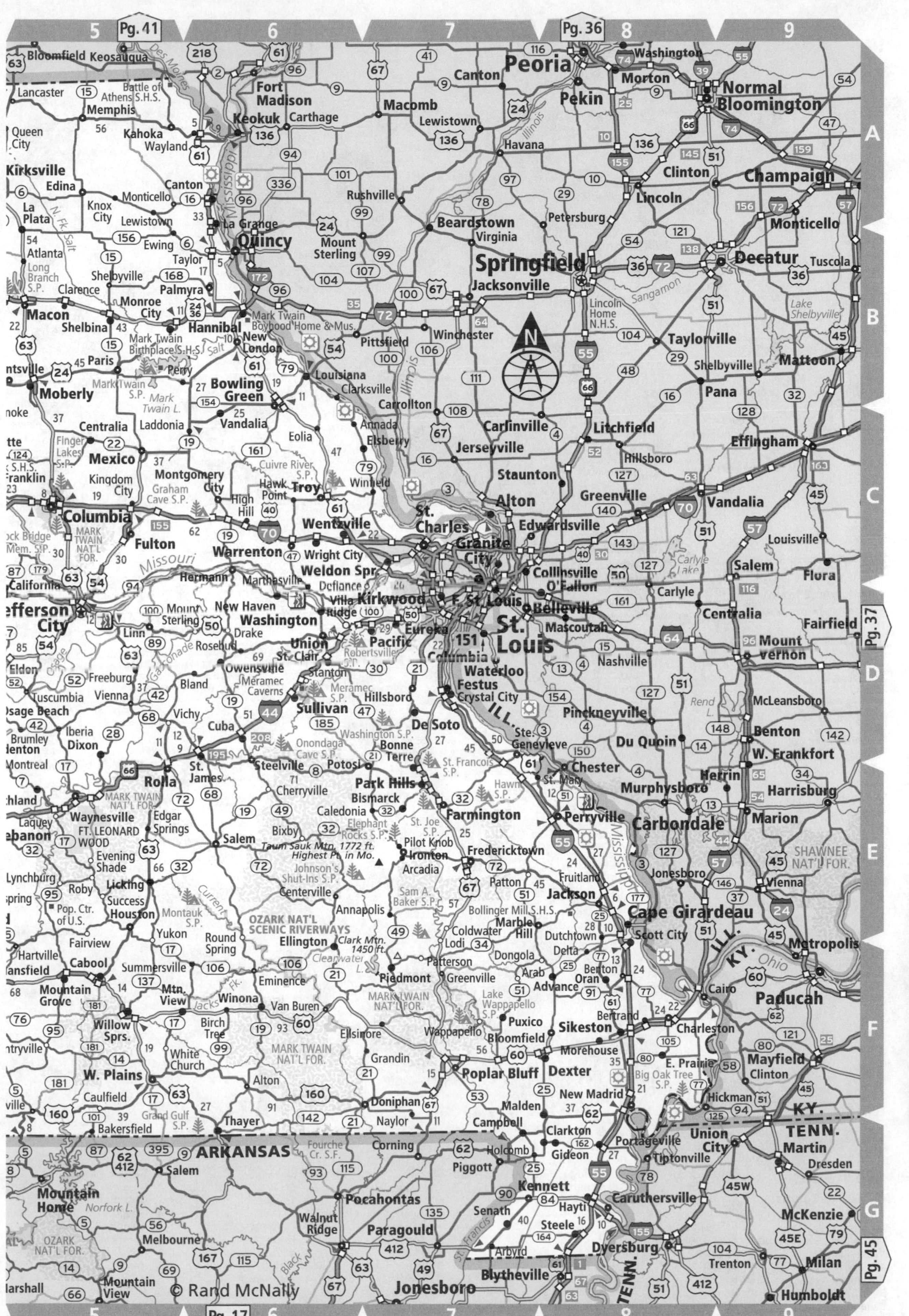

Travel planning & on-the-road resources

Tourism Information
Missouri Division of Tourism
(573) 751-4133
www.visitmo.com

Road Conditions & Construction
(888) 275-6636, (866) 831-6277
traveler.modot.org/map
www.modot.org

Montana

Montana state facts

Nickname: The Treasure State
Capital: Helena, D-4

Population: 1,084,225 (rank: 44th)
Largest city: Billings, 117,116, E-7

Land area: 145,509 sq. mi. (rank: 4th)
Highest point: Granite Peak, 12,799 ft., E-6

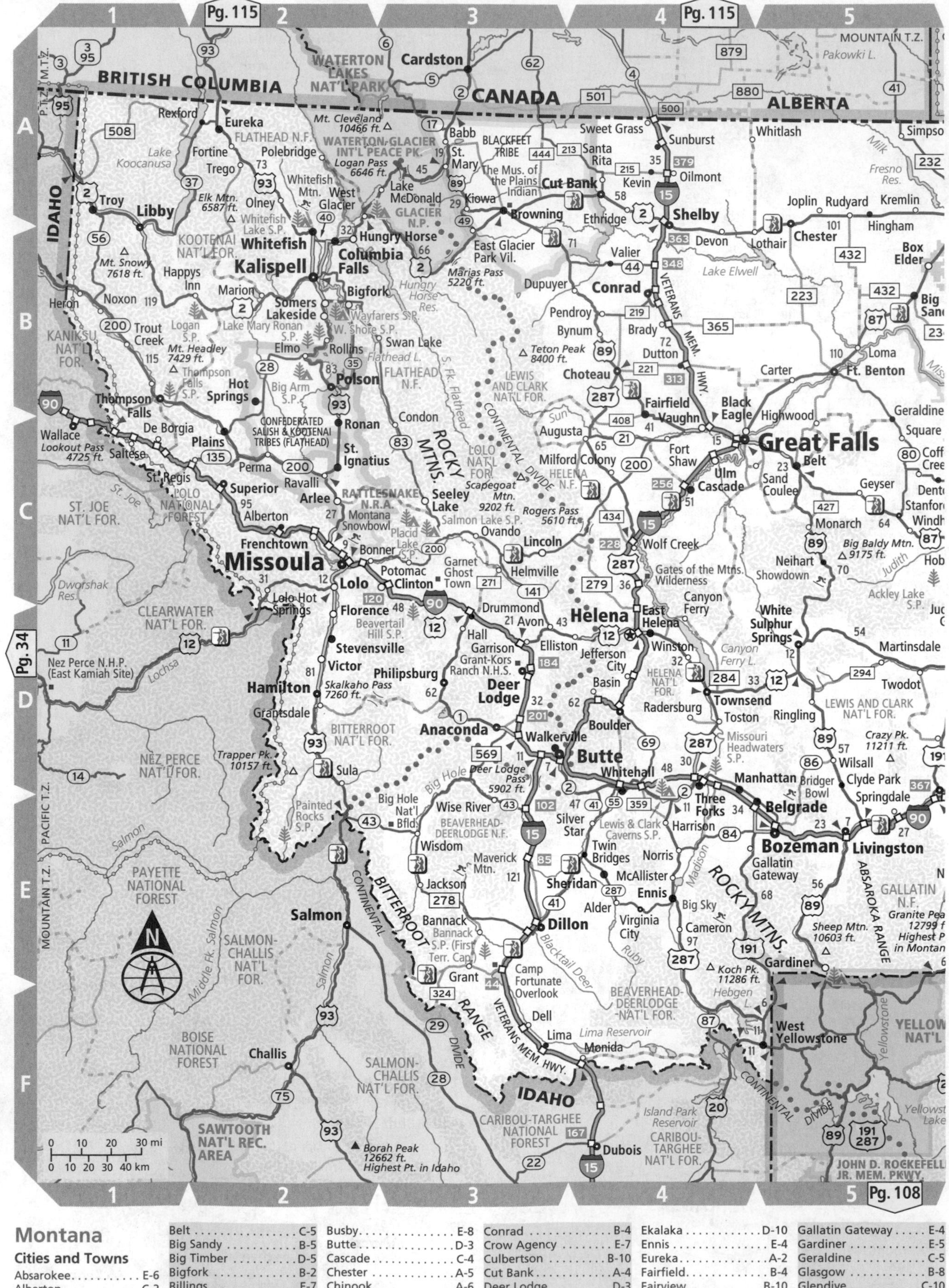

Montana

Cities and Towns

Absarokee E-6
Alberton C-2
Anaconda D-3
Arlee C-2
Ashland E-8
Augusta C-4
Baker D-10
Ballantine D-7
Belgrade E-5
Belt C-5
Big Sandy B-5
Big Timber D-5
Bigfork B-2
Billings E-7
Black Eagle C-4
Boulder D-4
Box Elder B-5
Bozeman E-5
Bridger E-6
Broadus E-9
Browning A-3
Busby E-8
Butte D-3
Cascade C-4
Chester A-5
Chinook A-6
Choteau B-4
Circle C-9
Clinton C-3
Clyde Park D-5
Colstrip D-8
Columbia Falls B-2
Columbus E-6
Conrad B-4
Crow Agency E-7
Culbertson B-10
Cut Bank A-4
Deer Lodge D-3
Denton C-5
Dillon E-3
Drummond D-3
Dutton B-4
East Glacier Park Village B-3
East Helena D-4
Ekalaka D-10
Ennis E-4
Eureka A-2
Fairfield B-4
Fairview B-10
Florence D-2
Forsyth D-8
Fort Belknap Agency . . B-6
Fort Benton B-5
Frazer B-8
Frenchtown C-2
Fromberg E-6
Gallatin Gateway E-4
Gardiner E-5
Geraldine C-5
Glasgow B-8
Glendive C-10
Great Falls C-4
Hamilton D-2
Hardin E-7
Harlem A-6
Harlowton D-6
Havre A-6
Hays B-6

NOTE: Maps are not always in alphabetical order.
See Page 1 for map location in this atlas.

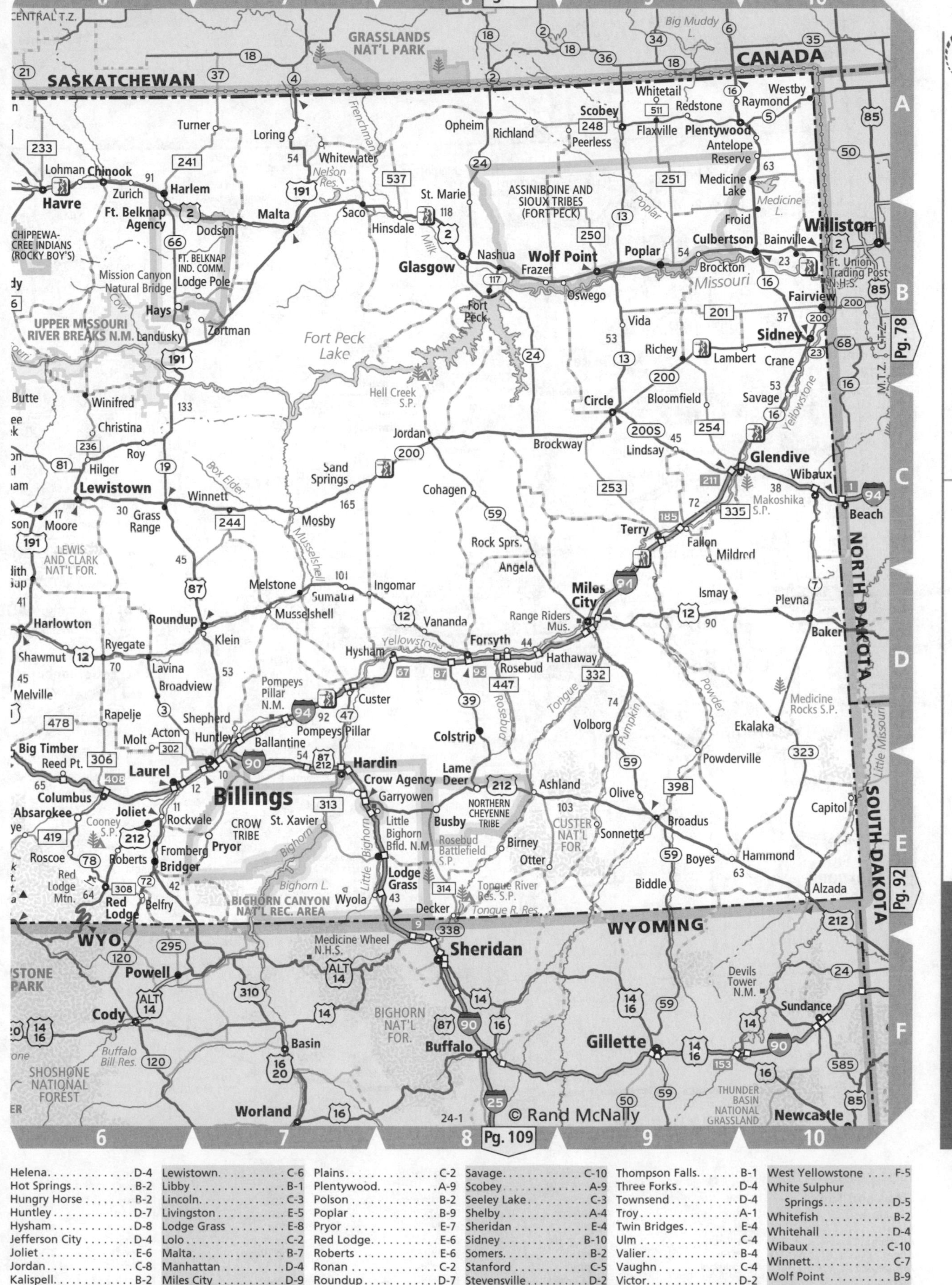

Road Conditions & Construction 511, (800) 226-7623, (406) 444-6200
www.511mt.net
www.mdt.mt.gov/travinfo

Tourism Information Montana Office of Tourism:
(800) 847-4868
www.visitmt.com

Travel planning & on-the-road resources

Helena . . . D-4
Hot Springs . . . B-2
Hungry Horse . . . B-2
Huntley . . . D-7
Hysham . . . D-8
Jefferson City . . . D-4
Joliet . . . E-6
Jordan . . . C-8
Kalispell . . . B-2
Lakeside . . . B-2
Lame Deer . . . E-8
Laurel . . . E-6
Lewistown . . . C-6
Libby . . . B-1
Lincoln . . . C-3
Livingston . . . E-5
Lodge Grass . . . E-8
Lolo . . . C-2
Malta . . . B-7
Manhattan . . . D-4
Miles City . . . D-9
Missoula . . . C-2
Nashua . . . B-8
Philipsburg . . . D-3
Plains . . . C-2
Plentywood . . . A-9
Polson . . . C-2
Poplar . . . B-9
Pryor . . . E-7
Red Lodge . . . E-6
Roberts . . . E-6
Ronan . . . C-2
Roundup . . . D-7
Ryegate . . . D-6
St. Ignatius . . . C-2
St. Regis . . . C-2
Savage . . . C-10
Scobey . . . A-9
Seeley Lake . . . C-3
Shelby . . . A-4
Sheridan . . . E-4
Sidney . . . B-10
Somers . . . B-2
Stanford . . . C-5
Stevensville . . . D-2
Sunburst . . . A-4
Superior . . . C-2
Terry . . . C-9
Thompson Falls . . . B-1
Three Forks . . . D-4
Townsend . . . D-4
Troy . . . A-1
Twin Bridges . . . E-4
Ulm . . . C-4
Valier . . . B-4
Vaughn . . . C-4
Victor . . . D-2
Virginia City . . . E-4
Walkerville . . . D-3
West Glacier . . . A-2
West Yellowstone . . . F-5
White Sulphur Springs . . . D-5
Whitefish . . . B-2
Whitehall . . . D-4
Wibaux . . . C-10
Winnett . . . C-7
Wolf Point . . . B-9

Nebraska state facts

Nickname: The Cornhusker State
Capital: Lincoln, D-9

Population: 1,961,504 (rank: 37th)
Largest city: Omaha, 486,051, D-9

Land area: 76,796 sq. mi. (rank: 15th)
Highest point: Panorama Point, 5,424 ft., D-1

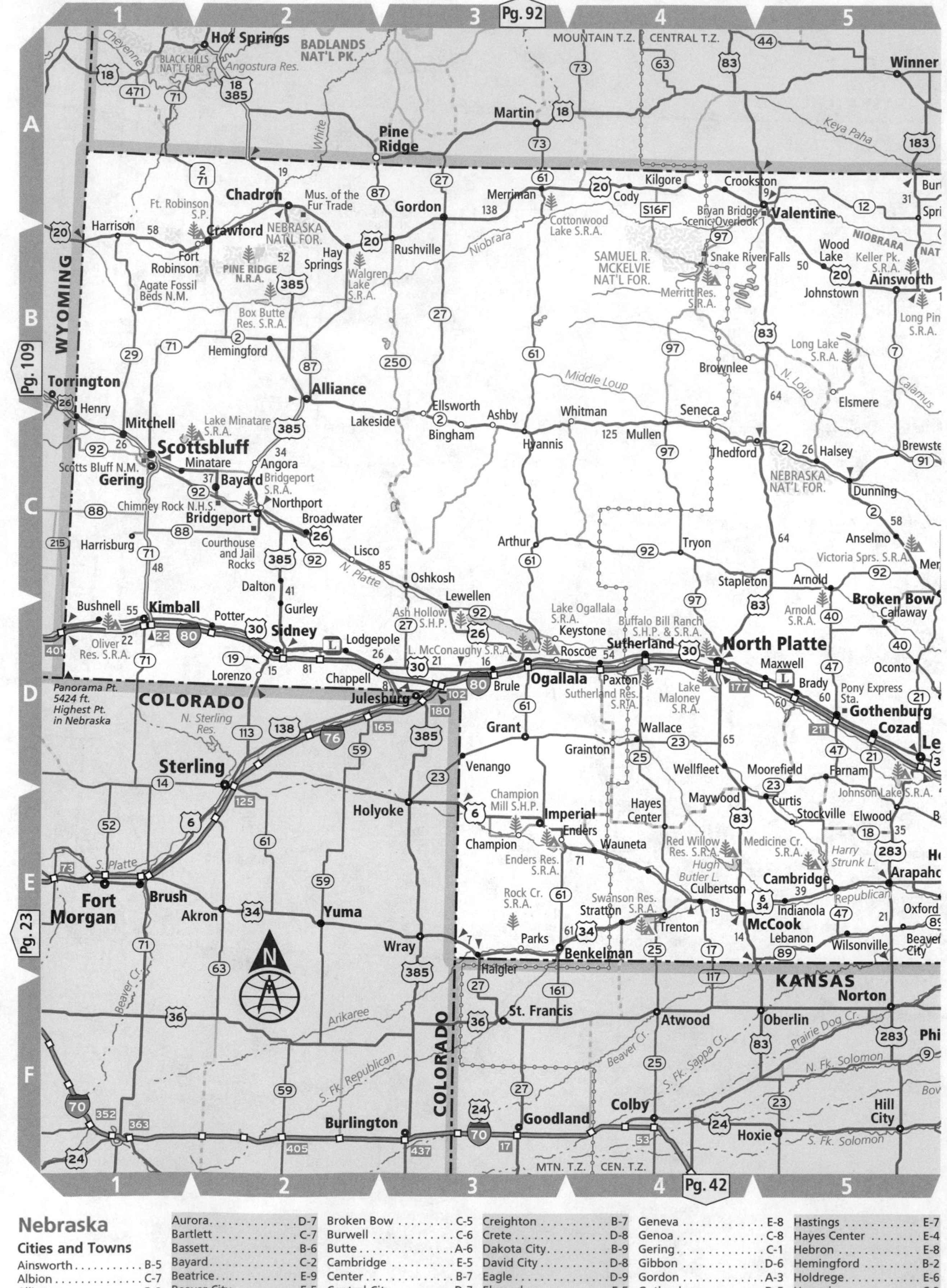

Nebraska

Cities and Towns

Ainsworth B-5
Albion C-7
Alliance B-2
Alma E-6
Arapahoe E-5
Arthur C-3
Ashland D-9
Atkinson B-6
Auburn E-10
Aurora D-7
Bartlett C-7
Bassett B-6
Bayard C-2
Beatrice E-9
Beaver City E-5
Bellevue D-9
Benkelman E-3
Blair C-9
Bloomfield B-8
Brewster C-5
Bridgeport C-2
Broken Bow C-5
Burwell C-6
Butte A-6
Cambridge E-5
Center B-7
Central City D-7
Chadron A-2
Chappell D-2
Clay Center E-7
Columbus C-8
Cozad D-5
Crawford B-2
Creighton B-7
Crete D-8
Dakota City B-9
David City D-8
Eagle D-9
Elwood E-5
Fairbury E-8
Falls City E-10
Franklin E-6
Fremont C-9
Friend D-8
Fullerton C-7
Geneva E-8
Genoa C-8
Gering C-1
Gibbon D-6
Gordon A-3
Gothenburg D-5
Grand Island D-7
Grant D-3
Greeley C-7
Harrisburg C-1
Harrison B-1
Hartington B-8
Hastings E-7
Hayes Center E-4
Hebron E-8
Hemingford B-2
Holdrege E-6
Hyannis C-3
Imperial E-3
Kearney D-6
Kimball D-1
Laurel B-8
Lexington D-5
Lincoln D-9

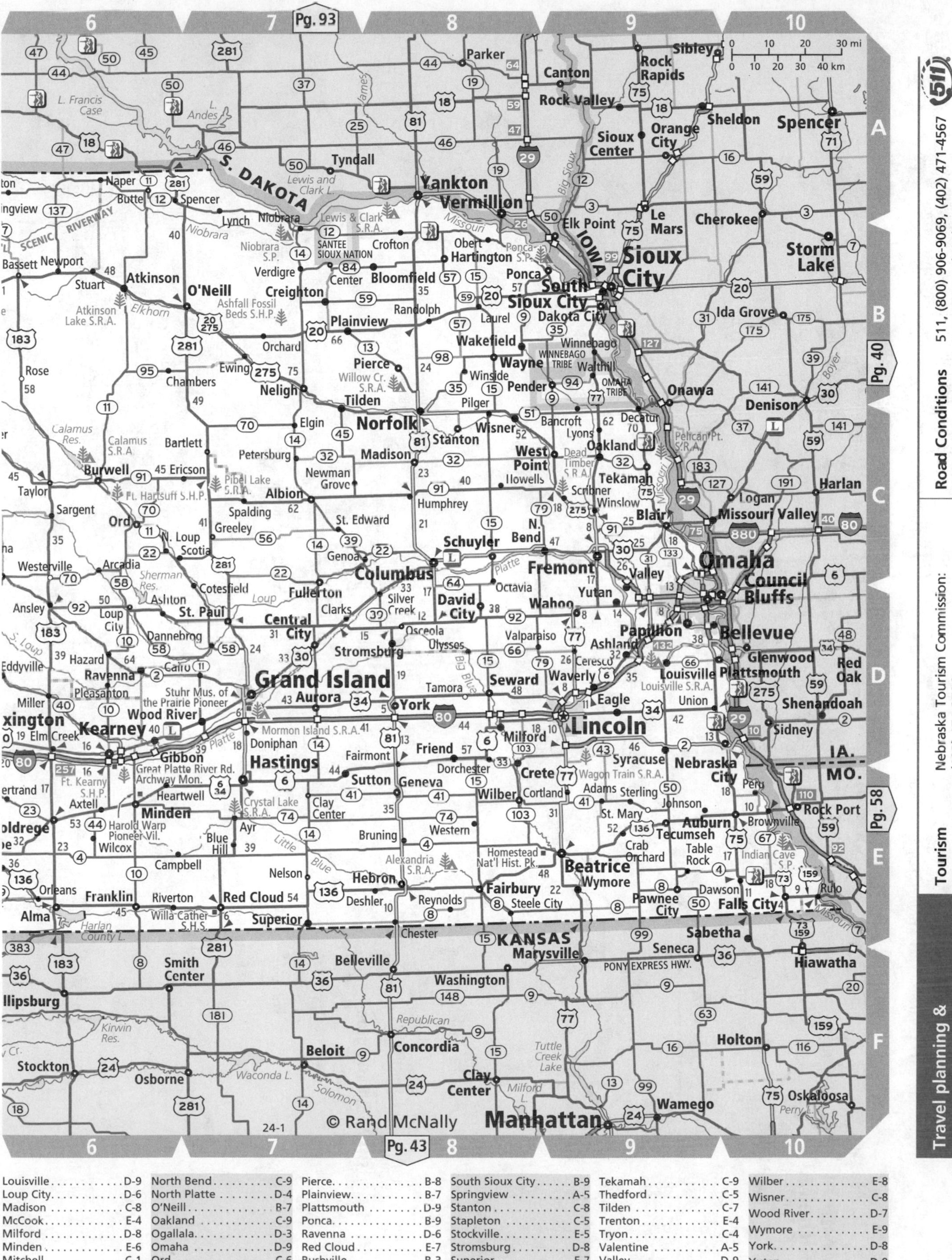

Road Conditions & Construction
511, (800) 906-9069, (402) 471-4567
www.511.nebraska.gov
dot.nebraska.gov/travel

Tourism Information
Nebraska Tourism Commission:
(402) 471-3796
visitnebraska.com

Travel planning & on-the-road resources

Louisville D-9
Loup City D-6
Madison C-8
McCook E-4
Milford D-8
Minden E-6
Mitchell C-1
Mullen C-4
Nebraska City D-10
Neligh B-7
Nelson E-7
Norfolk C-8
North Bend C-9
North Platte D-4
O'Neill B-7
Oakland C-9
Ogallala D-3
Omaha D-9
Ord C-6
Osceola D-8
Oshkosh C-3
Papillion D-9
Pawnee City E-9
Pender B-9
Pierce B-8
Plainview B-7
Plattsmouth D-9
Ponca B-9
Ravenna D-6
Red Cloud E-7
Rushville B-3
St. Paul D-7
Schuyler C-8
Scottsbluff C-1
Seward D-8
Sidney D-2
South Sioux City B-9
Springview A-5
Stanton C-8
Stapleton C-5
Stockville E-5
Stromsburg D-8
Superior E-7
Sutherland D-4
Sutton E-7
Syracuse D-9
Taylor C-6
Tecumseh E-9
Tekamah C-9
Thedford C-5
Tilden C-7
Trenton E-4
Tryon C-4
Valentine A-5
Valley D-9
Wahoo D-9
Wakefield B-8
Waverly D-9
Wayne B-8
West Point C-9
Wilber E-8
Wisner C-8
Wood River D-7
Wymore E-9
York D-8
Yutan D-9

New Hampshire state facts

Nickname: The Granite State
Capital: Concord, H-5
Population: 1,377,529 (rank: 41st)
Largest city: Manchester, 115,644, H-5
Land area: 8,951 sq. mi. (rank: 44th)
Highest point: Mt. Washington, 6,288 ft., D-6

Travel planning & on-the-road resources

Tourism Information
N.H. Div. of Travel & Tourism Dev.:
(603) 271-2665
www.visitnh.gov

Road Conditions & Construction
(603) 271-3734
newengland511.org
www.dot.nh.gov

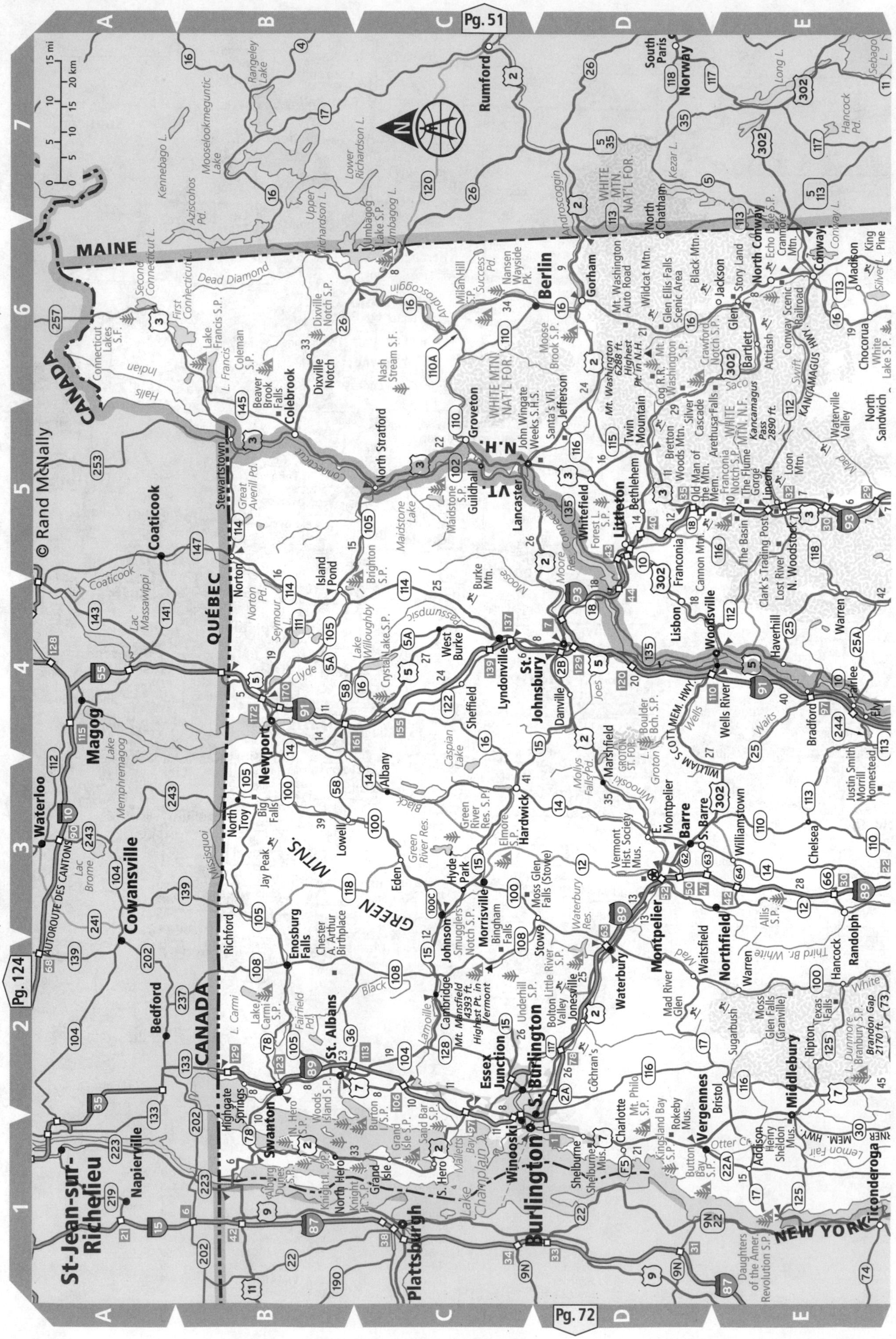

Pg. 124
Pg. 51
Pg. 72

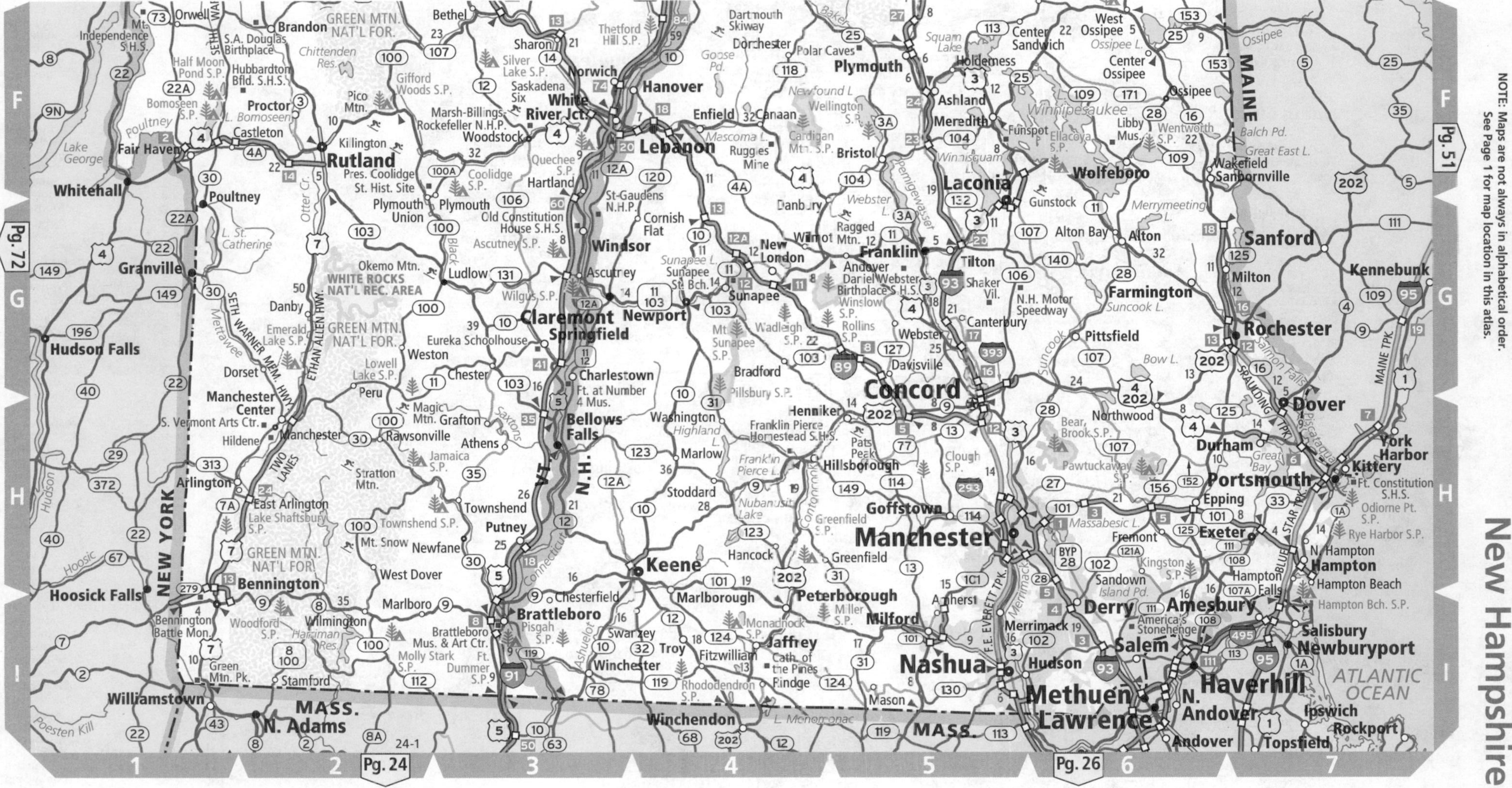

New Hampshire

Cities and Towns

- Berlin . . . D-6
- Bristol . . . F-5
- Claremont . . . G-3
- Concord . . . H-5
- Conway . . . E-6
- Derry . . . I-6
- Dover . . . H-7
- Durham . . . H-7
- Enfield . . . F-4
- Epping . . . H-6
- Exeter . . . H-7
- Farmington . . . G-6
- Franklin . . . G-5
- Goffstown . . . H-5
- Gorham . . . D-6
- Hampton . . . H-7
- Hanover . . . F-4
- Henniker . . . H-5
- Hudson . . . I-5
- Jaffrey . . . I-4
- Keene . . . H-4
- Laconia . . . G-5
- Lancaster . . . C-5
- Lebanon . . . F-4
- Littleton . . . D-5
- Manchester . . . H-5
- Meredith . . . F-5
- Merrimack . . . I-5
- Milford . . . I-5
- Nashua . . . I-5
- Newport . . . G-4
- North Conway . . . E-6
- North Hampton . . . H-7
- Ossipee . . . F-6
- Peterborough . . . I-4
- Pittsfield . . . G-6
- Plymouth . . . F-5
- Portsmouth . . . H-7
- Rochester . . . G-7
- Salem . . . I-6
- Swanzey . . . I-4
- Winchester . . . I-3
- Wolfeboro . . . F-6
- Woodsville . . . E-4

Vermont

Cities and Towns

- Arlington . . . H-1
- Barre . . . D-3
- Bellows Falls . . . H-3
- Bennington . . . I-1
- Bethel . . . F-3
- Brandon . . . F-2
- Brattleboro . . . I-3
- Burlington . . . C-1
- Chelsea . . . E-3
- Enosburg Falls . . . B-2
- Essex Junction . . . C-2
- Fair Haven . . . F-1
- Guildhall . . . C-5
- Hardwick . . . C-3
- Hyde Park . . . C-3
- Johnson . . . C-3
- Lyndonville . . . C-4
- Manchester . . . H-2
- Manchester Center . . . H-2
- Middlebury . . . E-1
- Montpelier . . . D-3
- Morrisville . . . C-3
- Newfane . . . H-3
- Newport . . . B-4
- North Hero . . . B-1
- Northfield . . . E-3
- Norwich . . . F-3
- Poultney . . . G-1
- Proctor . . . F-2
- Putney . . . H-3
- Randolph . . . E-3
- Rutland . . . F-2
- St. Albans . . . B-2
- St. Johnsbury . . . D-4
- South Barre . . . D-3
- South Burlington . . . D-2
- Springfield . . . G-3
- Swanton . . . B-2
- Vergennes . . . D-1
- Waterbury . . . D-2
- White River Junction . . . F-3
- Windsor . . . G-3
- Winooski . . . C-1
- Woodstock . . . F-3

Vermont state facts

Nickname: The Green Mtn. State
Capital: Montpelier, D-3
Population: 643,077 (rank: 49th)

Largest city: Burlington, 44,743, C-1
Land area: 9,215 sq. mi. (rank: 43rd)
Highest point: Mt. Mansfield, 4,393 ft., C-2

Travel planning & on-the-road resources

Tourism Information Vt. Dept. of Tourism & Mktg.: (800) 837-6668 www.vermontvacation.com

Road Conditions & Construction (802) 917-2458 newengland511.org www.vtrans.vermont.gov

New Jersey state facts

Nickname: The Garden State
Capital: Trenton, E-3

Population: 9,288,994 (rank: 11th)
Largest city: Newark, 311,549, C-5

Land area: 7,353 sq. mi. (rank: 46th)
Highest point: High Point, 1,803 ft., A-4

New Jersey

Cities and Towns

Absecon	H-4
Asbury Park	E-5
Atlantic City	H-4
Atlantic Highlands	D-5
Audubon	F-2
Avalon	I-3
Beachwood	F-5
Belleville	C-5
Belvidere	C-2
Berlin	G-3
Bernardsville	C-4
Blackwood	G-2
Boonton	C-4
Bordentown	E-3
Bound Brook	D-4
Bridgeton	H-2
Brigantine	H-4
Browns Mills	F-4
Budd Lake	C-3
Buena	H-3
Burlington	F-3
Caldwell	C-5
Camden	F-2
Cape May	J-3
Cape May Court House	I-3
Clifton	C-5
Clinton	D-3
Cranbury	E-4
Denville	C-4
Dover	C-4
Eatontown	E-5
Edison	D-4
Egg Harbor City	H-4
Elizabeth	D-5
Elmer	H-2
Ewing	E-3
Flemington	D-3
Folsom	H-3
Forked River	G-5
Franklin	B-4
Freehold	E-5
Glassboro	G-2
Hackensack	C-5
Hackettstown	C-3
Hamburg	B-4
Hammonton	G-3
High Bridge	D-3
Highland Park	D-4
Highlands	E-5
Hightstown	E-4
Hopatcong	B-4
Hope	C-3
Hopewell	E-3
Jamesburg	E-4
Keansburg	D-5
Kinnelon	B-4
Lakehurst	F-5
Lakewood	F-5
Lambertville	E-3
Lawrenceville	E-3
Lebanon	D-3
Linden	D-5
Little Silver	E-5
Long Branch	E-6
Madison	C-4
Mahwah	B-5
Malaga	H-2
Manahawkin	G-5
Manville	D-4
Margate City	I-4

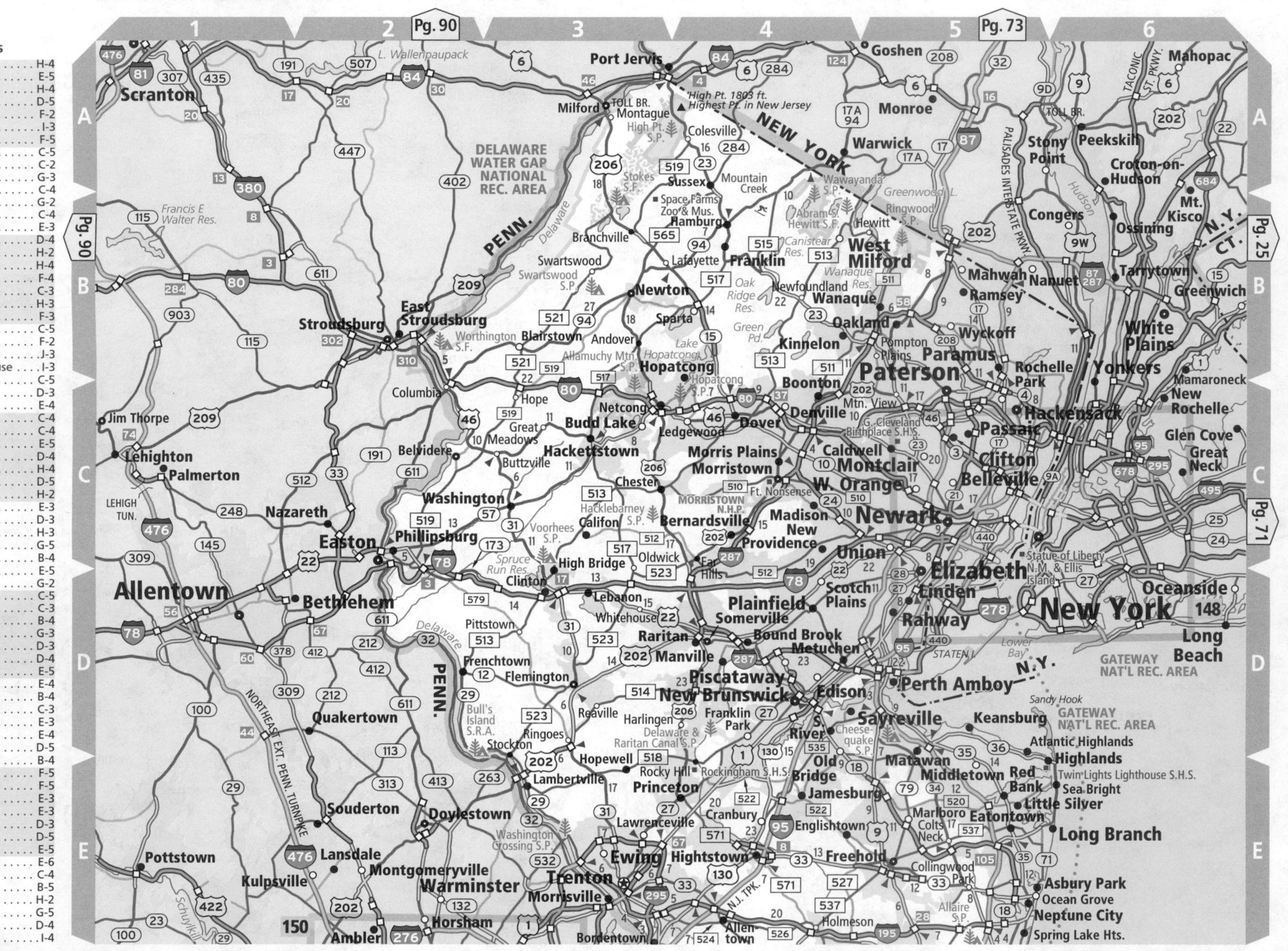

NOTE: Maps are not always in alphabetical order. See Page 1 for map location in this atlas.

Marlton F-3
Matawan D-5
Mays Landing H-3
Medford F-3
Metuchen D-4
Middletown E-5
Millville H-2
Montclair C-5
Morris Plains C-4
Morristown C-4
Mount Holly F-3
Neptune City E-5
Netcong C-3
New Brunswick D-4
New Egypt F-4
New Providence C-4
Newark C-5
Newton B-3
Oakland B-5
Ocean City I-4
Ocean Grove E-5
Old Bridge D-4
Paramus B-5
Passaic C-5
Paterson C-5
Paulsboro G-2
Penns Grove G-1
Pennsville G-1
Perth Amboy D-5
Phillipsburg C-2
Piscataway D-4
Plainfield D-4
Pleasantville H-4
Point Pleasant F-5
Princeton E-4
Rahway D-5
Ramsey B-5
Raritan D-4
Red Bank E-5
Rio Grande J-3
Rochelle Park C-5
Salem H-1
Sayreville D-4
Scotch Plains D-4
Sea Girt F-5
Sea Isle City I-3
Seaside Heights F-5
Seaside Park F-5
Somerdale G-3
Somers Point I-4
Somerville D-4
South River D-4
Spring Lake Heights E-5
Sussex A-4
Toms River F-5
Trenton E-3
Tuckerton H-4
Union C-5
Ventnor City I-4
Villas J-3
Vineland H-2
Wanaque B-5
Washington C-3
West Milford B-4
West Orange C-5
Wildwood J-3
Williamstown G-3
Woodbury G-2
Woodstown G-2
Wyckoff B-5

Travel planning & on-the-road resources	Tourism Information	New Jersey Division of Travel and Tourism: (609) 599-6540 visitnj.org	Road Conditions & Construction	511, (866) 511-6538 511nj.org www.state.nj.us/transportation

511

New Mexico state facts

Nickname: Land of Enchantment
Capital: Santa Fe, C-4

Population: 2,117,522 (rank: 36th)
Largest city: Albuquerque, 564,559, D-3

Land area: 121,280 sq. mi. (rank: 5th)
Highest point: Wheeler Peak, 13,161 ft., B-5

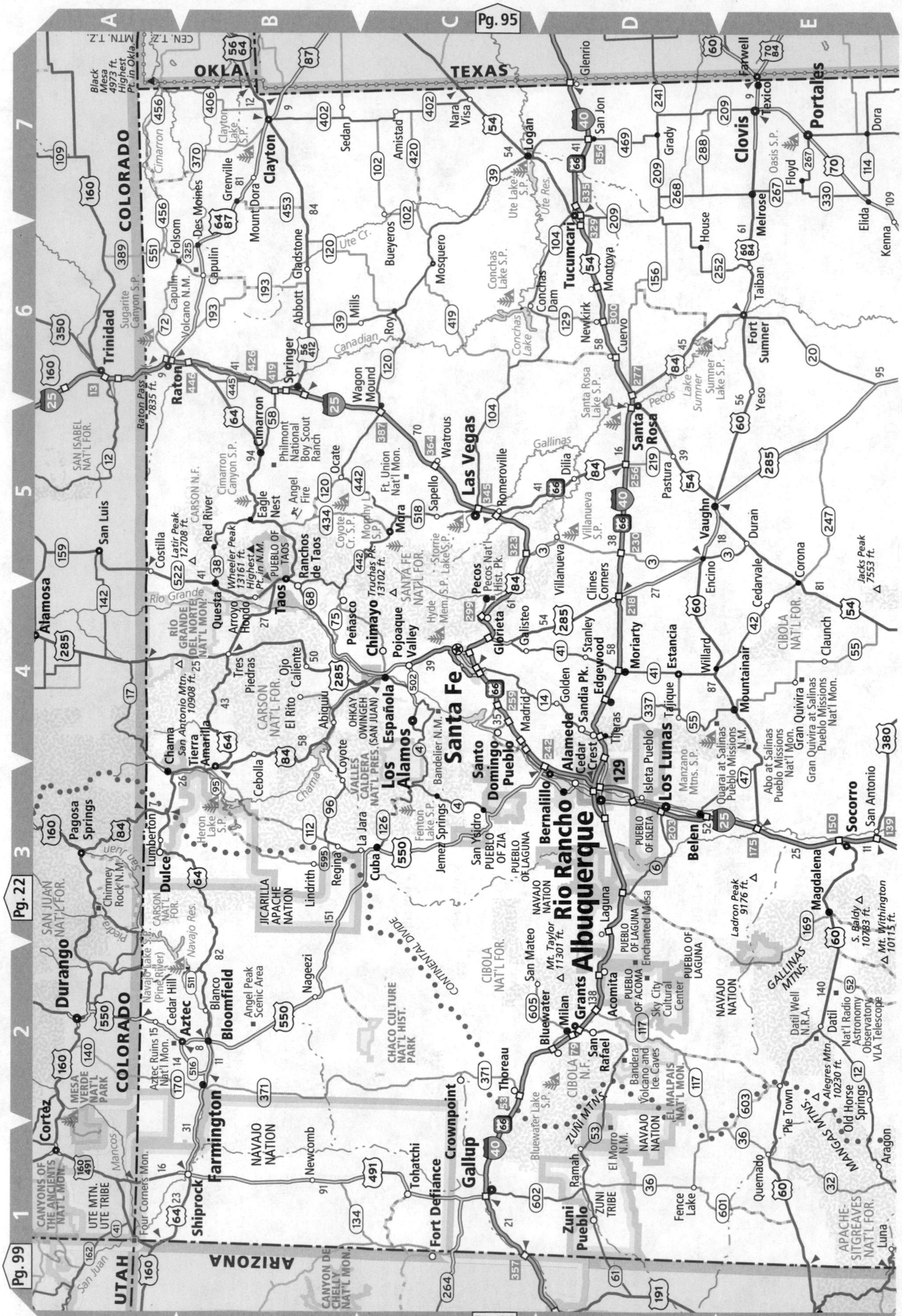

NOTE: Maps are not always in alphabetical order. See Page 1 for map location in this atlas.

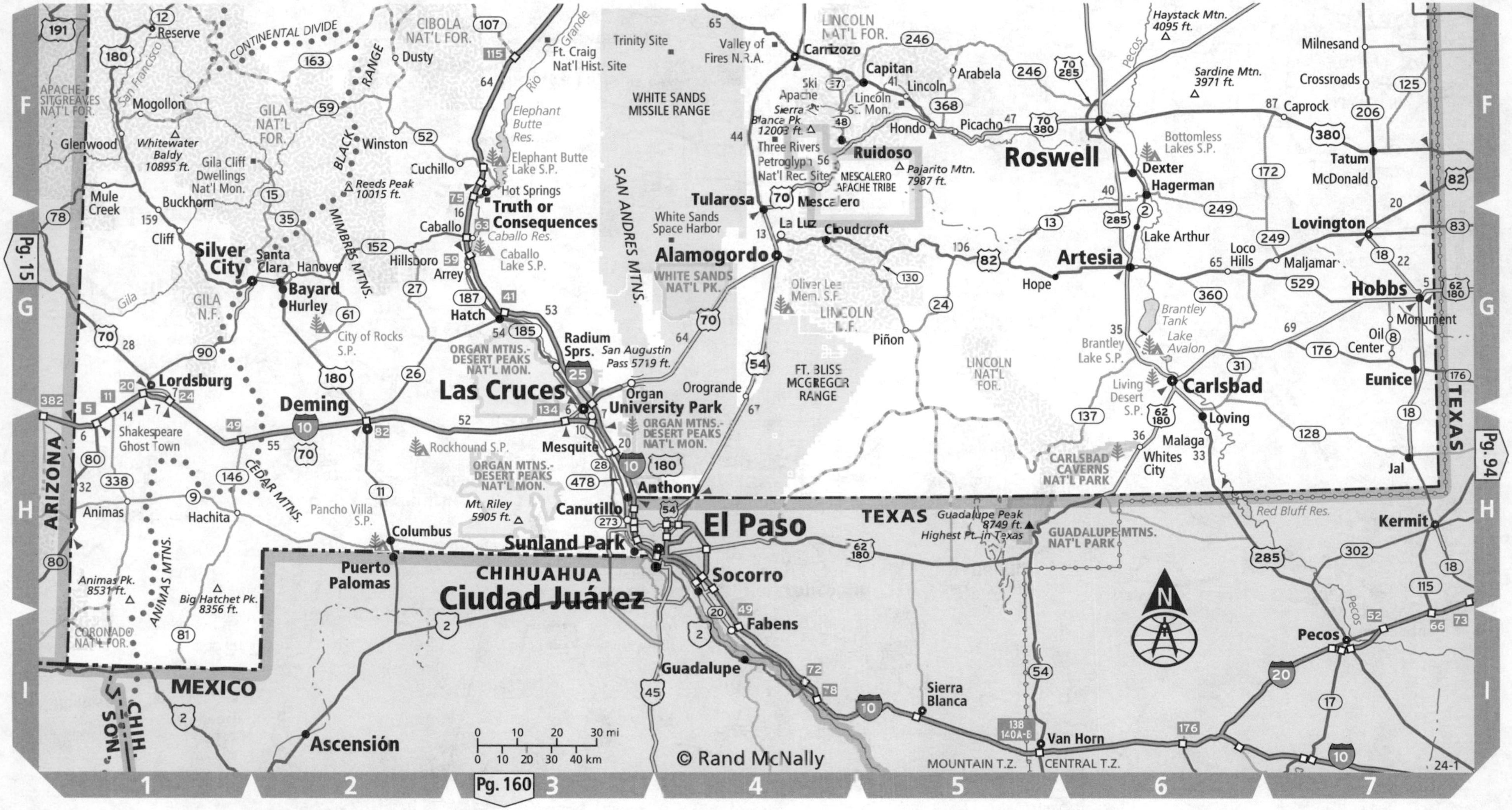

Pg. 15
Pg. 94
Pg. 160

New Mexico

Cities and Towns

Acomita D-2
Alameda D-3
Alamogordo G-4
Albuquerque D-3
Anthony H-3
Artesia G-6
Aztec B-2
Bayard G-2
Belen D-3
Bernalillo D-3
Bloomfield B-2
Bluewater D-2
Capitan F-5
Carlsbad G-6
Carrizozo F-4
Cedar Crest D-4
Chama A-3
Chimayo C-4
Cimarron B-5
Clayton B-7
Cloudcroft G-4
Clovis E-7
Columbus H-2
Crownpoint C-2
Cuba C-3
Deming H-2
Dexter F-6
Dulce A-3
Edgewood D-4
Española C-4
Estancia D-4
Eunice G-7
Farmington B-2
Fort Sumner E-6
Gallup C-1
Glorieta C-4
Grants D-2
Hagerman F-6
Hatch G-3
Hobbs G-7
Hurley G-2
Jal H-7
La Luz G-4
Las Cruces G-3
Las Vegas C-5
Logan C-7
Lordsburg G-1
Los Alamos C-4
Los Lunas D-3
Loving H-6
Lovington G-7
Magdalena E-3
Melrose E-7
Mescalero F-4
Mesquite H-3
Milan D-2
Mora C-5
Moriarty D-4
Mosquero C-6
Mountainair E-4
Organ G-3
Pecos C-4
Peñasco B-4
Pojoaque Valley C-4
Portales E-7
Questa B-4
Radium Springs G-3
Ranchos de Taos B-4
Raton A-6
Reserve F-1
Rio Rancho D-3
Roswell F-6
Ruidoso F-4
San Rafael D-2
Sandia Park D-4
Santa Clara G-2
Santa Fe C-4
Santa Rosa D-5
Santo Domingo Pueblo . . C-4
Shiprock B-1
Silver City G-2
Socorro E-3
Springer B-6
Sunland Park H-3
Taos B-5
Tatum F-7
Texico E-7
Thoreau C-2
Tierra Amarilla B-3
Tohatchi C-1
Truth or Consequences . . F-3
Tucumcari D-7
Tularosa G-4
University Park H-3
Vaughn D-5
Zuni Pueblo D-1

Travel planning & on-the-road resources

Tourism Information
New Mexico Tourism Department:
(505) 795-0343
www.newmexico.org

Road Conditions & Construction
511
(800) 432-4269, (505) 795-1401
www.nmroads.com, www.dot.nm.gov

New York state facts

Nickname: The Empire State
Capital: Albany, F-11

Population: 20,201,249 (rank: 4th)
Largest city: New York, 8,804,190, J-1

Land area: 47,111 sq. mi. (rank: 30th)
Highest point: Mount Marcy, 5,344 ft., C-11

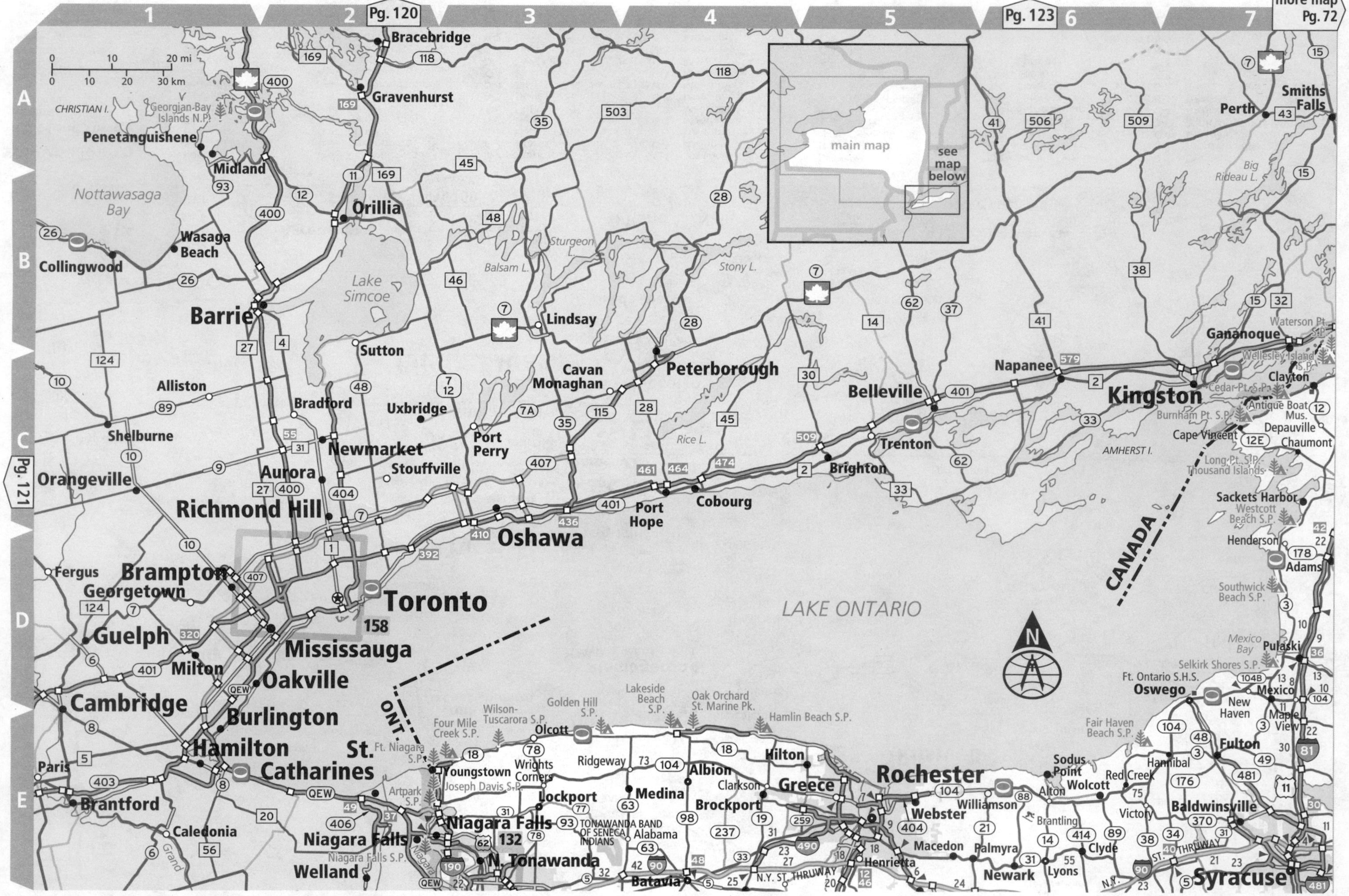

more map Pg. 72
Pg. 120
Pg. 123
Pg. 121

LAKE ONTARIO

NOTE: Maps are not always in alphabetical order.
See Page 1 for map location in this atlas.

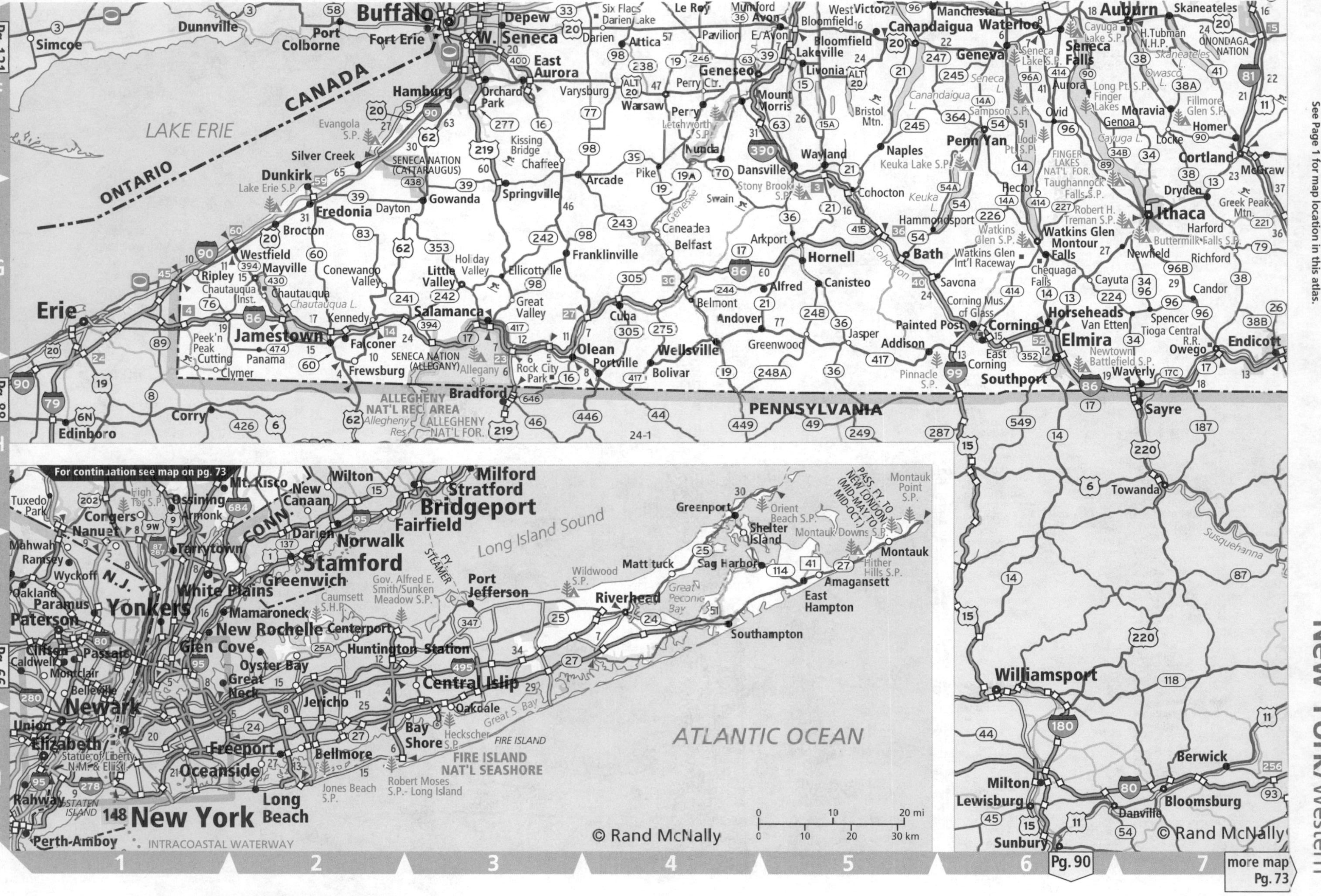

Travel planning & on-the-road resources

Tourism Information
New York State Division of Tourism:
(800) 225-5697
www.iloveny.com

Road Conditions & Construction
511, (888) 465-1169
www.511ny.org, www.dot.ny.gov
Thruway: (800) 847-8929, www.thruway.ny.gov

Nickname: The Empire State
Capital: Albany, F-11
Population: 20,201,249 (rank: 4th)
Largest city: New York, 8,804,190, J-1
Land area: 47,111 sq. mi. (rank: 30th)
Highest point: Mount Marcy, 5,344 ft., C-11

New York state facts

more map Pg. 70
Pg. 123
Pg. 124
Pg. 64

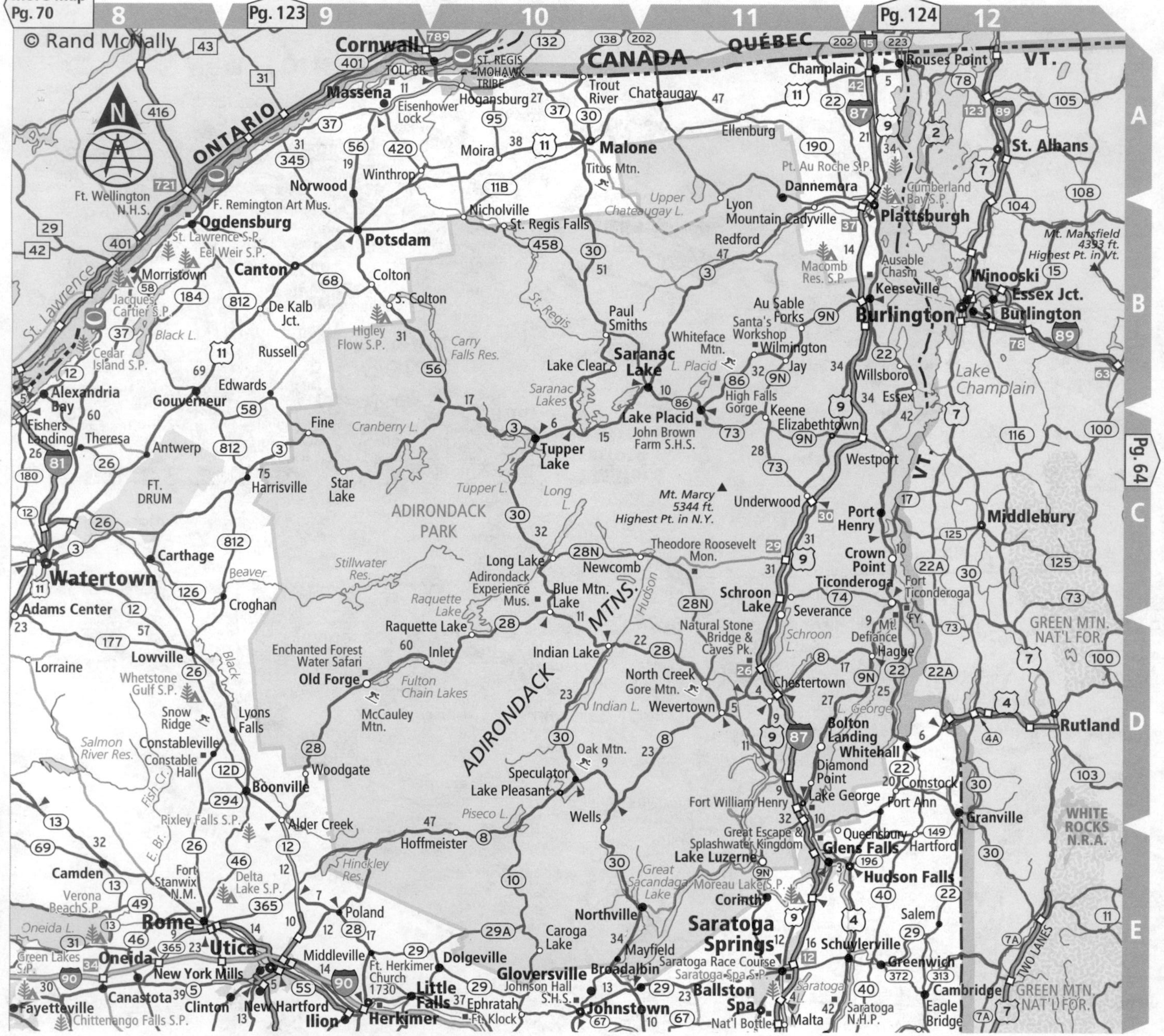

New York

Cities and Towns

Adams . . . D-7
Adams Center . . . D-8
Addison . . . G-5
Albany . . . F-11
Albion . . . E-4
Alexandria Bay . . . B-8
Alfred . . . G-5
Amagansett . . . I-5
Amenia . . . H-12
Amherst . . . E-3
Amsterdam . . . F-11
Andover . . . G-5
Arcade . . . F-3
Arkport . . . G-5
Armonk . . . J-11
Attica . . . F-4
Auburn . . . F-7
Avon . . . F-5
Bainbridge . . . G-8
Baldwinsville . . . E-7
Ballston Spa . . . E-11
Batavia . . . E-4
Bath . . . G-5
Bay Shore . . . J-3
Beacon . . . I-11
Belfast . . . G-4
Bellmore . . . J-2
Belmont . . . G-4
Binghamton . . . G-8
Bolivar . . . H-4
Bolton Landing . . . D-11
Boonville . . . D-9
Brewster . . . I-12
Brockport . . . E-4
Brocton . . . G-2
Buffalo . . . F-3
Cadyville . . . B-11
Cairo . . . G-11
Cambridge . . . E-12
Camden . . . E-8
Canajoharie . . . F-10
Canandaigua . . . F-5
Canastota . . . E-8
Candor . . . G-7
Canisteo . . . G-5
Canton . . . B-9
Carthage . . . C-8
Catskill . . . G-11
Cayuta . . . G-6
Cazenovia . . . F-8
Centerport . . . I-2
Central Islip . . . I-3
Champlain . . . A-12
Chestertown . . . D-11
Claverack . . . G-11
Clayton . . . C-7
Clinton . . . E-9
Clyde . . . E-6
Cobleskill . . . F-10
Cohocton . . . G-5
Cohoes . . . F-11
Congers . . . H-1
Cooperstown . . . F-9
Corinth . . . E-11
Corning . . . G-6
Cornwall-on-Hudson . . . I-11
Cortland . . . F-7
Croton Falls . . . I-12
Croton-on-Hudson . . . I-11
Crown Point . . . C-12
Le Roy . . . E-4
Liberty . . . H-10
Little Falls . . . E-9
Little Valley . . . G-3
Livingston Manor . . . H-9
Livonia . . . F-5
Loch Sheldrake . . . H-10
Lockport . . . E-3
Long Beach . . . J-2
Lowville . . . D-8
Lyons . . . E-6
Macedon . . . E-5
Mahopac . . . I-11
Malone . . . A-10
Mamaroneck . . . J-11
Manchester . . . F-5
Massena . . . A-9
Mattituck . . . I-4
Mayville . . . G-2
McGraw . . . F-7
Mechanicville . . . F-11
Medina . . . E-4
Mexico . . . D-7
Middleburgh . . . F-10
Middletown . . . I-10
Millbrook . . . H-11
Millerton . . . H-12
Monroe . . . I-11
Montauk . . . I-5
Monticello . . . H-10
Montour Falls . . . G-6
Moravia . . . F-7
Mount Kisco . . . I-11
Mount Morris . . . F-4
Naples . . . F-5
New Berlin . . . F-9
New Hartford . . . E-9
New Lebanon . . . G-12
New Paltz . . . H-11
New Rochelle . . . J-11
New Windsor . . . I-11
New York . . . J-1
New York Mills . . . E-9
Newark . . . E-6
Newburgh . . . I-11
Niagara Falls . . . E-3
North Tonawanda . . . E-3
Northville . . . E-11
Norwich . . . F-8
Norwood . . . A-9
Nunda . . . F-4
Oakdale . . . I-3
Oceanside . . . J-2
Ogdensburg . . . B-8
Olcott . . . E-3
Old Forge . . . D-9
Olean . . . H-3
Oneida . . . E-8
Oneonta . . . G-9
Orchard Park . . . F-3
Ossining . . . J-11
Oswego . . . D-7
Owego . . . G-7
Oxford . . . G-8
Oyster Bay . . . I-2
Painted Post . . . G-6
Palmyra . . . E-5
Pawling . . . I-12
Peekskill . . . I-11
Penn Yan . . . F-6
Perry . . . F-4
Plattsburgh . . . B-12
Port Henry . . . C-12
Port Jefferson . . . I-3

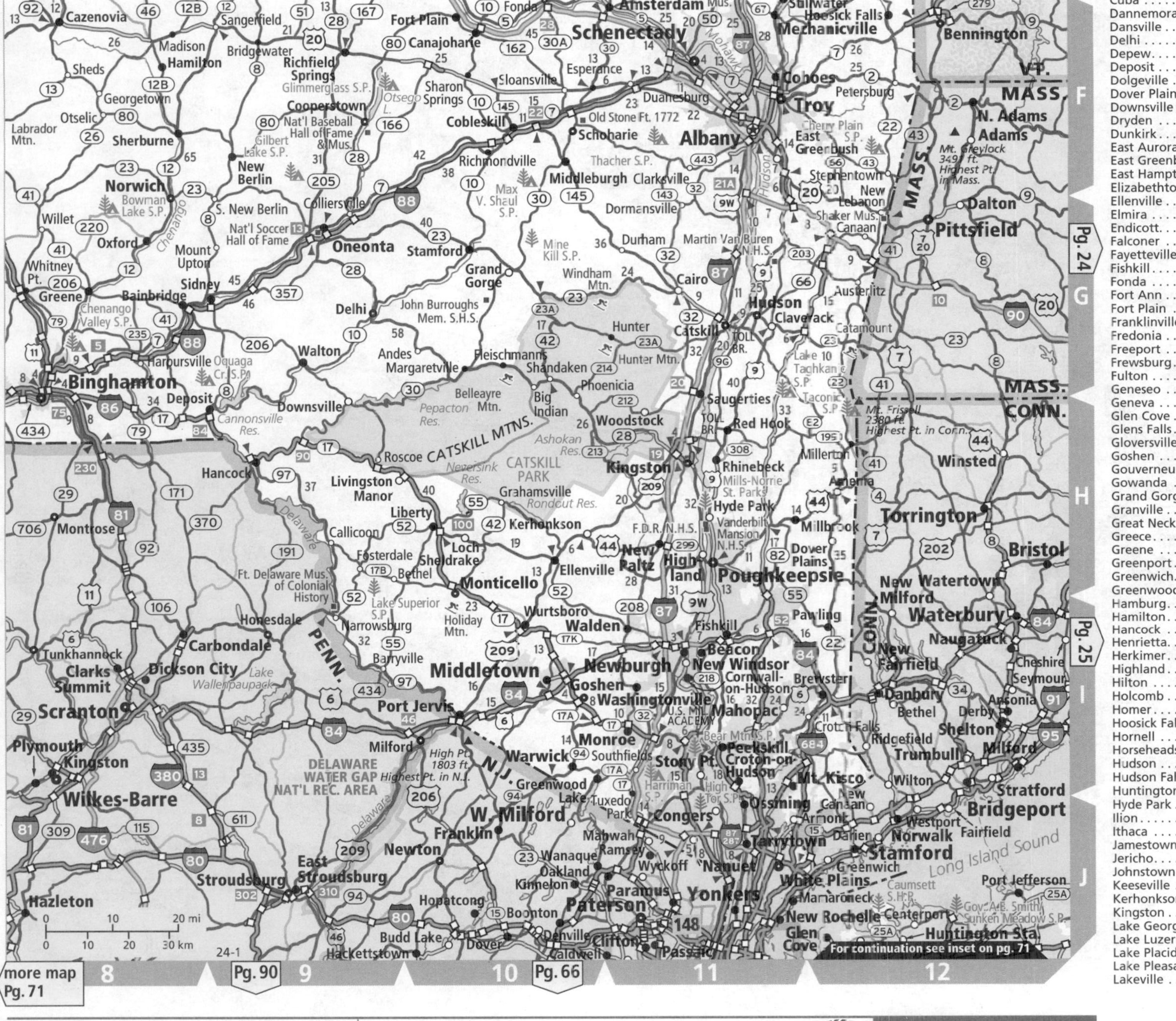

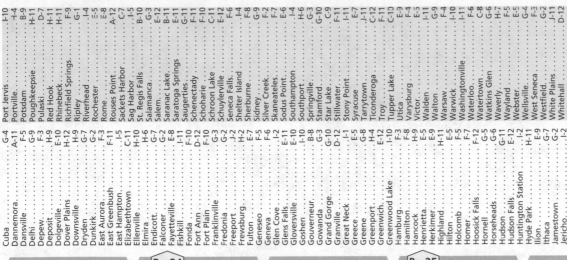

Cuba G-4
Dannemora. A-11
Dansville F-5
Delhi G-9
Depew. F-3
Deposit H-9
Dolgeville E-10
Dover Plains H-12
Downsville H-9
Dryden G-7
Dunkirk G-2
East Aurora. F-3
East Greenbush F-11
East Hampton. I-5
Elizabethtown C-11
Ellenville H-10
Elmira H-6
Endicott. G-7
Falconer G-2
Fayetteville. E-8
Fishkill. I-11
Fonda F-10
Fort Ann D-12
Fort Plain F-10
Franklinville G-3
Fredonia G-2
Freeport J-2
Frewsburg. H-2
Fulton E-7
Geneseo F-5
Geneva F-6
Glen Cove I-2
Glens Falls. E-11
Gloversville. E-10
Goshen I-10
Gouverneur. B-8
Gowanda G-3
Grand Gorge. G-10
Granville D-12
Great Neck I-1
Greece. E-5
Greene G-8
Greenport. H-4
Greenwich. E-12
Greenwood Lake I-10
Hamburg. F-3
Hamilton. F-8
Hancock H-9
Henrietta. E-5
Herkimer. E-9
Highland. H-11
Hilton E-5
Holcomb F-5
Homer. F-7
Hoosick Falls. F-12
Hornell G-5
Horseheads. G-6
Hudson G-11
Hudson Falls. E-12
Huntington Station I-2
Hyde Park H-11
Ilion. E-9
Ithaca G-7
Jamestown G-2
Jericho. I-2
Johnstown E-10
Keeseville B-12
Kerhonkson H-10
Kingston H-11
Lake George. D-11
Lake Luzerne E-11
Lake Placid C-11
Lake Pleasant D-10
Lakeville F-5
Port Jervis. I-10
Portville. I-4
Potsdam B-9
Poughkeepsie. H-11
Pulaski. D-7
Red Hook H-11
Rhinebeck H-11
Richfield Springs. F-9
Ripley G-1
Riverhead I-4
Rochester E-5
Rome. E-8
Rouses Point. A-12
Sackets Harbor C-7
Sag Harbor I-5
St. Regis Falls B-10
Salamanca. G-3
Salem. E-12
Saranac Lake. B-11
Saratoga Springs E-11
Saugerties. G-11
Schenectady F-11
Schoharie F-10
Schroon Lake C-11
Schuylerville E-12
Seneca Falls. F-6
Shelter Island I-4
Sherburne. F-8
Sidney G-9
Silver Creek. F-2
Skaneateles. F-7
Sodus Point. E-6
Southampton I-4
Southport H-6
Springville. G-3
Stamford. G-10
Star Lake. C-9
Stillwater. F-11
Stony Point I-11
Syracuse E-7
Tarrytown. J-11
Ticonderoga C-12
Troy. F-11
Tupper Lake C-10
Utica E-9
Varysburg F-4
Victor. E-5
Walden I-11
Walton G-9
Warsaw. F-4
Warwick I-10
Washingtonville I-11
Waterloo. F-6
Watertown C-8
Watkins Glen G-6
Waverly. H-7
Wayland F-5
Webster. E-5
Wellsville. G-4
West Seneca F-3
Westfield. G-2
White Plains J-11
Whitehall D-12
Whitney Point G-8
Williamson E-6
Willsboro. B-12
Wolcott. E-6
Woodbury. I-2
Woodstock H-11
Wurtsboro. I-10
Yonkers. J-11
Youngstown. E-2

Tourism Information N.Y. State Division of Tourism: (800) 225-5697 www.iloveny.com

Road Conditions & Construction 511, (888) 465-1169 www.511ny.org, www.dot.ny.gov Thruway: (800) 847-8929, www.thruway.ny.gov

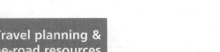

511

Travel planning & on-the-road resources

North Carolina state facts

Nickname: The Tar Heel State
Capital: Raleigh, C-8

Population: 10,439,388 (rank: 9th)
Largest city: Charlotte, 874,579, D-5

Land area: 48,607 sq. mi. (rank: 29th)
Highest point: Mount Mitchell, 6,684 ft., C-3

more map Pg. 76
Pg. 46
Pg. 101
Pg. 47
Pg. 32

NOTE: Maps are not always in alphabetical order.
See Page 1 for map location in this atlas.

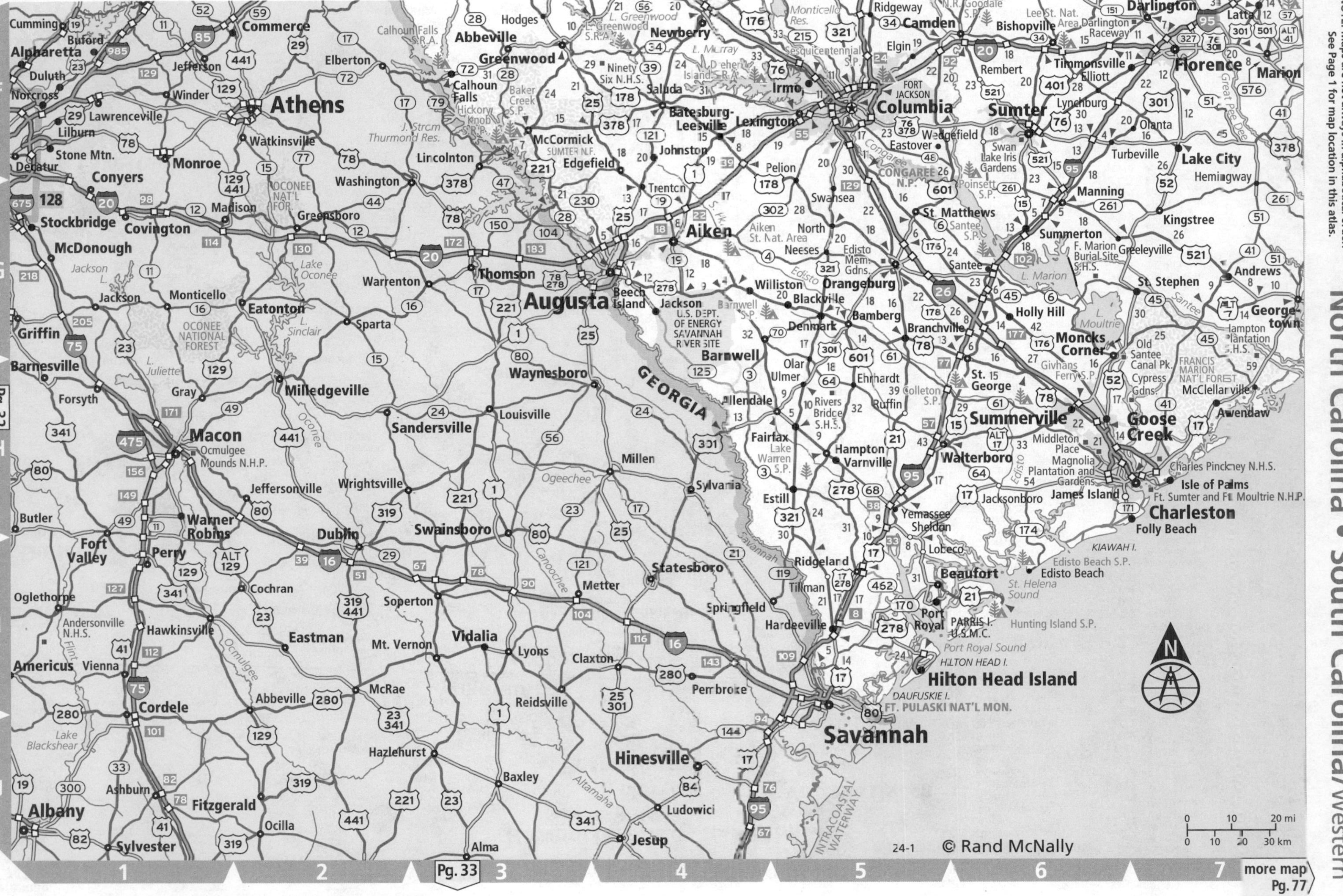

Travel planning & on-the-road resources

Tourism Information
Visit North Carolina:
(800) 847-4862
www.visitnc.com

Road Conditions & Construction
511, (877) 511-4662
drivenc.gov
www.ncdot.gov/travel-maps

South Carolina state facts

Nickname: The Palmetto State
Capital: Columbia, F-5
Population: 5,118,425 (rank: 23rd)
Largest city: Charleston, 150,227, H-7
Land area: 30,056 sq. mi. (rank: 40th)
Highest point: Sassafras Mtn., 3,560 ft., D-3

more map Pg. 74
Pg. 103

North Carolina

Cities and Towns

Aberdeen D-7
Ahoskie B-11
Albemarle D-6
Apex C-8
Asheboro C-7
Asheville C-3
Bayboro D-11
Beaufort E-11
Benson D-8
Black Mountain C-3
Bolivia F-9
Boone B-4
Brevard D-3
Bryson City D-2
Burgaw E-9
Burlington C-7
Burnsville C-3
Canton C-2
Carolina Beach F-9
Carthage D-7
Cary C-8
Chapel Hill C-8
Charlotte D-5
Cherokee D-2
Cherryville D-5
Clayton C-9
Clinton D-9
Columbia C-12
Columbus D-3
Concord D-6
Currituck B-12
Danbury B-6
Dobson B-5
Dunn D-8
Durham C-8
East Flat Rock D-3
Eden B-7
Edenton C-11
Elizabeth City B-12
Elizabethtown E-8
Elkin B-5
Enfield B-10
Erwin D-8
Fairview D-6
Farmville C-10
Fayetteville D-8
Forest City D-4
Franklin D-2
Fuquay-Varina C-8
Garner C-8
Gastonia D-5
Goldsboro D-9
Graham C-7
Granite Falls C-4
Greensboro C-7
Greenville C-10
Hamlet E-7
Harbinger B-12
Havelock E-11
Hayesville D-1
Henderson B-9
Hendersonville D-3
Hertford B-11
Hickory C-5
High Point C-6
Hillsborough C-8
Hope Mills D-8
Jackson B-10
Jacksonville E-10
Jefferson B-4
Wallace E-9
Warrenton B-9
Warsaw D-9
Washington C-11
Waynesville D-2
Whiteville F-8
Wilkesboro B-5
Williamston C-11
Wilmington F-9
Wilson C-9
Windsor C-11
Winston-Salem C-6
Winterville C-10
Winton B-11
Wrightsville Beach F-10
Yadkinville B-6
Yanceyville B-7
Zebulon C-9

South Carolina

Cities and Towns

Abbeville F-3
Aiken G-4
Allendale H-5
Anderson E-3
Andrews G-7
Awendaw H-7
Bamberg G-5
Barnwell G-4
Batesburg-Leesville F-4
Beaufort I-5
Beech Island G-4
Belton E-3
Bennettsville E-7
Bishopville F-6
Blackville G-5
Branchville G-5
Calhoun Falls F-3
Camden F-6
Charleston H-7
Cheraw E-7
Chesnee D-4
Chester E-5
Chesterfield E-6
Clemson E-2
Clinton E-4
Columbia F-5
Conway F-8
Cowpens D-4
Darlington F-7
Denmark G-5
Dillon E-7
Easley E-3
Eastover F-5
Edgefield F-4
Elgin F-5
Enoree E-4
Estill H-5
Fairfax H-5
Florence F-7
Folly Beach H-7
Fort Lawn E-5
Fountain Inn E-3
Gaffney D-4
Garden City Beach G-8
Georgetown G-7
Goose Creek H-6
Great Falls E-5
Greenville E-3
Greenwood F-3
Greer D-3
Hampton H-5
Hardeeville I-5

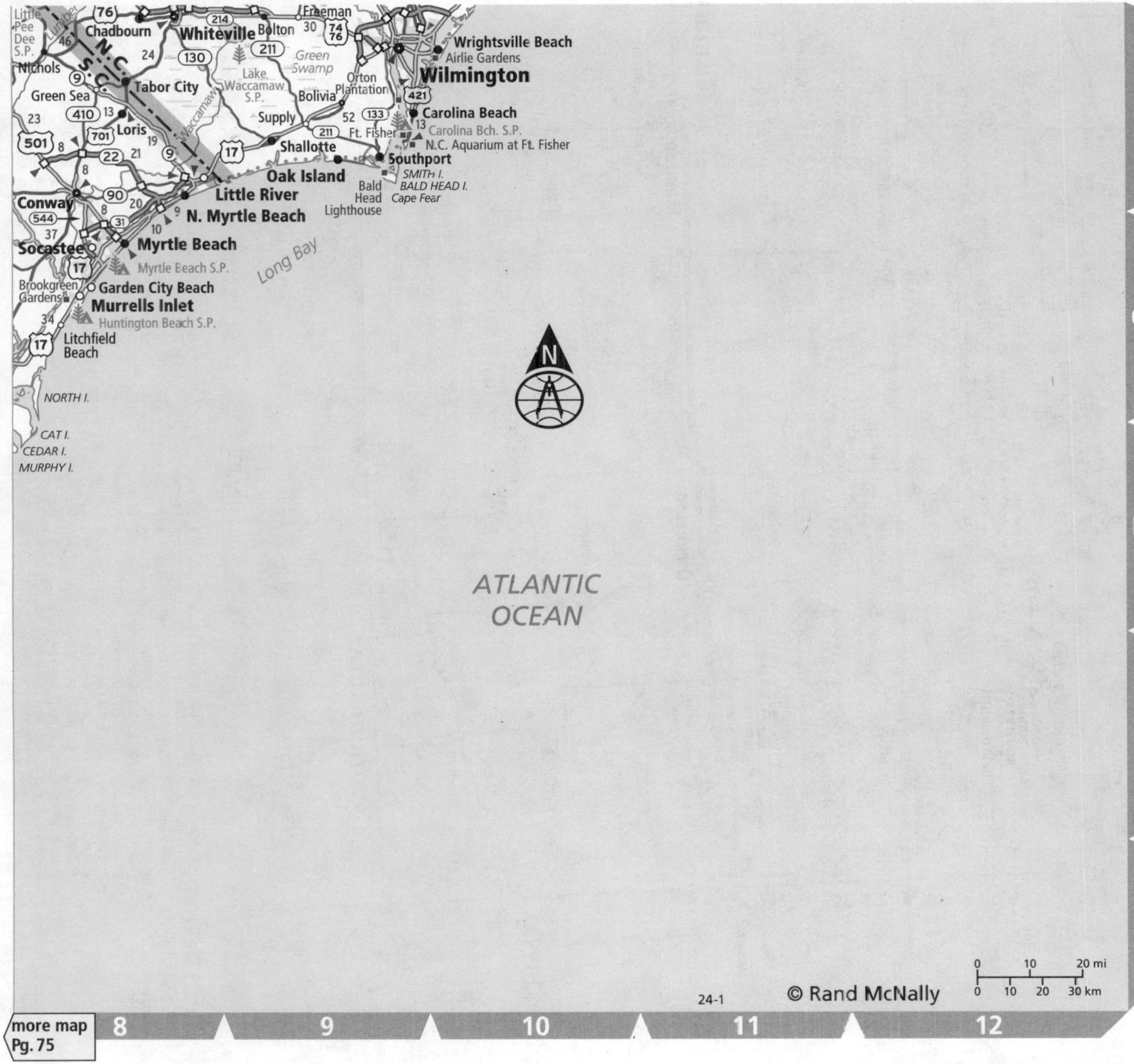

more map Pg. 75

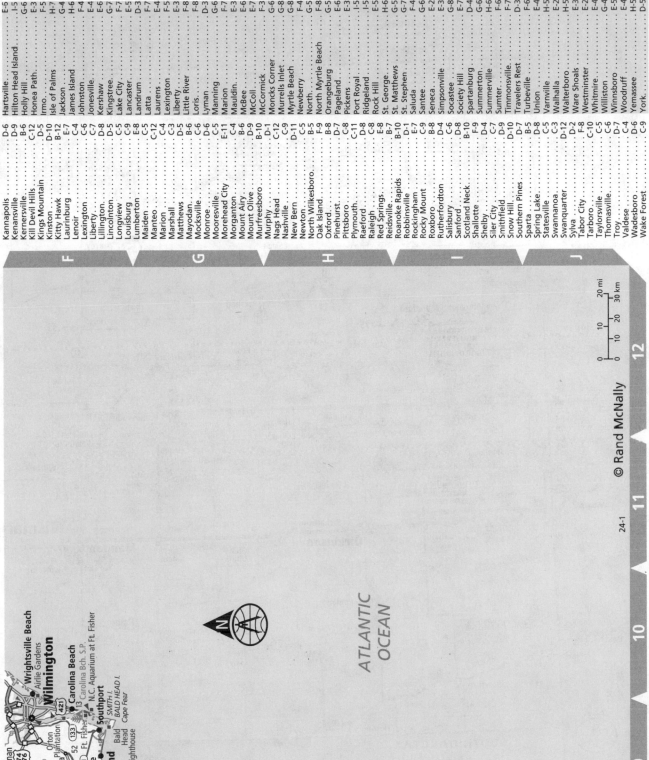

ATLANTIC OCEAN

24-1

© Rand McNally

0 10 20 mi
0 10 20 30 km

North Carolina	
Kannapolis	D-6
Kenansville	D-9
Kernersville	B-6
Kill Devil Hills	C-12
Kings Mountain	D-5
Kinston	D-10
Kitty Hawk	B-12
Laurinburg	E-7
Lenoir	C-4
Lexington	C-6
Liberty	C-7
Lillington	D-8
Lincolnton	D-5
Longview	C-5
Louisburg	C-9
Lumberton	E-8
Maiden	C-5
Manteo	C-12
Marion	C-4
Marshall	C-3
Matthews	D-5
Mayodan	B-6
Mocksville	C-6
Monroe	D-6
Mooresville	C-5
Morehead City	E-11
Morganton	C-4
Mount Airy	B-6
Mount Olive	D-9
Murfreesboro	B-10
Murphy	D-1
Nags Head	C-12
Nashville	C-9
New Bern	D-11
Newton	C-5
North Wilkesboro	B-5
Oak Island	F-9
Oxford	B-8
Pinehurst	D-7
Pittsboro	C-8
Plymouth	C-11
Raeford	D-8
Raleigh	C-8
Red Springs	E-8
Reidsville	B-7
Roanoke Rapids	B-10
Robbinsville	D-1
Rockingham	E-7
Rocky Mount	C-9
Roxboro	B-8
Rutherfordton	D-4
Salisbury	C-6
Sanford	D-8
Scotland Neck	B-10
Shallotte	F-9
Shelby	D-4
Siler City	C-7
Smithfield	D-9
Snow Hill	D-10
Southern Pines	D-7
Sparta	B-5
Spring Lake	D-8
Statesville	C-5
Swannanoa	C-3
Swanquarter	D-12
Sylva	D-2
Tabor City	F-8
Tarboro	C-10
Taylorsville	C-5
Thomasville	C-6
Troy	D-7
Valdese	C-4
Wadesboro	D-6
Wake Forest	C-9

South Carolina	
Hartsville	E-6
Hilton Head Island	I-5
Holly Hill	G-6
Honea Path	E-3
Irmo	F-5
Isle of Palms	H-7
Jackson	G-4
James Island	H-6
Johnston	F-4
Jonesville	E-4
Kershaw	E-6
Kingstree	G-7
Lake City	F-7
Lancaster	E-5
Landrum	D-3
Latta	F-7
Laurens	E-4
Lexington	F-5
Liberty	E-3
Little River	F-8
Loris	F-8
Lyman	D-3
Manning	G-6
Marion	F-7
Mauldin	E-3
McBee	E-6
McColl	E-7
McCormick	F-3
Moncks Corner	G-6
Murrells Inlet	G-8
Myrtle Beach	G-8
Newberry	F-4
North	G-5
North Myrtle Beach	F-8
Orangeburg	G-5
Pageland	E-6
Pickens	E-3
Port Royal	I-5
Ridgeland	I-5
Rock Hill	E-5
St. George	H-6
St. Matthews	G-5
St. Stephen	G-7
Saluda	F-4
Santee	G-6
Seneca	E-2
Simpsonville	E-3
Socastee	G-8
Society Hill	E-7
Spartanburg	D-4
Summerton	G-6
Summerville	H-6
Sumter	F-6
Timmonsville	F-7
Travelers Rest	D-3
Turbeville	F-6
Union	E-4
Varnville	H-5
Walhalla	E-2
Walterboro	H-5
Ware Shoals	E-3
Westminster	E-2
Whitmire	E-4
Williston	G-4
Winnsboro	E-5
Woodruff	E-4
Yemassee	H-5
York	D-5

North Dakota

North Dakota state facts

Nickname: The Peace Garden State
Capital: Bismarck, E-5
Population: 779,094 (rank: 47th)
Largest city: Fargo, 125,990, D-10
Land area: 68,977 sq. mi. (rank: 17th)
Highest point: White Butte, 3,506 ft., E-2

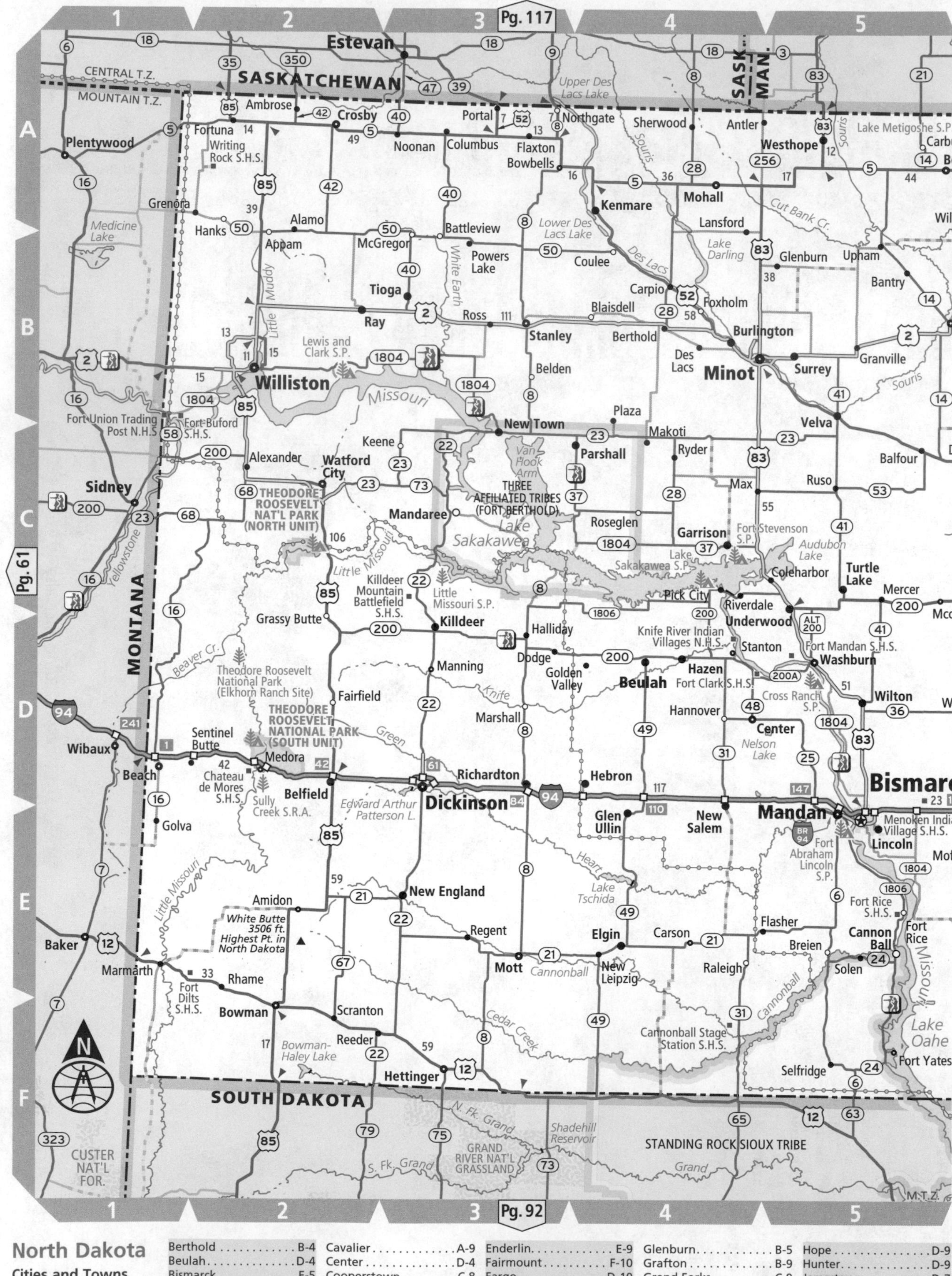

North Dakota

Cities and Towns

Abercrombie E-10
Amidon E-2
Anamoose C-6
Aneta C-8
Arthur D-9
Ashley F-7
Beach D-1
Belcourt A-6
Belfield D-2
Berthold B-4
Beulah D-4
Bismarck E-5
Bottineau A-5
Bowbells A-3
Bowman F-2
Burlington B-4
Cando B-7
Cannon Ball E-5
Carrington C-7
Carson E-4
Casselton D-9
Cavalier A-9
Center D-4
Cooperstown C-8
Crosby A-2
Devils Lake B-7
Dickinson D-3
Drake C-6
Drayton B-9
Dunseith A-6
Edgeley E-7
Elgin E-4
Ellendale F-8
Enderlin E-9
Fairmount F-10
Fargo D-10
Fessenden C-6
Finley C-8
Flasher E-5
Forman F-9
Fort Totten C-7
Fort Yates F-5
Gackle E-7
Garrison C-4
Glen Ullin E-4
Glenburn B-5
Grafton B-9
Grand Forks C-9
Granville B-5
Gwinner F-9
Hankinson F-10
Harvey C-6
Hatton C-9
Hazen D-4
Hebron D-4
Hettinger F-3
Hillsboro C-9
Hope D-9
Hunter D-9
Jamestown D-7
Kenmare A-4
Killdeer D-3
Kindred E-9
Kulm E-7
Lakota B-8
Lamoure E-8
Langdon A-8
Larimore C-9
Leeds B-7

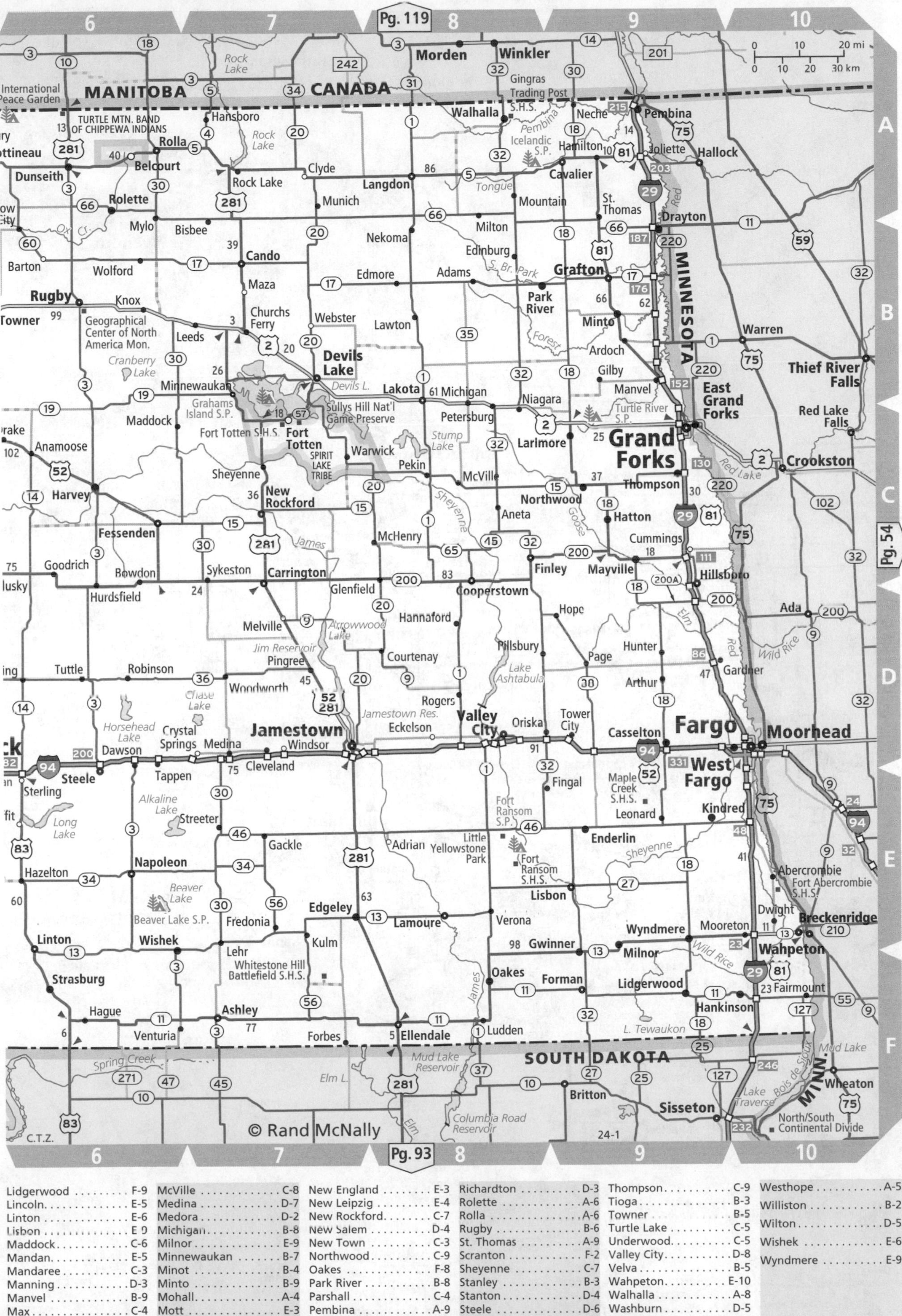

Road Conditions & Construction
511, (866) 696-3511
travel.dot.nd.gov
www.dot.nd.gov/travel

Tourism Information
North Dakota Tourism Division:
(800) 435-5663
www.ndtourism.com

Travel planning & on-the-road resources

Lidgerwood F-9
Lincoln. E-5
Linton E-6
Lisbon E-9
Maddock. C-6
Mandan. E-5
Mandaree C-3
Manning D-3
Manvel B-9
Max C-4
Mayville. C-9
Mcclusky C-5
McVille C-8
Medina D-7
Medora D-2
Michigan. B-8
Milnor E-9
Minnewaukan B-7
Minot B-4
Minto B-9
Mohall. A-4
Mott E-3
Napoleon E-6
Neche A-9
New England E-3
New Leipzig E-4
New Rockford. C-7
New Salem D-4
New Town C-3
Northwood C-9
Oakes F-8
Park River B-8
Parshall C-4
Pembina A-9
Powers Lake B-3
Ray. B-2
Richardton D-3
Rolette A-6
Rolla A-6
Rugby B-6
St. Thomas A-9
Scranton F-2
Sheyenne C-7
Stanley B-3
Stanton D-4
Steele D-6
Strasburg. F-6
Surrey B-5
Thompson. C-9
Tioga B-3
Towner B-5
Turtle Lake C-5
Underwood. C-5
Valley City. D-8
Velva B-5
Wahpeton. E-10
Walhalla A-8
Washburn D-5
Watford City. C-2
West Fargo D-10
Westhope A-5
Williston B-2
Wilton. D-5
Wishek E-6
Wyndmere E-9

Ohio state facts

Nickname: The Buckeye State
Capital: Columbus, G-5

Population: 11,799,448 (rank: 7th)
Largest city: Columbus, 905,748, G-5

Land area: 40,848 sq. mi. (rank: 35th)
Highest point: Campbell Hill, 1,550 ft., F-3

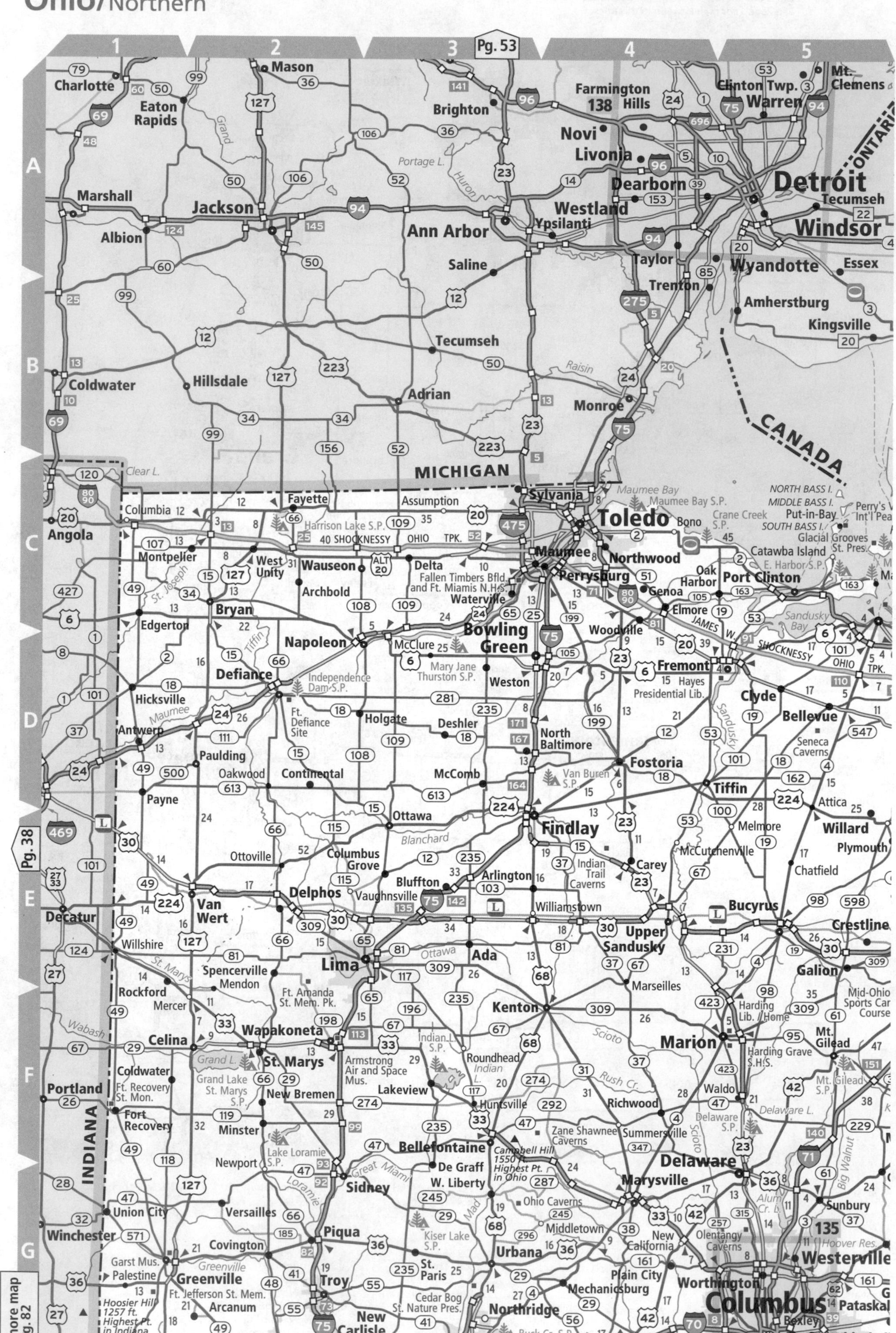

NOTE: Maps are not always in alphabetical order.
See Page 1 for map location in this atlas.

Road Conditions & Construction
511, (855) 511-6446; www.ohgo.com, transportation.ohio.gov
Ohio Turnpike: (440) 234-2081; www.ohioturnpike.org

Tourism Information
Tourism Ohio: (800) 282-5393
ohio.org

Travel planning & on-the-road resources

Ohio state facts

Nickname: The Buckeye State
Capital: Columbus, G-5
Population: 11,799,448 (rank: 7th)
Largest city: Columbus, 905,748, G-5
Land area: 40,848 sq. mi. (rank: 35th)
Highest point: Campbell Hill, 1,550 ft., F-3

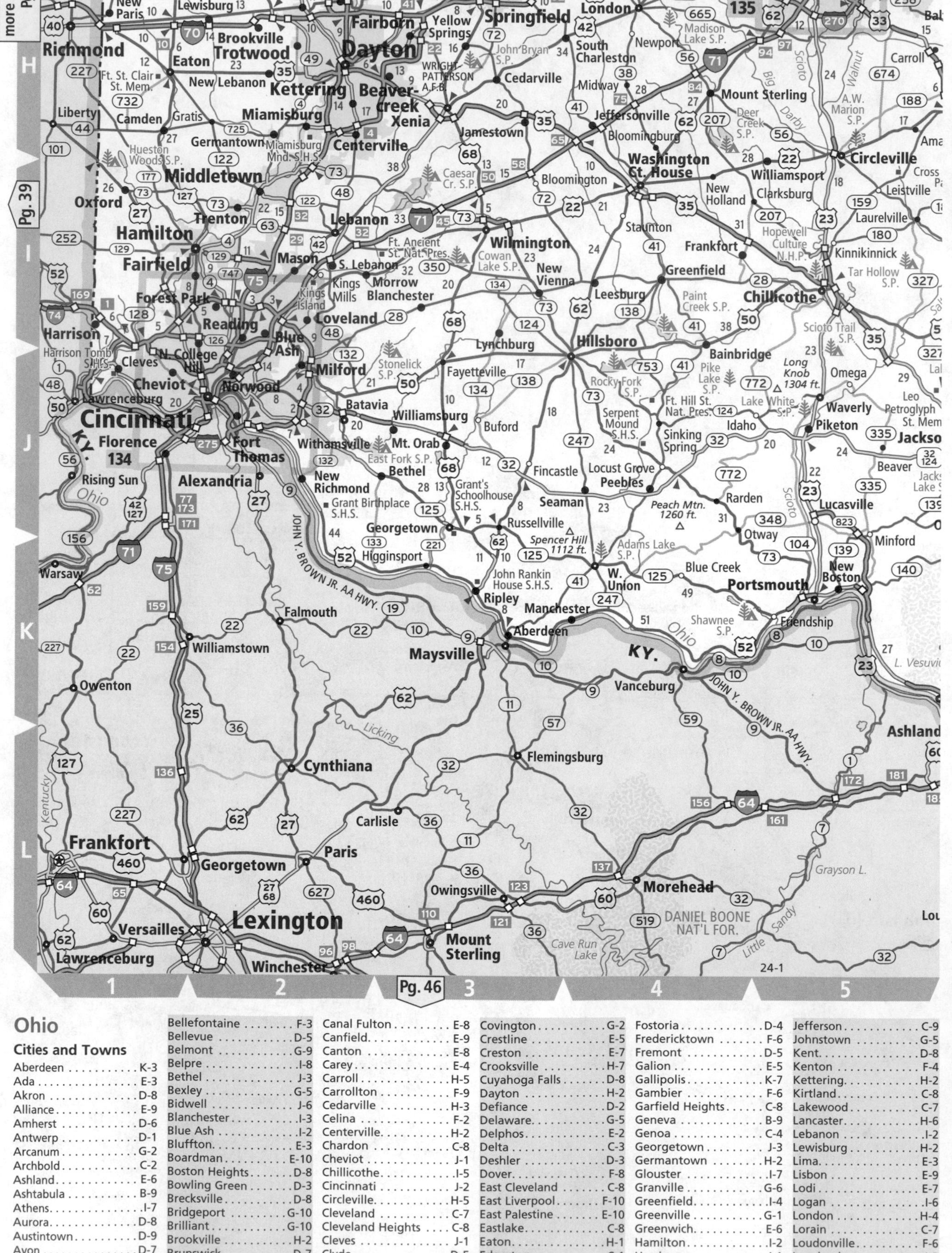

Ohio

Cities and Towns

Aberdeen K-3
Ada E-3
Akron D-8
Alliance E-9
Amherst D-6
Antwerp D-1
Arcanum G-2
Archbold C-2
Ashland E-6
Ashtabula B-9
Athens I-7
Aurora D-8
Austintown D-9
Avon D-7
Baltimore H-6
Barberton E-8
Barnesville G-9
Batavia J-2
Beavercreek H-3
Bedford Heights D-8
Bellaire G-9
Bellefontaine F-3
Bellevue D-5
Belmont G-9
Belpre I-8
Bethel J-3
Bexley G-5
Bidwell J-6
Blanchester I-3
Blue Ash I-2
Bluffton E-3
Boardman E-10
Boston Heights D-8
Bowling Green D-3
Brecksville D-8
Bridgeport G-10
Brilliant G-10
Brookville H-2
Brunswick D-7
Bryan C-2
Bucyrus E-5
Byesville G-8
Cadiz G-9
Caldwell H-8
Cambridge G-8
Camden H-1
Canal Fulton E-8
Canfield E-9
Canton E-8
Carey E-4
Carroll H-5
Carrollton F-9
Cedarville H-3
Celina F-2
Centerville H-2
Chardon C-8
Cheviot J-1
Chillicothe I-5
Cincinnati J-2
Circleville H-5
Cleveland C-7
Cleveland Heights C-8
Cleves J-1
Clyde D-5
Coldwater F-1
Columbiana E-10
Columbus G-5
Columbus Grove E-3
Conneaut B-10
Cortland D-9
Coshocton G-7
Covington G-2
Crestline E-5
Creston E-7
Crooksville H-7
Cuyahoga Falls D-8
Dayton H-2
Defiance D-2
Delaware G-5
Delphos E-2
Delta C-3
Deshler D-3
Dover F-8
East Cleveland C-8
East Liverpool F-10
East Palestine E-10
Eastlake C-8
Eaton H-1
Edgerton C-1
Elyria D-7
Englewood H-2
Euclid C-8
Fairborn H-3
Fairfield I-2
Findlay E-3
Forest Park I-2
Fostoria D-4
Fredericktown F-6
Fremont D-5
Galion E-5
Gallipolis K-7
Gambier F-6
Garfield Heights C-8
Geneva B-9
Genoa C-4
Georgetown J-3
Germantown H-2
Glouster I-7
Granville G-6
Greenfield I-4
Greenville G-1
Greenwich E-6
Hamilton I-2
Harrison I-1
Hicksville D-1
Hillsboro J-4
Hudson D-8
Huron D-6
Ironton K-5
Jackson J-6
Jamestown H-3
Jefferson C-9
Johnstown G-5
Kent D-8
Kenton F-4
Kettering H-2
Kirtland C-8
Lakewood C-7
Lancaster H-6
Lebanon I-2
Lewisburg H-2
Lima E-3
Lisbon E-9
Lodi E-7
Logan I-6
London H-4
Lorain C-7
Loudonville F-6
Loveland I-2
Lucasville J-5
Manchester K-4
Mansfield E-6
Mantua D-8
Marietta I-8
Marion F-5
Martins Ferry G-10

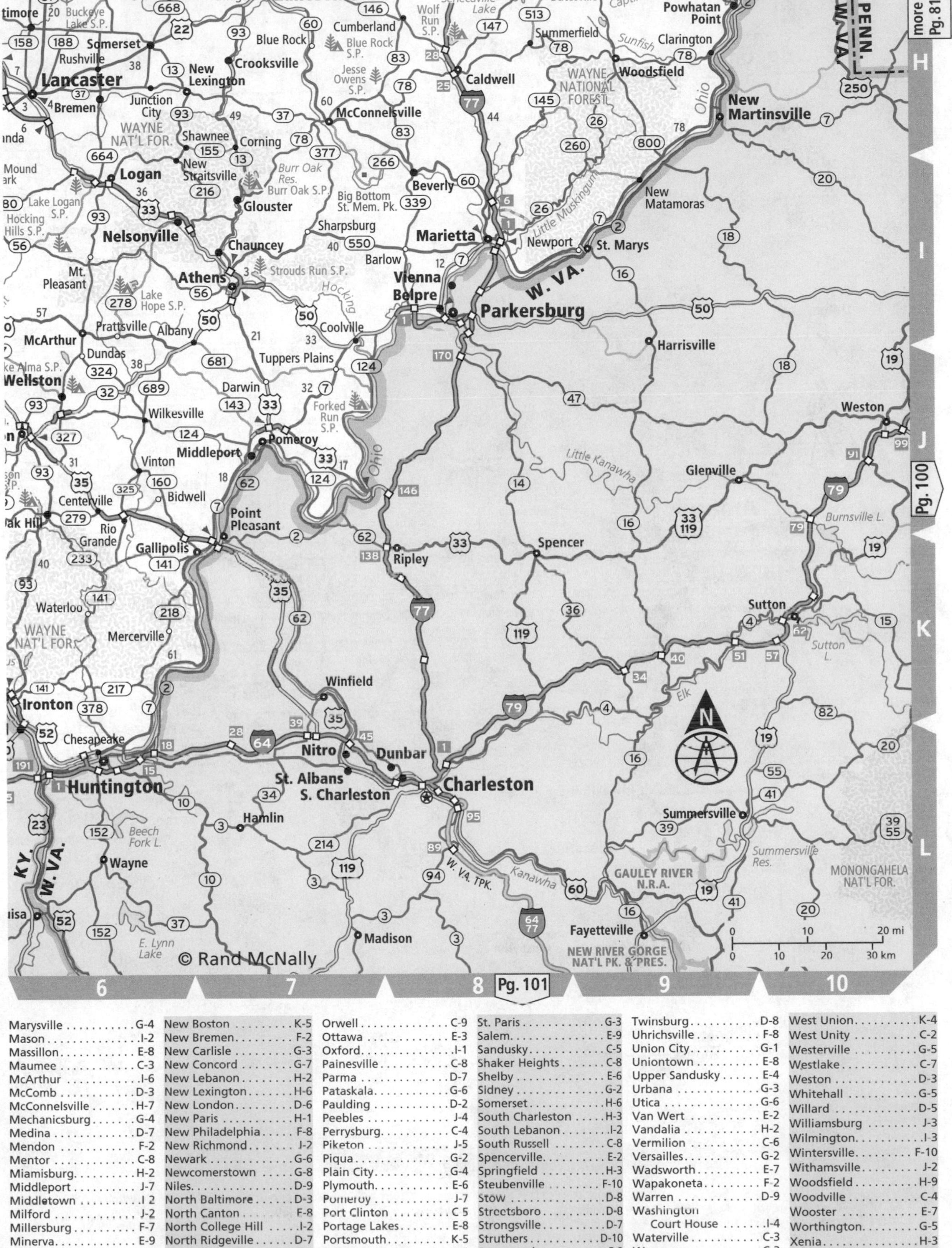

Road Conditions & Construction
511, (855) 511-6446; www.ohgo.com, transportation.ohio.gov
Ohio Turnpike:
(440) 234-2081; www.ohioturnpike.org

Tourism Information
Tourism Ohio:
(800) 282-5393
ohio.org

Travel planning & on-the-road resources

Marysville G-4
Mason I-2
Massillon E-8
Maumee C-3
McArthur I-6
McComb D-3
McConnelsville H-7
Mechanicsburg G-4
Medina D-7
Mendon F-2
Mentor C-8
Miamisburg H-2
Middleport J-7
Middletown I-2
Milford J-2
Millersburg F-7
Minerva E-9
Minster F-2
Montpelier C-2
Mount Gilead F-5
Mount Orab J-3
Mount Sterling H-4
Mount Vernon F-6
Napoleon D-3
Nelsonville I-6
New Boston K-5
New Bremen F-2
New Carlisle G-3
New Concord G-7
New Lebanon H-2
New Lexington H-6
New London D-6
New Paris H-1
New Philadelphia F-8
New Richmond J-2
Newark G-6
Newcomerstown G-8
Niles D-9
North Baltimore D-3
North Canton F-8
North College Hill I-2
North Ridgeville D-7
Northridge G-3
Northwood C-4
Norwalk D-6
Norwood J-2
Oak Harbor C-5
Oak Hill J-6
Oberlin D-6
Orrville E-7
Orwell C-9
Ottawa E-3
Oxford I-1
Painesville C-8
Parma D-7
Pataskala G-6
Paulding D-2
Peebles J-4
Perrysburg C-4
Piketon J-5
Piqua G-2
Plain City G-4
Plymouth E-6
Pomeroy J-7
Port Clinton C-5
Portage Lakes E-8
Portsmouth K-5
Powhatan Point H-9
Ravenna D-8
Reading I-2
Richwood F-4
Ripley K-3
Rittman E-7
St. Clairsville G-9
St. Marys F-2
St. Paris G-3
Salem E-9
Sandusky C-5
Shaker Heights C-8
Shelby E-6
Sidney G-2
Somerset H-6
South Charleston H-3
South Lebanon I-2
South Russell C-8
Spencerville E-2
Springfield H-3
Steubenville F-10
Stow D-8
Streetsboro D-8
Strongsville D-7
Struthers D-10
Sugarcreek F-8
Sunbury G-5
Sylvania C-3
Tiffin D-4
Toledo C-4
Trenton I-2
Trotwood H-2
Troy G-2
Twinsburg D-8
Uhrichsville F-8
Union City G-1
Uniontown E-8
Upper Sandusky E-4
Urbana G-3
Utica G-6
Van Wert E-2
Vandalia H-2
Vermilion C-6
Versailles G-2
Wadsworth E-7
Wapakoneta F-2
Warren D-9
Washington Court House I-4
Waterville C-3
Wauseon C-3
Waverly J-5
Wellington D-6
Wellston J-6
Wellsville F-10
West Lafayette G-7
West Liberty G-3
West Salem E-7
West Union K-4
West Unity C-2
Westerville G-5
Westlake C-7
Weston D-3
Whitehall G-5
Willard D-5
Williamsburg J-3
Wilmington I-3
Wintersville F-10
Withamsville J-2
Woodsfield H-9
Woodville C-4
Wooster E-7
Worthington G-5
Xenia H-3
Yellow Springs H-3
Youngstown D-10
Zanesville H-7

Oklahoma state facts

Nickname: The Sooner State
Capital: Oklahoma City, C-7

Population: 3,959,353 (rank: 28th)
Largest city: Oklahoma City, 681,054, C-7

Land area: 68,578 sq. mi. (rank: 19th)
Highest point: Black Mesa, 4,973 ft., A-1

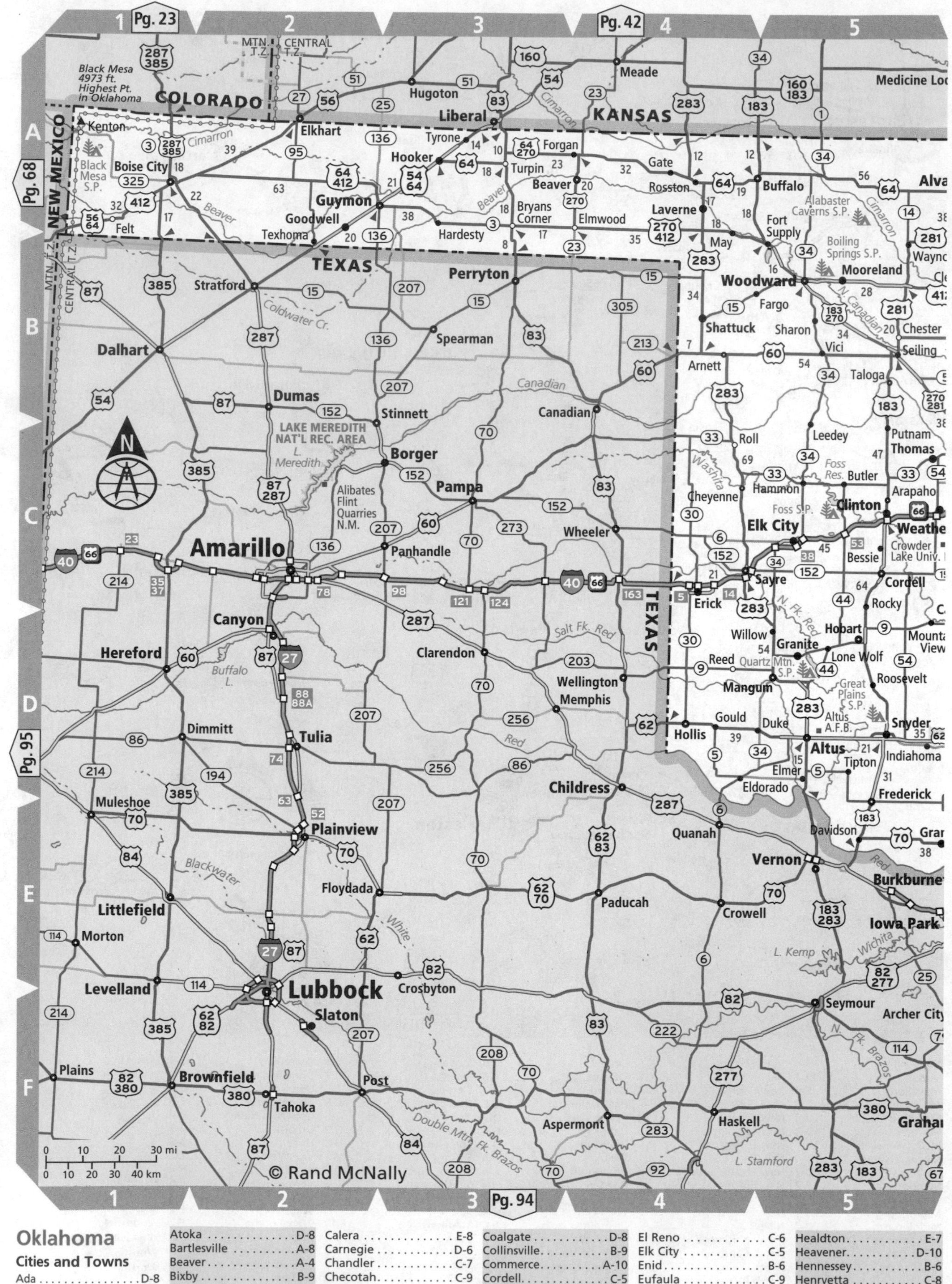

Oklahoma

Cities and Towns

Ada D-8
Altus D-5
Alva A-6
Anadarko D-6
Antlers E-9
Apache D-6
Arapaho C-5
Ardmore E-7
Arnett B-4
Atoka D-8
Bartlesville A-8
Beaver A-4
Bixby B-9
Blackwell A-7
Blanchard C-7
Boise City A-1
Bristow C-8
Broken Arrow B-9
Broken Bow E-10
Buffalo A-4
Cache D-6
Calera E-8
Carnegie D-6
Chandler C-7
Checotah C-9
Chelsea B-9
Cherokee A-6
Cheyenne C-4
Chickasha D-6
Chouteau B-9
Claremore B-9
Cleveland B-8
Clinton C-5
Coalgate D-8
Collinsville B-9
Commerce A-10
Cordell C-5
Coweta B-9
Cushing B-8
Davis D-7
Dewey A-8
Drumright B-8
Duncan D-6
Durant E-8
Edmond C-7
El Reno C-6
Elk City C-5
Enid B-6
Eufaula C-9
Fairview B-6
Frederick D-5
Granite D-5
Grove A-10
Guthrie B-7
Guymon A-2
Harrah C-7
Haskell C-9
Healdton E-7
Heavener D-10
Hennessey B-6
Henryetta C-8
Hinton C-6
Hobart D-5
Holdenville D-8
Hollis D-4
Hominy B-8
Hooker A-3
Hugo E-9
Idabel E-10

NOTE: Maps are not always in alphabetical order.
See Page 1 for map location in this atlas.

Road Conditions & Construction
(844) 465-4997
okroads.org
oklahoma.gov/odot

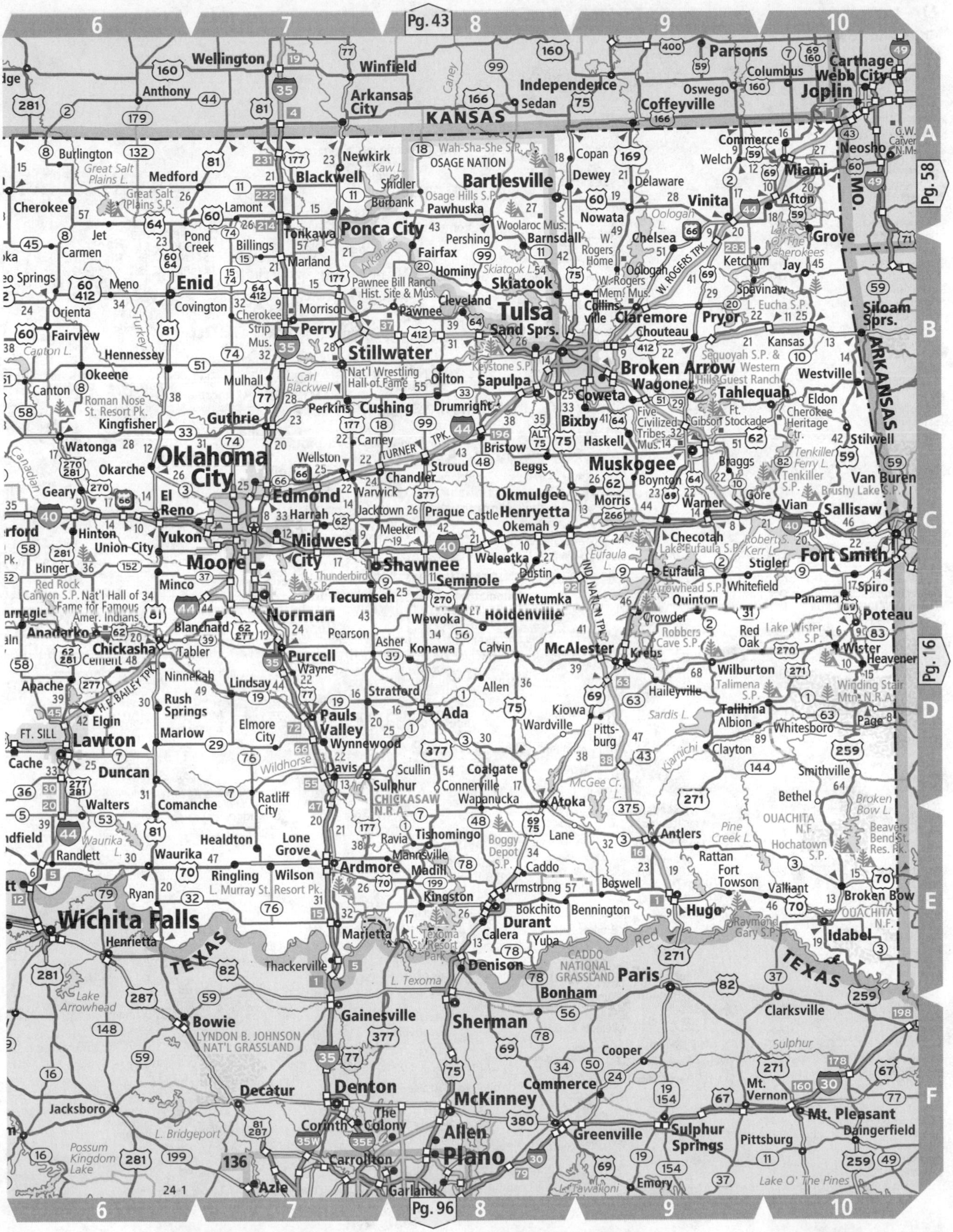

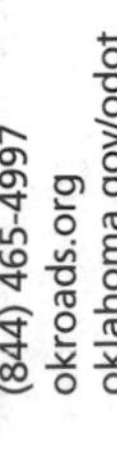

Tourism Information
Oklahoma Tourism & Recreation Dept.:
(800) 652-6552, (405) 522-950C
www.travelok.com

Travel planning & on-the-road resources

Jay ... B-10
Kingfisher ... C-6
Krebs ... D-9
Lawton ... D-6
Lindsay ... D-7
Lone Grove ... E-7
Madill ... E-8
Mangum ... D-5
Marietta ... E-7
Marlow ... D-6
McAlester ... D-9
Medford ... A-7
Miami ... A-10
Midwest City ... C-7
Minco ... C-6
Moore ... C-7
Muskogee ... C-9
Newkirk ... A-7
Norman ... C-7
Nowata ... A-9
Okemah ... C-8
Oklahoma City ... C-7
Okmulgee ... C-8
Pauls Valley ... D-7
Pawhuska ... A-8
Pawnee ... B-8
Perkins ... B-7
Perry ... B-7
Picher ... A-10
Ponca City ... A-8
Poteau ... D-10
Prague ... C-8
Pryor ... B-9
Purcell ... D-7
Sallisaw ... C-10
Sand Springs ... B-8
Sapulpa ... B-8
Sayre ... C-4
Seminole ... C-8
Shawnee ... C-7
Skiatook ... B-8
Spiro ... C-10
Stigler ... C-9
Stillwater ... B-7
Stilwell ... C-10
Stroud ... C-8
Sulphur ... D-7
Tahlequah ... B-10
Taloga ... B-5
Tecumseh ... C-7
Tishomingo ... E-8
Tonkawa ... A-7
Tulsa ... B-8
Vinita ... A-9
Wagoner ... B-9
Walters ... E-6
Watonga ... C-6
Waurika ... E-6
Weatherford ... C-5
Westville ... B-10
Wewoka ... C-8
Wilburton ... D-9
Wilson ... E-7
Woodward ... B-5
Wynnewood ... D-7
Yukon ... C-7

Oregon state facts

Nickname: The Beaver State
Capital: Salem, C-2
Population: 4,237,256 (rank: 27th)
Largest city: Portland, 652,503, B-3
Land area: 95,963 sq. mi. (rank: 10th)
Highest point: Mount Hood, 11,239 ft., B-4

Oregon

Cities and Towns

Albany . . . C-2
Amity . . . C-2
Ashland . . . G-3
Astoria . . . A-2
Athena . . . B-7
Baker City . . . C-8
Bandon . . . E-1
Beaverton . . . B-3
Bend . . . D-4
Boardman . . . B-6
Brookings . . . G-1
Bunker Hill . . . E-1
Burns . . . E-7
Cannon Beach . . . A-2
Canyon City . . . D-7
Canyonville . . . F-2
Cave Junction . . . G-2
Central Point . . . G-2
Clatskanie . . . A-2
Condon . . . B-5
Coos Bay . . . E-1
Coquille . . . E-1
Corvallis . . . C-2
Cottage Grove . . . E-2
Dallas . . . C-2
Eagle Point . . . F-3
Elgin . . . B-8
Enterprise . . . B-8
Estacada . . . B-3
Eugene . . . D-2
Florence . . . D-1
Fossil . . . C-5
Gladstone . . . B-3
Glide . . . E-2
Gold Beach . . . F-1
Grants Pass . . . F-2
Heppner . . . B-6
Hermiston . . . B-6
Hillsboro . . . B-3
Hood River . . . B-4
Jacksonville . . . G-2
John Day . . . D-7
Junction City . . . D-2
Klamath Falls . . . G-4
La Grande . . . B-8
La Pine . . . E-4
Lakeside . . . E-1
Lakeview . . . G-5
Lebanon . . . C-3
Lincoln City . . . C-1
Madras . . . C-4
McMinnville . . . B-2
Medford . . . G-3
Mill City . . . C-3
Milton-Freewater . . . A-7
Molalla . . . C-3
Monmouth . . . C-2
Moro . . . B-5
Myrtle Creek . . . F-2
Myrtle Point . . . F-1
Newberg . . . B-3
Newport . . . C-1
North Bend . . . E-1
Nyssa . . . D-9
Oakridge . . . E-3
Ontario . . . D-9
Oregon City . . . B-3
Pendleton . . . B-7
Philomath . . . C-2
Phoenix . . . G-3
Pilot Rock . . . B-7
Portland . . . B-3
Prineville . . . D-5
Rainier . . . A-3
Redmond . . . D-4
Reedsport . . . E-1
Rockaway Beach . . . B-2
Roseburg . . . E-2
St. Helens . . . B-3
Salem . . . C-2
Sandy . . . B-3
Scappoose . . . B-3
Seaside . . . A-2
Silverton . . . C-3
Springfield . . . D-2
Stayton . . . C-3
Sublimity . . . C-3
Sutherlin . . . E-2
Sweet Home . . . D-3
The Dalles . . . B-4
Tigard . . . B-3
Tillamook . . . B-2
Toledo . . . C-2
Umatilla . . . A-6
Union . . . B-8
Vale . . . D-9
Veneta . . . D-2
Vernonia . . . A-2
Waldport . . . D-1
Warm Springs . . . C-4
Warrenton . . . A-2
Winston . . . E-2
Woodburn . . . C-3

Pg. 104

Pg. 18

NOTE: Maps are not always in alphabetical order.
See Page 1 for map location in this atlas.

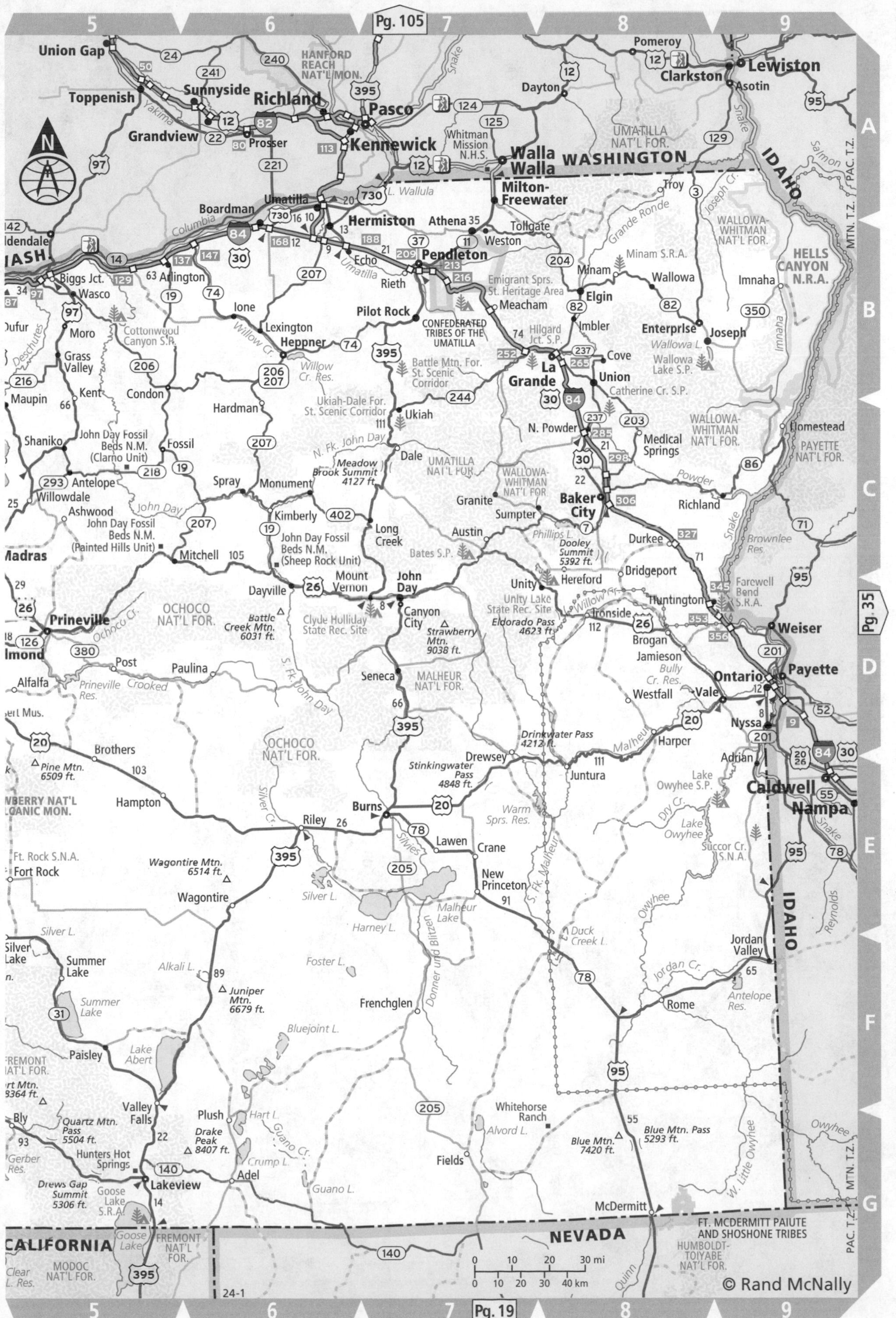

Road Conditions & Construction
511, (800) 977-6368
(503) 588-2941, (888) 275-6368
www.tripcheck.com, www.oregon.gov/odot

Tourism Information
Travel Oregon:
(800) 547-7842
traveloregon.com

Travel planning & on-the-road resources

Pennsylvania state facts

Nickname: The Keystone State
Capital: Harrisburg, G-9
Population: 13,002,700 (rank: 5th)
Largest city: Philadelphia, 1,603,797, H-13
Land area: 44,730 sq. mi. (rank: 32nd)
Highest point: Mount Davis, 3,213 ft., I-4

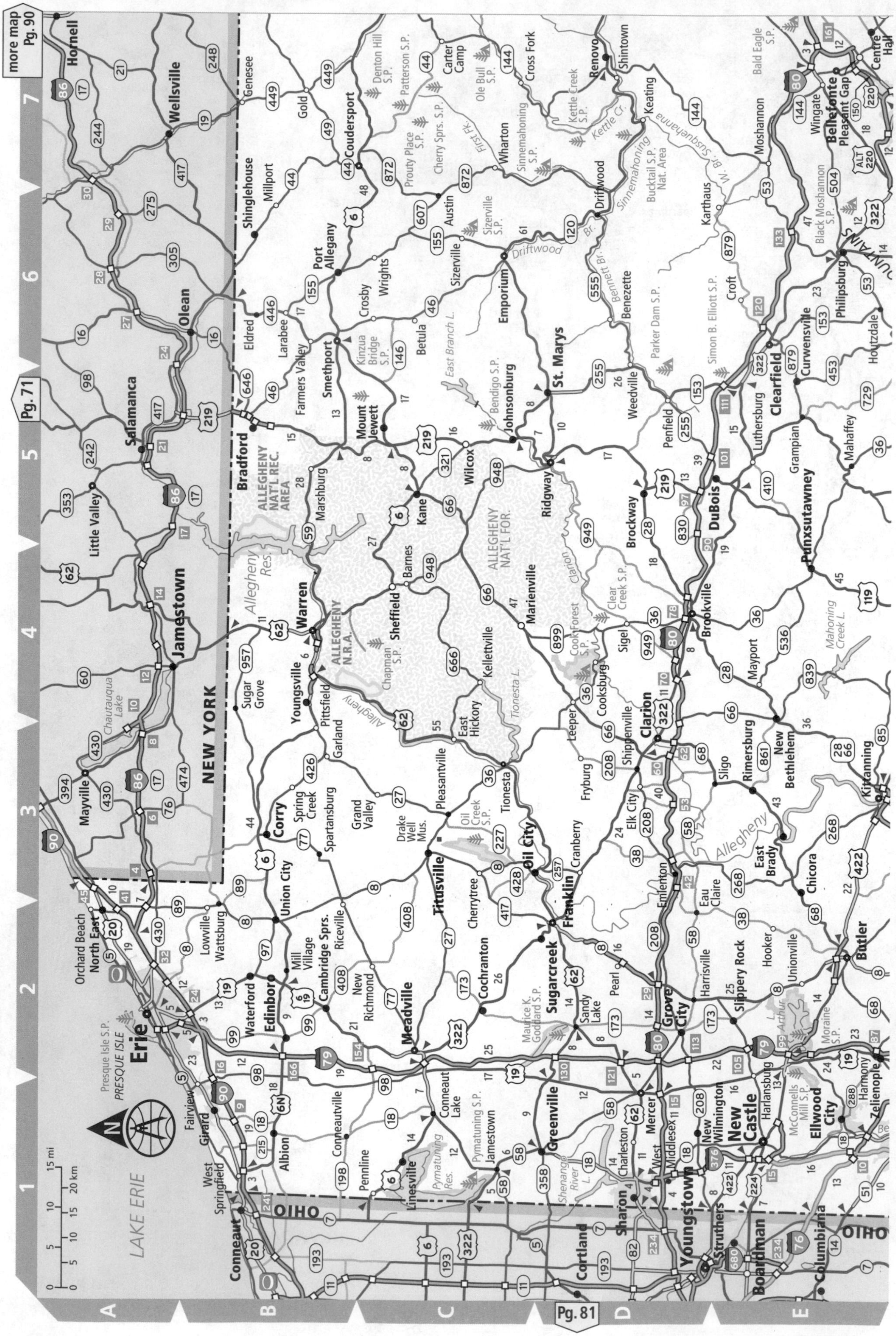

more map Pg. 90
Pg. 71
Pg. 81

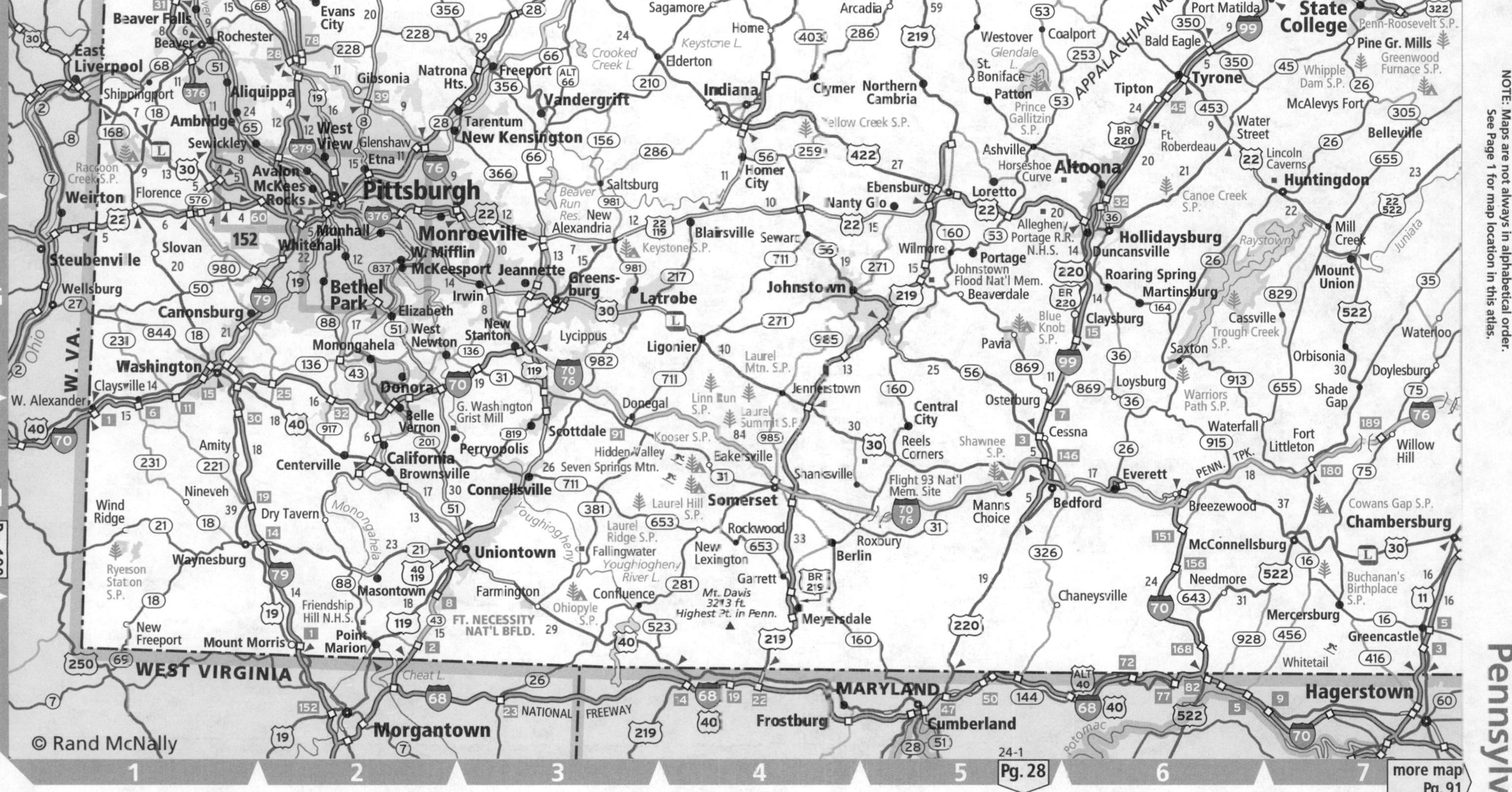

Pennsylvania

Cities and Towns

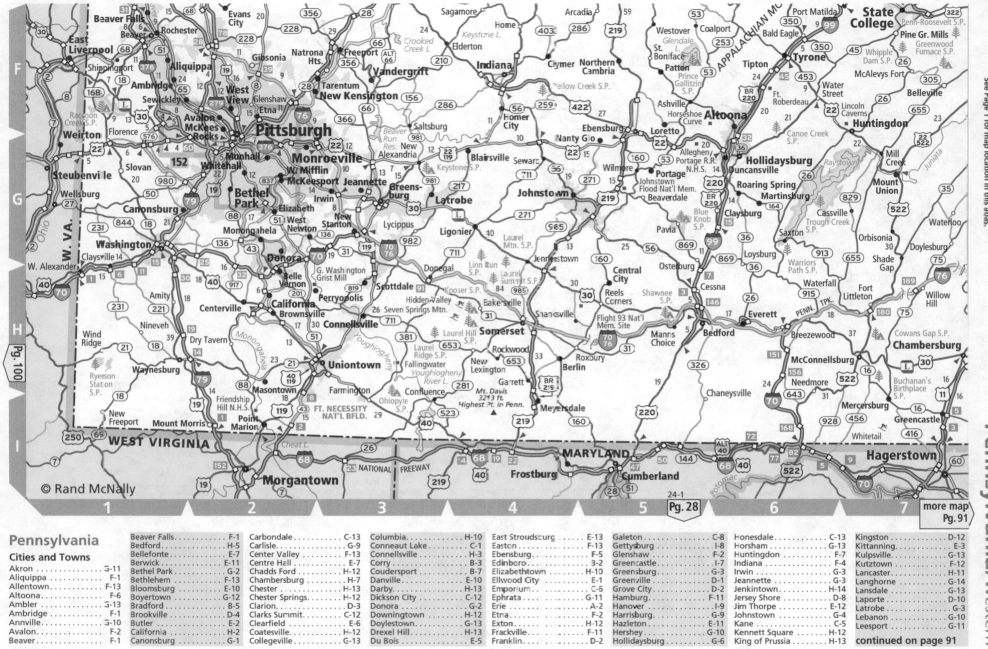

Akron G-11
Aliquippa F-1
Allentown F-13
Altoona F-6
Ambler G-13
Ambridge F-1
Annville G-10
Avalon F-2
Beaver F-1
Beaver Falls F-1
Bedford H-5
Bellefonte E-7
Berwick E-11
Bethel Park G-2
Bethlehem F-13
Bloomsburg E-10
Boyertown G-12
Bradford B-5
Brookville D-4
Butler E-2
California H-2
Canonsburg G-1
Carbondale C-13
Carlisle G-9
Center Valley F-13
Centre Hall E-7
Chadds Ford H-12
Chambersburg H-7
Chester H-13
Chester Springs H-12
Clarion D-3
Clarks Summit C-12
Clearfield E-6
Coatesville H-12
Collegeville G-13
Columbia H-10
Conneaut Lake C-1
Connellsville H-3
Corry B-3
Coudersport B-7
Danville E-10
Darby H-13
Dickson City C-12
Donora G-2
Downingtown H-12
Doylestown G-13
Drexel Hill H-13
Du Bois E-5
East Stroudsburg E-13
Easton F-13
Ebensburg F-5
Edinboro B-2
Elizabethtown H-10
Ellwood City E-1
Emporium C-6
Ephrata G-11
Erie A-2
Etna F-2
Exton H-12
Frackville F-11
Franklin D-2
Galeton C-8
Gettysburg I-8
Glenshaw F-2
Greencastle I-7
Greensburg G-3
Greenville D-1
Grove City D-2
Hamburg F-11
Hanover I-9
Harrisburg G-9
Hazleton E-11
Hershey G-10
Hollidaysburg G-6
Honesdale C-13
Horsham G-13
Huntingdon F-7
Indiana F-4
Irwin G-3
Jeannette G-3
Jenkintown H-14
Jersey Shore D-8
Jim Thorpe E-12
Johnstown G-4
Kane C-5
Kennett Square H-12
King of Prussia H-13
Kingston D-12
Kittanning E-3
Kulpsville G-13
Kutztown F-12
Lancaster H-11
Langhorne G-14
Lansdale G-13
Laporte D-10
Latrobe G-3
Lebanon G-10
Leesport G-11
continued on page 91

Travel planning & on-the-road resources

Tourism Information Pennsylvania Tourism Office: visitpa.com

Road Conditions & Construction 511, (877) 511-7366 www.511pa.com, www.penndot.pa.gov

Pennsylvania state facts

Nickname: The Keystone State
Capital: Harrisburg, G-9

Population: 13,002,700 (rank: 5th)
Largest city: Philadelphia, 1,603,797, H-13

Land area: 44,730 sq. mi. (rank: 32nd)
Highest point: Mount Davis, 3,213 ft., I-4

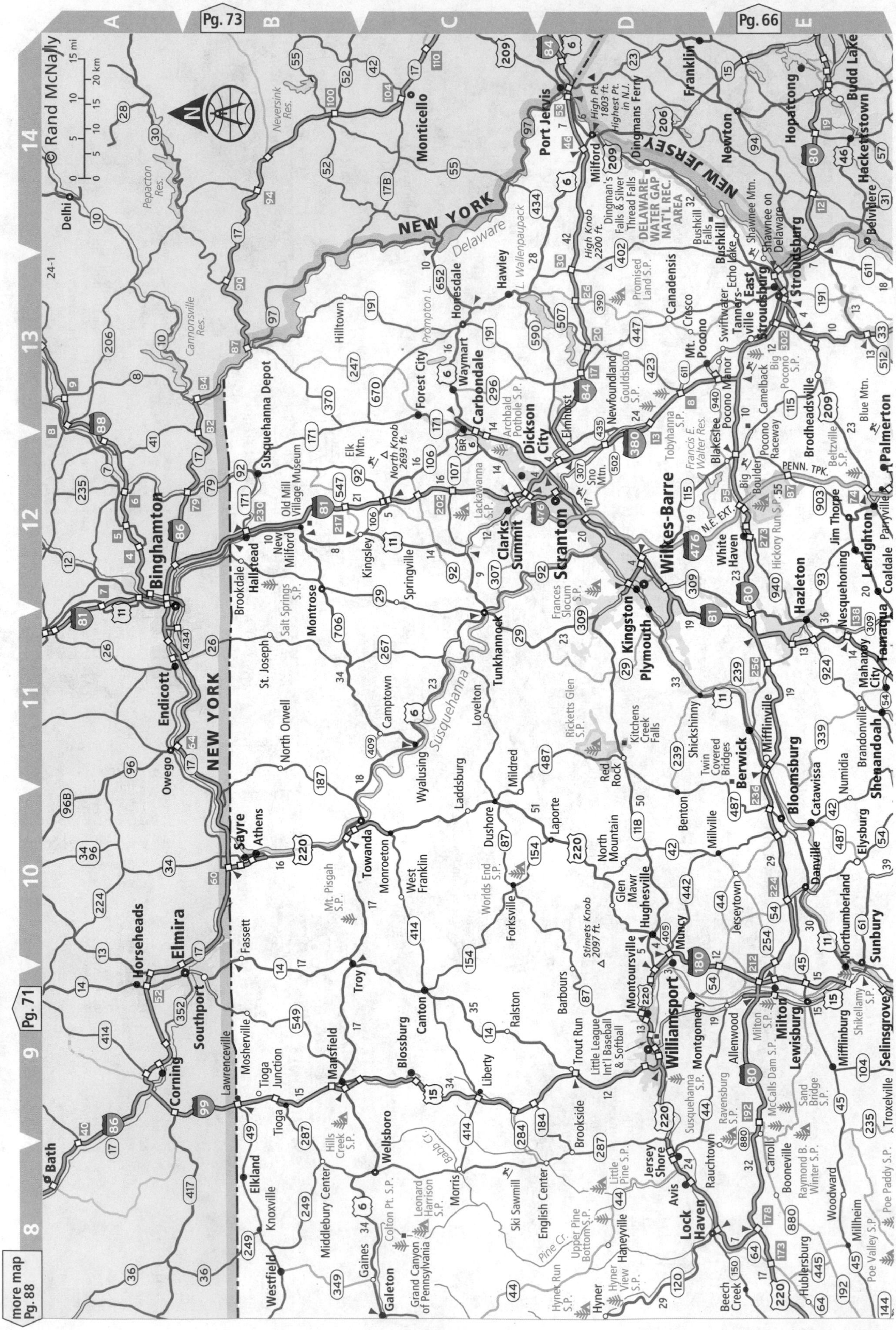

Pg. 73
Pg. 66
Pg. 71
more map Pg. 88

NEW YORK
NEW JERSEY
Binghamton
Endicott
Owego
Elmira
Horseheads
Corning
Bath
Southport
Delhi
Monticello
Port Jervis
Milford
Scranton
Wilkes-Barre
Kingston
Plymouth
Dickson City
Carbondale
Clarks Summit
Hazleton
Williamsport
Lock Haven
Jersey Shore
Bloomsburg
Berwick
Danville
Sunbury
Lewisburg
Milton
Selinsgrove
Shamokin
Shenandoah
Stroudsburg
East Stroudsburg
Towanda
Sayre
Athens
Montrose
Tunkhannock
Honesdale
Hawley
Wellsboro
Mansfield
Galeton
Lehighton
Palmerton
Jim Thorpe
Tamaqua
DELAWARE WATER GAP NAT'L REC. AREA
Susquehanna
Delaware

NOTE: Maps are not always in alphabetical order. See Page 1 for map location in this atlas.

more map Pg. 89

Pg. 29 Pg. 67

continued from page 89

Lehighton . . . E-12
Lewisburg . . . E-9
Lewistown . . . F-8
Lititz . . . H-11
Littlestown . . . I-9
Lock Haven . . . D-8
Mahanoy City . . . E-11
Manheim . . . G-10
Mansfield . . . B-9
McConnellsburg . . . H-7
McKees Rocks . . . F-2
McKeesport . . . G-2
Meadville . . . C-2
Mechanicsburg . . . G-9
Media . . . H-13
Mercer . . . D-1
Middleburg . . . F-9
Middletown . . . G-10
Mifflintown . . . F-8
Milford . . . D-14
Milton . . . E-9
Monongahela . . . G-2
Monroeville . . . G-2
Montgomeryville . . . G-13
Montoursville . . . D-9
Montrose . . . B-12
Morrisville . . . G-14
Mount Carmel . . . F-10
Mount Joy . . . H-10
Munhall . . . G-2
Nazareth . . . F-13
New Bloomfield . . . G-9
New Castle . . . E-1
New Holland . . . H-11
New Kensington . . . F-2
Norristown . . . H-13
North East . . . A-2
Northern Cambria . . . F-5
Oil City . . . C-3
Orwigsburg . . . F-11
Oxford . . . I-11
Palmerton . . . E-12
Paoli . . . H-13
Parryville . . . E-12
Philadelphia . . . H-13
Phoenixville . . . H-13
Pittsburgh . . . F-2
Plains . . . D-12
Plymouth . . . D-11
Pottstown . . . G-12
Pottsville . . . F-11
Punxsutawney . . . E-4
Quakertown . . . G-13
Reading . . . G-12
Red Lion . . . H-10
Ridgway . . . D-5
Rochester . . . F-1
St. Marys . . . D-5
Sayre . . . B-10
Schuylkill Haven . . . F-11
Scottdale . . . H-3
Scranton . . . D-12
Selinsgrove . . . F-9
Sellersville . . . G-13
Sewickley . . . F-1
Shamokin . . . F-10
Sharon . . . D-1
Shenandoah . . . E-11
Shippensburg . . . H-8
Smethport . . . B-6
Somerset . . . H-4
Souderton . . . G-13
State College . . . F-7
Stroudsburg . . . E-13
Sugarcreek . . . D-2
Sunbury . . . E-10
Tamaqua . . . F-11
Tarentum . . . F-3
Tionesta . . . C-3
Titusville . . . C-3
Towanda . . . C-10
Tunkhannock . . . C-11
Tyrone . . . F-6
Uniontown . . . H-3
Valley Forge . . . H-13
Vandergrift . . . F-3
Warminster . . . G-14
Warren . . . B-4
Washington . . . G-1
Waynesboro . . . I-8
Waynesburg . . . H-1
Wellsboro . . . C-8
West Chester . . . H-12
West Mifflin . . . G-2
West View . . . F-2
West York . . . H-10
Whitehall . . . G-2
Wilkes-Barre . . . D-12
Williamsport . . . D-9
Willow Street . . . H-11
York . . . H-10
Zelienople . . . E-2

Travel planning & on-the-road resources

Tourism Information — Pennsylvania Tourism Office: visitpa.com

Road Conditions & Construction — 511, (877) 511-7366 www.511pa.com, www.penndot.pa.gov

South Dakota state facts

Nickname: The Mount Rushmore State
Capital: Pierre, C-5

Population: 886,667 (rank: 46th)
Largest city: Sioux Falls, 192,517, E-10

Land area: 75,790 sq. mi. (rank: 16th)
Highest point: Black Elk Peak, 7,242 ft., D-2

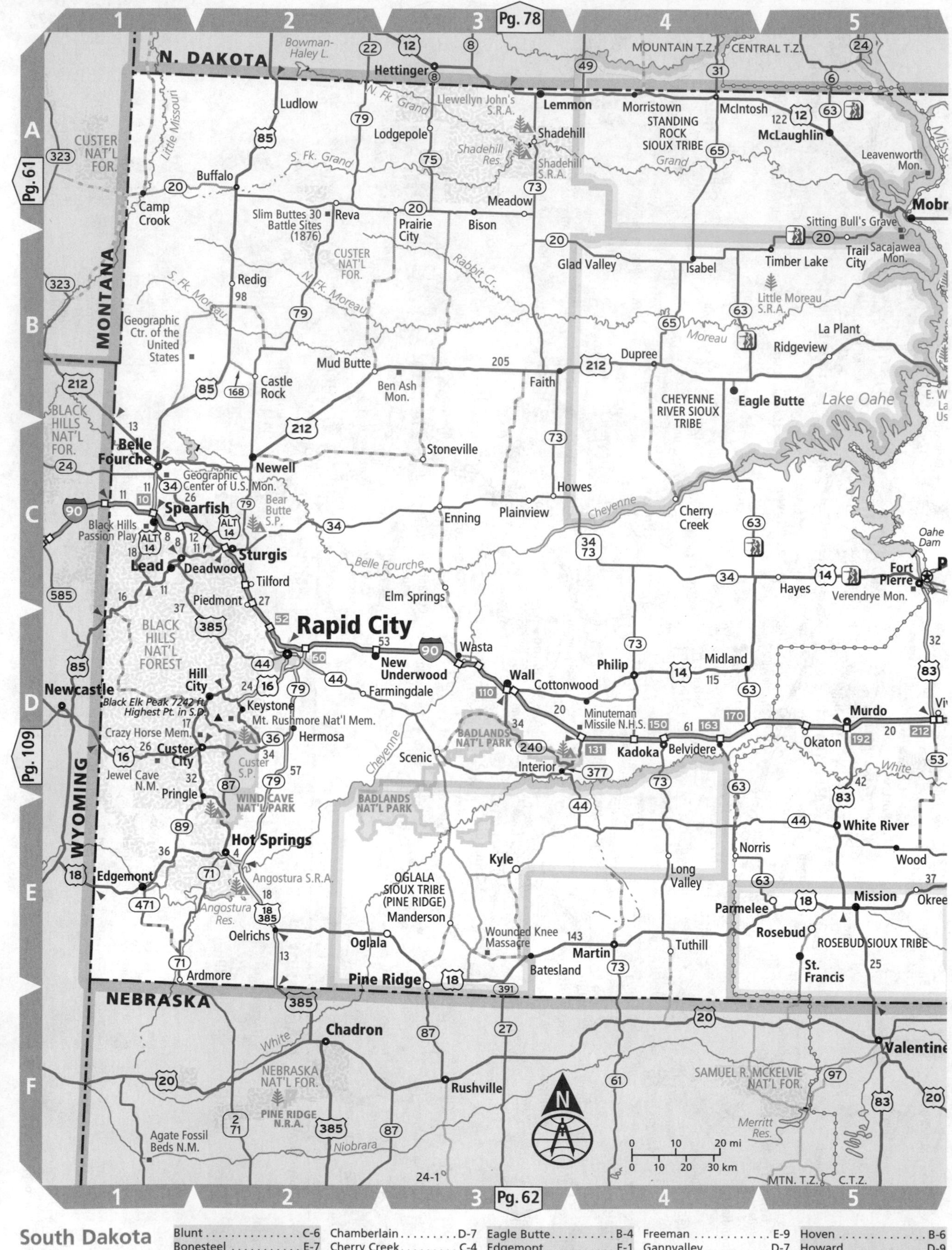

South Dakota

Cities and Towns

Aberdeen B-8
Alexandria D-8
Arlington C-9
Armour E-8
Avon F-8
Belle Fourche C-1
Beresford E-10
Big Stone City....... B-10
Bison A-3
Blunt C-6
Bonesteel E-7
Bowdle B-6
Bridgewater E-9
Bristol B-8
Britton.............. A-8
Brookings C-10
Bryant C-9
Buffalo A-2
Burke................ E-7
Canton E-10
Castlewood C-9
Chamberlain.......... D-7
Cherry Creek......... C-4
Clark B-8
Clear Lake.......... C-10
Colman D-10
Colome E-6
Custer D-2
De Smet C-9
Deadwood C-1
Dell Rapids......... D-10
Doland B-8
Dupree B-4
Eagle Butte.......... B-4
Edgemont............. E-1
Elk Point F-10
Elkton C-10
Estelline............ C-9
Ethan................ E-8
Eureka............... A-6
Faith B-3
Faulkton B-7
Flandreau D-10
Fort Pierre.......... C-5
Fort Thompson........ D-6
Freeman E-9
Gannvalley D-7
Gettysburg B-6
Gregory.............. E-6
Groton............... B-8
Harrisburg.......... E-10
Hecla A-8
Hermosa D-2
Herreid A-6
Highmore C-6
Hill City............ D-2
Hot Springs.......... E-2
Hoven B-6
Howard............... D-9
Huron C-8
Ipswich B-7
Kadoka D-4
Kennebec D-6
Keystone............. D-2
Kimball D-7
Kyle E-3
Lake Andes........... E-8
Lake Preston......... C-9
Langford............. A-8

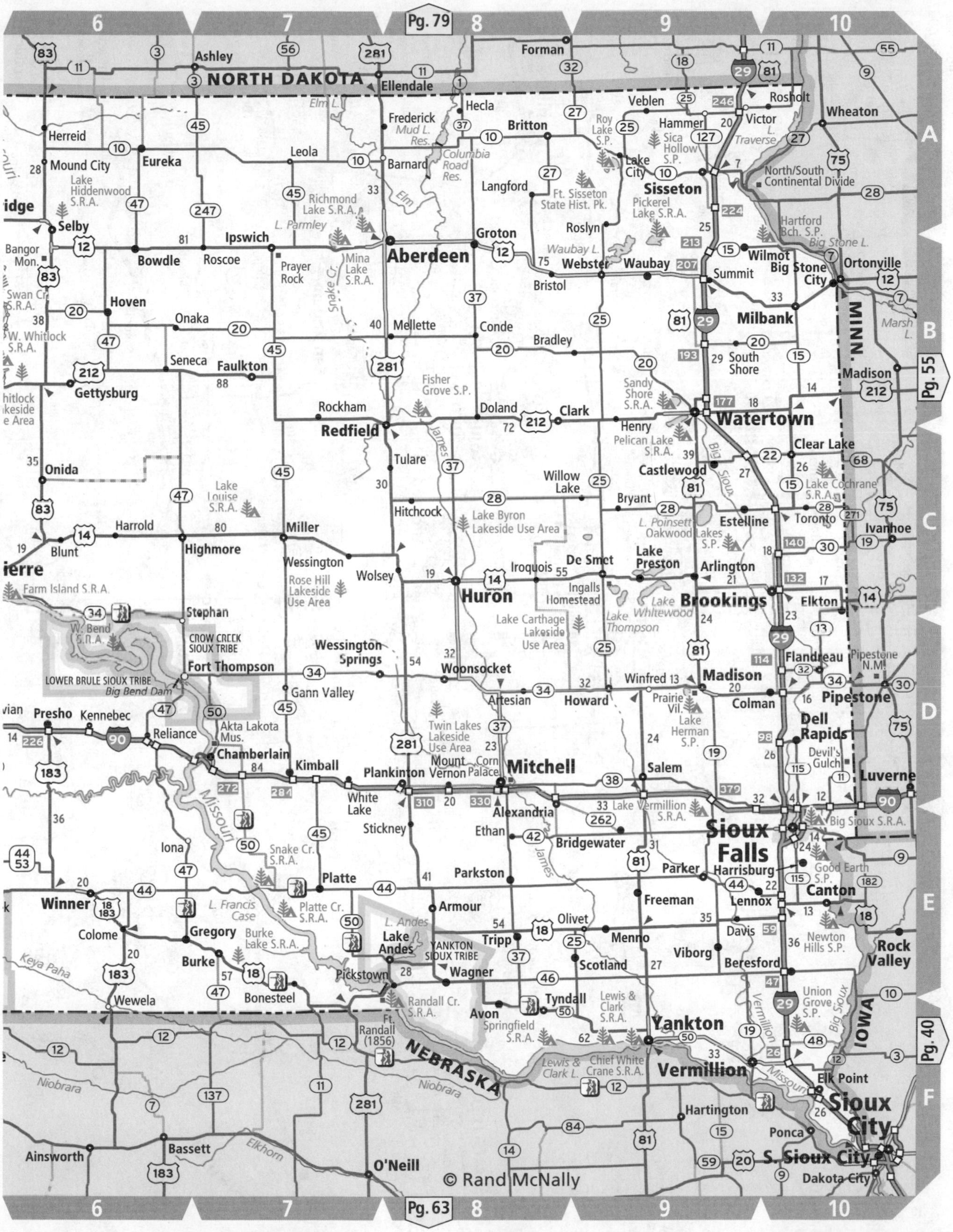

NOTE: Maps are not always in alphabetical order.
See Page 1 for map location in this atlas.

Pg. 79 · Pg. 55 · Pg. 40 · Pg. 63

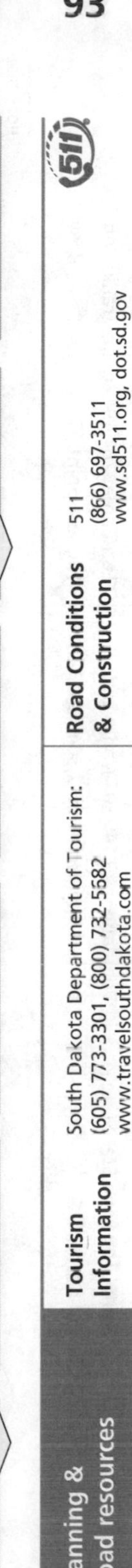

Lead C-1
Lemmon A-3
Lennox E-9
Leola A-7
Madison D-9
Martin E-4
McIntosh A-4
McLaughlin A-5
Menno E-9
Milbank B-10
Miller C-7
Mission E-5
Mitchell D-8
Mobridge A-5
Mound City A-6
Mount Vernon D-8
Murdo D-5
New Underwood D-2
Newell C-2
Oglala E-3
Olivet E-9
Onida C-6
Parker E-9
Parkston E-8
Parmelee E-5
Philip D-4
Piedmont C-2
Pierre C-5
Pine Ridge E-3
Plankinton D-8
Platte E-7
Presho D-6
Rapid City D-2
Redfield B-8
Roscoe B-7
Rosebud E-5
Rosholt A-10
St. Francis E-5
Salem D-9
Scotland E-9
Selby A-6
Sioux Falls E-10
Sisseton A-9
Spearfish C-1
Stickney E-8
Sturgis C-2
Summit B-9
Timber Lake B-5
Tripp E-8
Tyndall F-8
Vermillion F-9
Viborg E-9
Wagner E-8
Wall D-3
Watertown B-9
Waubay B-9
Webster B-9
Wessington Springs D-7
White Lake D-7
White River E-5
Willow Lake C-9
Wilmot B-9
Winner E-6
Wolsey C-8
Woonsocket D-8
Yankton F-9

Texas state facts

Nickname: The Lone Star State
Capital: Austin, E-9
Population: 29,145,505 (rank: 2nd)
Largest city: Houston, 2,304,580, F-11
Land area: 261,194 sq. mi. (rank: 2nd)
Highest point: Guadalupe Peak, 8,749 ft., C-2

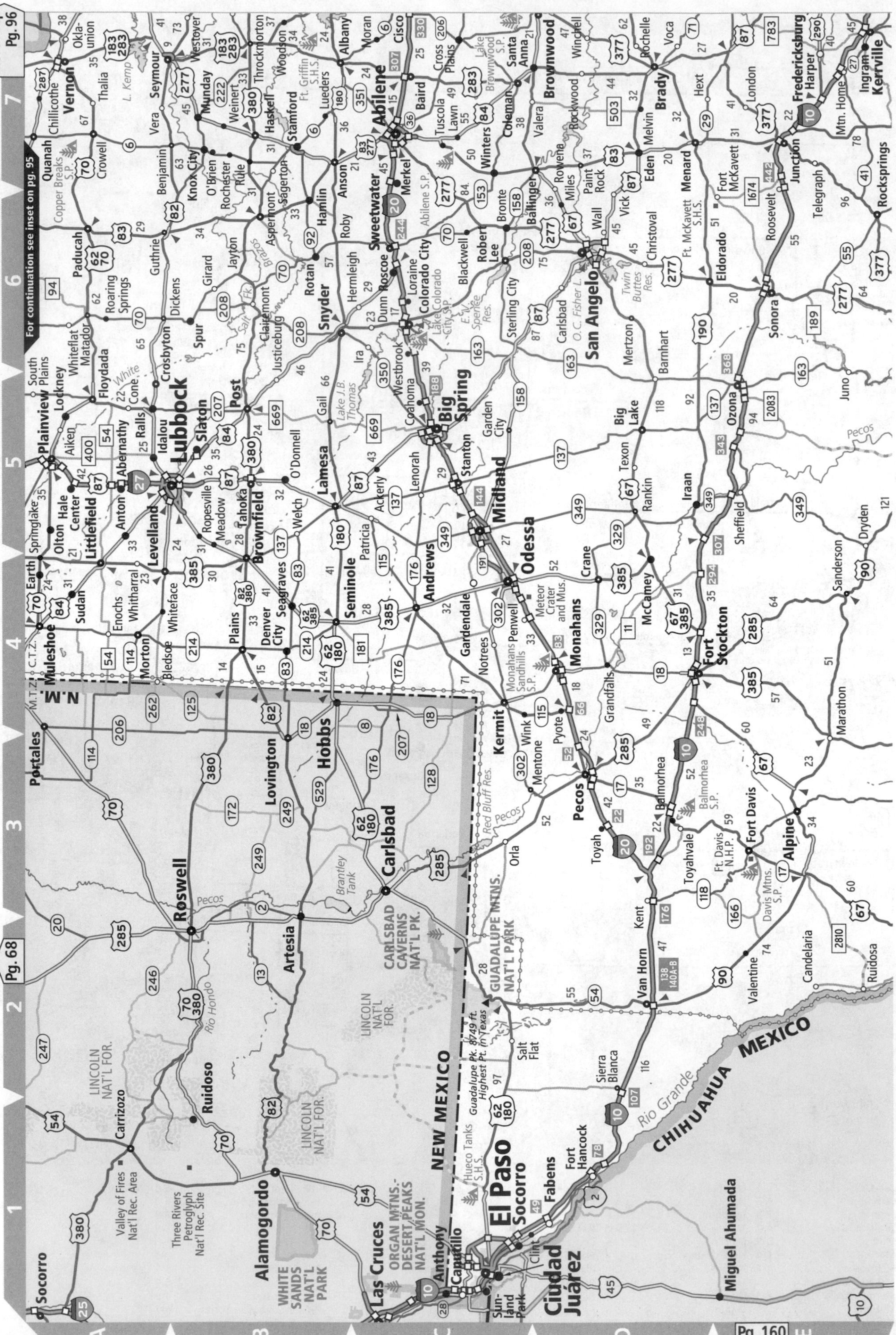

more map Pg. 96
Pg. 68
For continuation see inset on pg. 95
Pg. 160

NOTE: Maps are not always in alphabetical order.
See Page 1 for map location in this atlas.

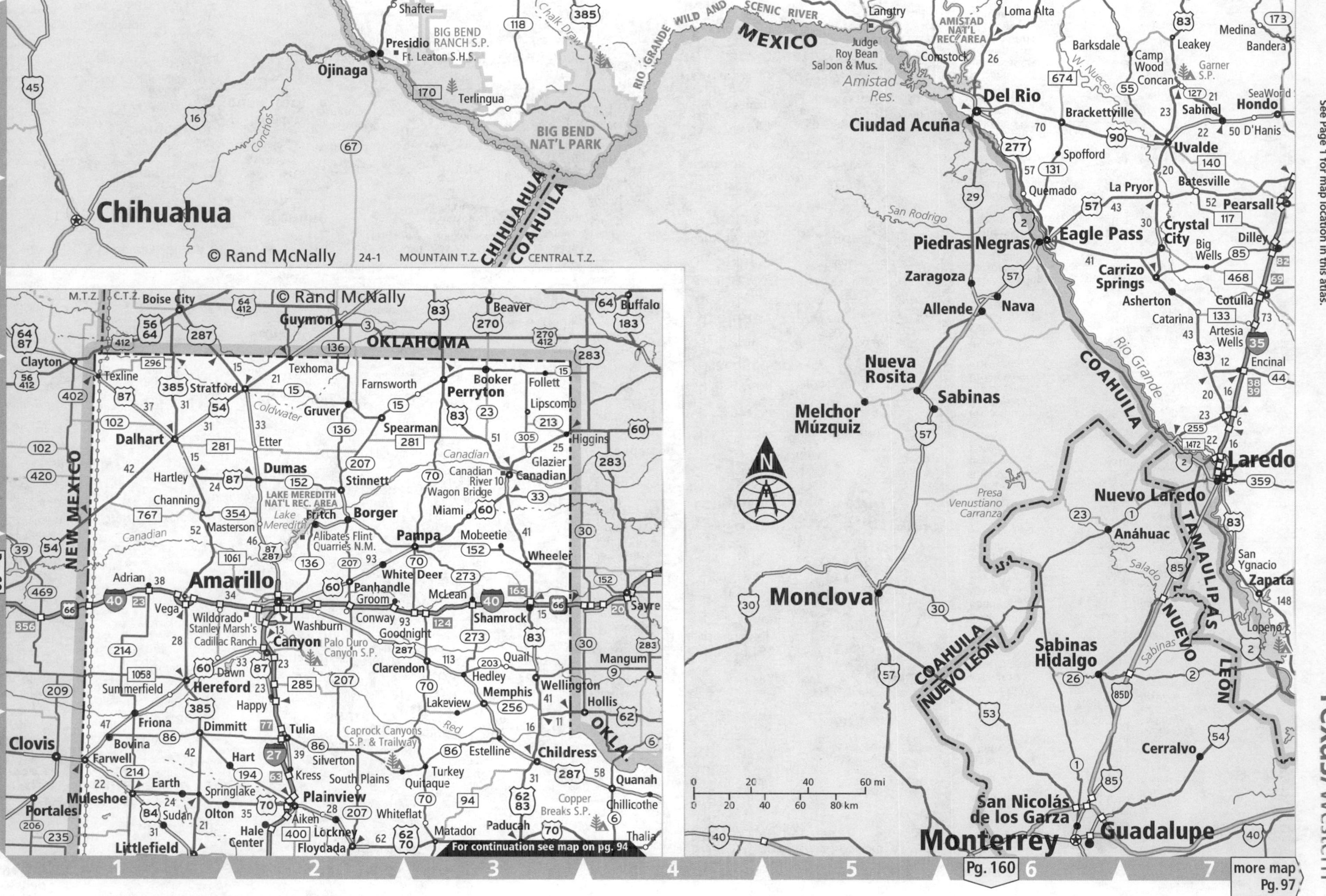

Travel planning & on-the-road resources

Tourism Information
Texas Tourism:
(512) 463-2000
www.traveltexas.com

Road Conditions & Construction
(800) 452-9292, (512) 463-8588
Dallas Metroplex: (877) 511-3255
drivetexas.org, 511dfw.org, www.txdot.gov

Texas state facts

Nickname: The Lone Star State
Capital: Austin, E-9
Population: 29,145,505 (rank: 2nd)
Largest city: Houston, 2,304,580, F-11
Land area: 261,194 sq. mi. (rank: 2nd)
Highest point: Guadalupe Peak, 8,749 ft., C-2

more map Pg. 94
Pg. 85
Pg. 16
Pg. 48

Texas

Cities and Towns

Abilene . . . C-7
Albany . . . B-7
Alice . . . H-8
Allen . . . B-10
Alpine . . . E-3
Alvin . . . F-11
Amarillo . . . I-2
Anahuac . . . F-12
Anderson . . . E-10
Andrews . . . C-4
Angleton . . . F-11
Anson . . . B-7
Archer City . . . A-8
Arlington . . . B-9
Aspermont . . . B-6
Athens . . . C-10
Austin . . . E-9
Baird . . . C-7
Ballinger . . . D-7
Bandera . . . F-7
Bastrop . . . E-9
Bay City . . . F-10
Baytown . . . F-11
Beaumont . . . E-12
Beeville . . . G-9
Bellville . . . E-10
Belton . . . D-9
Benjamin . . . B-7
Big Lake . . . D-5
Big Spring . . . C-5
Boerne . . . F-8
Bonham . . . A-10
Borger . . . H-2
Brackettville . . . F-6
Brady . . . D-7
Breckenridge . . . B-8
Brownfield . . . B-4
Brownsville . . . J-9
Brownwood . . . D-7
Bryan . . . E-10
Burnet . . . E-8
Caldwell . . . E-10
Cameron . . . D-9
Canadian . . . H-3
Canton . . . C-10
Canyon . . . I-2
Carrizo Springs . . . G-7
Carthage . . . C-12
Cedar Park . . . E-9
Center . . . C-12
Centerville . . . D-10
Channing . . . H-1
Childress . . . J-3
Clarendon . . . I-3
Clarksville . . . A-11
Cleburne . . . C-9
Coldspring . . . E-11
Coleman . . . C-7
College Station . . . E-10
Colorado City . . . C-6
Columbus . . . F-10
Comanche . . . C-8
Conroe . . . E-11
Cooper . . . B-11
Copperas Cove . . . D-9
Corinth . . . B-9
Corpus Christi . . . H-9
Corsicana . . . C-10
Cotulla . . . G-7
Crane . . . D-4
Jefferson . . . B-12
Johnson City . . . E-8
Jourdanton . . . G-8
Junction . . . E-7
Karnes City . . . G-9
Kaufman . . . C-10
Kermit . . . C-4
Kerrville . . . E-7
Killeen . . . D-9
Kingsville . . . H-9
Kingwood . . . E-11
Kountze . . . E-12
La Grange . . . E-10
La Porte . . . F-11
Lake Jackson . . . F-11
Lamesa . . . B-5
Lampasas . . . D-8
Laredo . . . H-7
Leakey . . . F-7
Levelland . . . A-4
Liberty . . . E-12
Linden . . . B-12
Lipscomb . . . H-3
Littlefield . . . A-4
Livingston . . . E-11
Llano . . . E-8
Lockhart . . . F-9
Longview . . . C-11
Lubbock . . . B-5
Lufkin . . . D-12
Madisonville . . . D-10
Marlin . . . D-9
Marshall . . . C-12
Matador . . . A-6
McAllen . . . J-8
McKinney . . . B-10
Memphis . . . I-3
Menard . . . D-7
Mentone . . . C-3
Mercedes . . . J-9
Meridian . . . C-9
Mertzon . . . D-6
Miami . . . H-3
Midland . . . C-5
Mineral Wells . . . B-8
Mission . . . J-8
Monahans . . . D-4
Montague . . . A-9
Morton . . . A-4
Mount Pleasant . . . B-11
Mount Vernon . . . B-11
Muleshoe . . . J-1
Nacogdoches . . . D-12
New Braunfels . . . F-8
Odessa . . . C-4
Orange . . . E-12
Ozona . . . E-5
Paducah . . . A-6
Paint Rock . . . D-7
Palestine . . . C-11
Palo Pinto . . . B-8
Pampa . . . I-3
Panhandle . . . I-2
Paris . . . A-11
Pearsall . . . G-7
Pecos . . . D-3
Perryton . . . H-3
Pharr . . . J-8
Pittsburg . . . B-11
Plains . . . B-4
Plainview . . . J-2
Plano . . . B-10
Port Arthur . . . E-12
Port Lavaca . . . G-10

NOTE: Maps are not always in alphabetical order.
See Page 1 for map location in this atlas.

Crockett	D-11	Post	B-5
Crosbyton	A-5	Quanah	I-4
Crowell	A-7	Quitman	B-11
Crystal City	G-7	Rankin	D-5
Cuero	F-9	Raymondville	I-9
Daingerfield	B-11	Refugio	G-9
Dalhart	H-1	Richmond	F-11
Dallas	B-10	Rio Grande City	I-8
Decatur	B-9	Robert Lee	C-6
Del Rio	F-6	Robstown	H-9
Denison	A-10	Roby	B-6
Denton	B-9	Rockport	H-9
Dickens	A-6	Rocksprings	E-6
Dickinson	F-11	Rockwall	B-10
Dimmitt	J-1	Rosenberg	F-11
Donna	J-9	Round Rock	E-9
Dumas	H-2	Rusk	C-11
Eagle Pass	G-6	San Angelo	D-6
Eastland	C-8	San Antonio	F-8
Edinburg	I-8	San Augustine	D-12
Edna	G-10	San Benito	J-9
El Paso	C-1	San Diego	H-8
Eldorado	D-6	San Marcos	F-9
Emory	B-10	San Saba	D-8
Ennis	C-10	Sanderson	E-4
Fairfield	C-10	Sarita	H-9
Falfurrias	H-8	Seguin	F-9
Farwell	J-1	Seminole	B-4
Floresville	F-8	Seymour	A-7
Floydada	A-5	Sherman	A-10
Fort Davis	E-3	Sierra Blanca	D-2
Fort Stockton	D-4	Silverton	J-2
Fort Worth	B-9	Sinton	H-9
Franklin	D-10	Snyder	B-6
Fredericksburg	E-8	Socorro	C-1
Gail	B-5	Sonora	E-5
Gainesville	A-9	Spearman	H-2
Galveston	F-12	Spring	E-11
Garden City	C-5	Stanton	C-5
Gatesville	D-9	Stephenville	C-8
George West	G-8	Sterling City	C-6
Georgetown	E-9	Stinnett	H-2
Giddings	E-9	Stratford	H-2
Gilmer	B-11	Sugar Land	F-11
Glen Rose	C-9	Sulphur Springs	B-11
Goldthwaite	D-8	Sweetwater	C-6
Goliad	G-9	Tahoka	B-5
Gonzales	F-9	Taylor	E-9
Graham	B-8	Temple	D-9
Granbury	C-9	Terrell	B-10
Greenville	B-10	Texarkana	B-12
Groesbeck	D-10	Texas City	F-11
Groveton	D-11	The Colony	B-9
Guthrie	A-6	The Woodlands	E-11
Hallettsville	F-10	Throckmorton	B-7
Hamilton	D-8	Tilden	G-8
Harker Heights	D-9	Tulia	J-2
Harlingen	J-9	Tyler	C-11
Haskell	B-7	Uvalde	F-7
Hebbronville	H-8	Van Horn	D-2
Hemphill	D-12	Vega	I-1
Hempstead	E-10	Victoria	G-9
Henderson	C-11	Waco	D-9
Henrietta	A-8	Waxahachie	C-9
Hereford	I-1	Weatherford	B-9
Hillsboro	C-9	Wellington	I-3
Hondo	F-7	Weslaco	J-9
Houston	F-11	Wharton	F-10
Huntsville	E-11	Wheeler	I-3
Jacksboro	B-8	Wichita Falls	A-8
Jacksonville	C-11	Woodville	D-12
Jasper	D-12	Zapata	I-7
Jayton	B-6		

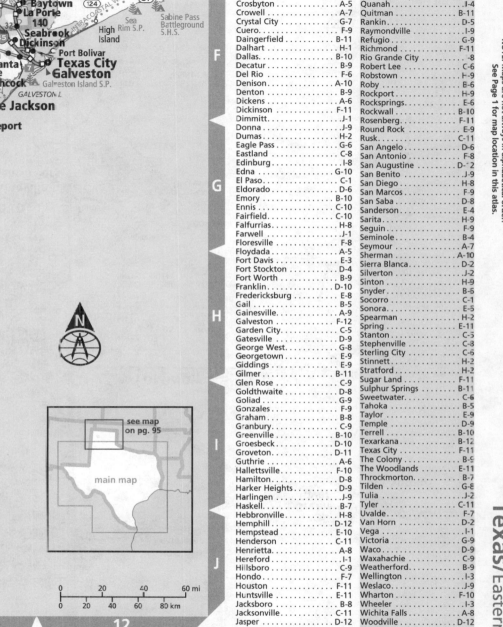

more map Pg. 95

Pg. 160

see map on pg. 95

Tourism Information Texas Tourism: (512) 463-2000 www.traveltexas.com

Road Conditions & Construction (800) 452-9292, (512) 463-8588 Dallas Metroplex: (877) 511-3255 drivetexas.org, 511dfw.org, www.txdot.gov

Travel planning & on-the-road resources

Utah state facts

Nickname: The Beehive State
Capital: Salt Lake City, C-4

Population: 3,271,616 (rank: 30th)
Largest city: Salt Lake City, 199,723, C-4

Land area: 82,355 sq. mi. (rank: 12th)
Highest point: Kings Peak, 13,528 ft., C-5

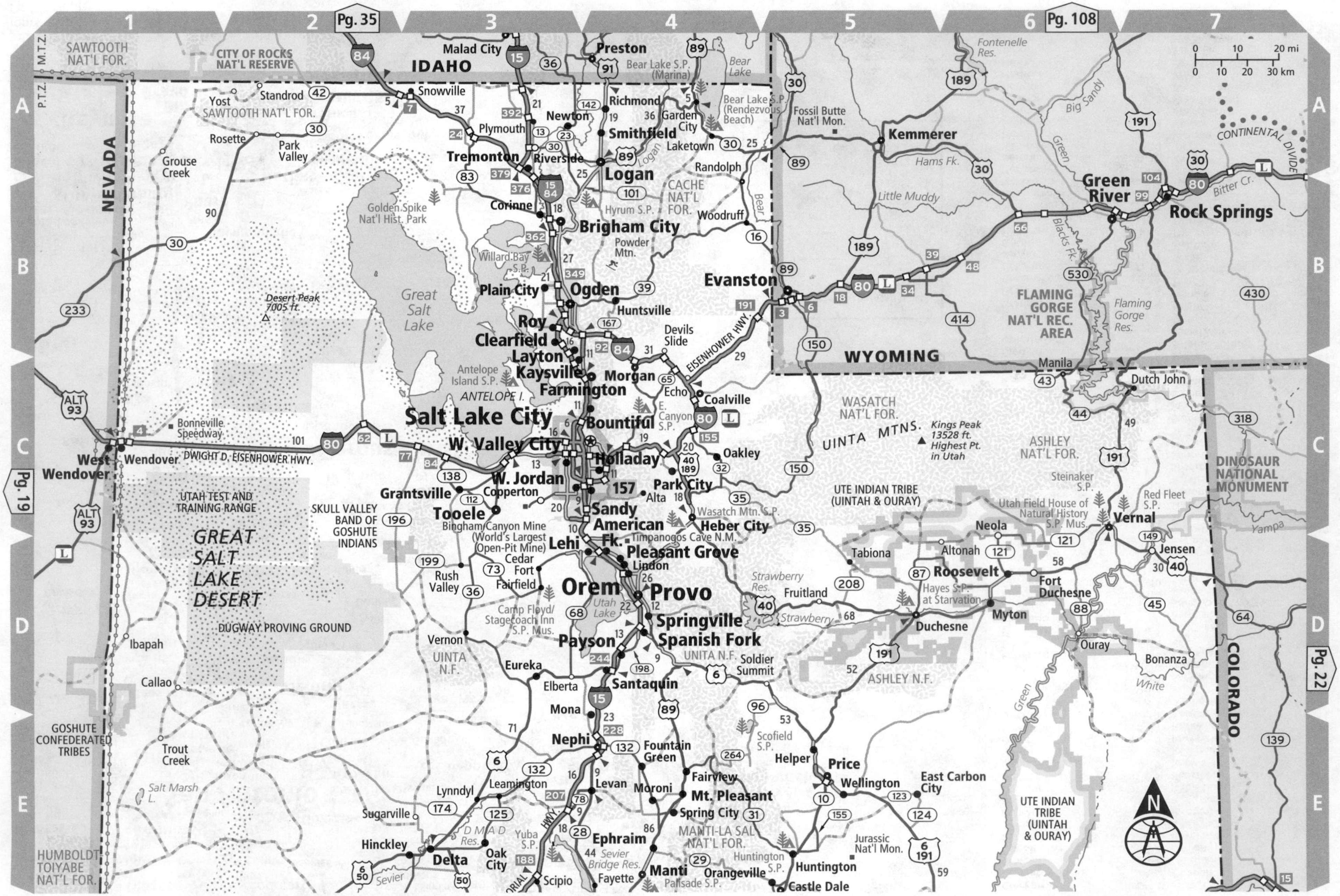

Pg. 35 Pg. 108 Pg. 19 Pg. 22

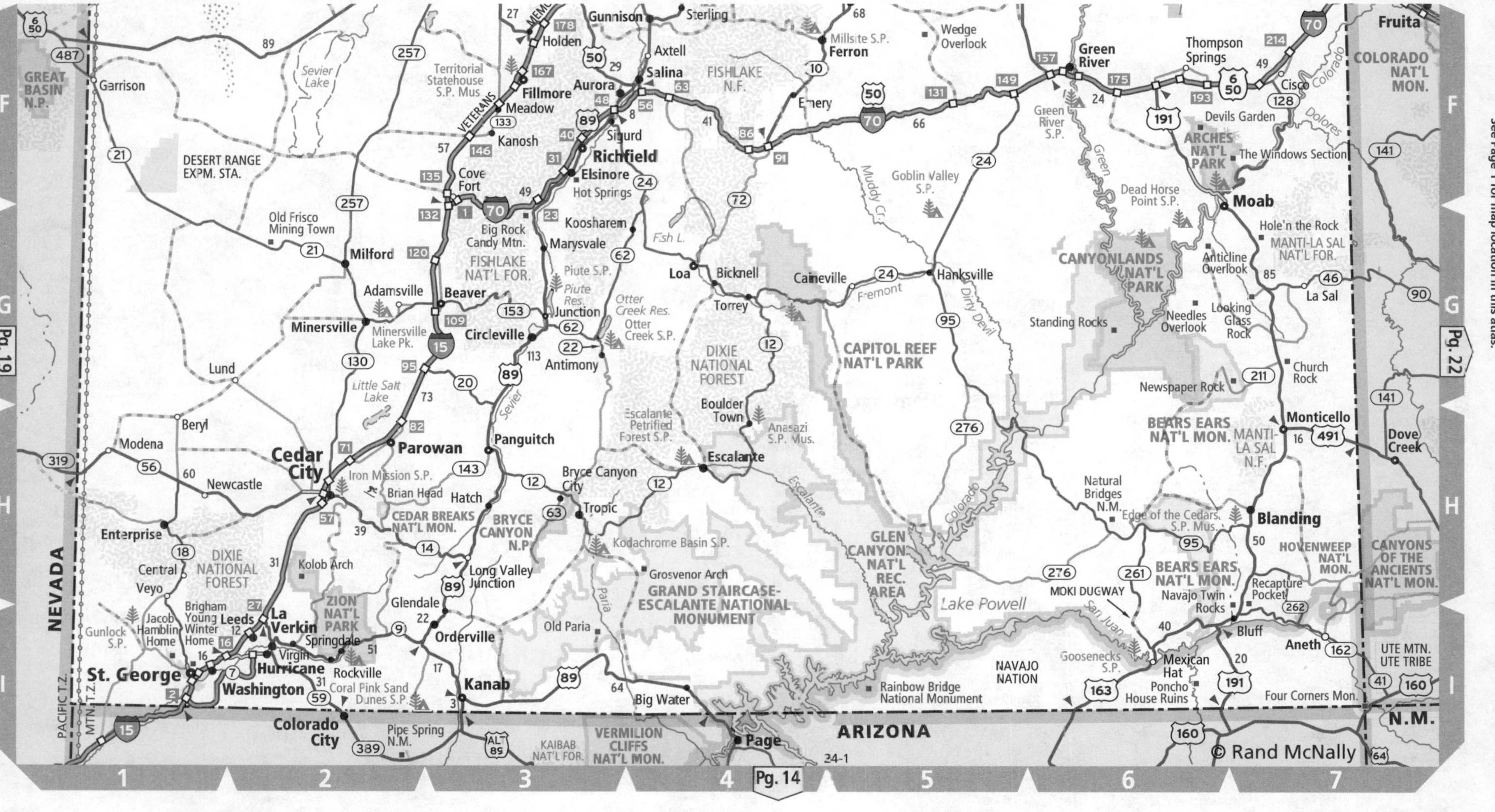

Utah

Cities and Towns

American Fork . . . D-4
Aneth . . . I-7
Aurora . . . F-3
Beaver . . . G-3
Blanding . . . H-7
Bountiful . . . C-4
Brigham City . . . B-3
Castle Dale . . . E-5
Cedar City . . . H-2
Clearfield . . . B-3
Coalville . . . C-4
Copperton . . . C-3
Corinne . . . B-3
Delta . . . E-3
Duchesne . . . D-5
East Carbon City . . . E-5
Elsinore . . . F-3
Enterprise . . . H-1
Ephraim . . . E-4
Escalante . . . H-4
Eureka . . . D-3
Fairview . . . E-4
Farmington . . . C-4
Ferron . . . F-4
Fillmore . . . F-3
Fort Duchesne . . . D-6
Fountain Green . . . E-4
Grantsville . . . C-3
Green River . . . F-6
Gunnison . . . F-4
Heber City . . . C-4
Helper . . . E-5
Hinckley . . . E-3
Holladay . . . C-4
Huntington . . . E-5
Huntsville . . . B-4
Hurricane . . . I-2
Junction . . . G-3
Kanab . . . I-3
Kaysville . . . C-3
La Verkin . . . I-2
Layton . . . B-3
Lehi . . . D-4
Levan . . . E-4
Lindon . . . D-4
Loa . . . G-4
Logan . . . A-4
Manila . . . C-6
Manti . . . E-4
Milford . . . G-2
Minersville . . . G-2
Moab . . . G-6
Mona . . . E-4
Monticello . . . H-7
Morgan . . . C-4
Moroni . . . E-4
Mount Pleasant . . . E-4
Nephi . . . E-4
Newton . . . A-3
Oak City . . . E-3
Oakley . . . C-4
Ogden . . . B-3
Orangeville . . . E-5
Orderville . . . I-3
Orem . . . D-4
Panguitch . . . H-3
Park City . . . C-4
Parowan . . . H-2
Payson . . . D-4
Plain City . . . B-3
Pleasant Grove . . . D-4
Price . . . E-5
Provo . . . D-4
Randolph . . . B-4
Richfield . . . F-3
Richmond . . . A-4
Riverside . . . A-3
Roosevelt . . . D-6
Roy . . . B-3
St. George . . . I-1
Salina . . . F-4
Salt Lake City . . . C-4
Sandy . . . C-4
Santaquin . . . D-4
Smithfield . . . A-4
Spanish Fork . . . D-4
Spring City . . . E-4
Springville . . . D-4
Tooele . . . C-3
Tremonton . . . A-3
Vernal . . . C-6
Washington . . . I-1
Wellington . . . E-5
Wendover . . . C-1
West Jordan . . . C-3
West Valley City . . . C-3

Travel planning & on-the-road resources

Tourism Information
Utah Office of Tourism:
(800) 200-1160, (801) 538-1900
www.visitutah.com

Road Conditions & Construction
511, (866) 511-8824, (801) 965-4000
udottraffic.utah.gov
www.udot.utah.gov

Virginia state facts

Nickname: Old Dominion
Capital: Richmond, G-11
Population: 8,631,393 (rank: 12th)
Largest city: Virginia Beach, 459,470, H-13
Land area: 39,472 sq. mi. (rank: 37th)
Highest point: Mount Rogers, 5,729 ft., I-4

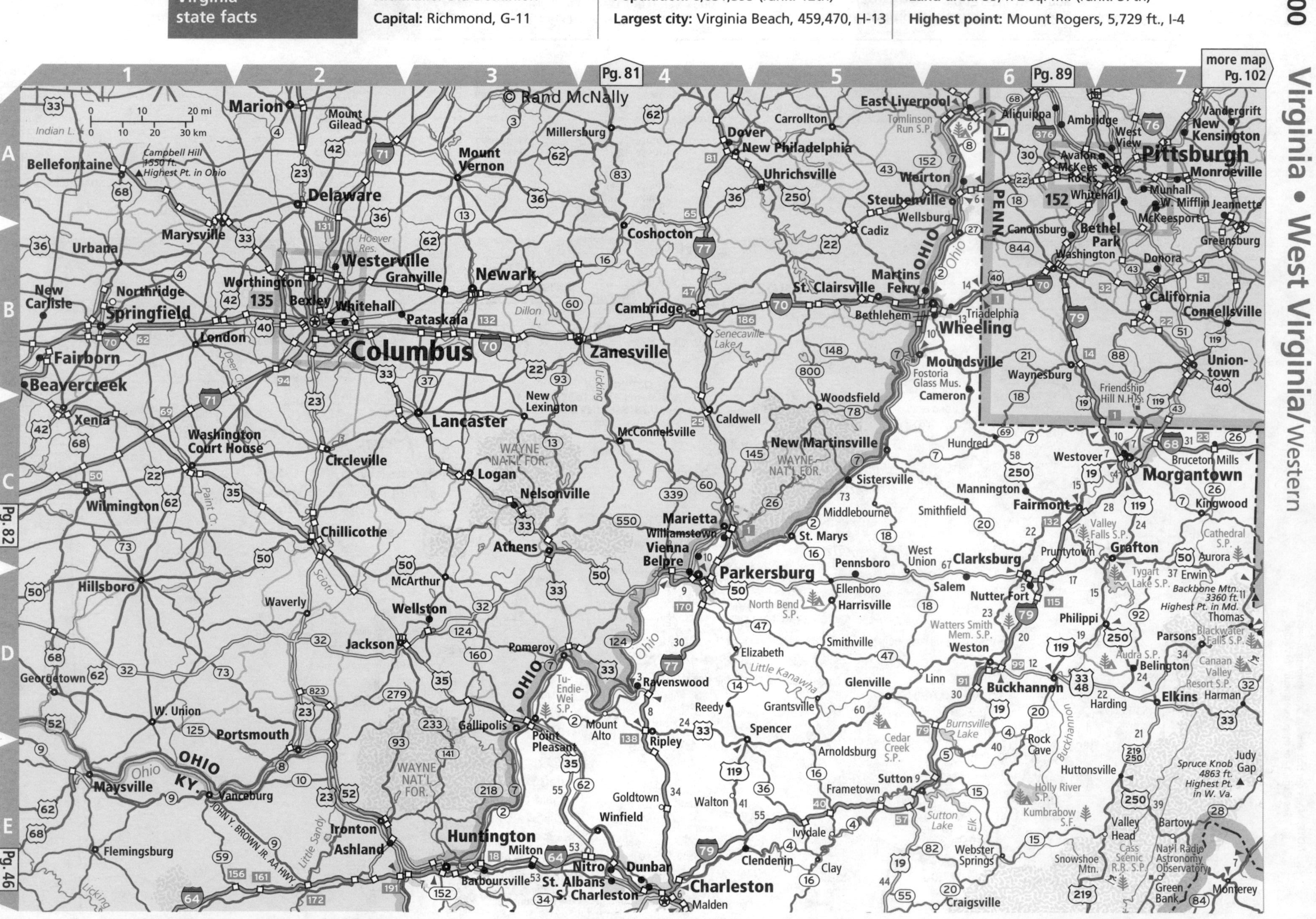

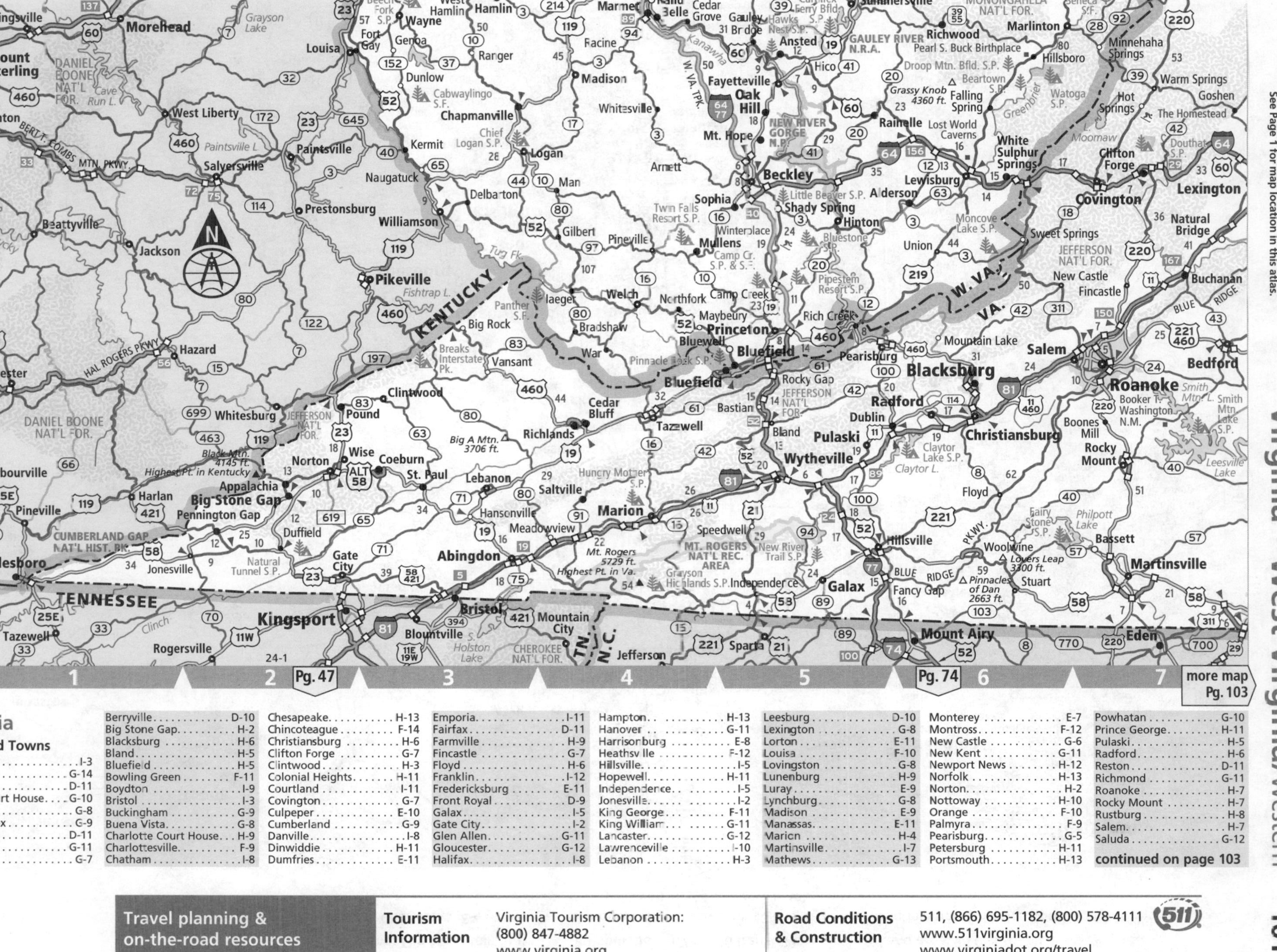

Virginia

Cities and Towns

Abingdon . . . I-3
Accomac . . . G-14
Alexandria . . . D-11
Amelia Court House . . . G-10
Amherst . . . G-8
Appomattox . . . G-9
Arlington . . . D-11
Ashland . . . G-11
Bedford . . . G-7
Berryville . . . D-10
Big Stone Gap . . . H-2
Blacksburg . . . H-6
Bland . . . H-5
Bluefield . . . H-5
Bowling Green . . . F-11
Boydton . . . I-9
Bristol . . . I-3
Buckingham . . . G-9
Buena Vista . . . G-8
Charlotte Court House . . . H-9
Charlottesville . . . F-9
Chatham . . . I-8
Chesapeake . . . H-13
Chincoteague . . . F-14
Christiansburg . . . H-6
Clifton Forge . . . G-7
Clintwood . . . H-3
Colonial Heights . . . H-11
Courtland . . . I-11
Covington . . . G-7
Culpeper . . . E-10
Cumberland . . . G-9
Danville . . . I-8
Dinwiddie . . . H-11
Dumfries . . . E-11
Emporia . . . I-11
Fairfax . . . D-11
Farmville . . . H-9
Fincastle . . . G-7
Floyd . . . H-6
Franklin . . . I-12
Fredericksburg . . . E-11
Front Royal . . . D-9
Galax . . . I-5
Gate City . . . I-2
Glen Allen . . . G-11
Gloucester . . . G-12
Halifax . . . I-8
Hampton . . . H-13
Hanover . . . G-11
Harrisonburg . . . E-8
Heathsville . . . F-12
Hillsville . . . I-5
Hopewell . . . H-11
Independence . . . I-5
Jonesville . . . I-2
King George . . . F-11
King William . . . G-11
Lancaster . . . G-12
Lawrenceville . . . I-10
Lebanon . . . H-3
Leesburg . . . D-10
Lexington . . . G-8
Lorton . . . E-11
Louisa . . . F-10
Lovingston . . . G-8
Lunenburg . . . H-9
Luray . . . E-9
Lynchburg . . . G-8
Madison . . . E-9
Manassas . . . E-11
Marion . . . H-4
Martinsville . . . I-7
Mathews . . . G-13
Monterey . . . E-7
Montross . . . F-12
New Castle . . . G-6
New Kent . . . G-11
Newport News . . . H-12
Norfolk . . . H-13
Norton . . . H-2
Nottoway . . . H-10
Orange . . . F-10
Palmyra . . . F-9
Pearisburg . . . G-5
Petersburg . . . H-11
Portsmouth . . . H-13
Powhatan . . . G-10
Prince George . . . H-11
Pulaski . . . H-5
Radford . . . H-6
Reston . . . D-11
Richmond . . . G-11
Roanoke . . . H-7
Rocky Mount . . . H-7
Rustburg . . . H-8
Salem . . . H-7
Saluda . . . G-12

continued on page 103

Travel planning & on-the-road resources

Tourism Information	Virginia Tourism Corporation: (800) 847-4882 www.virginia.org	**Road Conditions & Construction**	511, (866) 695-1182, (800) 578-4111 www.511virginia.org www.virginiadot.org/travel

West Virginia state facts

Nickname: The Mountain State
Capital: Charleston, E-4

Population: 1,793,716 (rank: 39th)
Largest city: Charleston, 48,864, E-4

Land area: 24,035 sq. mi. (rank: 41st)
Highest point: Spruce Knob, 4,863 ft., E-7

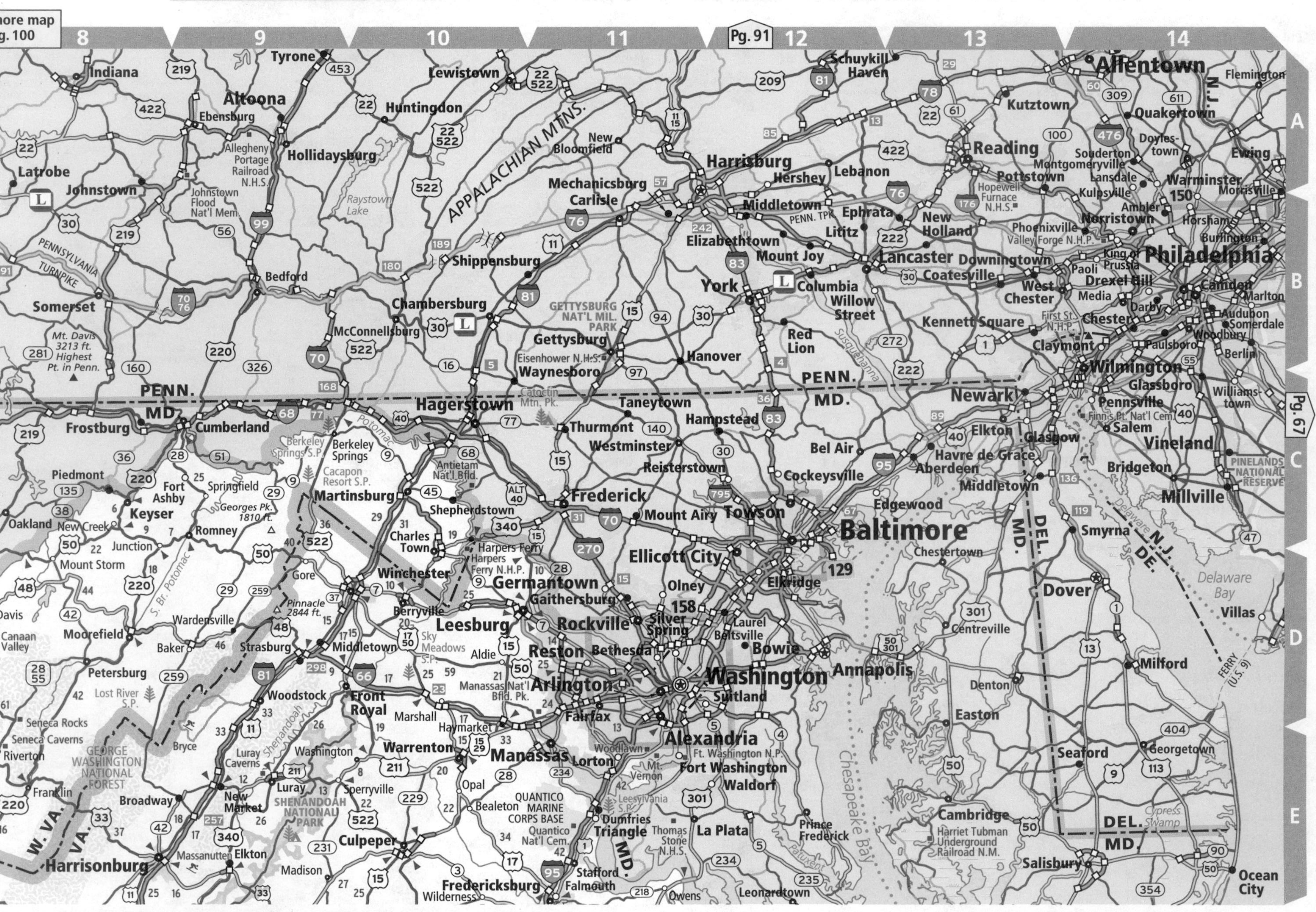

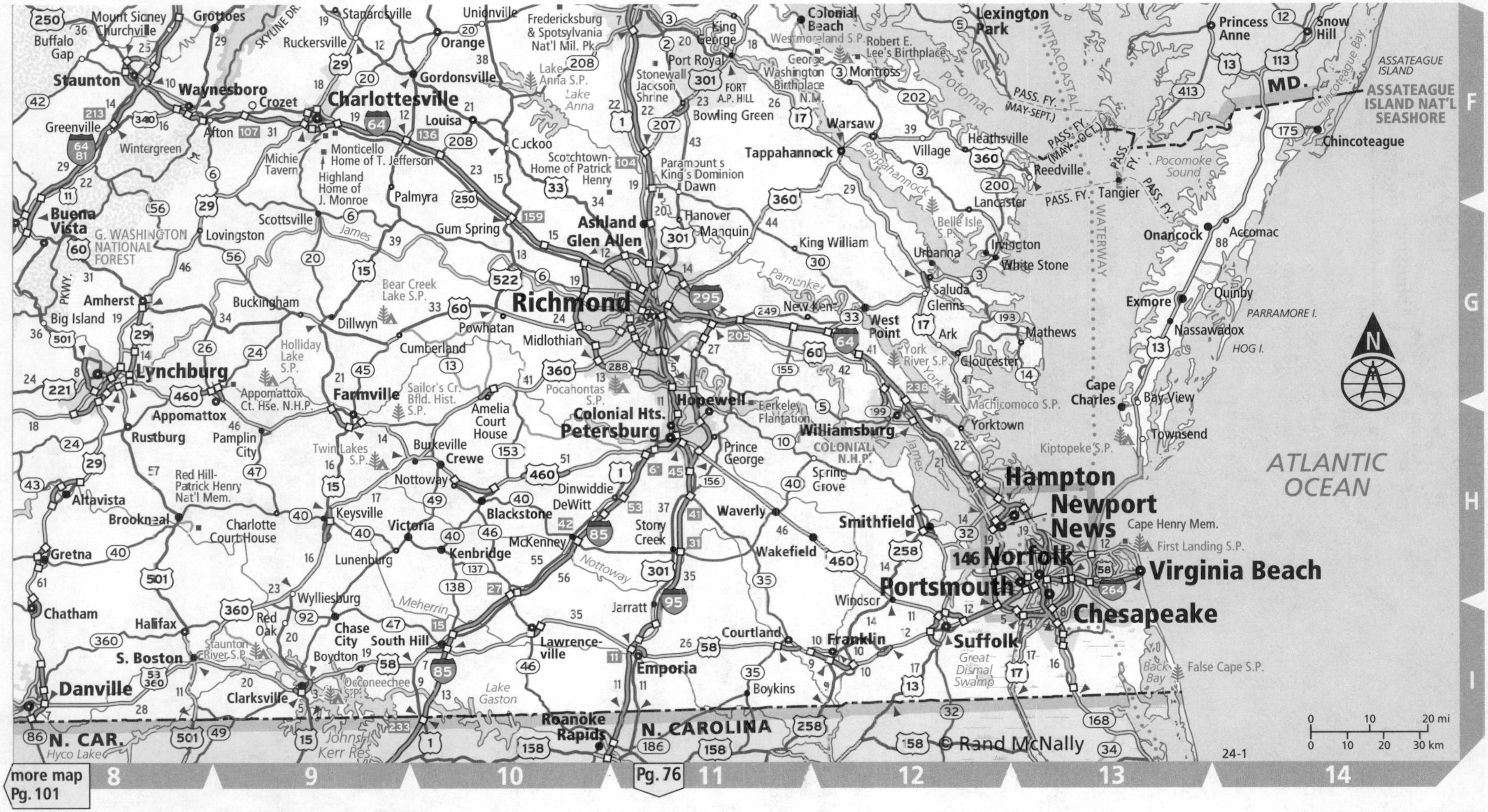

more map Pg. 101

Pg. 76

continued from page 101

Smithfield H-12
South Boston I-8
South Hill I-10
Stafford E-11
Stanardsville F-9
Staunton F-8
Stuart I-6
Suffolk I-12
Tappahannock F-12
Tazewell H-4
Triangle E-11
Virginia Beach H-13
Warm Springs F-7
Warrenton E-10
Warsaw F-12
Washington E-10
Waynesboro F-8
Williamsburg H-12
Winchester D-10
Wise H-2
Woodbridge E-11
Woodstock D-9
Wytheville H-5
Yorktown H-12

West Virginia

Cities and Towns

Barboursville E-3
Beckley G-5
Berkeley Springs C-9
Bethlehem B-6
Bluefield H-5
Buckhannon D-6
Charles Town D-10
Charleston E-4
Clay E-5
Delbarton G-3
Dunbar E-4
Elizabeth D-4
Elkins D-7
Fairmont C-6
Fayetteville F-5
Franklin E-8
Glenville D-5
Grafton C-7
Grantsville D-5
Hamlin F-3
Harrisville D-5
Hico F-5
Hinton G-5
Huntington E-3
Keyser C-8
Kingwood C-7
Lewisburg G-6
Logan F-3
Madison F-4
Marlinton F-6
Martinsburg C-10
Middlebourne C-5
Milton E-3
Moorefield D-8
Morgantown C-7
Moundsville B-5
New Martinsville C-5
Nitro E-4
Nutter Fort D-6
Oak Hill F-5
Parsons D-7
Petersburg D-8
Philippi D-7
Pineville G-4
Point Pleasant D-3
Princeton G-5
Ravenswood D-4
Richwood F-6
Ripley D-4
Romney C-9
St. Albans E-4
St. Marys C-5
South Charleston E-4
Spencer D-4
Summersville F-5
Sutton E-6
Union G-6
Vienna C-4
Wayne F-3
Webster Springs E-6
Weirton A-6
Welch G-4
Wellsburg B-6
West Union D-5
Weston D-6
Wheeling B-6
White Sulphur Springs G-6
Williamson G-3
Williamstown C-4
Winfield E-4

Travel planning & on-the-road resources

Tourism Information
West Virginia Tourism Office:
(304) 558-2200
wvtourism.com

Road Conditions & Construction
511, (855) 699-8511
www.wv511.org
transportation.wv.gov

Washington state facts

Nickname: The Evergreen State
Capital: Olympia, D-3

Population: 7,705,281 (rank: 13th)
Largest city: Seattle, 737,015, C-4

Land area: 66,438 sq. mi. (rank: 20th)
Highest point: Mount Rainier, 14,411 ft., D-4

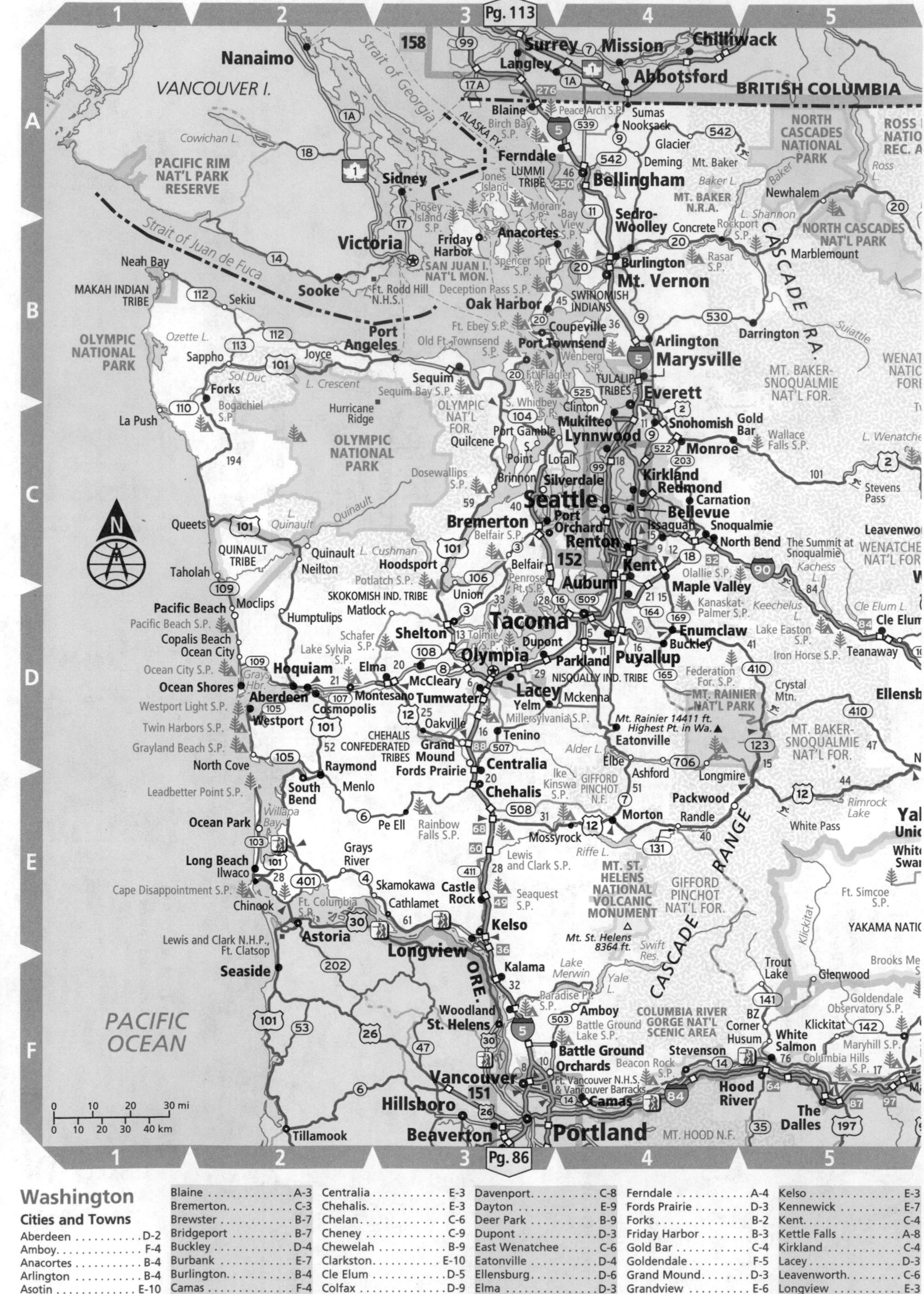

Washington

Cities and Towns

Aberdeen D-2
Amboy. F-4
Anacortes B-4
Arlington B-4
Asotin E-10
Auburn D-4
Battle Ground. F-3
Bellevue C-4
Bellingham A-4
Blaine A-3
Bremerton. C-3
Brewster B-7
Bridgeport B-7
Buckley D-4
Burbank E-7
Burlington. B-4
Camas F-4
Carnation C-4
Cashmere C-6
Castle Rock E-3
Cathlamet E-3
Centralia E-3
Chehalis. E-3
Chelan C-6
Cheney C-9
Chewelah B-9
Clarkston. E-10
Cle Elum D-5
Colfax D-9
Colville B-9
Connell E-8
Cosmopolis D-2
Coupeville. B-3
Davenport. C-8
Dayton E-9
Deer Park B-9
Dupont D-3
East Wenatchee C-6
Eatonville D-4
Ellensburg. D-6
Elma D-3
Entiat. C-6
Enumclaw D-4
Ephrata D-7
Everett. C-4
Ferndale A-4
Fords Prairie D-3
Forks B-2
Friday Harbor B-3
Gold Bar C-4
Goldendale F-5
Grand Mound. D-3
Grandview E-6
Granger. E-6
Hoquiam. D-2
Issaquah C-4
Kalama F-3
Kelso E-3
Kennewick E-7
Kent. C-4
Kettle Falls A-8
Kirkland C-4
Lacey D-3
Leavenworth. C-6
Longview E-3
Lynnwood. C-4
Mabton. E-6
Maple Valley. C-4
Marysville B-4

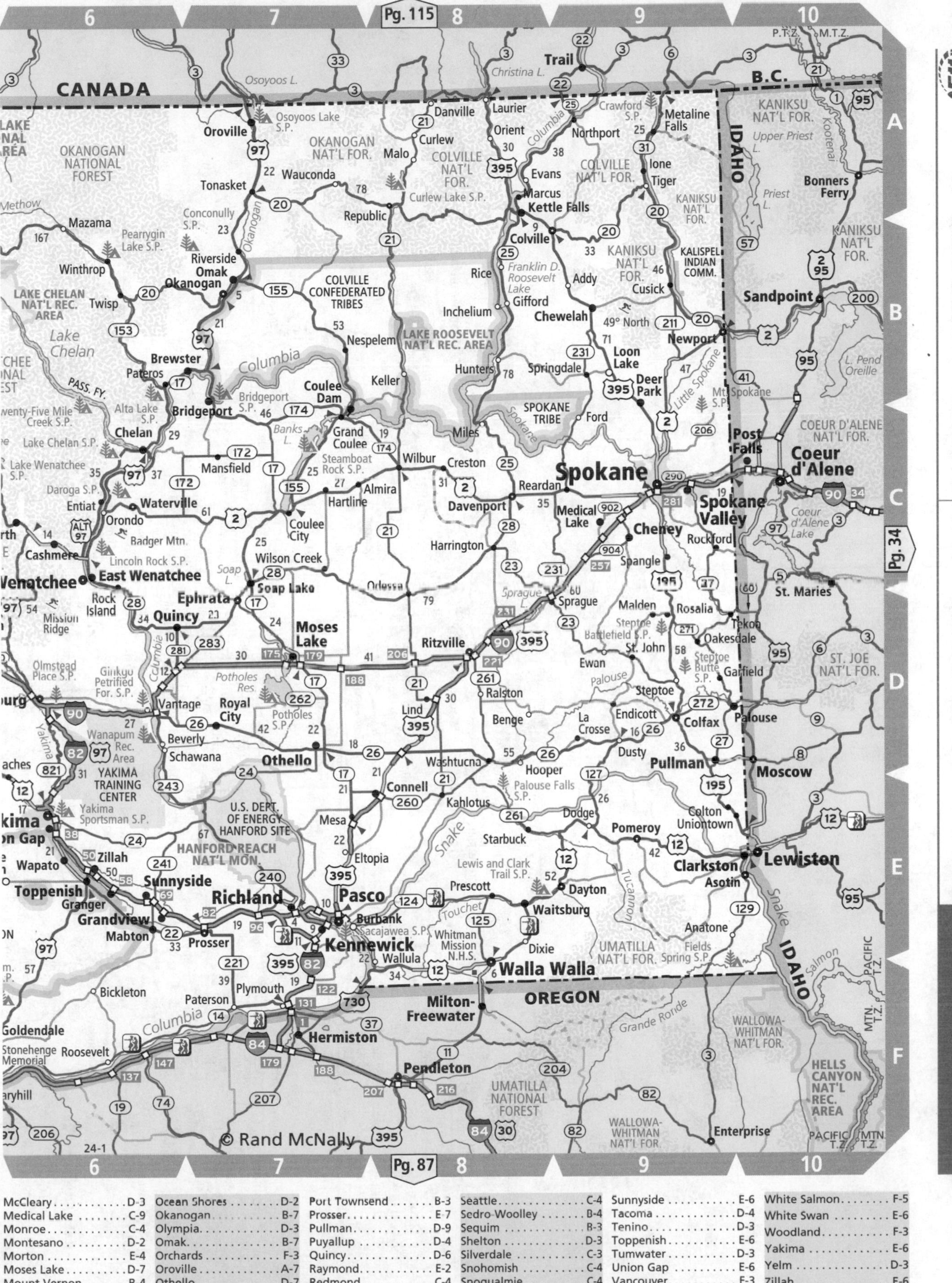

McCleary D-3
Medical Lake C-9
Monroe C-4
Montesano D-2
Morton E-4
Moses Lake D-7
Mount Vernon B-4
Mukilteo C-4
Newport B-9
North Bend C-4
Oak Harbor B-3
Ocean Park E-2
Ocean Shores D-2
Okanogan B-7
Olympia D-3
Omak B-7
Orchards F-3
Oroville A-7
Othello D-7
Parkland D-4
Pasco E-7
Pomeroy E-9
Port Angeles B-3
Port Orchard C-3
Port Townsend B-3
Prosser E-7
Pullman D-9
Puyallup D-4
Quincy D-6
Raymond E-2
Redmond C-4
Renton C-4
Republic A-8
Richland E-7
Ritzville D-8
Royal City D-7
Seattle C-4
Sedro-Woolley B-4
Sequim B-3
Shelton D-3
Silverdale C-3
Snohomish C-4
Snoqualmie C-4
Soap Lake C-7
South Bend E-2
Spokane C-9
Spokane Valley C-9
Stevenson F-4
Sunnyside E-6
Tacoma D-4
Tenino D-3
Toppenish E-6
Tumwater D-3
Union Gap E-6
Vancouver F-3
Walla Walla F-8
Wapato E-6
Waterville C-6
Wenatchee C-6
Westport D-2
White Salmon F-5
White Swan E-6
Woodland F-3
Yakima E-6
Yelm D-3
Zillah E-6

Road Conditions & Construction
511, (800) 695-7623
wsdot.com/travel

Tourism Information
Washington Tourism Alliance:
(800) 544-1800
stateofwatourism.com

Travel planning & on-the-road resources

Wisconsin state facts

Nickname: The Badger State
Capital: Madison, G-4
Population: 5,893,718 (rank: 20th)
Largest city: Milwaukee, 577,222, G-6
Land area: 54,153 sq. mi. (rank: 25th)
Highest point: Timms Hill, 1,951 ft., D-4

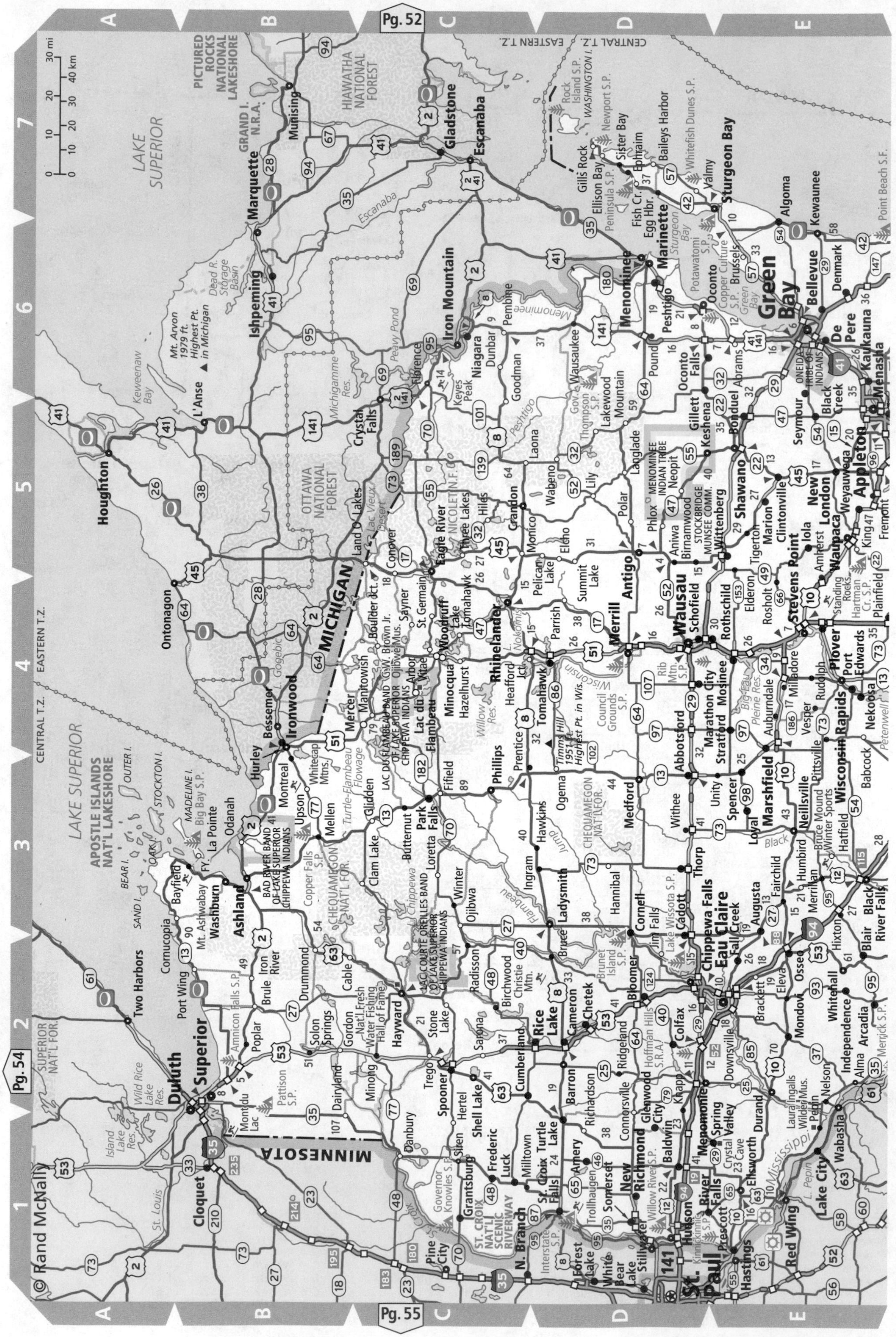

Pg. 52
Pg. 54
Pg. 55

NOTE: Maps are not always in alphabetical order.
See Page 1 for map location in this atlas.

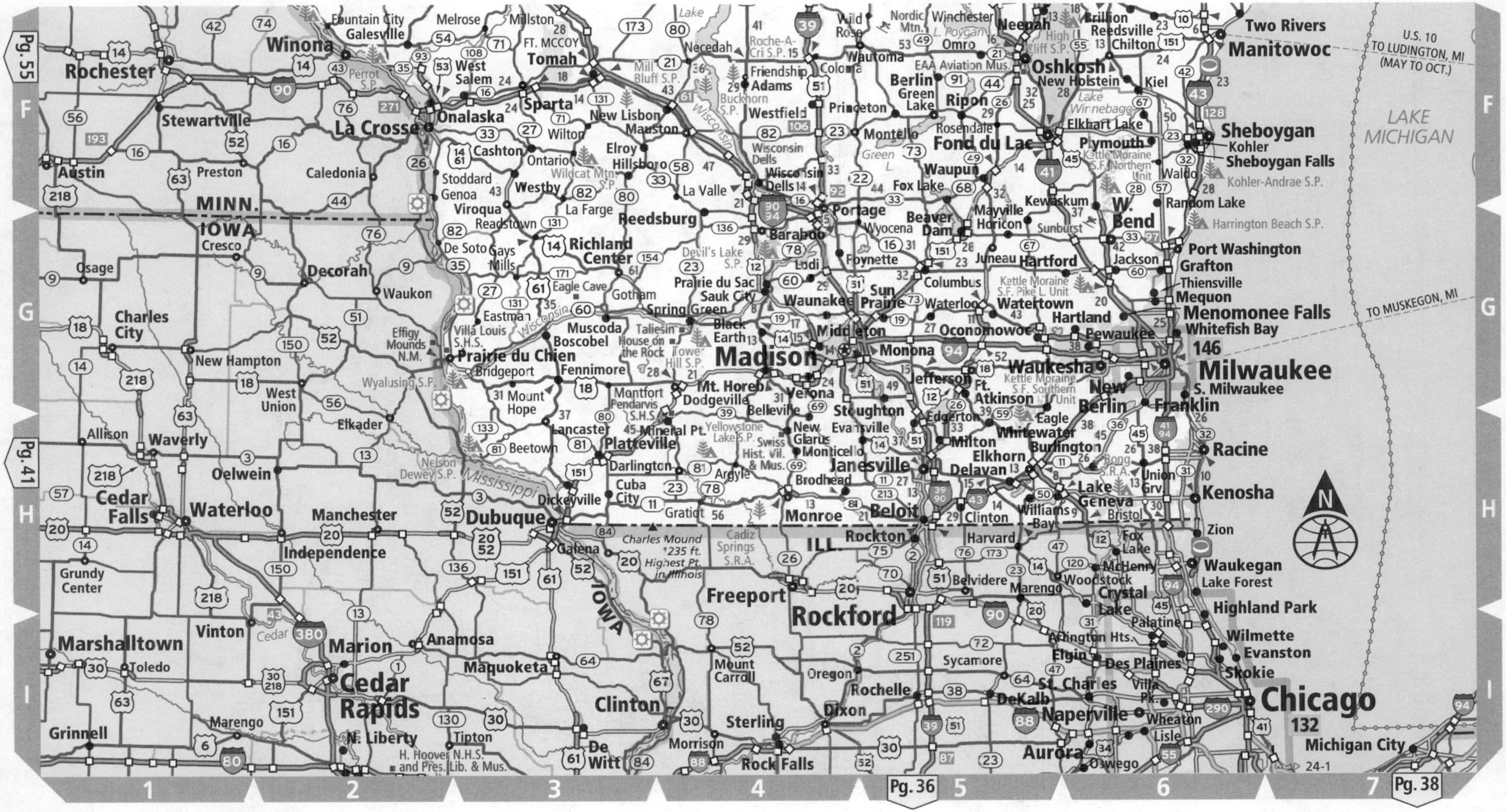

Pg. 55 · Pg. 41 · Pg. 36 · Pg. 38

Wisconsin

Cities and Towns

Antigo . . . D-5
Appleton . . . E-5
Arbor Vitae . . . C-4
Ashland . . . B-3
Baraboo . . . G-4
Barron . . . D-2
Beaver Dam . . . G-5
Bellevue . . . E-6
Beloit . . . H-5
Black River Falls . . . E-3
Bonduel . . . E-5
Chilton . . . F-6
Chippewa Falls . . . D-2
Darlington . . . H-4
De Pere . . . E-6
Dodgeville . . . G-4
Eau Claire . . . E-2
Elkhorn . . . H-5
Ellsworth . . . E-1
Fond du Lac . . . F-5
Fort Atkinson . . . G-5
Franklin . . . G-6
Grafton . . . G-6
Green Bay . . . E-6
Hartford . . . G-6
Hayward . . . C-2
Hudson . . . D-1
Janesville . . . H-5
Jefferson . . . G-5
Juneau . . . G-5
Kaukauna . . . E-6
Kenosha . . . H-6
Kewaunee . . . E-6
La Crosse . . . F-2
Ladysmith . . . D-3
Lancaster . . . H-3
Madison . . . G-4
Manitowoc . . . F-6
Marinette . . . D-6
Marshfield . . . E-4
Mauston . . . F-4
Medford . . . D-3
Menasha . . . E-5
Menomonee Falls . . . G-6
Menomonie . . . D-2
Mequon . . . G-6
Merrill . . . D-4
Middleton . . . G-4
Milwaukee . . . G-6
Monroe . . . H-4
Neenah . . . F-5
Neillsville . . . E-3
New Berlin . . . G-6
New Richmond . . . D-1
Oconomowoc . . . G-5
Oconto . . . D-6
Onalaska . . . F-2
Oshkosh . . . F-5
Peshtigo . . . D-6
Pewaukee . . . G-6
Plover . . . E-4
Port Washington . . . G-6
Portage . . . G-4
Prairie du Chien . . . G-2
Racine . . . H-6
Rhinelander . . . C-4
Rice Lake . . . D-2
Richland Center . . . G-3
River Falls . . . D-1
Rothschild . . . E-4
Sauk City . . . G-4
Shawano . . . E-5
Sheboygan . . . F-6
South Milwaukee . . . G-6
Sparta . . . F-3
Stevens Point . . . E-4
Stoughton . . . G-5
Sturgeon Bay . . . E-7
Sun Prairie . . . G-5
Superior . . . B-2
Thiensville . . . G-6
Two Rivers . . . F-6
Viroqua . . . F-3
Washburn . . . B-3
Watertown . . . G-5
Waukesha . . . G-6
Waupaca . . . E-5
Waupun . . . F-5
Wausau . . . D-4
Wautoma . . . F-5
West Bend . . . G-6
Whitefish Bay . . . G-6
Whitewater . . . H-5
Wisconsin Dells . . . F-4
Wisconsin Rapids . . . E-4

Travel planning & on-the-road resources

Tourism Information
Wisconsin Department of Tourism:
(800) 432-8747, (608) 266-2161
www.travelwisconsin.com

Road Conditions & Construction
511
(866) 511-9472
511wi.gov

Wyoming

Cities and Towns

City	Grid
Afton	D-1
Albin	F-9
Alpine	C-1
Baggs	G-5
Bairoil	E-5
Bar Nunn	D-6
Basin	B-4
Beulah	A-9
Big Horn	A-6
Big Piney	D-2
Bondurant	C-2
Buffalo	B-6
Burlington	B-4
Burns	F-9
Carpenter	G-9
Casper	D-6
Centennial	F-7
Cheyenne	F-8
Chugwater	F-8
Clearmont	A-6
Cody	A-3
Cokeville	E-1
Daniel	D-2
Dayton	A-5
Deaver	A-4
Diamondville	F-2
Douglas	D-7
Dubois	C-3
Eden	E-3
Edgerton	C-6
Elk Mountain	F-6
Evanston	F-1
Evansville	D-6
Farson	E-3
Fort Bridger	F-2
Fort Laramie	E-8
Fort Washakie	D-4
Freedom	D-1
Garland	A-4
Gillette	B-7
Glendo	D-8
Granger	F-2
Green River	F-3
Greybull	B-4
Guernsey	E-8
Hanna	E-6
Horse Creek	F-8
Hudson	D-4
Hulett	A-8
Jackson	C-1
Jeffrey City	D-5
Kaycee	C-6
Kemmerer	E-2
Kinnear	D-4
La Barge	E-2
LaGrange	F-9
Lander	D-4
Laramie	F-7
Linch	C-6
Lingle	E-9
Lovell	A-4
Lucerne	C-4
Lusk	D-8
Lyman	F-2
Manderson	B-5
Manville	D-8
Marbleton	D-2
McFadden	F-7
Medicine Bow	E-6
Meeteetse	B-4
Midwest	C-6
Moorcroft	B-8
Moose	C-2
Mountain View	F-2
Newcastle	B-9
Opal	F-2
Osage	B-8
Pavillion	C-4
Pine Bluffs	F-9
Pinedale	D-2
Powell	A-4
Ranchester	A-5
Rawlins	F-5
Riverton	D-4
Rock River	F-7
Rock Springs	F-3
Saratoga	F-6
Sheridan	A-6
Shoshoni	C-4
Sinclair	F-5
Smoot	D-1
Sundance	B-8
Superior	F-3
Ten Sleep	B-5
Teton Village	C-1
Thayne	D-1
Thermopolis	C-4
Torrington	E-9
Upton	B-8
Wamsutter	F-5
Wheatland	E-8
Worland	B-5
Wright	C-7

Wyoming state facts

Nickname: The Equality State

Capital: Cheyenne, F-8

Population: 576,851 (rank: 50th)

Largest city: Cheyenne, 65,132, F-8

Land area: 97,063 sq. mi. (rank: 9th)

Highest point: Gannett Peak, 13,804 ft., C-3

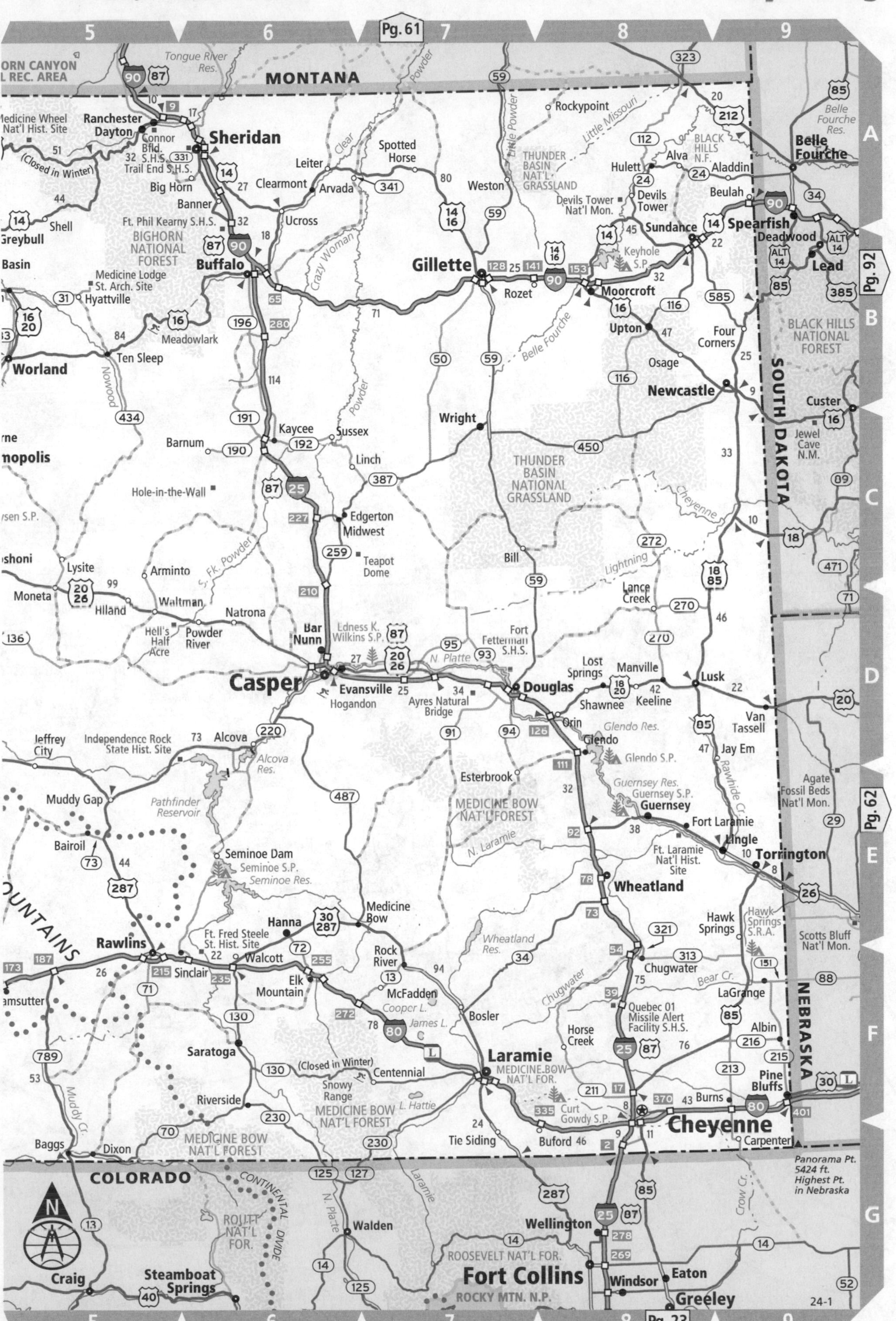

Road Conditions & Construction
511
(888) 996-7623
www.wyoroad.info

Tourism Information
Wyoming Office of Tourism:
(800) 225-5996, (307) 777-7777
travelwyoming.com

Travel planning & on-the-road resources

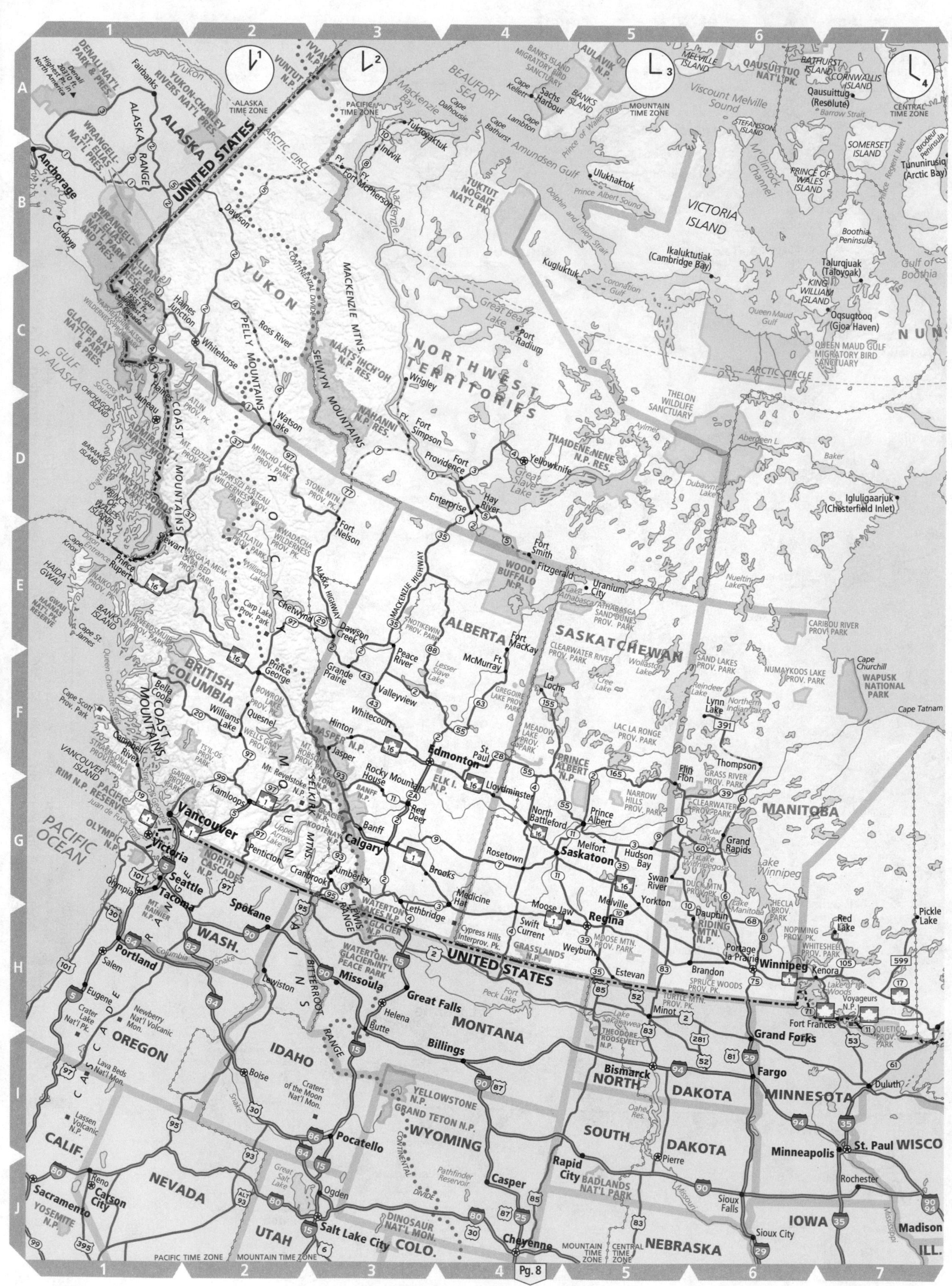
ALASKA
UNITED STATES
YUKON
NORTHWEST TERRITORIES
BRITISH COLUMBIA
ALBERTA
SASKATCHEWAN
MANITOBA
VICTORIA ISLAND
PACIFIC OCEAN
GULF OF ALASKA
BEAUFORT SEA
WASH.
OREGON
IDAHO
MONTANA
WYOMING
NEVADA
UTAH
COLO.
CALIF.
NORTH DAKOTA
SOUTH DAKOTA
NEBRASKA
MINNESOTA
IOWA
Vancouver
Victoria
Seattle
Calgary
Edmonton
Saskatoon
Regina
Winnipeg
Whitehorse
Yellowknife
Anchorage
Fairbanks
Juneau
Spokane
Portland
Boise
Salt Lake City
Missoula
Great Falls
Billings
Bismarck
Fargo
Minneapolis
St. Paul
Pierre
Cheyenne
ALASKA TIME ZONE
PACIFIC TIME ZONE
MOUNTAIN TIME ZONE
CENTRAL TIME ZONE
PACIFIC TIME ZONE
MOUNTAIN TIME ZONE
CENTRAL TIME ZONE
Pg. 8

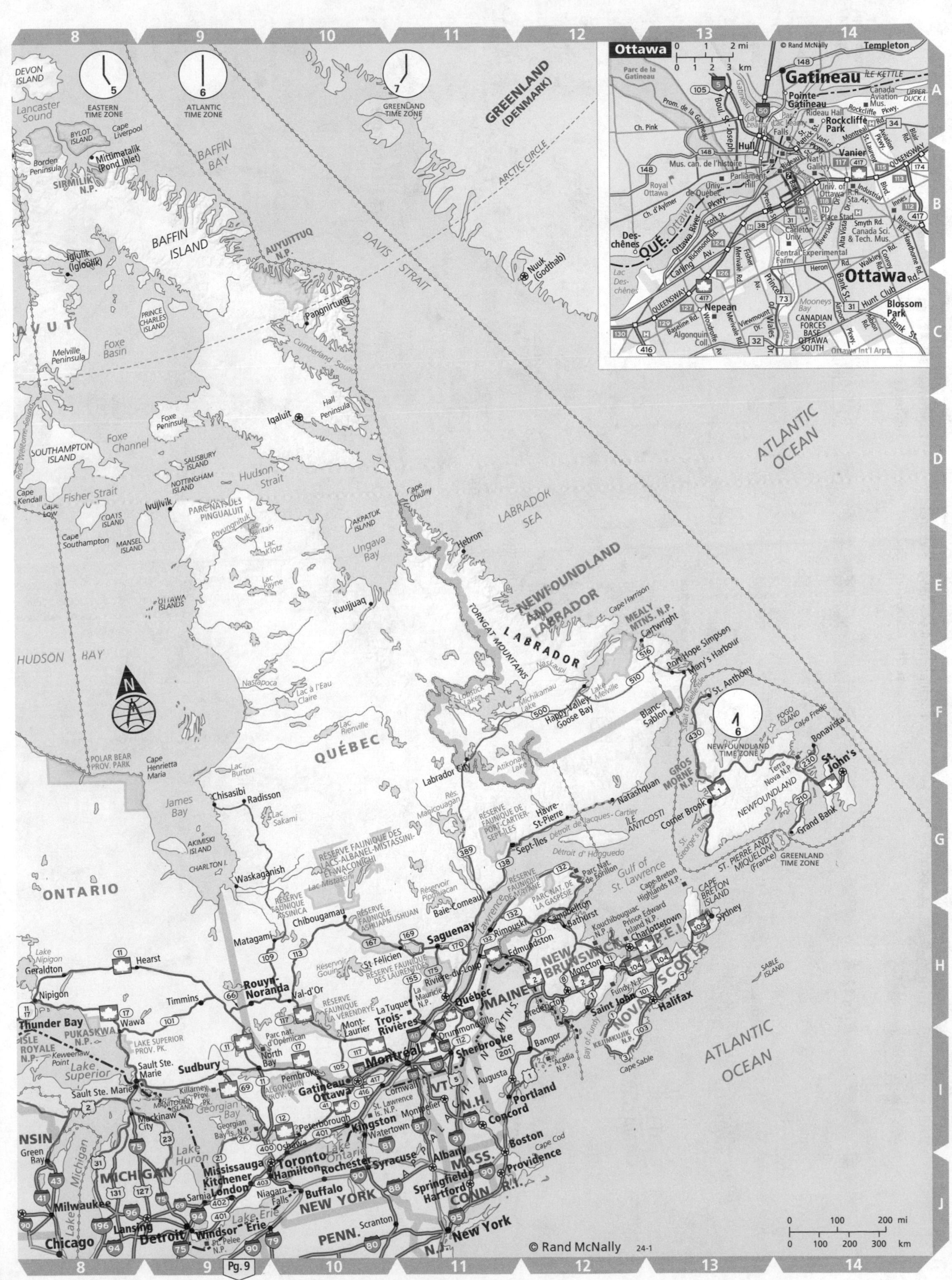
Ottawa
Gatineau
Ottawa
EASTERN TIME ZONE
ATLANTIC TIME ZONE
GREENLAND TIME ZONE
NEWFOUNDLAND TIME ZONE
GREENLAND (DENMARK)
BAFFIN ISLAND
BAFFIN BAY
DAVIS STRAIT
ARCTIC CIRCLE
LABRADOR SEA
ATLANTIC OCEAN
HUDSON BAY
QUÉBEC
ONTARIO
NEWFOUNDLAND AND LABRADOR
LABRADOR
NEWFOUNDLAND
NEW BRUNSWICK
NOVA SCOTIA
P.E.I.
MAINE
NEW YORK
Iqaluit
Nuuk (Godthab)
Montréal
Québec
Toronto
Halifax
St. John's
Detroit
Chicago
Boston
New York
© Rand McNally
24-1
Pg. 9

British Columbia provincial facts

Capital: Victoria, I-6

Population: 4,648,055 (rank: 3rd)

Largest city: Vancouver, 662,248, H-6

Land area: 355,477 sq. mi. (rank: 4th)

Highest point: Mt. Fairweather, 15,300 ft.

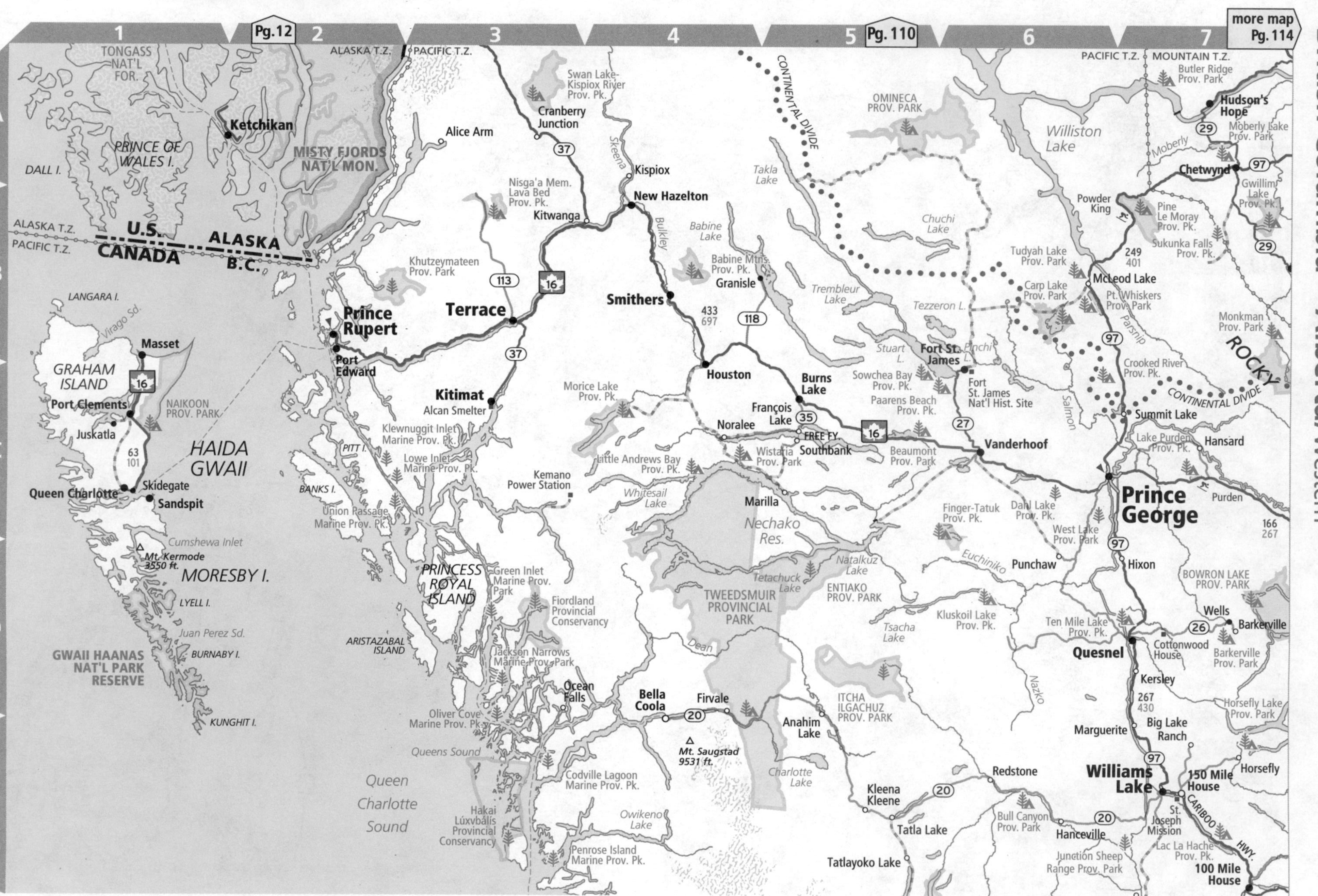

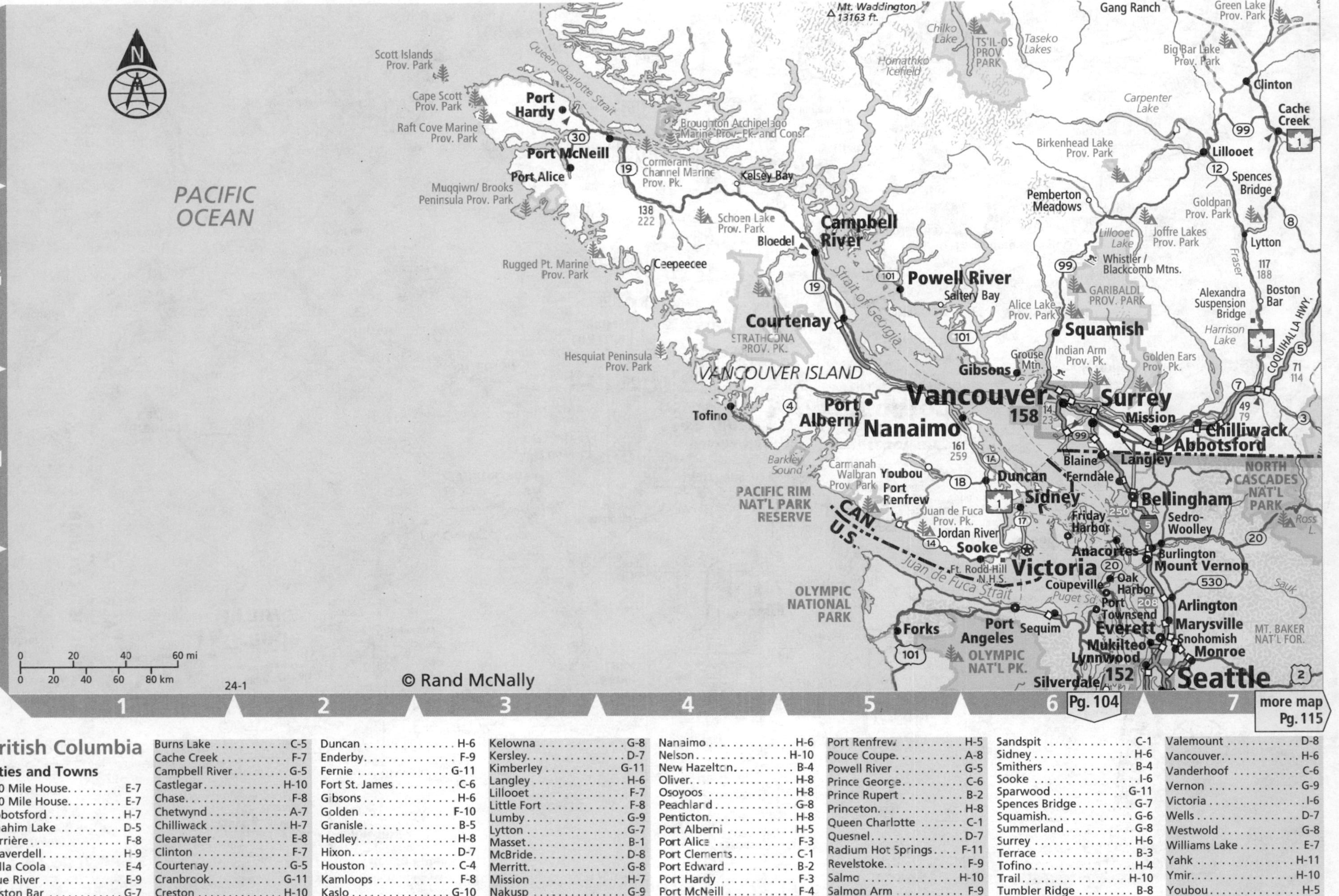

British Columbia

Cities and Towns

100 Mile House . . . E-7
150 Mile House . . . E-7
Abbotsford . . . H-7
Anahim Lake . . . D-5
Barrière . . . F-8
Beaverdell . . . H-9
Bella Coola . . . E-4
Blue River . . . E-9
Boston Bar . . . G-7
Burns Lake . . . C-5
Cache Creek . . . F-7
Campbell River . . . G-5
Castlegar . . . H-10
Chase . . . F-8
Chetwynd . . . A-7
Chilliwack . . . H-7
Clearwater . . . E-8
Clinton . . . F-7
Courtenay . . . G-5
Cranbrook . . . G-11
Creston . . . H-10
Duncan . . . H-6
Enderby . . . F-9
Fernie . . . G-11
Fort St. James . . . C-6
Gibsons . . . H-6
Golden . . . F-10
Granisle . . . B-5
Hedley . . . H-8
Hixon . . . D-7
Houston . . . C-4
Kamloops . . . F-8
Kaslo . . . G-10
Kelowna . . . G-8
Kersley . . . D-7
Kimberley . . . G-11
Langley . . . H-6
Lillooet . . . F-7
Little Fort . . . F-8
Lumby . . . G-9
Lytton . . . G-7
Masset . . . B-1
McBride . . . D-8
Merritt . . . G-8
Mission . . . H-7
Nakusp . . . G-9
Nanaimo . . . H-6
Nelson . . . H-10
New Hazelton . . . B-4
Oliver . . . H-8
Osoyoos . . . H-8
Peachland . . . G-8
Penticton . . . H-8
Port Alberni . . . H-5
Port Alice . . . F-3
Port Clements . . . C-1
Port Edward . . . B-2
Port Hardy . . . F-3
Port McNeill . . . F-4
Port Renfrew . . . H-5
Pouce Coupe . . . A-8
Powell River . . . G-5
Prince George . . . C-6
Prince Rupert . . . B-2
Princeton . . . H-8
Queen Charlotte . . . C-1
Quesnel . . . D-7
Radium Hot Springs . . . F-11
Revelstoke . . . F-9
Salmo . . . H-10
Salmon Arm . . . F-9
Sandspit . . . C-1
Sidney . . . H-6
Smithers . . . B-4
Sooke . . . I-6
Sparwood . . . G-11
Spences Bridge . . . G-7
Squamish . . . G-6
Summerland . . . G-8
Surrey . . . H-6
Terrace . . . B-3
Tofino . . . H-4
Trail . . . H-10
Tumbler Ridge . . . B-8
Valemount . . . D-8
Vancouver . . . H-6
Vanderhoof . . . C-6
Vernon . . . G-9
Victoria . . . I-6
Wells . . . D-7
Westwold . . . G-8
Williams Lake . . . E-7
Yahk . . . H-11
Ymir . . . H-10
Youbou . . . H-5

Travel planning & on-the-road resources

Tourism Information	Destination British Columbia: www.hellobc.com	**Road Conditions & Construction**	(800) 550-4997 www.drivebc.ca www2.gov.bc.ca/gov/content/transportation

Alberta provincial facts

Capital: Edmonton, C-12

Population: 4,067,175 (rank: 4th)

Largest city: Calgary, 1,306,784, F-12

Land area: 245,042 sq. mi. (rank: 6th)

Highest point: Mount Columbia, 12,294 ft., E-10

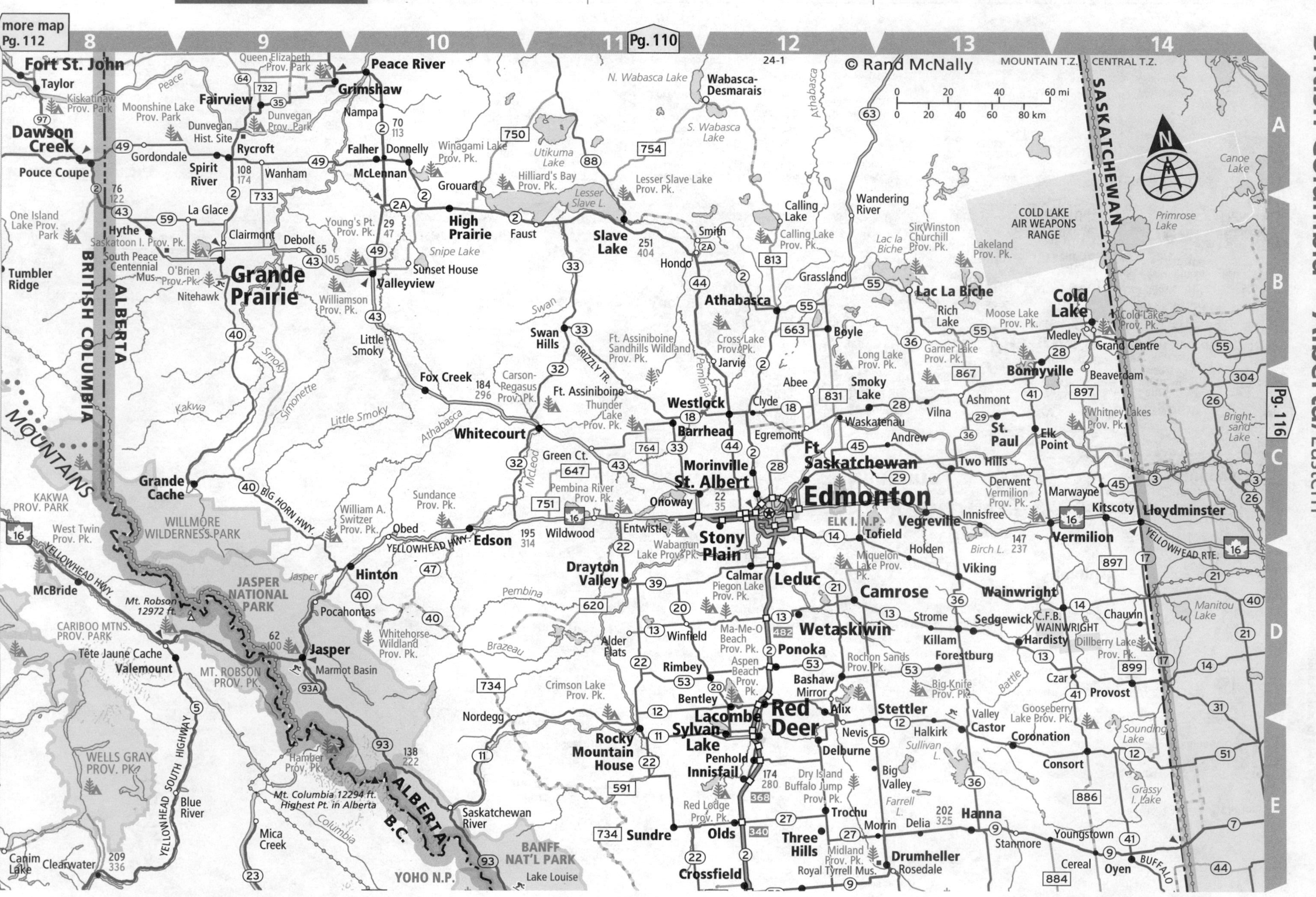

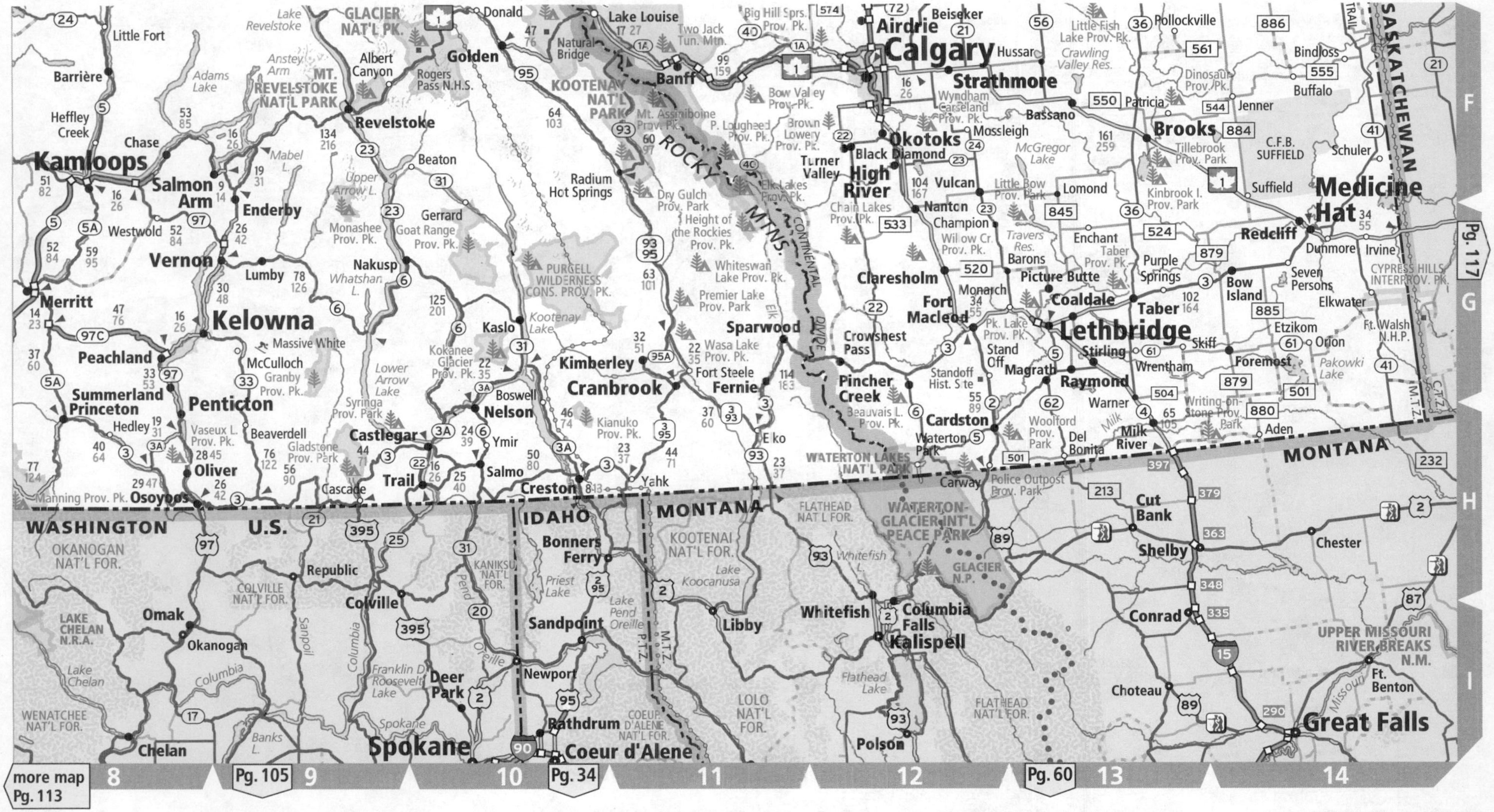

Pg. 117
more map Pg. 113
Pg. 105
Pg. 34
Pg. 60

Alberta

Cities and Towns

City	Grid
Airdrie	F-12
Alix	D-12
Athabasca	B-12
Banff	F-11
Barrhead	C-11
Bassano	F-13
Beiseker	E-12
Bentley	D-12
Black Diamond	F-12
Bonnyville	B-13
Bow Island	G-14
Boyle	B-12
Brooks	F-13
Calgary	F-12
Calmar	D-12
Camrose	D-12
Cardston	H-12
Castor	E-13
Claresholm	G-12
Coaldale	G-13
Cold Lake	B-14
Coronation	E-13
Crossfield	E-12
Crowsnest Pass	G-12
Drayton Valley	D-11
Drumheller	E-13
Dunmore	G-14
Edmonton	C-12
Edson	C-10
Elk Point	C-13
Falher	A-10
Forestburg	D-13
Fort Macleod	G-12
Fort Saskatchewan	C-12
Fox Creek	C-10
Grande Cache	C-9
Grande Prairie	B-9
Hanna	E-13
High Prairie	B-10
High River	F-12
Hinton	D-10
Hythe	B-8
Innisfail	E-12
Jasper	D-9
Killam	D-13
Lac La Biche	B-13
Lacombe	D-12
Leduc	D-12
Lethbridge	G-13
Lloydminster	C-14
Magrath	G-13
McLennan	A-10
Medicine Hat	G-14
Morinville	C-12
Nanton	G-12
Okotoks	F-12
Olds	E-12
Onoway	C-12
Oyen	E-14
Penhold	E-12
Picture Butte	G-13
Pincher Creek	G-12
Ponoka	D-12
Provost	D-14
Raymond	G-13
Red Deer	E-12
Redcliff	G-14
Rimbey	D-12
Rocky Mountain House	E-11
St. Albert	C-12
St. Paul	C-13
Sedgewick	D-13
Slave Lake	B-11
Smoky Lake	C-12
Stettler	E-13
Stirling	G-13
Stony Plain	C-12
Sundre	E-11
Swan Hills	B-11
Sylvan Lake	E-12
Taber	G-13
Three Hills	E-12
Tofield	C-12
Trochu	E-12
Turner Valley	F-12
Two Hills	C-13
Valleyview	B-10
Vegreville	C-13
Vermilion	C-14
Viking	D-13
Vulcan	F-12
Wainwright	D-14
Westlock	C-12
Wetaskiwin	D-12
Whitecourt	C-11

Travel planning & on-the-road resources

Tourism Information
Travel Alberta:
(403) 648-1000
www.travelalberta.com/us

Road Conditions & Construction
511
(855) 391-9743
511.alberta.ca

Saskatchewan provincial facts

Capital: Regina, H-5

Population: 1,098,352 (rank: 6th)

Largest city: Saskatoon, 266,141, F-4

Land area: 222,803 sq. mi. (rank: 7th)

Highest point: Cypress Hills, 4,817 ft., I-1

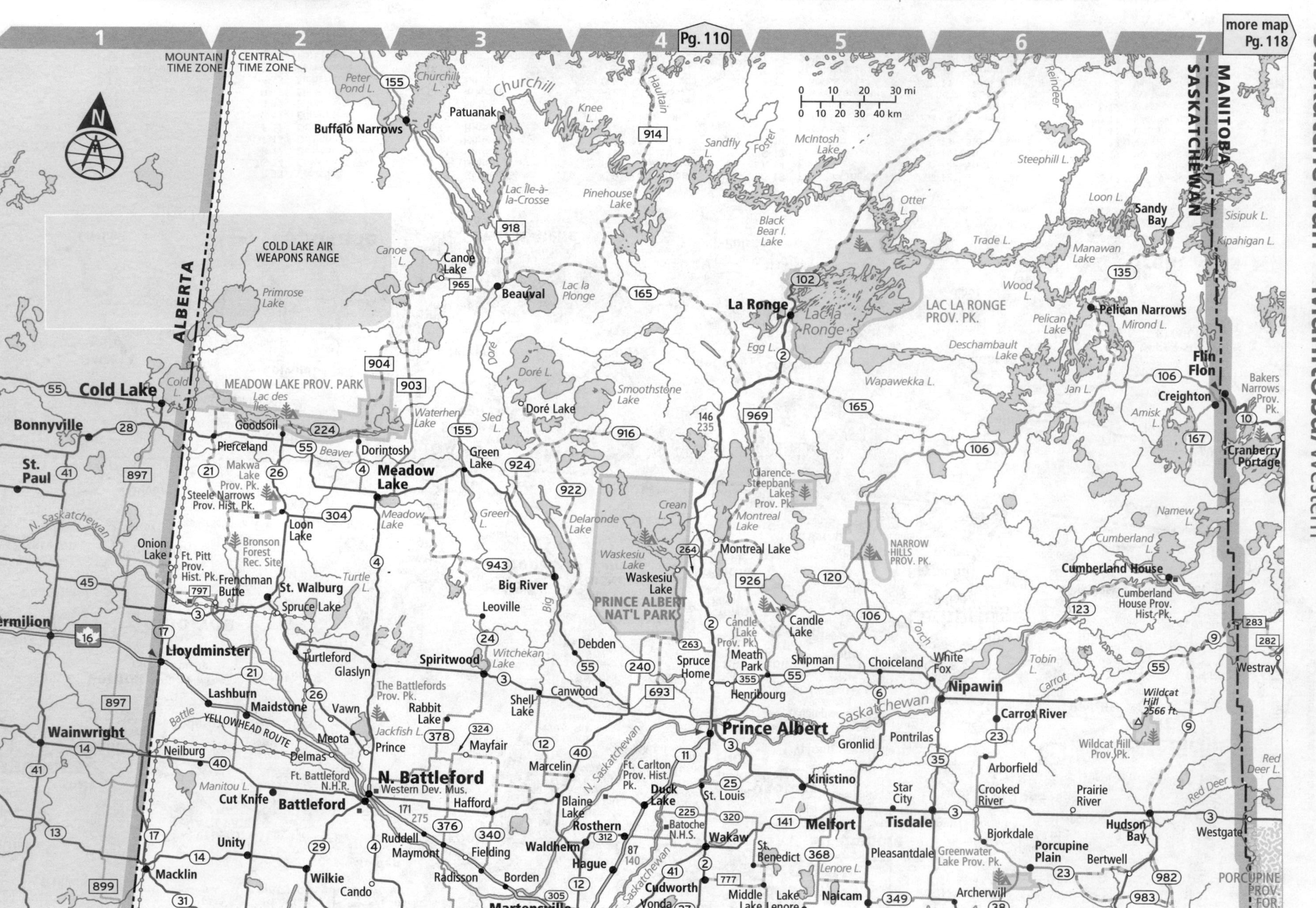

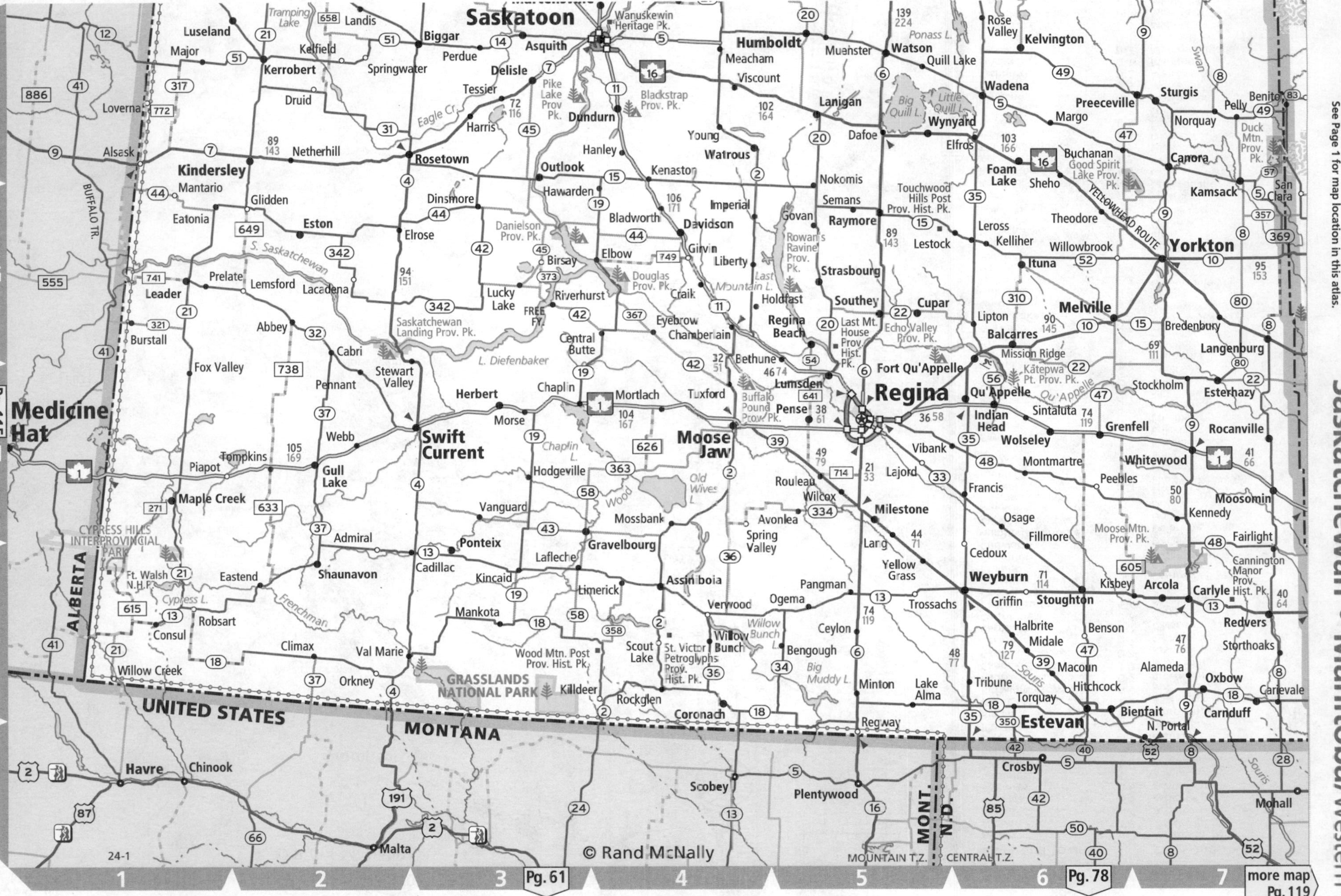

Travel planning & on-the-road resources

Tourism Information Tourism Saskatchewan: (877) 237-2273, (306) 787-9600 www.tourismsaskatchewan.com

Road Conditions & Construction (888) 335-7623, Saskatoon area: (306) 933-8333 Regina area: (306) 787-7623 www.saskatchewan.ca/residents/transportation/highways/highway-hotline

Capital: Winnipeg, H-11 | **Population:** 1,278,365 (rank: 5th) | **Largest city:** Winnipeg, 749,607, H-11 | **Land area:** 208,614 sq. mi. (rank: 8th) | **Highest point:** Baldy Mountain, 2,730 ft., G-8

Manitoba provincial facts

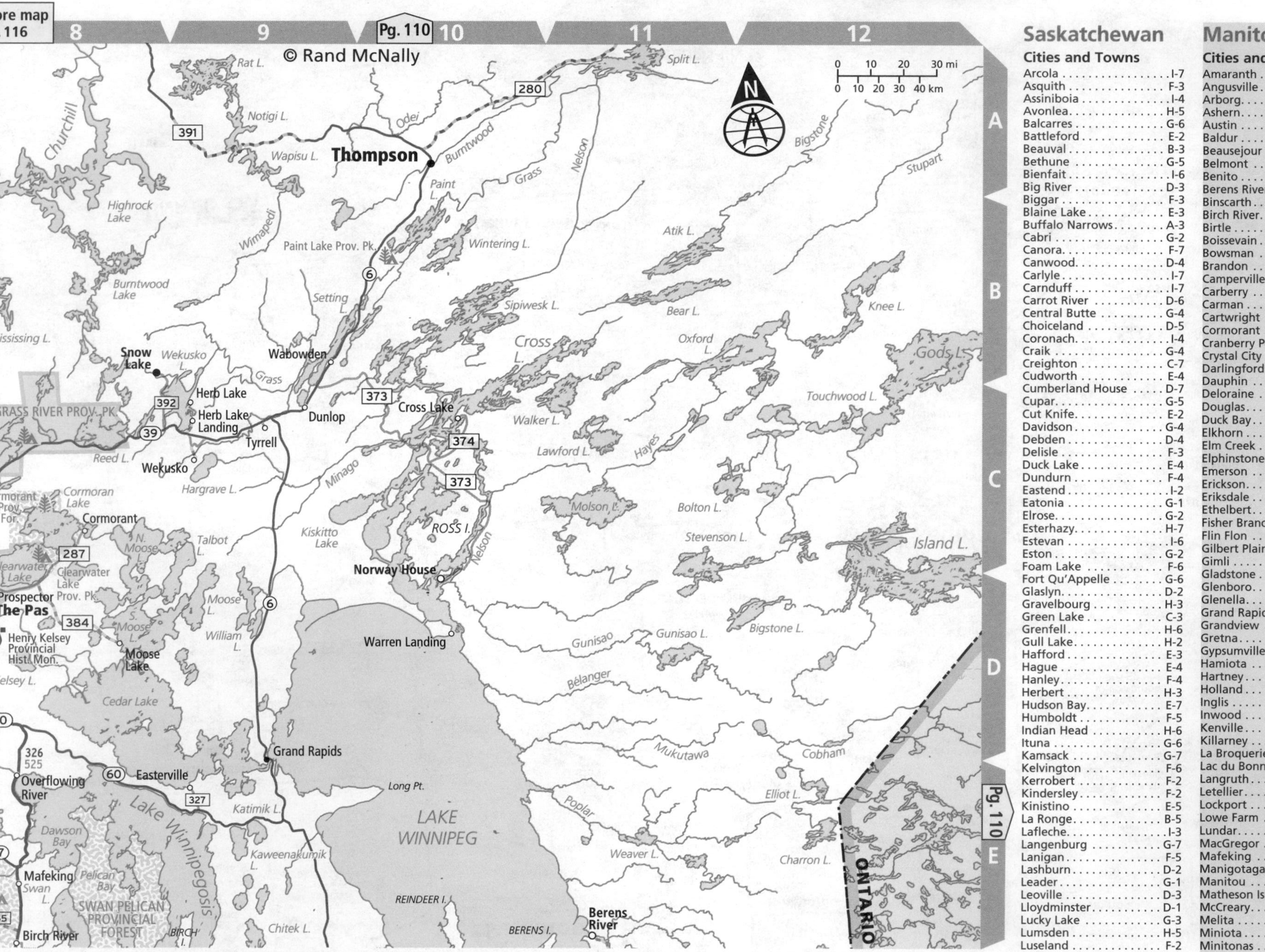

Saskatchewan

Cities and Towns

Arcola . . . I-7
Asquith . . . F-3
Assiniboia . . . I-4
Avonlea . . . H-5
Balcarres . . . G-6
Battleford . . . E-2
Beauval . . . B-3
Bethune . . . G-5
Bienfait . . . I-6
Big River . . . D-3
Biggar . . . F-3
Blaine Lake . . . E-3
Buffalo Narrows . . . A-3
Cabri . . . G-2
Canora . . . F-7
Canwood . . . D-4
Carlyle . . . I-7
Carnduff . . . I-7
Carrot River . . . D-6
Central Butte . . . G-4
Choiceland . . . D-5
Coronach . . . I-4
Craik . . . G-4
Creighton . . . C-7
Cudworth . . . E-4
Cumberland House . . . D-7
Cupar . . . G-5
Cut Knife . . . E-2
Davidson . . . G-4
Debden . . . D-4
Delisle . . . F-3
Duck Lake . . . E-4
Dundurn . . . F-4
Eastend . . . I-2
Eatonia . . . G-1
Elrose . . . G-2
Esterhazy . . . H-7
Estevan . . . I-6
Eston . . . G-2
Foam Lake . . . F-6
Fort Qu'Appelle . . . G-6
Glaslyn . . . D-2
Gravelbourg . . . H-3
Green Lake . . . C-3
Grenfell . . . H-6
Gull Lake . . . H-2
Hafford . . . E-3
Hague . . . E-4
Hanley . . . F-4
Herbert . . . H-3
Hudson Bay . . . E-7
Humboldt . . . F-5
Indian Head . . . H-6
Ituna . . . G-6
Kamsack . . . G-7
Kelvington . . . F-6
Kerrobert . . . F-2
Kindersley . . . F-2
Kinistino . . . E-5
La Ronge . . . B-5
Lafleche . . . I-3
Langenburg . . . G-7
Lanigan . . . F-5
Lashburn . . . D-2
Leader . . . G-1
Leoville . . . D-3
Lloydminster . . . D-1
Lucky Lake . . . G-3
Lumsden . . . H-5
Luseland . . . F-2

Manitoba

Cities and Towns

Amaranth . . . H-10
Angusville . . . H-8
Arborg . . . G-11
Ashern . . . G-10
Austin . . . H-9
Baldur . . . I-9
Beausejour . . . H-11
Belmont . . . I-9
Benito . . . F-7
Berens River . . . E-11
Binscarth . . . H-8
Birch River . . . E-8
Birtle . . . H-8
Boissevain . . . I-9
Bowsman . . . F-8
Brandon . . . I-9
Camperville . . . F-8
Carberry . . . I-9
Carman . . . I-10
Cartwright . . . I-9
Cormorant . . . C-8
Cranberry Portage . . . C-7
Crystal City . . . I-9
Darlingford . . . I-10
Dauphin . . . G-9
Deloraine . . . I-8
Douglas . . . H-9
Duck Bay . . . F-8
Elkhorn . . . H-8
Elm Creek . . . I-10
Elphinstone . . . H-8
Emerson . . . I-11
Erickson . . . H-9
Eriksdale . . . G-10
Ethelbert . . . G-8
Fisher Branch . . . G-10
Flin Flon . . . C-7
Gilbert Plains . . . G-8
Gimli . . . G-11
Gladstone . . . H-9
Glenboro . . . I-9
Glenella . . . H-9
Grand Rapids . . . E-9
Grandview . . . G-8
Gretna . . . I-11
Gypsumville . . . F-10
Hamiota . . . H-8
Hartney . . . I-8
Holland . . . I-9
Inglis . . . G-8
Inwood . . . H-11
Kenville . . . F-8
Killarney . . . I-9
La Broquerie . . . I-11
Lac du Bonnet . . . H-12
Langruth . . . H-10
Letellier . . . I-11
Lockport . . . H-11
Lowe Farm . . . I-11
Lundar . . . G-10
MacGregor . . . H-10
Mafeking . . . E-8
Manigotagan . . . G-11
Manitou . . . I-10
Matheson Island . . . F-11
McCreary . . . G-9
Melita . . . I-8
Miniota . . . H-8
Minitonas . . . F-8

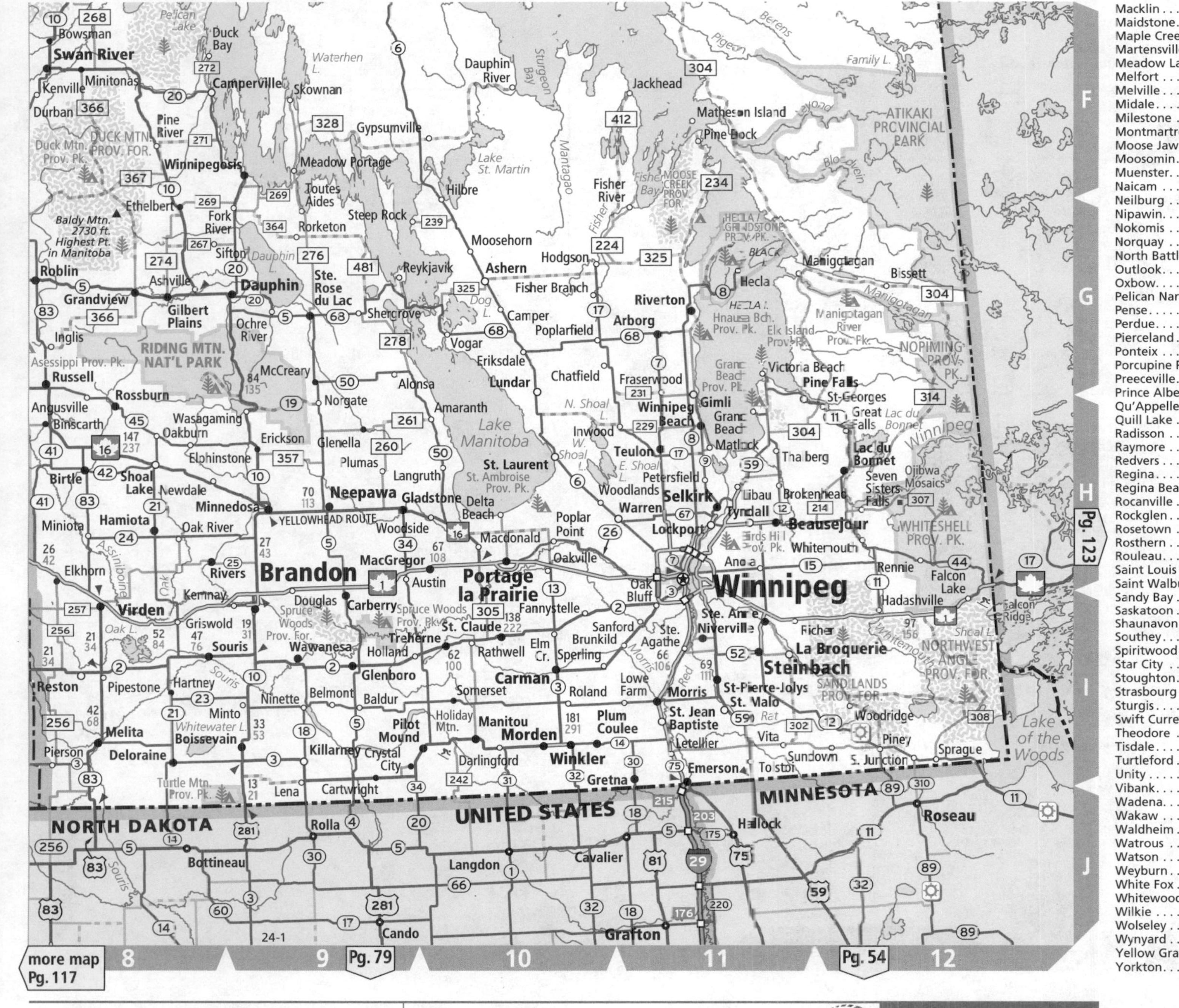

Macklin E-1
Maidstone D-2
Maple Creek H-1
Martensville F-4
Meadow Lake C-2
Melfort E-5
Melville G-6
Midale I-6
Milestone H-5
Montmartre H-6
Moose Jaw H-4
Moosomin H-7
Muenster F-5
Naicam E-5
Neilburg E-1
Nipawin D-6
Nokomis G-5
Norquay F-7
North Battleford E-2
Outlook F-3
Oxbow I-7
Pelican Narrows B-6
Pense H-5
Perdue F-3
Pierceland C-2
Ponteix I-3
Porcupine Plain E-6
Preeceville F-7
Prince Albert D-4
Qu'Appelle H-6
Quill Lake F-5
Radisson E-3
Raymore G-5
Redvers I-7
Regina H-5
Regina Beach G-5
Rocanville H-7
Rockglen I-4
Rosetown F-3
Rosthern E-4
Rouleau H-5
Saint Louis E-4
Saint Walburg D-2
Sandy Bay B-7
Saskatoon F-4
Shaunavon I-2
Southey G-5
Spiritwood D-3
Star City E-5
Stoughton I-6
Strasbourg G-5
Sturgis F-7
Swift Current H-3
Theodore G-6
Tisdale E-6
Turtleford D-2
Unity E-2
Vibank H-6
Wadena F-6
Wakaw E-4
Waldheim E-4
Watrous F-4
Watson F-5
Weyburn I-6
White Fox D-6
Whitewood H-7
Wilkie E-2
Wolseley H-6
Wynyard F-5
Yellow Grass I-5
Yorkton G-7
Minnedosa H-9
Moose Lake D-8
Moosehorn G-10
Morden I-10
Morris I-11
Neepawa H-9
Newdale H-8
Ninette I-9
Niverville I-11
Norway House D-10
Oak River H-8
Oakburn H-8
Oakville H-10
Ochre River G-9
Petersfield H-11
Pierson I-8
Pilot Mound I-10
Pine Falls H-11
Pine River F-8
Pipestone I-8
Plum Coulee I-10
Plumas H-9
Poplar Point H-10
Portage la Prairie H-10
Rathwell I-10
Rennie H-12
Reston I-8
Richer I-11
Rivers H-8
Riverton G-11
Roblin G-8
Roland I-10
Rorketon G-9
Rossburn H-8
Russell G-8
Saint Claude I-10
Saint Jean Baptiste I-11
Saint Laurent H-10
Saint Malo I-11
Saint-Georges H-12
Saint-Pierre-Jolys I-11
Sainte Agathe I-11
Sainte Anne I-11
Sainte Rose du Lac G-9
Sanford I-11
Selkirk H-11
Shoal Lake H-8
Sifton G-8
Snow Lake B-8
Somerset I-10
Souris I-8
Sprague I-12
Steinbach I-11
Swan River F-8
Teulon H-11
The Pas D-8
Thompson A-10
Treherne I-10
Tyndall H-11
Victoria Beach G-11
Virden I-8
Vita I-11
Wabowden B-9
Warren H-11
Wawanesa I-9
Whitemouth H-12
Winkler I-10
Winnipeg H-11
Winnipeg Beach H-11
Winnipegosis F-9
Woodridge I-12

Tourism Information Travel Manitoba: (800) 665-0040, (204) 927-7800 www.travelmanitoba.com

Road Conditions & Construction 511 (877) 627-6237, (204) 945-3704 www.manitoba511.ca/en

511 Travel planning & on-the-road resources

Ontario provincial facts

Capital: Toronto, G-6

Population: 13,448,494 (rank: 1st)

Largest city: Toronto, 2,794,356, G-6

Land area: 344,561 sq. mi. (rank: 5th)

Highest point: Ishpatina Ridge, 2,275 ft., J-12

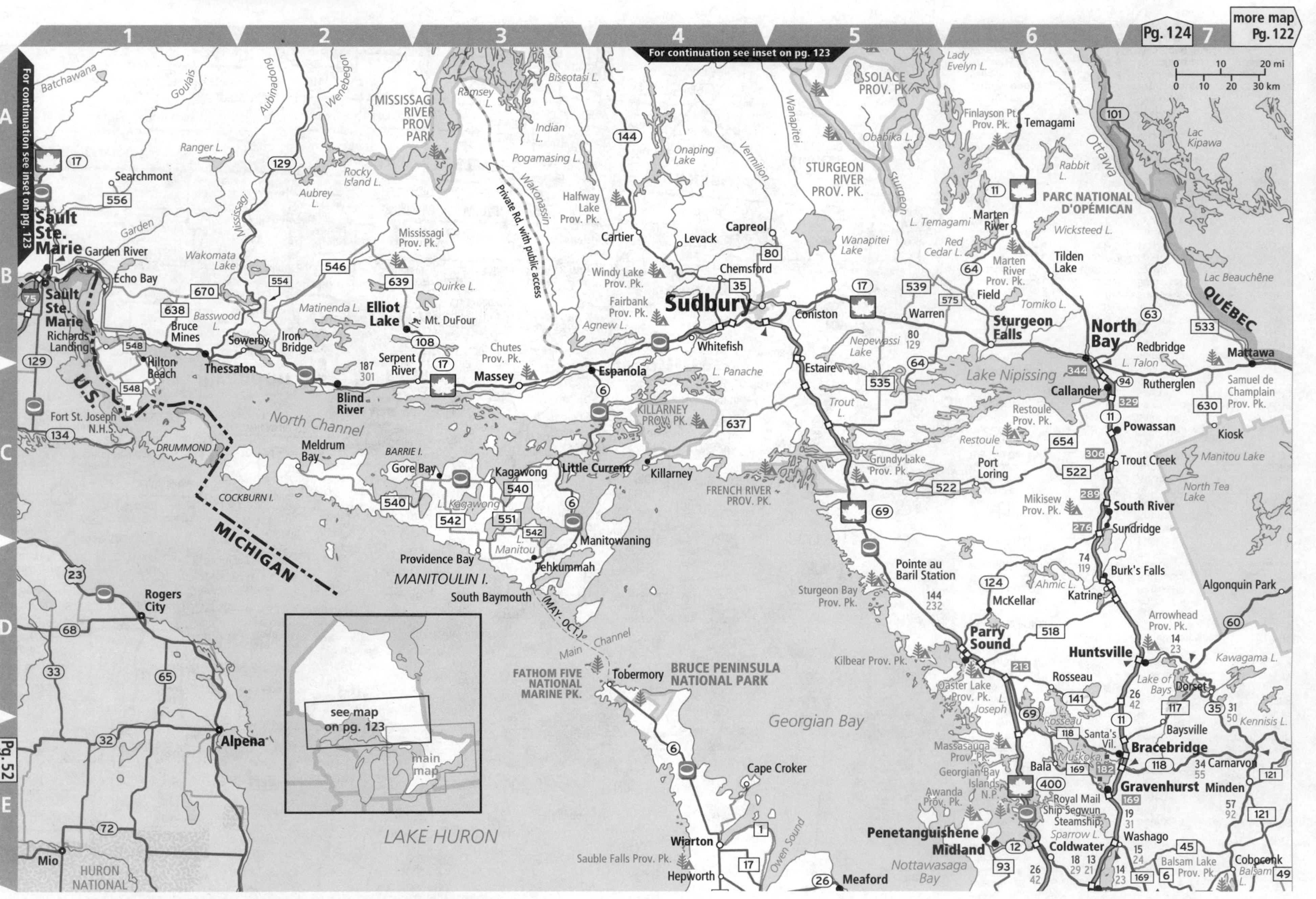

NOTE: Maps are not always in alphabetical order.
See Page 1 for map location in this atlas.

Capital: Toronto, G-6

Population: 13,448,494 (rank: 1st)
Largest city: Toronto, 2,794,356, G-6

Land area: 344,561 sq. mi. (rank: 5th)
Highest point: Ishpatina Ridge, 2,275 ft., J-12

Ontario provincial facts

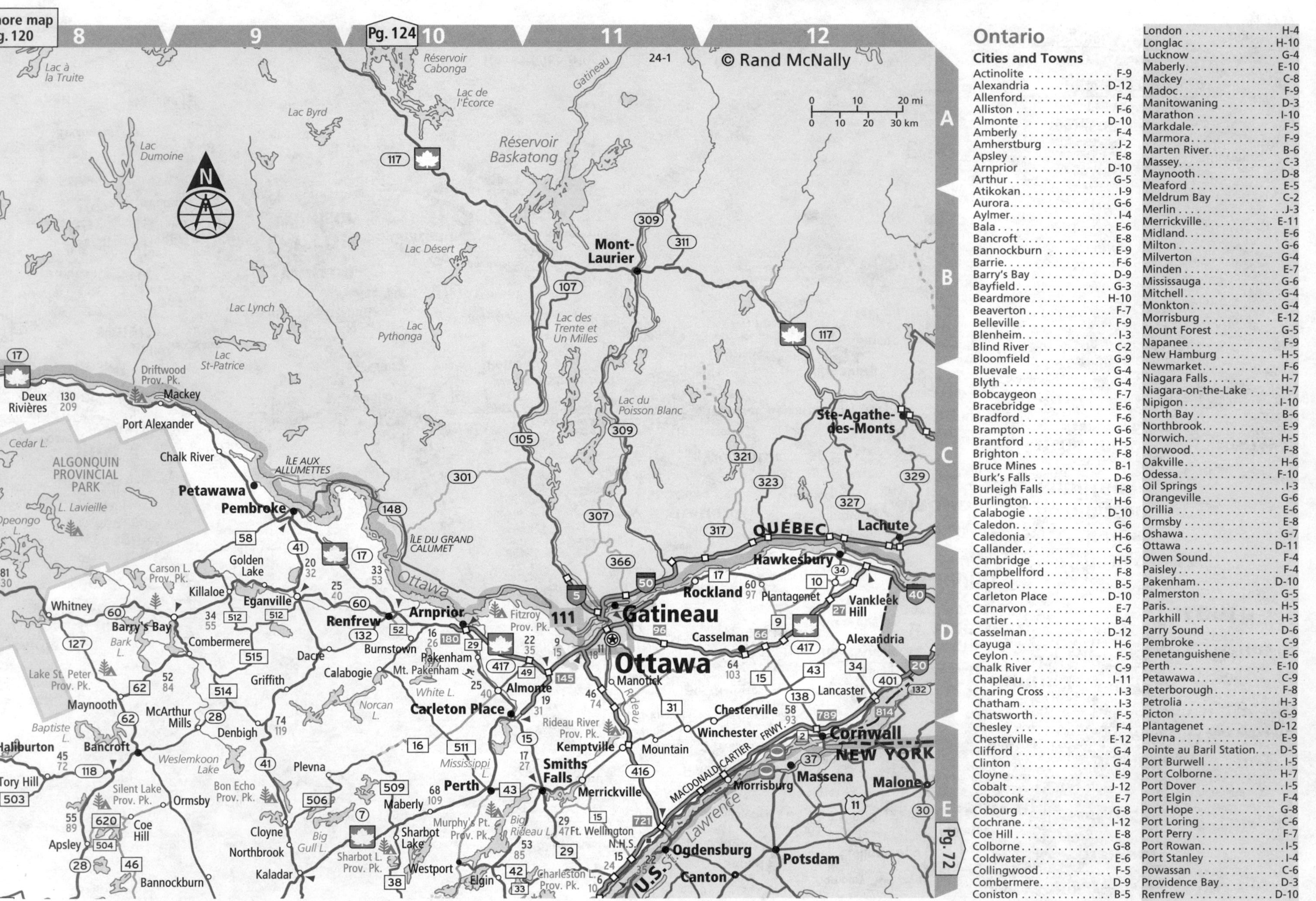

Ontario

Cities and Towns

Place	Grid
Actinolite	F-9
Alexandria	D-12
Allenford	F-4
Alliston	F-6
Almonte	D-10
Amberly	F-4
Amherstburg	J-2
Apsley	E-8
Arnprior	D-10
Arthur	G-5
Atikokan	I-9
Aurora	G-6
Aylmer	I-4
Bala	E-6
Bancroft	E-8
Bannockburn	E-9
Barrie	F-6
Barry's Bay	D-9
Bayfield	G-3
Beardmore	H-10
Beaverton	F-7
Belleville	F-9
Blenheim	I-3
Blind River	C-2
Bloomfield	G-9
Bluevale	G-4
Blyth	G-4
Bobcaygeon	F-7
Bracebridge	E-6
Bradford	F-6
Brampton	G-6
Brantford	H-5
Brighton	F-8
Bruce Mines	B-1
Burk's Falls	D-6
Burleigh Falls	F-8
Burlington	H-6
Calabogie	D-10
Caledon	G-6
Caledonia	H-6
Callander	C-6
Cambridge	H-5
Campbellford	F-8
Capreol	B-5
Carleton Place	D-10
Carnarvon	E-7
Cartier	B-4
Casselman	D-12
Cayuga	H-6
Ceylon	F-5
Chalk River	C-9
Chapleau	I-11
Charing Cross	I-3
Chatham	I-3
Chatsworth	F-5
Chesley	F-4
Chesterville	E-12
Clifford	G-4
Clinton	G-4
Cloyne	E-9
Cobalt	J-12
Coboconk	E-7
Cobourg	G-8
Cochrane	I-12
Coe Hill	E-8
Colborne	G-8
Coldwater	E-6
Collingwood	F-5
Combermere	D-9
Coniston	B-5
London	H-4
Longlac	H-10
Lucknow	G-4
Maberly	E-10
Mackey	C-8
Madoc	F-9
Manitowaning	D-3
Marathon	I-10
Markdale	F-5
Marmora	F-9
Marten River	B-6
Massey	C-3
Maynooth	D-8
Meaford	E-5
Meldrum Bay	C-2
Merlin	J-3
Merrickville	E-11
Midland	E-6
Milton	G-6
Milverton	G-4
Minden	E-7
Mississauga	G-6
Mitchell	G-4
Monkton	G-4
Morrisburg	E-12
Mount Forest	G-5
Napanee	F-9
New Hamburg	H-5
Newmarket	F-6
Niagara Falls	H-7
Niagara-on-the-Lake	H-7
Nipigon	I-10
North Bay	B-6
Northbrook	E-9
Norwich	H-5
Norwood	F-8
Oakville	H-6
Odessa	F-10
Oil Springs	I-3
Orangeville	G-6
Orillia	E-6
Ormsby	E-8
Oshawa	G-7
Ottawa	D-11
Owen Sound	F-4
Paisley	F-4
Pakenham	D-10
Palmerston	G-5
Paris	H-5
Parkhill	H-3
Parry Sound	D-6
Pembroke	C-9
Penetanguishene	E-6
Perth	E-10
Petawawa	C-9
Peterborough	F-8
Petrolia	H-3
Picton	G-9
Plantagenet	D-12
Plevna	E-9
Pointe au Baril Station	D-5
Port Burwell	I-5
Port Colborne	H-7
Port Dover	I-5
Port Elgin	F-4
Port Hope	G-8
Port Loring	C-6
Port Perry	F-7
Port Rowan	I-5
Port Stanley	I-4
Powassan	C-6
Providence Bay	D-3
Renfrew	D-10

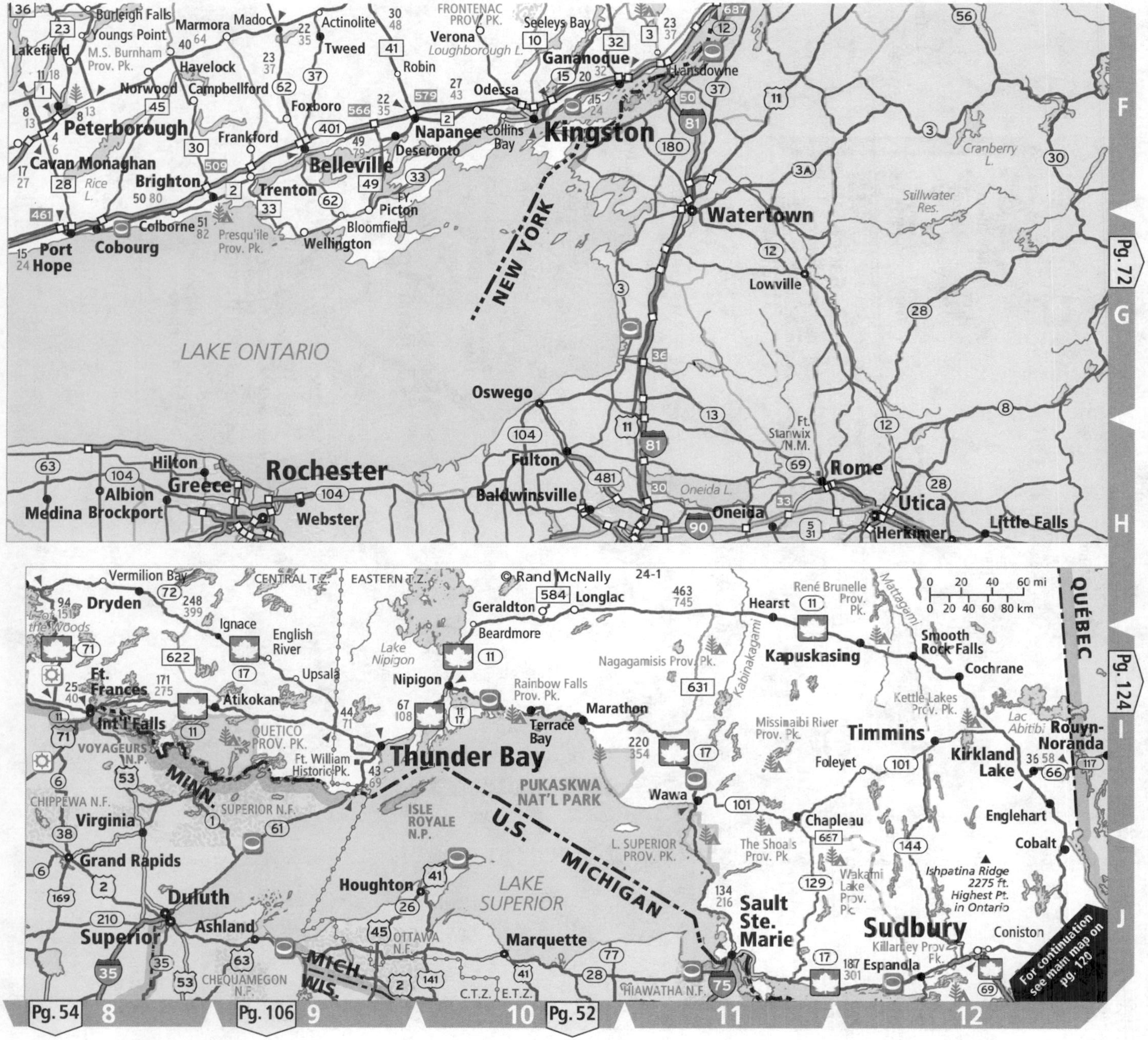

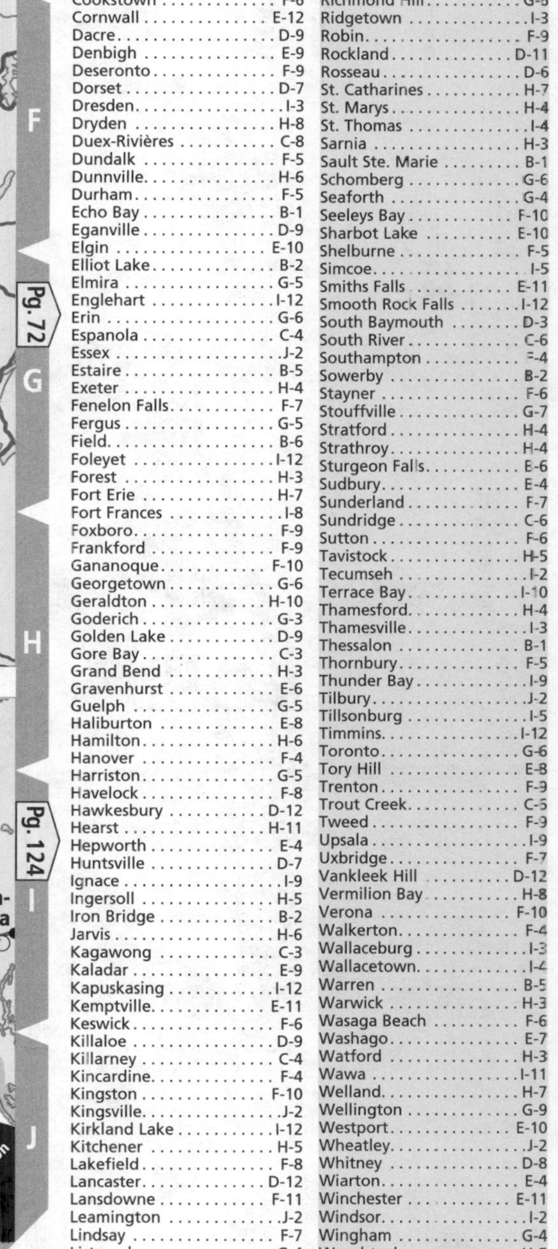

Cookstown . . . F-6
Cornwall . . . E-12
Dacre . . . D-9
Denbigh . . . E-9
Deseronto . . . F-9
Dorset . . . D-7
Dresden . . . I-3
Dryden . . . H-8
Duex-Rivières . . . C-8
Dundalk . . . F-5
Dunnville . . . H-6
Durham . . . F-5
Echo Bay . . . B-1
Eganville . . . D-9
Elgin . . . E-10
Elliot Lake . . . B-2
Elmira . . . G-5
Englehart . . . I-12
Erin . . . G-6
Espanola . . . C-4
Essex . . . J-2
Estaire . . . B-5
Exeter . . . H-4
Fenelon Falls . . . F-7
Fergus . . . G-5
Field . . . B-6
Foleyet . . . I-12
Forest . . . H-3
Fort Erie . . . H-7
Fort Frances . . . I-8
Foxboro . . . F-9
Frankford . . . F-9
Gananoque . . . F-10
Georgetown . . . G-6
Geraldton . . . H-10
Goderich . . . G-3
Golden Lake . . . D-9
Gore Bay . . . C-3
Grand Bend . . . H-3
Gravenhurst . . . E-6
Guelph . . . G-5
Haliburton . . . E-8
Hamilton . . . H-6
Hanover . . . F-4
Harriston . . . G-5
Havelock . . . F-8
Hawkesbury . . . D-12
Hearst . . . H-11
Hepworth . . . E-4
Huntsville . . . D-7
Ignace . . . I-9
Ingersoll . . . H-5
Iron Bridge . . . B-2
Jarvis . . . H-6
Kagawong . . . C-3
Kaladar . . . E-9
Kapuskasing . . . I-12
Kemptville . . . E-11
Keswick . . . F-6
Killaloe . . . D-9
Killarney . . . C-4
Kincardine . . . F-4
Kingston . . . F-10
Kingsville . . . J-2
Kirkland Lake . . . I-12
Kitchener . . . H-5
Lakefield . . . F-8
Lancaster . . . D-12
Lansdowne . . . F-11
Leamington . . . J-2
Lindsay . . . F-7
Listowel . . . G-4
Little Current . . . C-3
Richmond Hill . . . G-6
Ridgetown . . . I-3
Robin . . . F-9
Rockland . . . D-11
Rosseau . . . D-6
St. Catharines . . . H-7
St. Marys . . . H-4
St. Thomas . . . I-4
Sarnia . . . H-3
Sault Ste. Marie . . . B-1
Schomberg . . . G-6
Seaforth . . . G-4
Seeleys Bay . . . F-10
Sharbot Lake . . . E-10
Shelburne . . . F-5
Simcoe . . . I-5
Smiths Falls . . . E-11
Smooth Rock Falls . . . I-12
South Baymouth . . . D-3
South River . . . C-6
Southampton . . . F-4
Sowerby . . . B-2
Stayner . . . F-6
Stouffville . . . G-7
Stratford . . . H-4
Strathroy . . . H-4
Sturgeon Falls . . . E-6
Sudbury . . . E-4
Sunderland . . . F-7
Sundridge . . . C-6
Sutton . . . F-6
Tavistock . . . H-5
Tecumseh . . . I-2
Terrace Bay . . . I-10
Thamesford . . . H-4
Thamesville . . . I-3
Thessalon . . . B-1
Thornbury . . . F-5
Thunder Bay . . . I-9
Tilbury . . . J-2
Tillsonburg . . . I-5
Timmins . . . I-12
Toronto . . . G-6
Tory Hill . . . E-8
Trenton . . . F-9
Trout Creek . . . C-5
Tweed . . . F-9
Upsala . . . I-9
Uxbridge . . . F-7
Vankleek Hill . . . D-12
Vermilion Bay . . . H-8
Verona . . . F-10
Walkerton . . . F-4
Wallaceburg . . . I-3
Wallacetown . . . I-4
Warren . . . B-5
Warwick . . . H-3
Wasaga Beach . . . F-6
Washago . . . E-7
Watford . . . H-3
Wawa . . . I-11
Welland . . . H-7
Wellington . . . G-9
Westport . . . E-10
Wheatley . . . J-2
Whitney . . . D-8
Wiarton . . . E-4
Winchester . . . E-11
Windsor . . . I-2
Wingham . . . G-4
Woodstock . . . H-5
Youngs Point . . . F-8

For continuation see main map on pg. 120

Tourism Information Destination Ontario: (800) 668-2746 www.destinationontario.com/en-ca

Road Conditions & Construction 511, (866) 929-4257 511on.ca

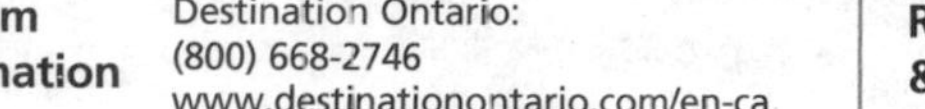

Québec

Cities and Towns

Acton Vale F-4
Alma B-5
Amos B-2
Baie-Comeau G-8
Baie-St-Paul. C-7
Beauceville E-6
Bécancour E-5
Berthierville E-4
Black Lake. F-6
Bromptonville. F-5
Cap-St-Ignace D-7
Chandler G-9
Chicoutimi. B-6
Châteauguay G-3
Coaticook G-5
Cowansville. G-4
Dégelis C-9
Delisle A-5
Dolbeau-Mistassini A-5
Donnacona E-5
Drummondville. F-4
Forestville A-8
Gaspé G-9
Gatineau. F-1
Granby F-4
Grand-Mère E-4
Havre-St-Pierre F-9
Joliette E-3
Jonquière B-6
La Malbaie C-7
La Pocatière C-7
La Sarre A-2
La Tuque C-4
Lac-Mégantic F-6
Lachute F-2
Laval F-3
Lebel-sur-Quévillon A-3
Lévis. D-6
Longueuil F-3
Louiseville E-4
Magog. G-5
Malartic. B-2
Maniwaki C-3
Matane G-8
Mont-Joli. B-9
Mont-Laurier E-1
Mont-Tremblant. E-2
Montmagny D-7
Montréal F-3
Napierville G-3
Nicolet. E-4
Plessisville E-5
Pohénégamook C-8
Port-Cartier. F-8
Princeville E-5
Québec D-6
Repentigny F-3
Richmond F-5
Rimouski B-9
Rivière-du-Loup C-8
Roberval B-5
Rouyn-Noranda B-2
Saguenay B-6
St-Alexis-des-Monts E-4
St-Eustache F-3
St-Félicien A-5
St-Georges E-6
St-Henri. D-6
St-Hyacinthe F-4
St-Jacques F-3
St-Jean-Port-Joli D-7
St-Jean-sur-Richelieu G-4
St-Jérôme F-3
St-Joseph-de-Beauce E-6
St-Nicéphore. F-5
St-Pamphile. D-7
St-Raymond D-5
St-Sauveur. F-3
Ste-Agathe-des-Monts E-2
Ste-Anne-de-Beaupré. D-6
Ste-Anne-des-Monts. G-8
Ste-Claire. E-6
Ste-Julie. E-5
Ste-Marie E-6
Salaberry-de-Valleyfield. . . G-3
Senneterre B-3
Sept-Îles. F-8
Shawinigan. E-4
Sherbrooke G-5
Sorel-Tracy E-4
Témiscaming. C-2
Thetford Mines. E-6
Trois-Pistoles B-8
Trois-Rivières. E-4
Val-des-Sources. F-5
Val-d'Or. B-2
Varennes. F-3
Vaudreuil-Dorion F-3
Victoriaville. E-5
Warwick F-5
Waterloo. G-4
Windsor. F-5

Québec provincial facts

Capital: Québec, D-6

Population: 8,164,361 (rank: 2nd)

Largest city: Montréal, 1,762,949, F-3

Land area: 501,390 sq. mi. (rank: 2nd)

Highest point: Mont d'Iberville, 5,420 ft.

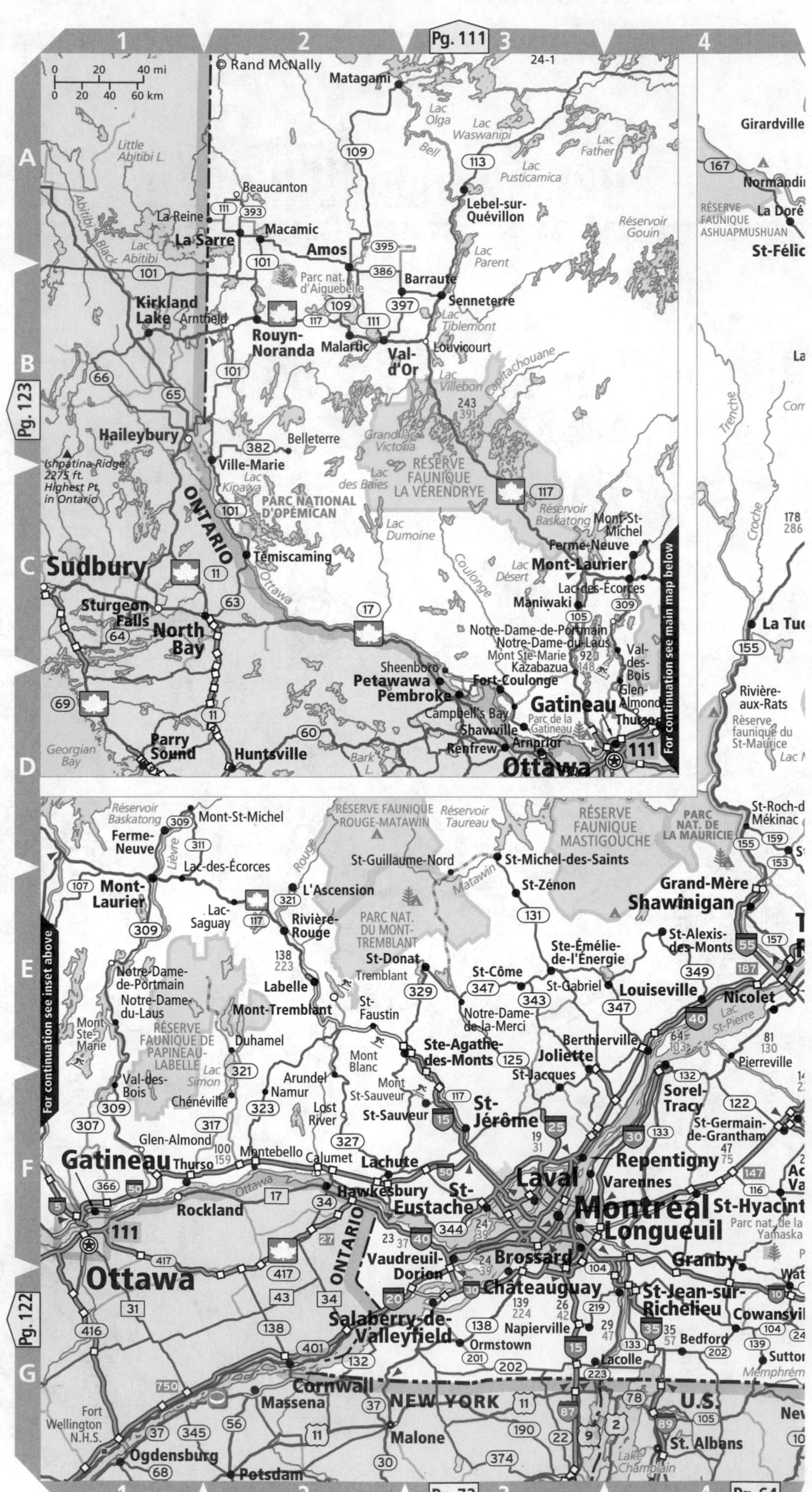

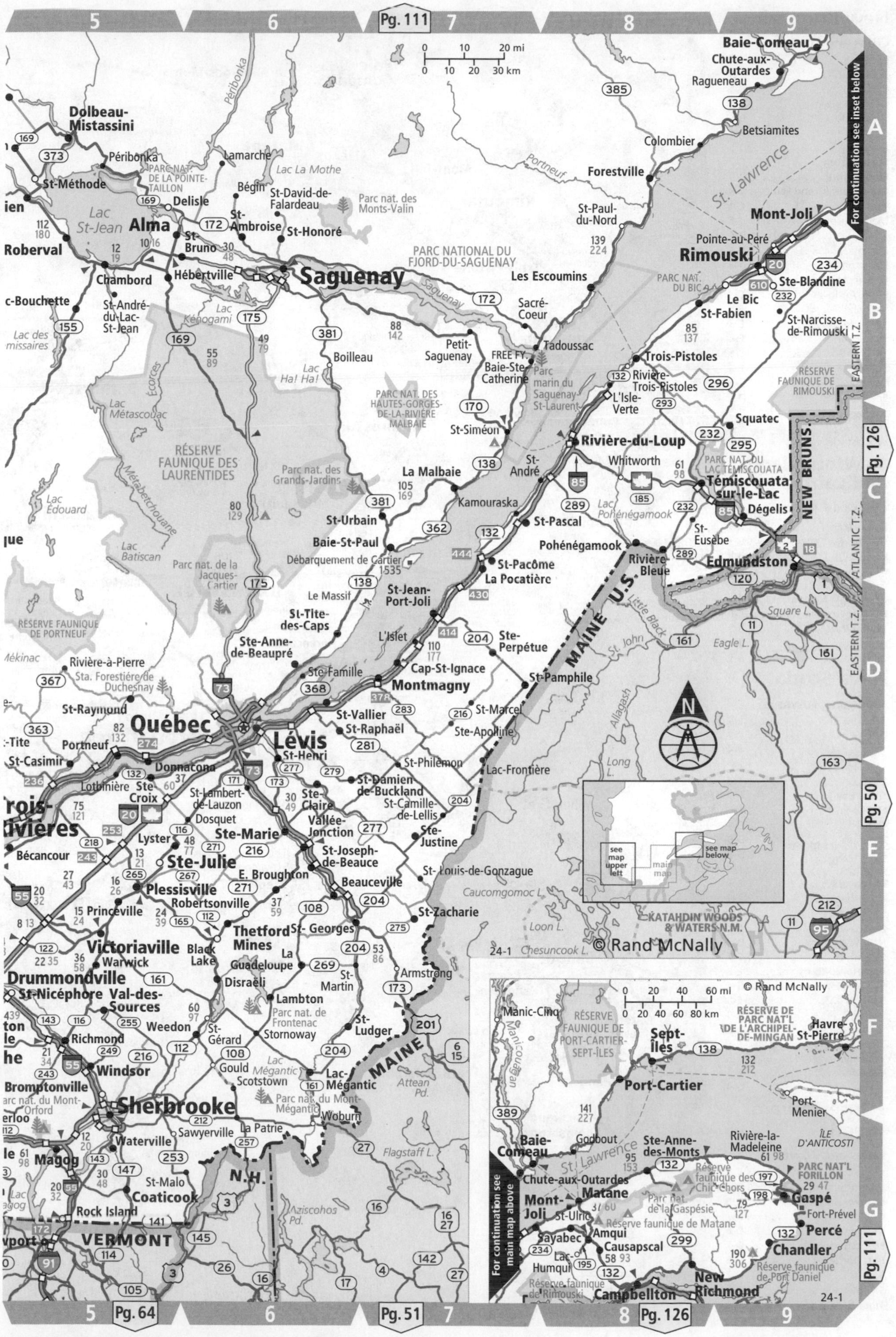

NOTE: Maps are not always in alphabetical order.
See Page 1 for map location in this atlas.

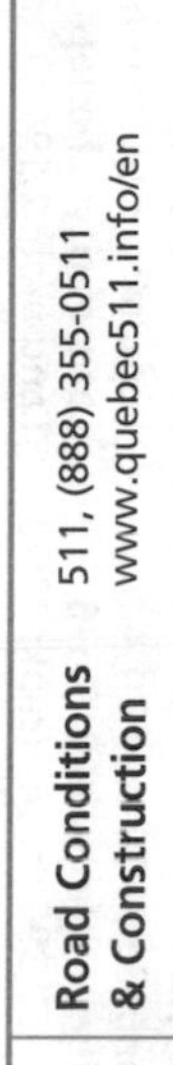

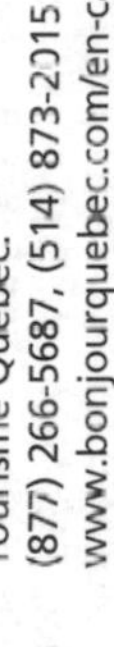

Travel planning & on-the-road resources

© Rand McNally

Atlantic Provinces

Provincial facts

NEW BRUNSWICK
Population: 747,101 (rank: 8th)
Largest city: Moncton, 79,470, D-5
Land area: 27,509 sq. mi. (rank: 11th)

NEWFOUNDLAND & LABRADOR
Population: 519,716 (rank: 9th)
Largest city: St. John's, 110,525, B-9
Land area: 138,290 sq. mi. (rank: 10th)

NOVA SCOTIA
Population: 923,598 (rank: 7th)
Largest city: Halifax, 439,819, F-6
Land area: 20,396 sq. mi. (rank: 12th)

PRINCE EDWARD ISLAND
Population: 142,907 (rank: 10th)
Largest city: Charlottetown, 38,809, D-6
Land area: 2,194 sq. mi. (rank: 13th)

New Brunswick

Cities and Towns

Bathurst C-4
Bouctouche. D-5
Campbellton. B-3
Cap-Pele D-5
Caraquet. B-5
Dalhousie B-4
Dieppe. D-5
Edmundston C-2
Fredericton D-3
Grand Falls (Grand Sault) . . C-3
Hampton. E-4
Memramcook D-5
Minto D-4
Miramichi C-4
Moncton D-5
Oromocto E-4
Perth-Andover C-3
Sackville E-5
St. Andrews E-3
Saint John. E-4
St-Quentin C-3
St. Stephen E-3
Salisbury D-5
Shediac D-5
Shippagan. B-5
Sussex E-4
Woodstock D-3

Newfoundland and Labrador

Cities and Towns

Bonavista B-9
Channel-Port aux Basques. . B-7
Corner Brook B-8
Deer Lake B-8
Gander B-8
Grand Falls-Windsor. B-8
Marystown C-8
Mount Pearl B-9
St. John's. B-9
Torbay. B-9

Nova Scotia

Cities and Towns

Amherst E-5
Antigonish E-7
Bridgewater F-5
Chester F-5
Digby. F-4
Glace Bay D-9
Halifax. F-6
Hebron G-4
Ingonish D-8
Inverness. D-8
Kentville F-5
Liverpool. G-5
Lunenburg F-5
Middleton. F-5
New Glasgow E-7
New Waterford D-9
Pictou E-7
Port Hawkesbury E-8
Shelburne G-4
Springhill. E-5
Sydney. D-9
Sydney Mines D-9
Truro E-6
Windsor. F-5
Wolfville E-5
Yarmouth G-4

Prince Edward Island

Cities and Towns

Alberton C-5
Charlottetown D-6
Cornwall D-6
Georgetown D-7
Kensington D-6
Montague. D-7
Port Borden D-6
Souris. D-7
Summerside D-6
Tignish. C-6

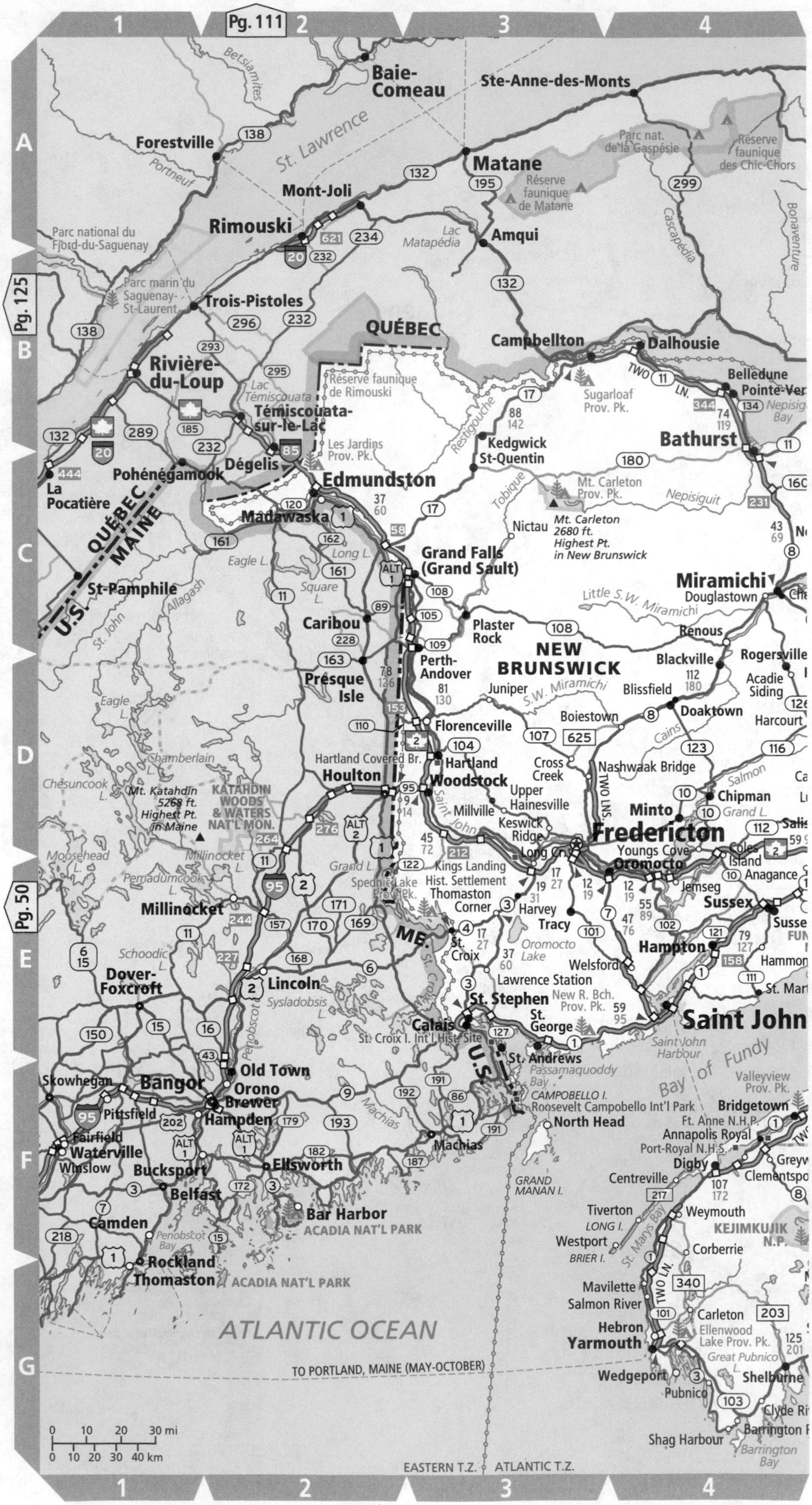

Pg. 111
Pg. 125
Pg. 50

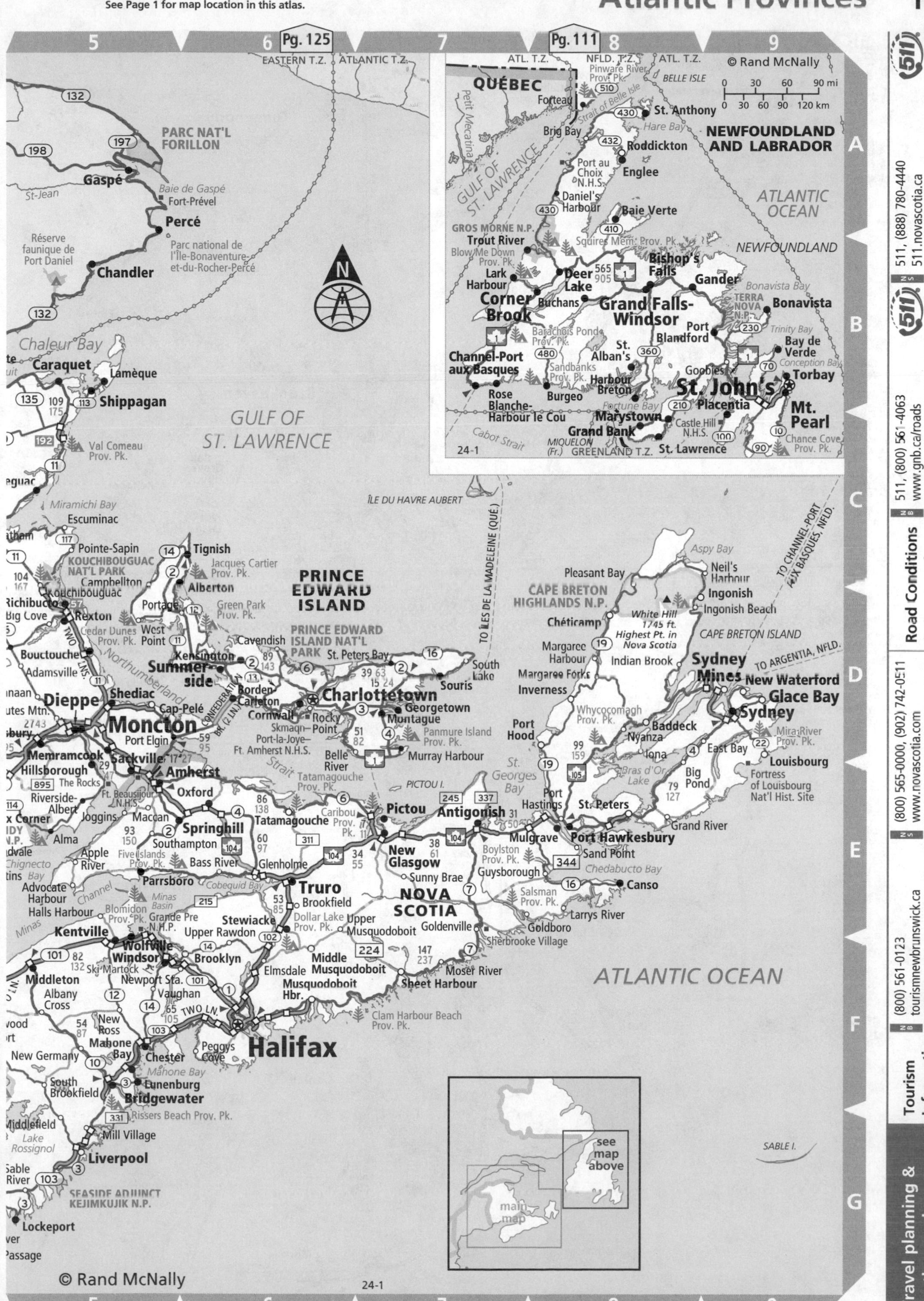

Travel planning & on-the-road resources

Tourism Information

NB (800) 561-0123 tourismnewbrunswick.ca
NL (800) 563-6353, (709) 729-2830 www.newfoundlandlabrador.com
NS (800) 565-0000, (902) 742-0511 www.novascotia.com
PE (800) 463-4734, (902) 437-8570 www.tourismpei.com

Road Conditions & Construction

NB 511, (800) 561-4063 www.gnb.ca/roads
NL 511, (833) 616-5511 www.511nl.ca/en
NS 511, (888) 780-4440 511.novascotia.ca
PE 511, (855) 241-2680 511.gov.pe.ca/en

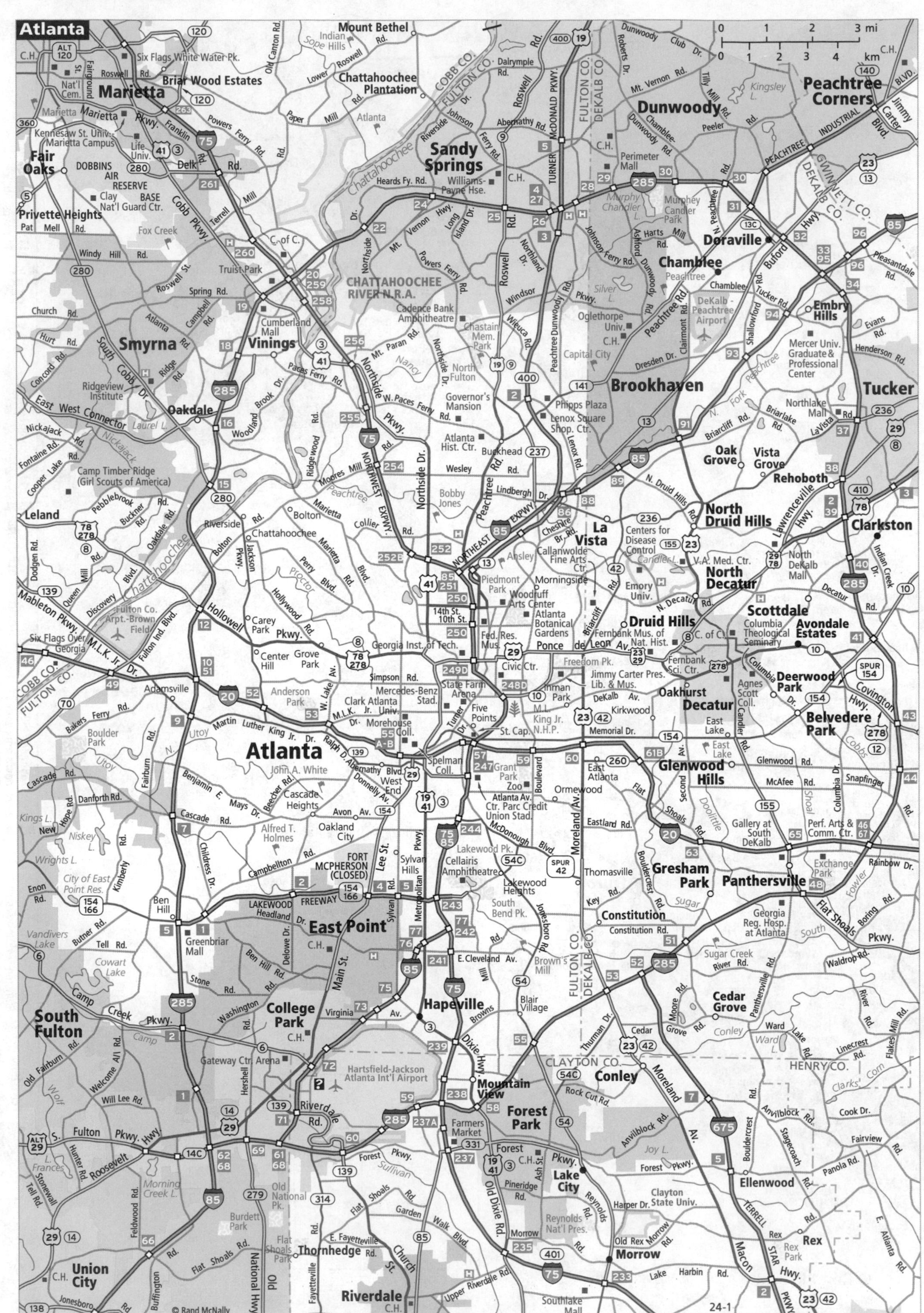
Atlanta
Mount Bethel
Indian Sope Hills
Six Flags White Water Pk.
Briar Wood Estates
Marietta
Chattahoochee Plantation
COBB CO.
FULTON CO.
FULTON CO.
DEKALB CO.
Dunwoody
Peachtree Corners
Kennesaw St. Univ.- Marietta Campus
Life Univ.
Fair Oaks
DOBBINS AIR RESERVE BASE
Clay Nat'l Guard Ctr.
Sandy Springs
Williams-Payne Hse.
Perimeter Mall
Murphey Candler Park
Privette Heights
Fox Creek
Truist Park
Doraville
Chamblee
CHATTAHOOCHEE RIVER N.R.A.
Cadence Bank Amphitheatre
Chastain Mem. Park
Oglethorpe Univ.
DeKalb - Peachtree Airport
Embry Hills
Smyrna
Cumberland Mall
Vinings
Mercer Univ. Graduate & Professional Center
Ridgeview Institute
North Fulton
Capital City
Brookhaven
Tucker
Oakdale
Governor's Mansion
Phipps Plaza
Lenox Square Shop. Ctr.
Northlake Mall
Atlanta Hist. Ctr.
Buckhead
Oak Grove
Vista Grove
Rehoboth
Camp Timber Ridge (Girl Scouts of America)
Bobby Jones
Leland
North Druid Hills
Clarkston
La Vista
Centers for Disease Control
V.A. Med. Ctr.
North DeKalb Mall
North Decatur
Piedmont Park
Woodruff Arts Center
Atlanta Botanical Gardens
Emory Univ.
Druid Hills
Fernbank Mus. of Nat. Hist.
Scottdale
Columbia Theological Seminary
Avondale Estates
Fulton Co. Arpt.-Brown Field
Six Flags Over Georgia
Carey Park
Center Hill
Grove Park
Georgia Inst. of Tech.
Fed. Res. Mus.
Civic Ctr.
Freedom Pk.
Jimmy Carter Pres. Lib. & Mus.
Fernbank Sci. Ctr.
Deerwood Park
Adamsville
Anderson Park
Mercedes-Benz Stad.
State Farm Arena
Clark Atlanta Univ.
Morehouse Coll.
Five Points
Inman Park
M.L. King Jr. N.H.P.
Oakhurst
Decatur
Agnes Scott Coll.
Belvedere Park
Boulder Park
Atlanta
St. Cap.
East Lake
John A. White
Spelman Coll.
Grant Park
Zoo
East Atlanta
Glenwood Hills
Cascade Heights
West End
Atlanta Av. Ctr. Parc Credit Union Stad.
Ormewood
Kings L.
Niskey L.
Alfred T. Holmes
Oakland City
Gallery at South DeKalb
Perf. Arts & Comm. Ctr.
Wrights L.
FORT MCPHERSON (CLOSED)
Sylvan Hills
Lakewood Pk.
Cellairis Amphitheatre
Lakewood Heights
Thomasville
Gresham Park
Panthersville
Exchange Park
City of East Point Res.
Ben Hill
South Bend Pk.
Constitution
Georgia Reg. Hosp. at Atlanta
East Point
Vandivers Lake
Greenbriar Mall
Cowart Lake
Brown's Mill
Sugar Creek
Hapeville
Cedar Grove
South Fulton
College Park
Blair Village
Conley
Gateway Ctr Arena
Hartsfield-Jackson Atlanta Int'l Airport
CLAYTON CO.
HENRY CO.
Mountain View
Riverdale
Farmers Market
Forest Park
L. Frances
Morning Creek L.
Joy L.
Ellenwood
Lake City
Burdett Park
Old National Pk.
Reynolds Nat'l Pres.
Clayton State Univ.
Union City
Flat Shoals Park
Thornhedge
Morrow
Rex Park
Rex
Riverdale
Southlake Mall
© Rand McNally
24-1
0 1 2 3 mi
0 1 2 3 4 km

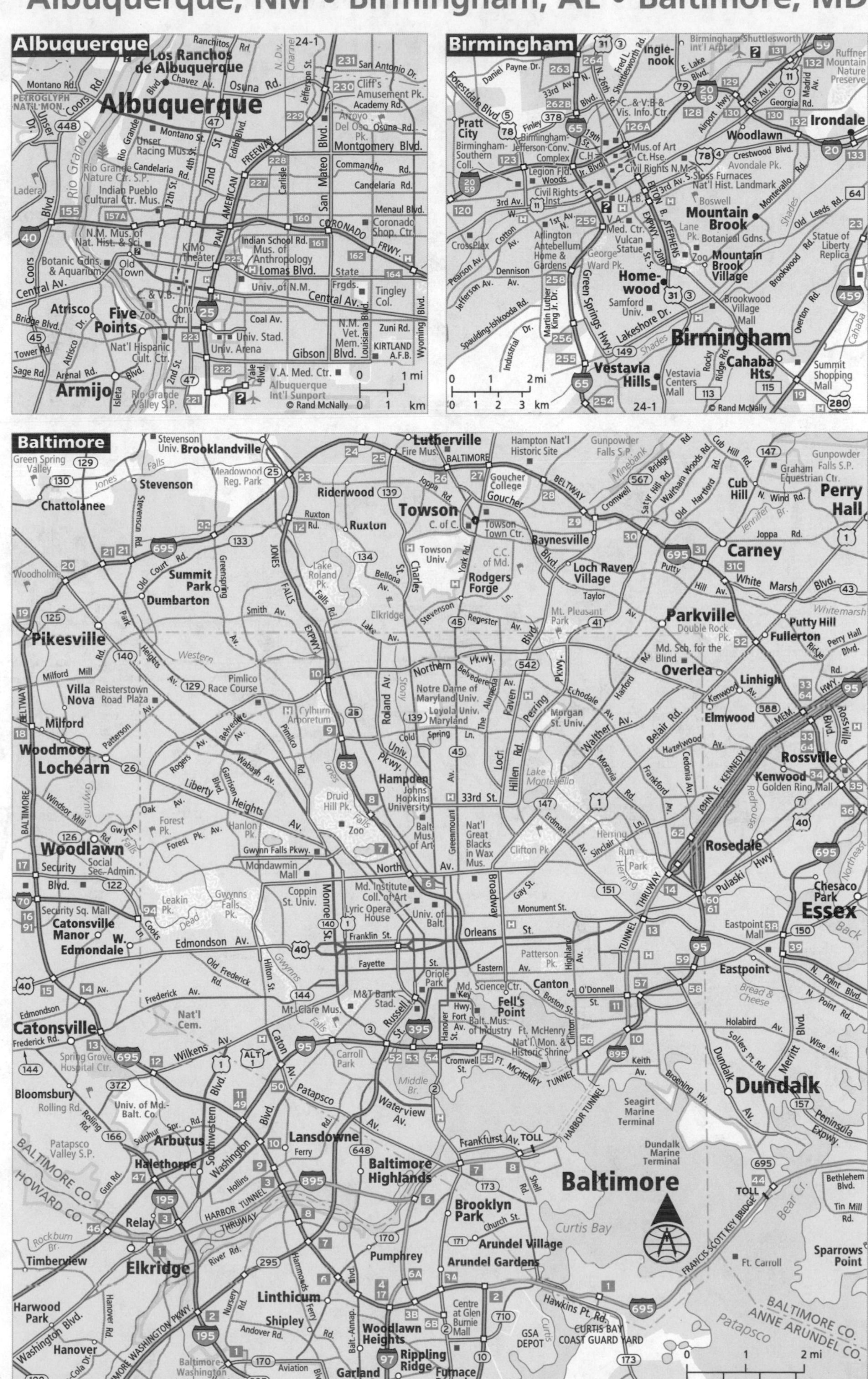
Albuquerque
Los Ranchos de Albuquerque
Albuquerque
Petroglyph Nat'l Mon.
Rio Grande Nature Ctr. S.P.
Indian Pueblo Cultural Ctr. Mus.
N.M. Mus. of Nat. Hist. & Sci.
Botanic Gdns. & Aquarium
Old Town
Atrisco
Five Points
Nat'l Hispanic Cult. Ctr.
Armijo
Rio Grande Valley S.P.
Univ. of N.M.
Tingley Col.
Univ. Stad.
Univ. Arena
N.M. Vet. Mem.
Kirtland A.F.B.
V.A. Med. Ctr.
Albuquerque Int'l Sunport
Cliff's Amusement Pk.
Montgomery Blvd.
Central Av.
Lomas Blvd.
Coronado Frwy.
Pan American Freeway
0 1 mi
0 1 km
© Rand McNally
24-1
Birmingham
Inglenook
Birmingham-Shuttlesworth Int'l Arpt.
Ruffner Mountain Nature Preserve
Irondale
Woodlawn
Pratt City
Birmingham-Southern Coll.
Birmingham-Jefferson Conv. Complex
Legion Fld.
Civil Rights Inst.
Mus. of Art
Civil Rights N.M.
Sloss Furnaces Nat'l Hist. Landmark
U.A.B.
Avondale Pk.
Mountain Brook
Botanical Gdns.
Vulcan Statue
Arlington Antebellum Home & Gardens
Mountain Brook Village
Homewood
Samford Univ.
Brookwood Village Mall
Birmingham
Statue of Liberty Replica
Vestavia Hills
Vestavia Centers Mall
Cahaba Hts.
Summit Shopping Mall
0 1 2 mi
0 1 2 3 km
24-1
© Rand McNally
Baltimore
Stevenson Univ.
Brooklandville
Lutherville
Hampton Nat'l Historic Site
Gunpowder Falls S.P.
Green Spring Valley
Stevenson
Chattolanee
Riderwood
Goucher College
Towson
Ruxton
Cub Hill
Perry Hall
Carney
Towson Univ.
Baynesville
Summit Park
Dumbarton
Loch Raven Village
Rodgers Forge
Parkville
Pikesville
Fullerton
Putty Hill
Overlea
Pimlico Race Course
Villa Nova
Milford
Woodmoor
Lochearn
Notre Dame of Maryland Univ.
Loyola Univ. Maryland
Morgan St. Univ.
Linhigh
Elmwood
Rossville
Kenwood
Golden Ring Mall
Hampden
Johns Hopkins University
Druid Hill Pk.
Zoo
Woodlawn
Social Security Admin.
Rosedale
Clifton Pk.
Chesaco Park
Essex
Md. Institute Coll. of Art
Lyric Opera House
Univ. of Balt.
Catonsville Manor
W. Edmondale
Eastpoint Mall
Eastpoint
Oriole Park
M&T Bank Stad.
Md. Science Ctr.
Canton
Fell's Point
Ft. McHenry Nat'l Mon. & Historic Shrine
Catonsville
Spring Grove Hospital Ctr.
Carroll Park
Fort McHenry Tunnel
Harbor Tunnel
Seagirt Marine Terminal
Dundalk
Dundalk Marine Terminal
Bloomsbury
Univ. of Md.-Balt. Co.
Arbutus
Lansdowne
Halethorpe
Baltimore Highlands
Baltimore
Relay
Brooklyn Park
Curtis Bay
Arundel Village
Arundel Gardens
Timberview
Elkridge
Pumphrey
Sparrows Point
Ft. Carroll
Francis Scott Key Bridge
Linthicum
Shipley
Harwood Park
Hanover
Woodlawn Heights
Centre at Glen Burnie Mall
GSA Depot
Curtis Bay Coast Guard Yard
Baltimore Co.
Anne Arundel Co.
Howard Co.
Rippling Ridge
Furnace Branch
Garland
Ferndale
Baltimore Washington International Thurgood Marshall Airport
0 1 2 mi
0 1 2 3 km
24-1
© Rand McNally

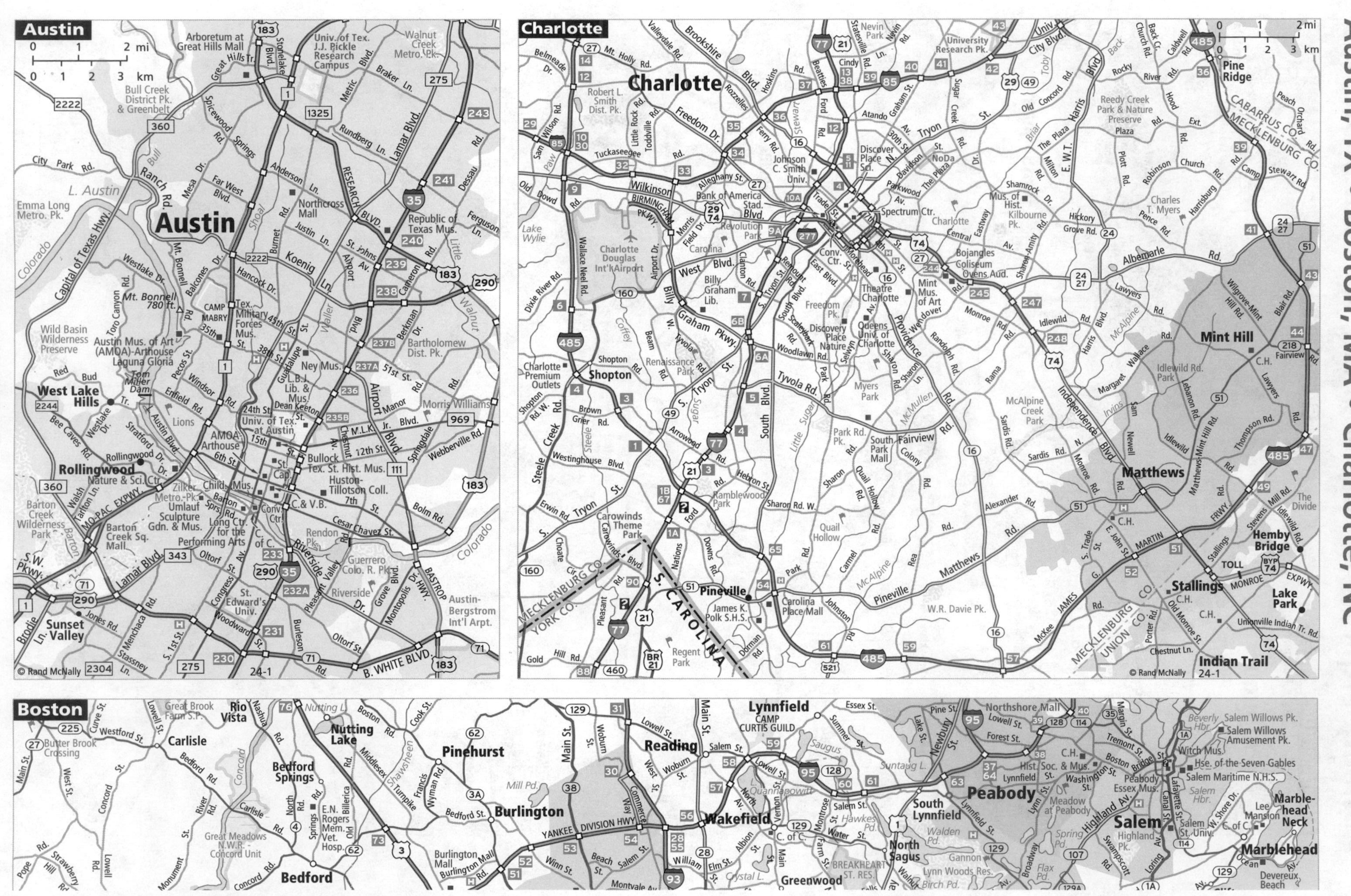
Austin
Charlotte
Boston
Mint Hill
Matthews
Stallings
Indian Trail
Pineville
Pine Ridge
Hemby Bridge
Lake Park
Shopton
S. CAROLINA
West Lake Hills
Rollingwood
Sunset Valley
Salem
Marblehead
Peabody
Lynnfield
Wakefield
Reading
Burlington
Bedford
Carlisle
Pinehurst
© Rand McNally

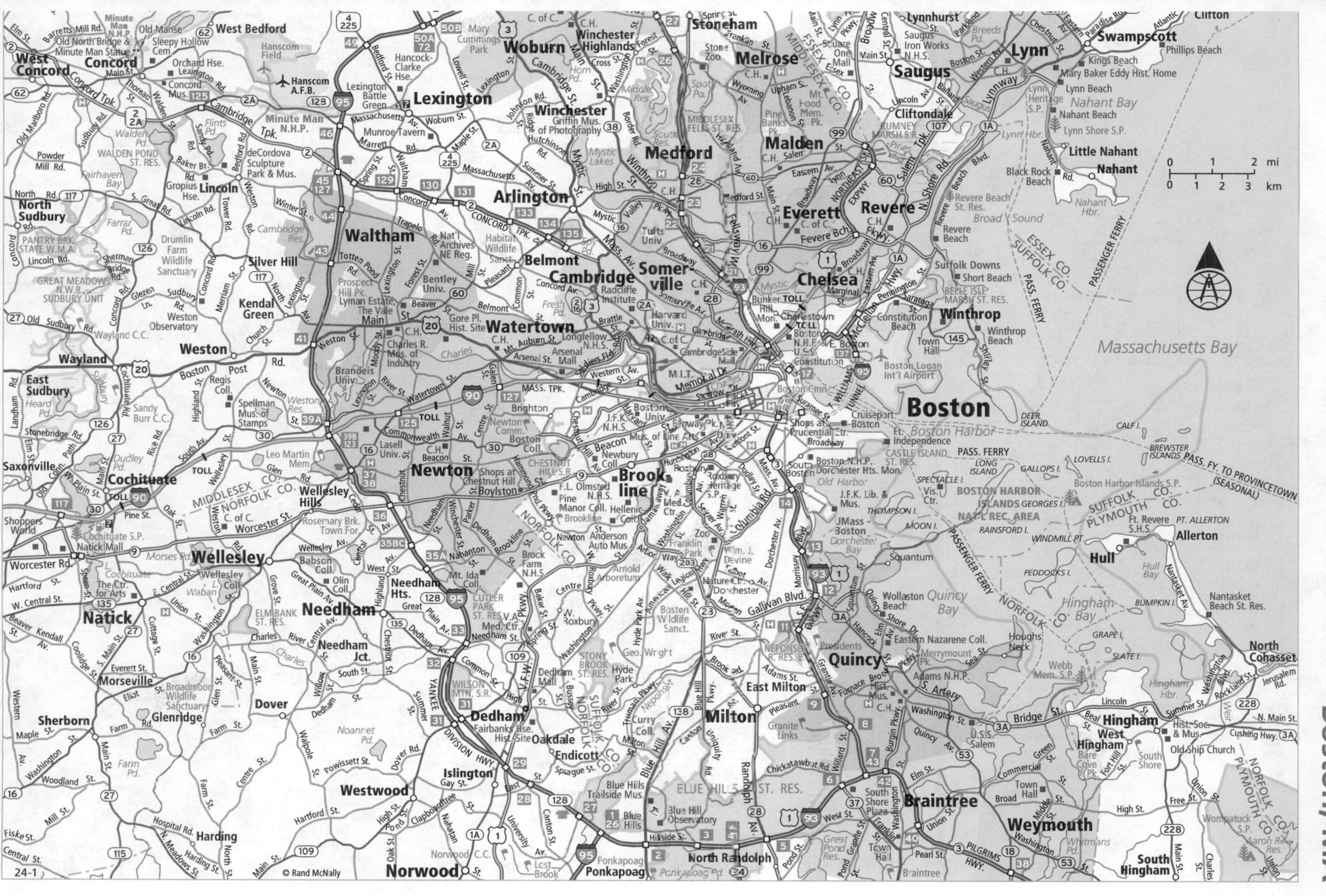

Massachusetts Bay
Boston
Boston Harbor
Boston Logan Int'l Airport
Cambridge
Somerville
Brookline
Newton
Watertown
Waltham
Belmont
Arlington
Medford
Malden
Everett
Chelsea
Revere
Winthrop
Saugus
Lynn
Swampscott
Nahant
Little Nahant
Melrose
Stoneham
Winchester
Woburn
Lexington
Concord
West Concord
Lincoln
Weston
Wayland
Wellesley
Needham
Dedham
Milton
Quincy
Braintree
Weymouth
Hingham
Hull
Norwood
Westwood
Dover
Natick
Sherborn
Cochituate
Saxonville
East Sudbury
North Sudbury
North Randolph
Islington
Glenridge
Harding
South Hingham
North Cohasset
Allerton
Squantum
East Milton
Oakdale
Endicott
Ponkapoag
Morseville
Boston Harbor Islands Nat'l Rec. Area
Blue Hills
Hanscom A.F.B.
Passenger Ferry
Pass. Fy. to Provincetown (Seasonal)
© Rand McNally
24-1

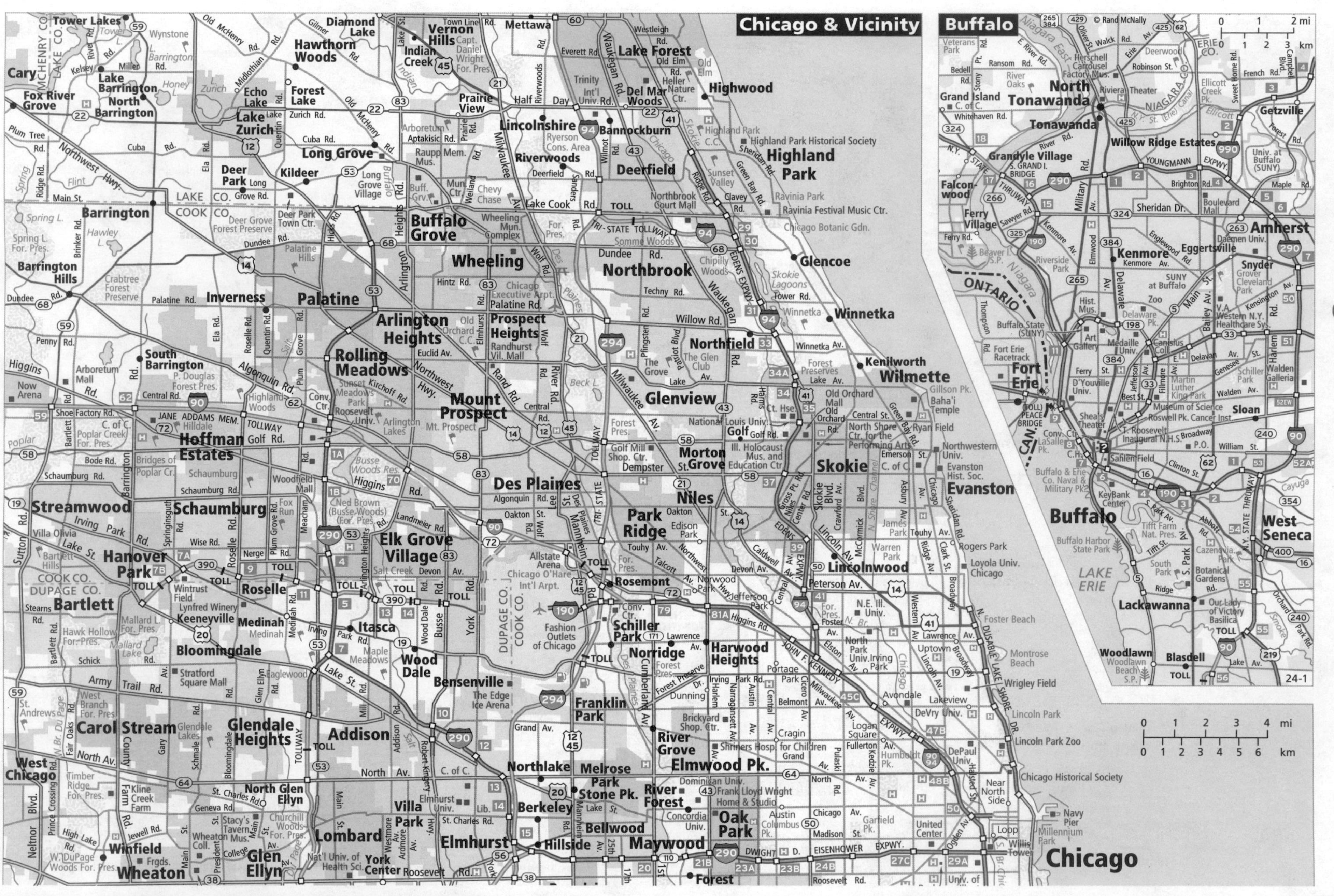
Chicago & Vicinity
Buffalo
© Rand McNally
North Tonawanda
Tonawanda
Kenmore
Amherst
Buffalo
Lackawanna
West Seneca
Fort Erie
ONTARIO
LAKE ERIE
Chicago
Evanston
Skokie
Wilmette
Winnetka
Glencoe
Highland Park
Highwood
Lake Forest
Northbrook
Glenview
Niles
Park Ridge
Des Plaines
Arlington Heights
Palatine
Schaumburg
Hoffman Estates
Elk Grove Village
Elmhurst
Oak Park
Maywood
Lombard
Wheaton
Glen Ellyn
Barrington

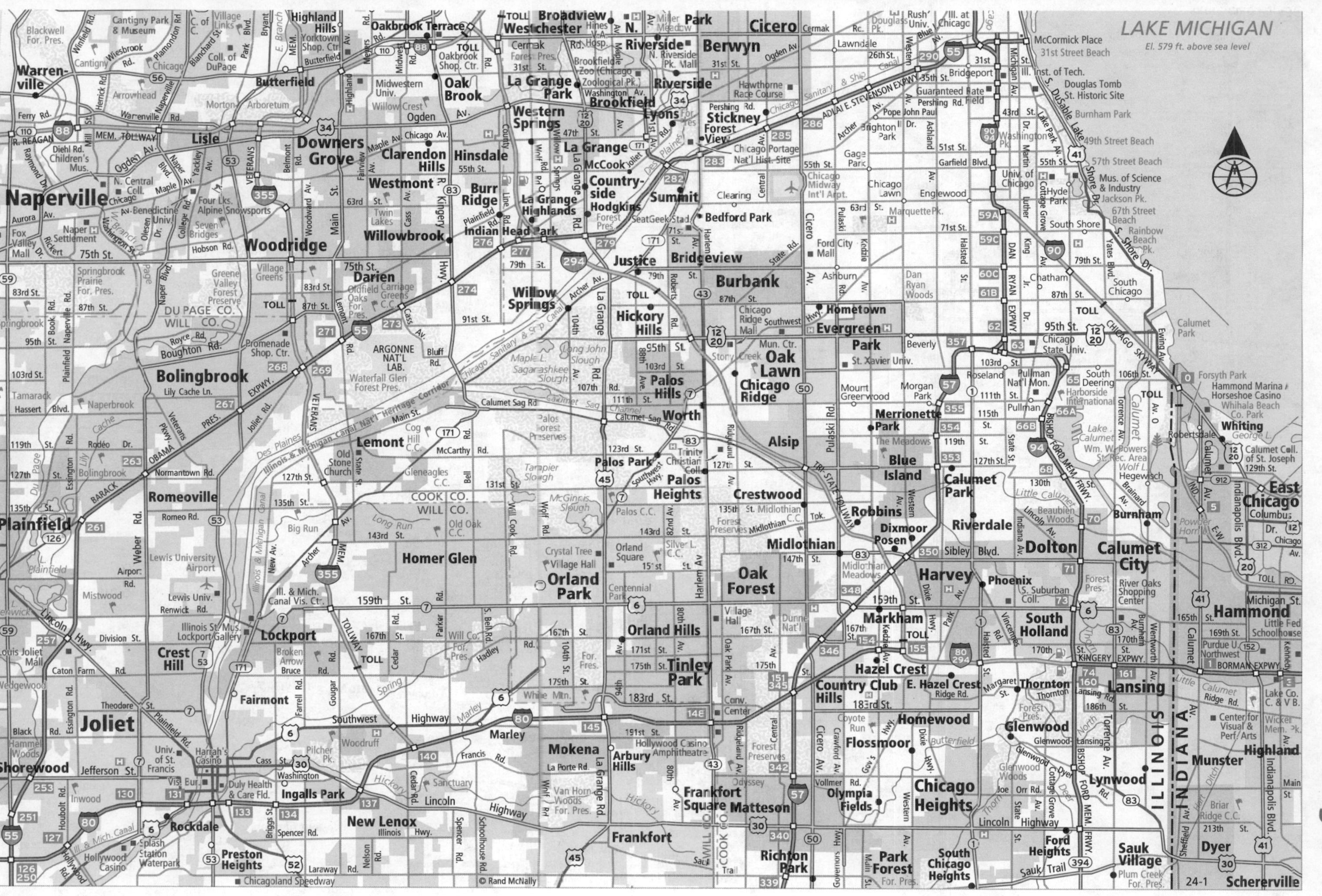
LAKE MICHIGAN
El. 579 ft. above sea level
INDIANA
ILLINOIS
East Chicago
Whiting
Hammond
Munster
Highland
Dyer
Schererville
Calumet City
Lansing
Burnham
Dolton
South Holland
Thornton
Riverdale
Calumet Park
Blue Island
Harvey
Phoenix
Markham
Hazel Crest
E. Hazel Crest
Homewood
Glenwood
Lynwood
Ford Heights
Sauk Village
Chicago Heights
South Chicago Heights
Flossmoor
Olympia Fields
Park Forest
Country Club Hills
Richton Park
Matteson
Dixmoor
Posen
Robbins
Midlothian
Oak Forest
Tinley Park
Orland Hills
Frankfort
Frankfort Square
Mokena
Arbury Hills
Orland Park
Palos Heights
Palos Park
Crestwood
Alsip
Oak Lawn
Chicago Ridge
Evergreen Park
Hometown
Merrionette Park
Worth
Palos Hills
Hickory Hills
Bridgeview
Justice
Burbank
Bedford Park
Summit
Stickney
Forest View
Cicero
Berwyn
Riverside
N. Riverside
Lyons
Brookfield
La Grange
La Grange Park
Countryside
Hodgkins
McCook
Willow Springs
Western Springs
La Grange Highlands
Indian Head Park
Burr Ridge
Hinsdale
Oak Brook
Oakbrook Terrace
Westchester
Broadview
Clarendon Hills
Westmont
Willowbrook
Darien
Downers Grove
Woodridge
Lisle
Bolingbrook
Lemont
Homer Glen
Lockport
Romeoville
Crest Hill
Joliet
Rockdale
Shorewood
Plainfield
Naperville
Warrenville
Butterfield
Highland Hills
New Lenox
Ingalls Park
Fairmont
Preston Heights
Marley
COOK CO.
WILL CO.
DU PAGE CO.
BISHOP FORD MEM. FRWY.
DAN RYAN EXPWY.
CHICAGO SKYWAY
TRI-STATE TOLLWAY
Chicago Midway Int'l Arpt.
Lewis University Airport
ARGONNE NAT'L LAB.
© Rand McNally

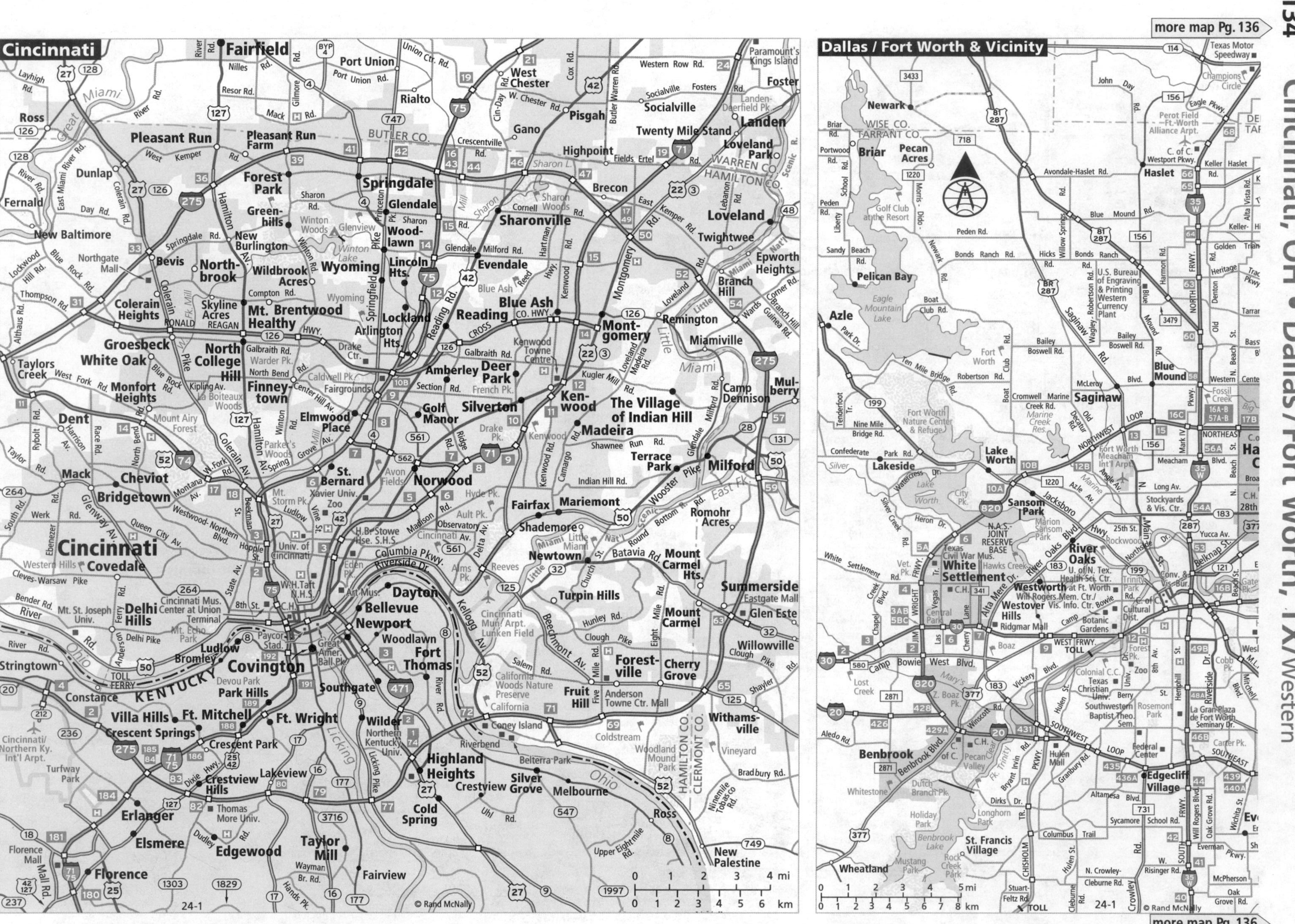

Cincinnati
Dallas / Fort Worth & Vicinity
more map Pg. 136
more map Pg. 136
Fairfield
Pleasant Run Farm
Pleasant Run
Forest Park
Springdale
Sharonville
Blue Ash
Evendale
Glendale
Wyoming
Lockland
Reading
Norwood
Cincinnati
Covington
Newport
Bellevue
Dayton
Fort Thomas
Highland Heights
Cold Spring
Erlanger
Elsmere
Florence
Taylor Mill
Edgewood
Crestview Hills
Villa Hills
Ludlow
Bromley
Cheviot
Bridgetown
Covedale
Delhi Hills
Mack
Dent
Taylors Creek
Ross
Fernald
New Baltimore
Dunlap
Colerain Heights
Groesbeck
White Oak
Monfort Heights
North College Hill
Mt. Healthy
Finneytown
Elmwood Place
St. Bernard
Silverton
Deer Park
Amberley
Golf Manor
Kenwood
Madeira
Montgomery
The Village of Indian Hill
Terrace Park
Milford
Mariemont
Fairfax
Newtown
Mount Carmel
Forestville
Cherry Grove
Summerside
Withamsville
Loveland
Landen
Twenty Mile Stand
Socialville
West Chester
Pisgah
Remington
Miamiville
Mulberry
New Palestine
Silver Grove
Melbourne
Fairview
Ohio
KENTUCKY
HAMILTON CO.
CLERMONT CO.
BUTLER CO.
WARREN CO.
© Rand McNally
24-1
Haslet
Saginaw
Blue Mound
Newark
Pecan Acres
Briar
Pelican Bay
Azle
Eagle Mountain Lake
Lake Worth
Sansom Park
River Oaks
White Settlement
Westworth
Westover Hills
Lakeside
Benbrook
Edgecliff Village
St. Francis Village
Wheatland
WISE CO.
TARRANT CO.
Texas Motor Speedway
Fort Worth Meacham Int'l Arpt.
N.A.S. JOINT RESERVE BASE
Benbrook Lake
© Rand McNally
24-1

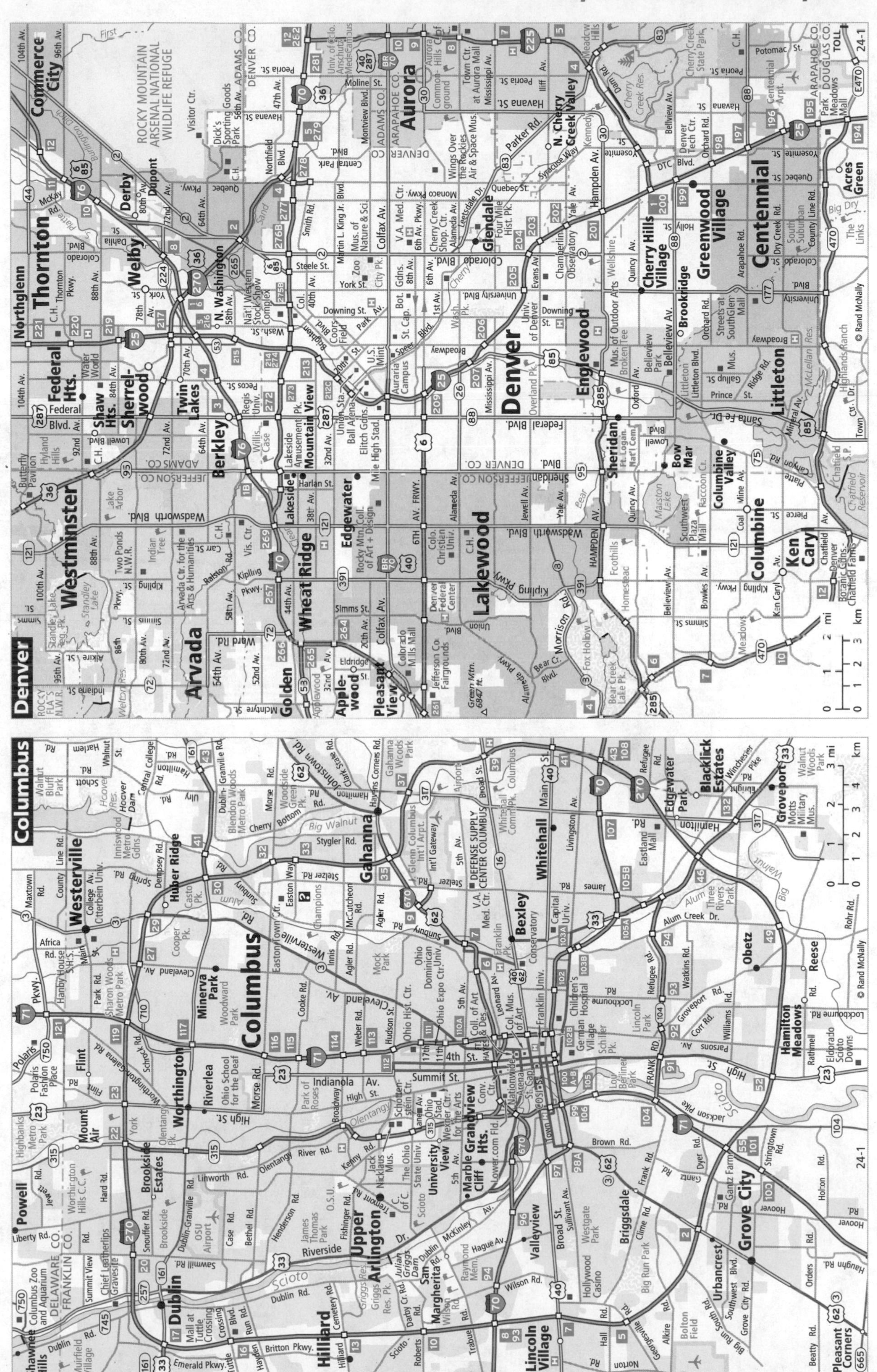
Columbus
Denver
Westerville
Huber Ridge
Gahanna
Columbus
Worthington
Minerva Park
Riverlea
Powell
Dublin
Brookside Estates
Upper Arlington
Hilliard
University View
Marble Cliff
Grandview Hts.
Valleyview
Lincoln Village
Bexley
Whitehall
Blacklick Estates
Groveport
Obetz
Reese
Hamilton Meadows
Briggsdale
Urbancrest
Grove City
Pleasant Corners
Edgewater Park
Shawnee Hills
Flint
Mount Air
Polaris
© Rand McNally
Westminster
Thornton
Northglenn
Commerce City
Federal Hts.
Shaw Hts.
Sherrelwood
Twin Lakes
Welby
Derby
Berkley
Arvada
Wheat Ridge
Mountain View
Lakeside
Edgewater
Golden
Applewood
Pleasant View
Lakewood
Denver
Aurora
Glendale
N. Cherry Creek Valley
Englewood
Sheridan
Bow Mar
Columbine Valley
Columbine
Ken Caryl
Littleton
Cherry Hills Village
Greenwood Village
Centennial
Acres Green
Brookridge
ROCKY MOUNTAIN ARSENAL NATIONAL WILDLIFE REFUGE
© Rand McNally
mi
km
24-1

Wylie
Murphy
Sachse
Rowlett
Garland
Sunnyvale
Mesquite
Seagoville
Plano
Richardson
Balch Springs
Dallas
Carrollton
Addison
Farmers Branch
University Park
Highland Park
Hutchins
Wilmer
Lancaster
DeSoto
Lewisville
Coppell
Irving
Cockrell Hill
Duncanville
Cedar Hill
Grand Prairie
Flower Mound
Grapevine
Euless
Mansfield
Southlake
Colleyville
Bedford
Arlington
Pantego
Dalworthington Gardens
Hurst
Kennedale
Marshall Creek
Trophy Club
Westlake
Roanoke
Keller
Watauga
N. Richland Hills
Richland Hills
Fort Worth
Forest Hill
Joe Pool Lake
Dallas/Ft. Worth International Airport
Dallas Love Field
more map Pg. 134
more map Pg. 134
© Rand McNally
24-1

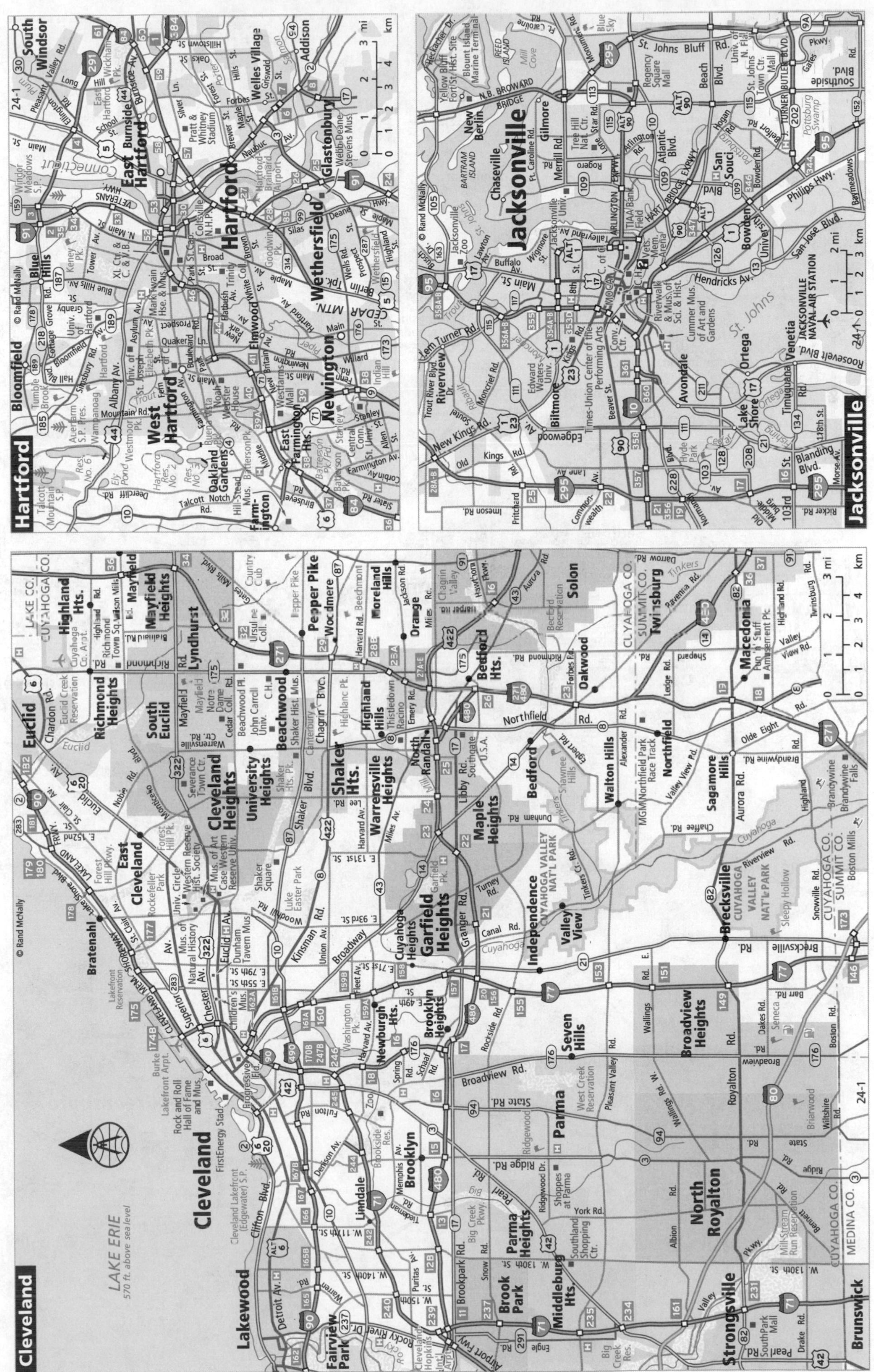
Hartford
© Rand McNally
Jacksonville
© Rand McNally
Cleveland
© Rand McNally
LAKE ERIE
570 ft. above sea level

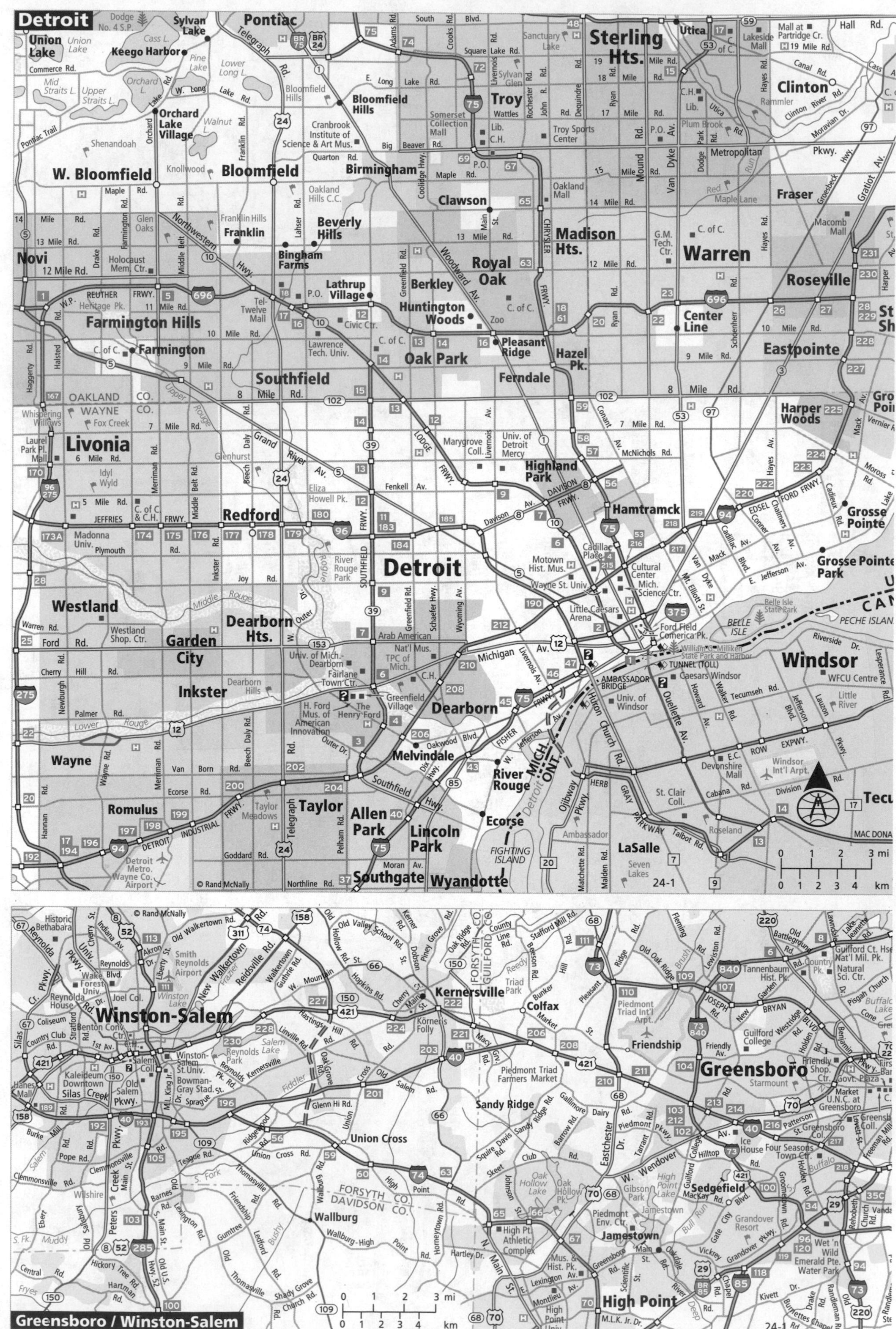
Detroit
Pontiac
Sterling Hts.
Troy
Bloomfield Hills
W. Bloomfield
Bloomfield
Birmingham
Clawson
Madison Hts.
Warren
Royal Oak
Berkley
Huntington Woods
Farmington Hills
Farmington
Southfield
Oak Park
Ferndale
Hazel Pk.
Center Line
Eastpointe
Roseville
Fraser
Clinton
Utica
Novi
Livonia
Redford
Highland Park
Hamtramck
Grosse Pointe
Grosse Pointe Park
Harper Woods
Westland
Garden City
Dearborn Hts.
Inkster
Dearborn
Melvindale
Wayne
Romulus
Taylor
Allen Park
Lincoln Park
Southgate
Wyandotte
Ecorse
River Rouge
Windsor
LaSalle
© Rand McNally
Greensboro / Winston-Salem
Winston-Salem
Kernersville
Colfax
Greensboro
Friendship
Union Cross
Wallburg
Sandy Ridge
Jamestown
High Point
Sedgefield
© Rand McNally

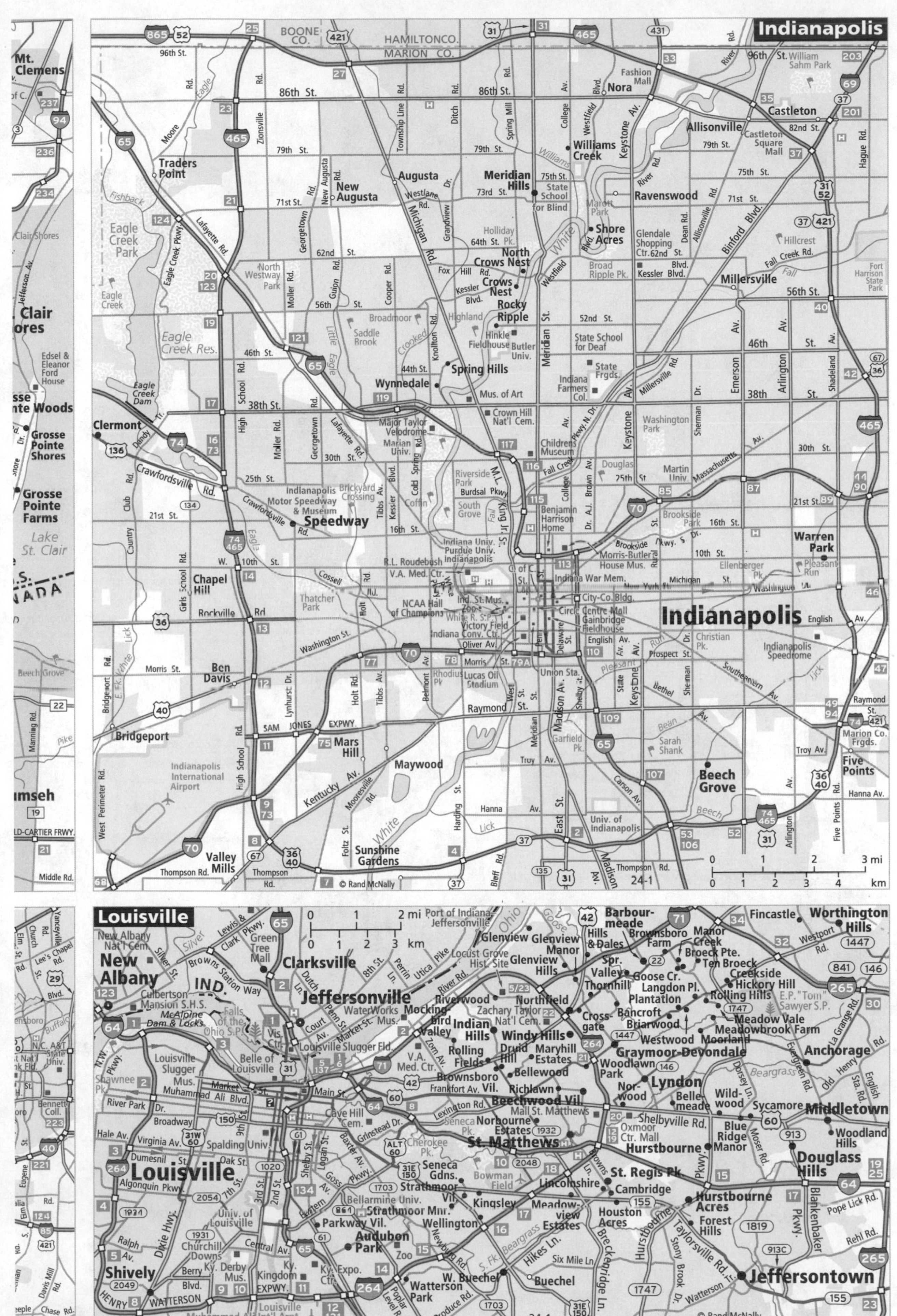
Indianapolis
Louisville
Mt. Clemens
St. Clair Shores
Grosse Pointe Woods
Grosse Pointe Shores
Grosse Pointe Farms
Lake St. Clair
Tecumseh
Traders Point
Eagle Creek Park
Eagle Creek Res.
Clermont
Speedway
Indianapolis Motor Speedway & Museum
Chapel Hill
Ben Davis
Bridgeport
Indianapolis International Airport
Valley Mills
Mars Hill
Maywood
Sunshine Gardens
Augusta
New Augusta
Meridian Hills
North Crows Nest
Crows Nest
Rocky Ripple
Spring Hills
Wynnedale
Williams Creek
Nora
Shore Acres
Ravenswood
Allisonville
Castleton
Castleton Square Mall
Millersville
Warren Park
Beech Grove
Five Points
Indianapolis Speedrome
Lucas Oil Stadium
Victory Field
Indiana Conv. Ctr.
Union Sta.
Circle Centre Mall
City-Co. Bldg.
Indiana War Mem.
Butler Univ.
Crown Hill Nat'l Cem.
State Fairgrounds
Univ. of Indianapolis
© Rand McNally
New Albany
Clarksville
Jeffersonville
Louisville Slugger Mus.
Shively
Audubon Park
Watterson Park
Buechel
Jeffersontown
St. Matthews
Lyndon
Middletown
Anchorage
Douglas Hills
Hurstbourne
Hurstbourne Acres
Graymoor-Devondale
Windy Hills
Indian Hills
Glenview
Barbourmeade
Worthington Hills
Fincastle
Muhammad Ali Int'l Arpt.
Univ. of Louisville
Churchill Downs
Ky. Expo. Ctr.
© Rand McNally

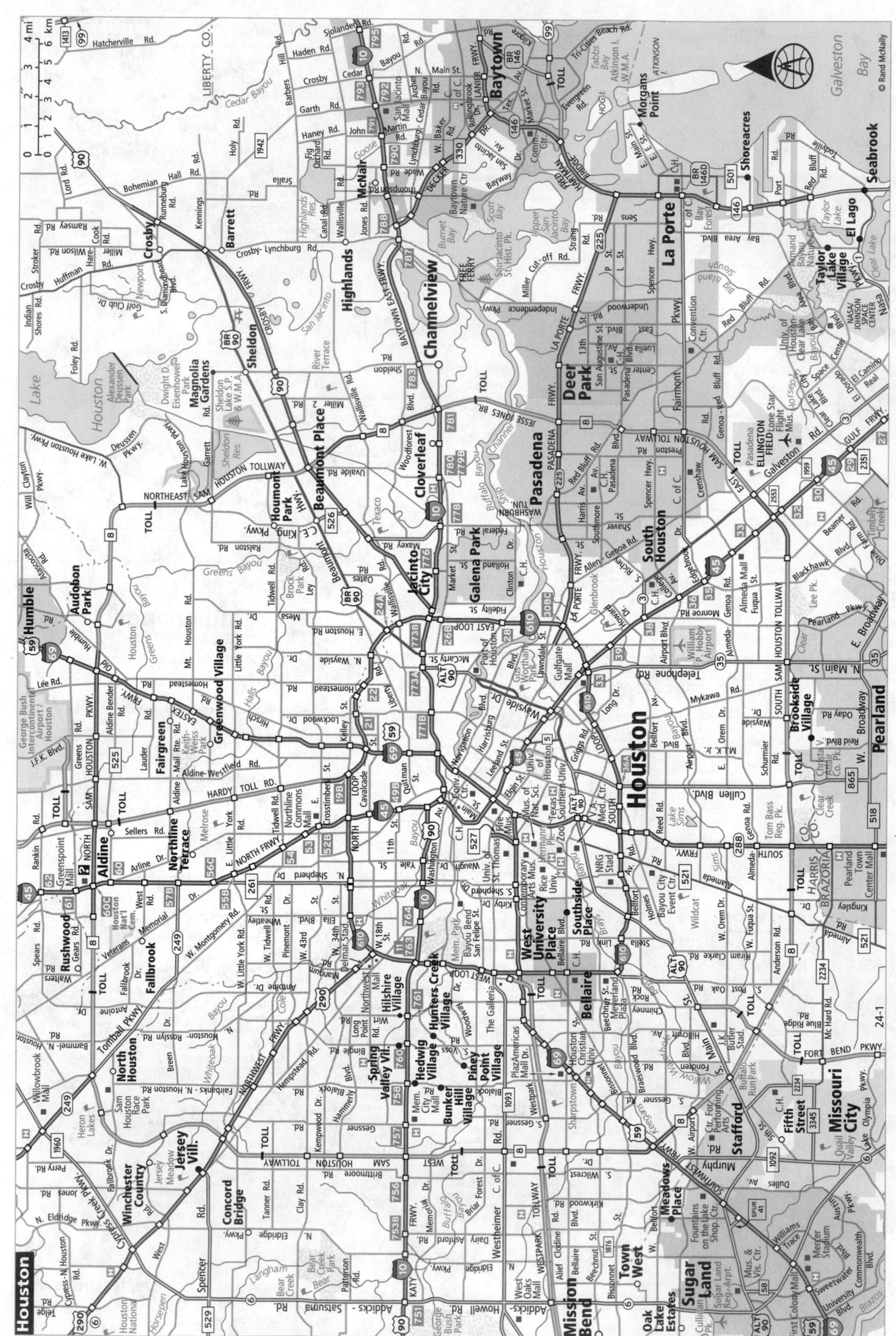
Houston
Humble
Aldine
Crosby
Sheldon
Highlands
Channelview
Baytown
McNair
Barrett
Cloverleaf
Jacinto City
Galena Park
Pasadena
Deer Park
La Porte
South Houston
Pearland
Missouri City
Stafford
Sugar Land
Bellaire
West University Place
Southside Place
Jersey Vil.
Fairbanks
Fallbrook
Rushwood
Fairgreen
Greenwood Village
Northline Terrace
North Houston
Winchester Country
Concord Bridge
Mission Bend
Town West
Meadows Place
Spring Valley Vil.
Hedwig Village
Hunters Creek Village
Piney Point Village
Bunker Hill Village
Hilshire Village
Seabrook
Shoreacres
El Lago
Taylor Lake Village
Morgans Point
Brookside Village
Fifth Street
Magnolia Gardens
Beaumont Place
Houmont Park
Audubon Park
Oak Lake Estates
Galveston Bay
Lake Houston
© Rand McNally
24-1

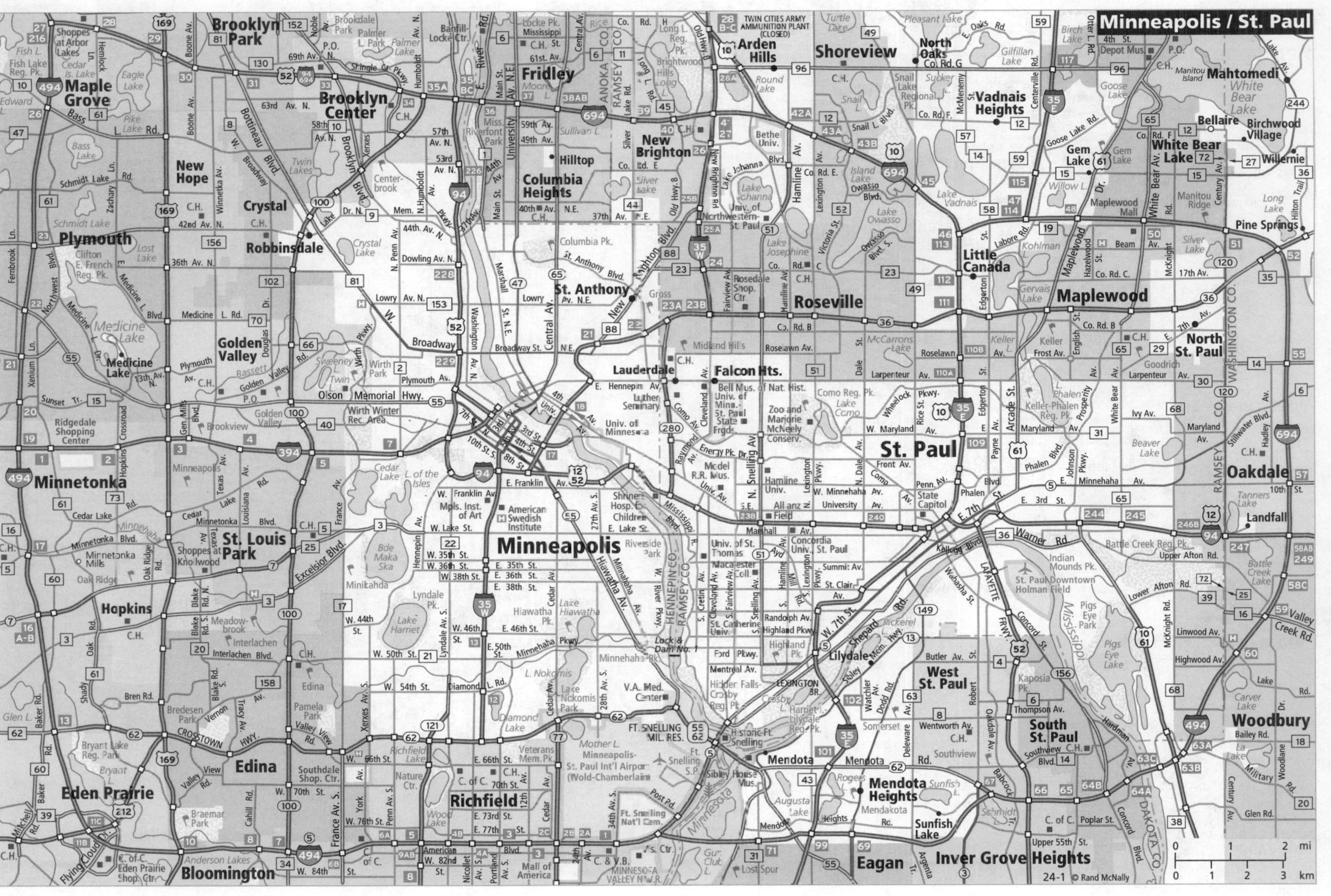
Minneapolis / St. Paul
Minneapolis
St. Paul
Maple Grove
Brooklyn Park
Brooklyn Center
Fridley
Arden Hills
Shoreview
North Oaks
Vadnais Heights
Mahtomedi
Bellaire
Birchwood Village
White Bear Lake
Willernie
Gem Lake
New Hope
Crystal
Robbinsdale
Plymouth
New Brighton
Hilltop
Columbia Heights
St. Anthony
Roseville
Little Canada
Maplewood
North St. Paul
Pine Springs
Oakdale
Landfall
Golden Valley
Medicine Lake
Lauderdale
Falcon Hts.
Minnetonka
St. Louis Park
Hopkins
Edina
Richfield
Eden Prairie
Bloomington
Lilydale
West St. Paul
South St. Paul
Mendota
Mendota Heights
Sunfish Lake
Eagan
Inver Grove Heights
Woodbury
Mississippi
Minnesota
WASHINGTON CO.
RAMSEY CO.
DAKOTA CO.
HENNEPIN CO.
ANOKA CO.
24-1 © Rand McNally

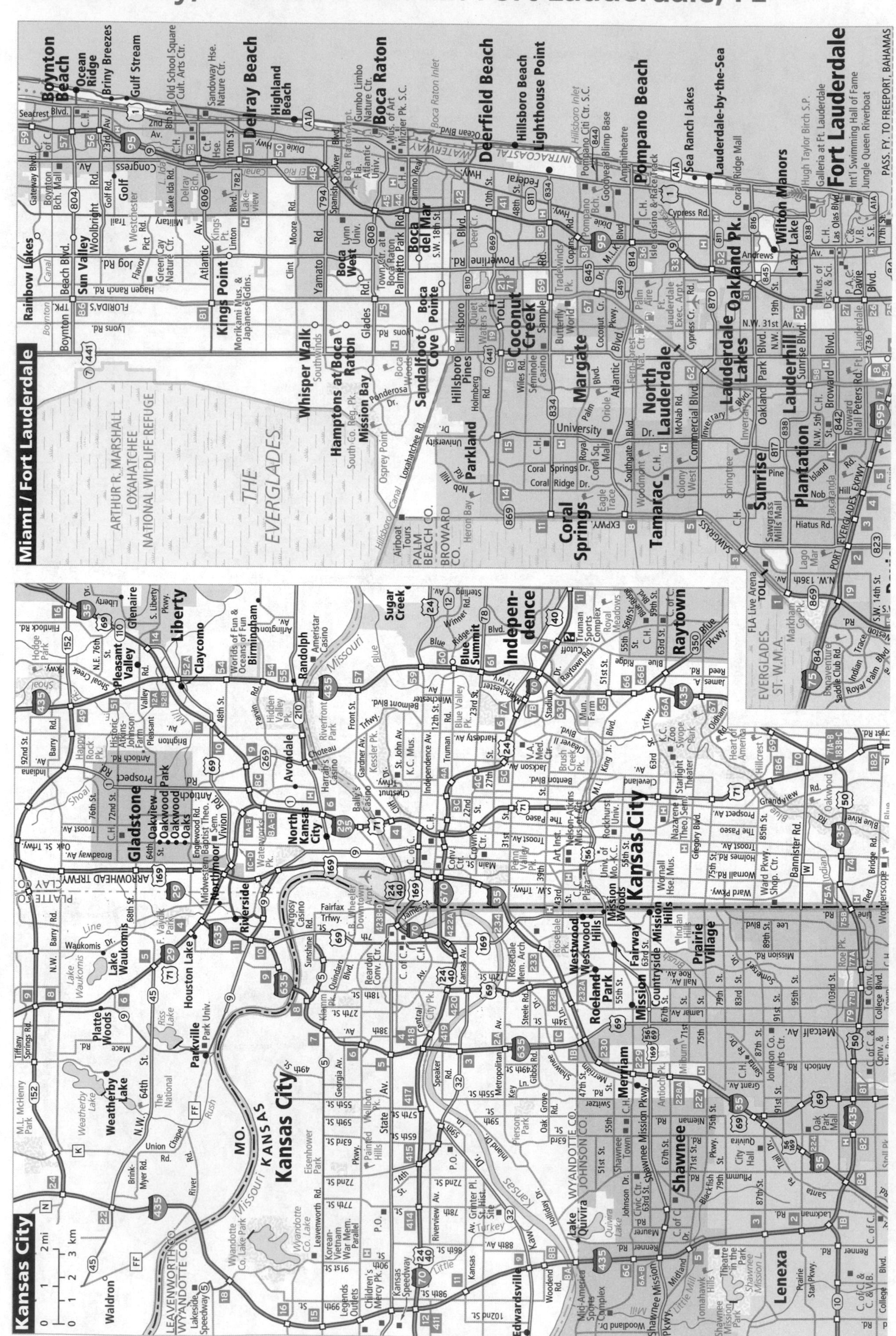
Kansas City
Miami / Fort Lauderdale
Kansas City
Independence
Liberty
Raytown
Gladstone
North Kansas City
Riverside
Parkville
Lenexa
Shawnee
Merriam
Prairie Village
Edwardsville
Fort Lauderdale
Boca Raton
Delray Beach
Pompano Beach
Deerfield Beach
Coral Springs
Margate
Tamarac
Sunrise
Plantation
Lauderhill
THE EVERGLADES
ARTHUR R. MARSHALL LOXAHATCHEE NATIONAL WILDLIFE REFUGE

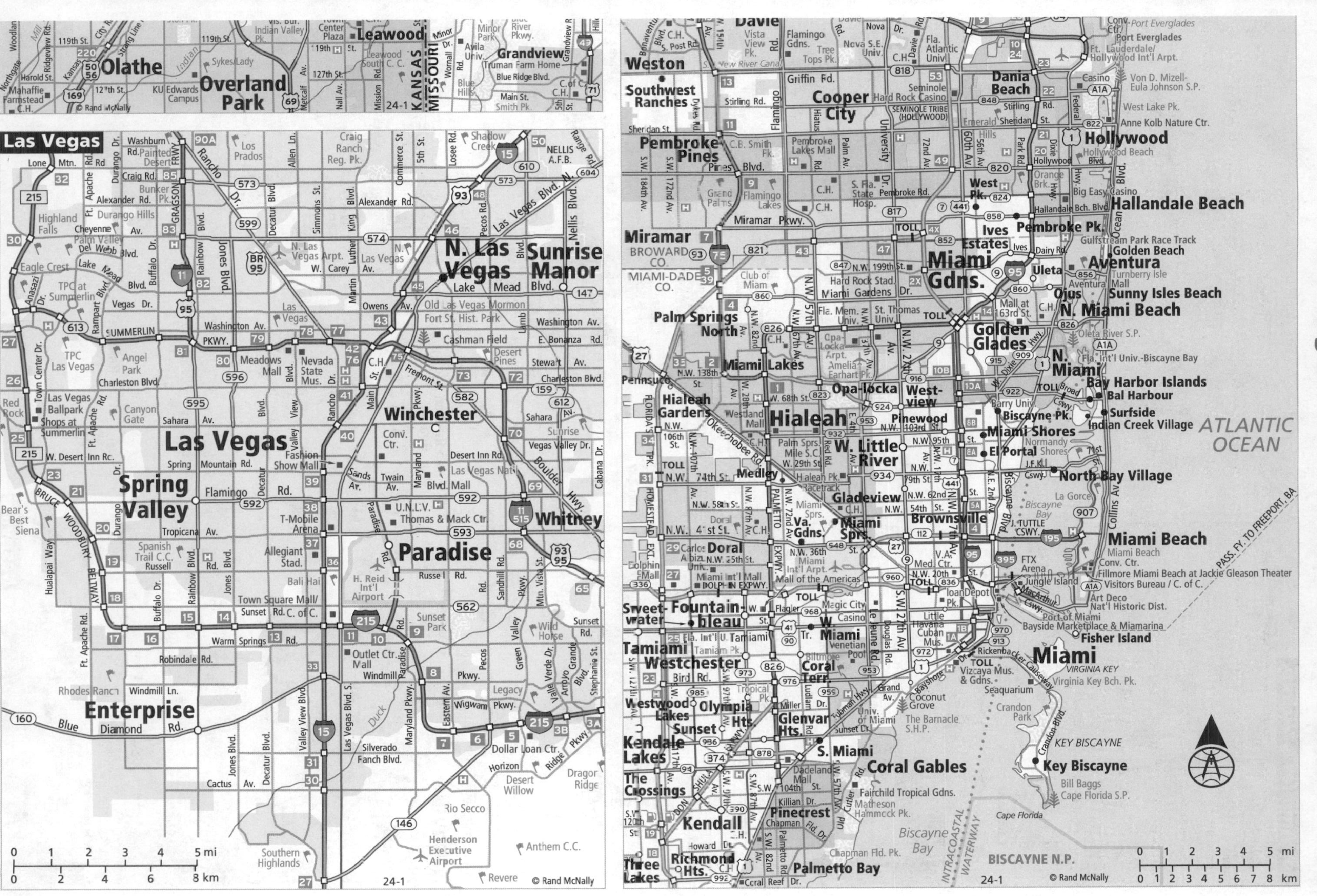
Las Vegas
Las Vegas
N. Las Vegas
Sunrise Manor
Winchester
Paradise
Whitney
Spring Valley
Enterprise
Overland Park
Olathe
Leawood
Grandview
KANSAS
MISSOURI
Hollywood
Hallandale Beach
Dania Beach
Cooper City
Davie
Weston
Southwest Ranches
Pembroke Pines
Miramar
Miami Gdns.
Golden Glades
N. Miami Beach
Sunny Isles Beach
Aventura
Opa-locka
Hialeah
Miami Lakes
Palm Springs North
Hialeah Gardens
Miami Beach
Miami
Coral Gables
Doral
Sweetwater
Fountainbleau
Westchester
Kendall
Palmetto Bay
Pinecrest
Key Biscayne
ATLANTIC OCEAN
BISCAYNE N.P.
© Rand McNally

Los Angeles & Vicinity
Simi Valley
Santa Susana
Chatsworth Lake Manor
Hidden Hills
Calabasas
Topanga Park
SANTA MONICA MOUNTAINS
SANTA MONICA MOUNTAINS NATIONAL RECREATION AREA
Topanga
Los Angeles
Beverly Hills
West Hollywood
Santa Monica
Culver City
Marina del Rey
Santa Monica Bay
Burbank
Glendale
La Cañada Flintridge
La Crescenta
Montrose
SAN FERNANDO VALLEY
VERDUGO MTNS.
Inglewood
El Segundo
Manhattan Beach
Hermosa Beach
Redondo Beach
Palos Verdes Estates
Rancho Palos Verdes
Rolling Hills Estates
Rolling Hills
Torrance
Gardena
Hawthorne
Lawndale
Compton
Carson
Lynwood
South Gate
Huntington Pk.
Florence
Vernon
Lomita
PACIFIC OCEAN
© Rand McNally
0 1 2 3 mi
0 1 2 3 4 km
Nashville
Madison
Inglewood
Bordeaux
Belle Meade
Berry Hill
Oak Hill
Forest Hills
Nashville
24-1
© Rand McNally

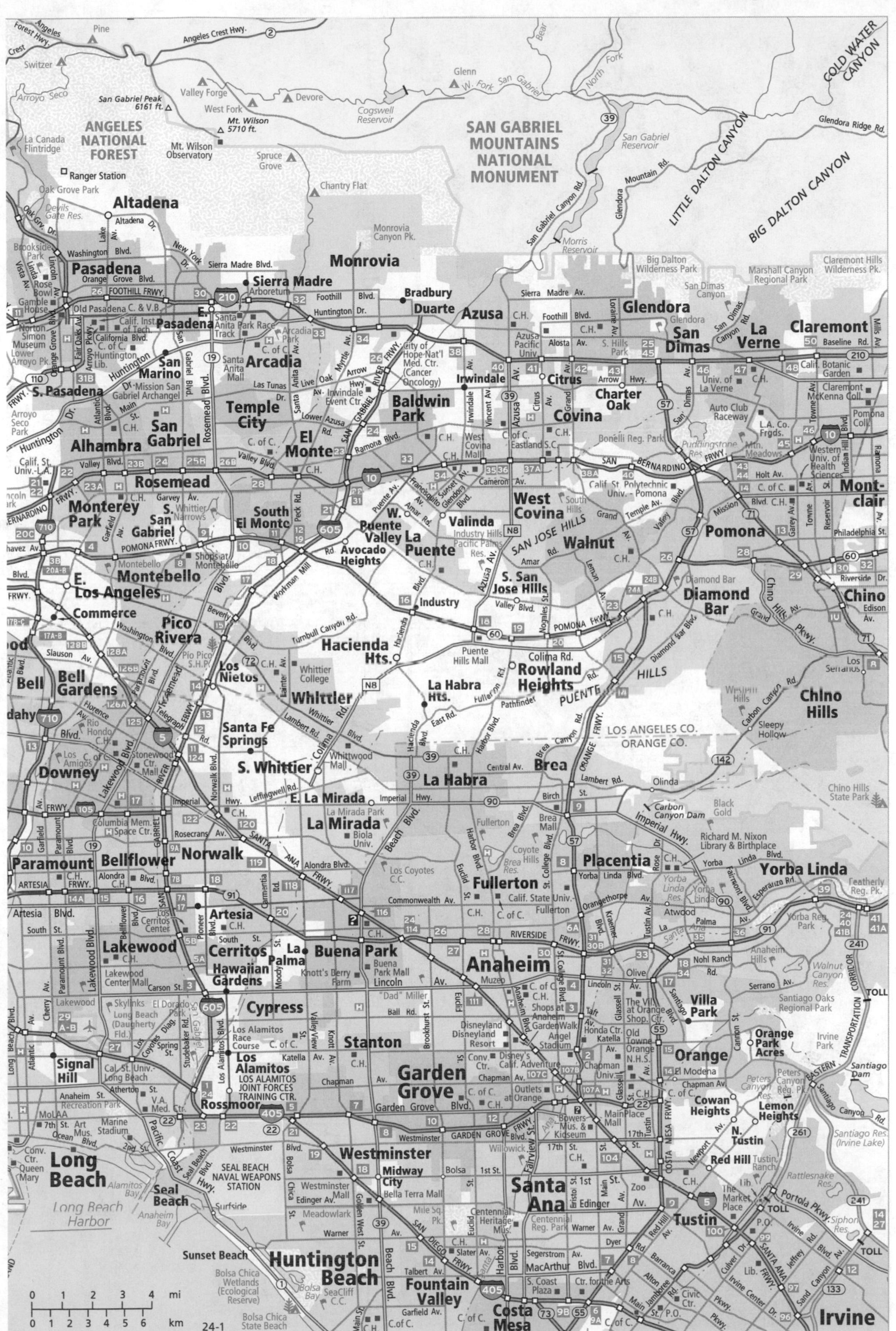

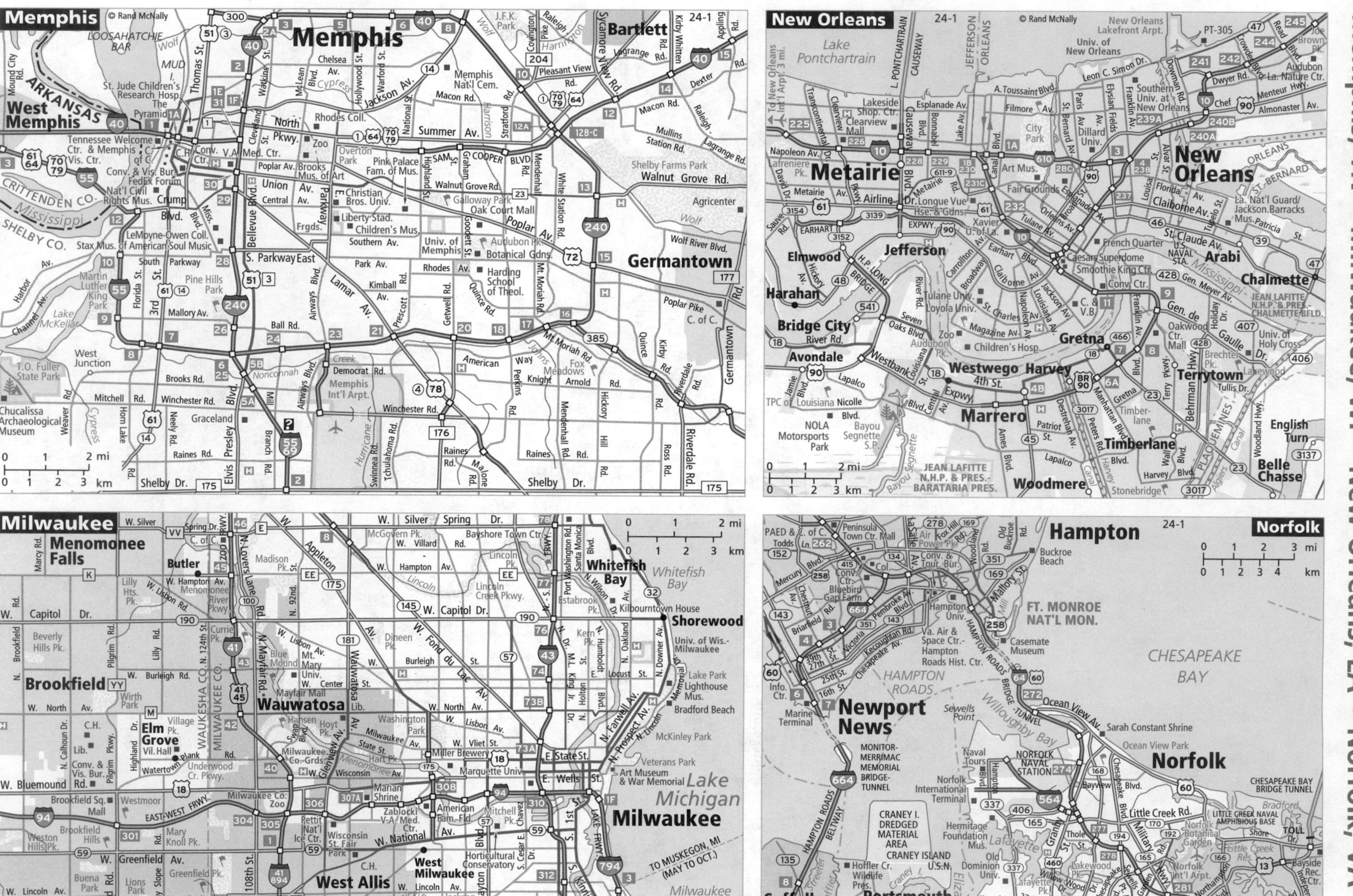
Memphis
© Rand McNally
Memphis
West Memphis
Bartlett
Germantown
ARKANSAS
CRITTENDEN CO.
SHELBY CO.
Mississippi
Memphis Int'l Arpt.
T.O. Fuller State Park
Chucalissa Archaeological Museum
New Orleans
© Rand McNally
Lake Pontchartrain
New Orleans
Metairie
Jefferson
Elmwood
Harahan
Bridge City
Avondale
Westwego
Harvey
Gretna
Marrero
Terrytown
Timberlane
Woodmere
Arabi
Chalmette
English Turn
Belle Chasse
Milwaukee
Menomonee Falls
Butler
Whitefish Bay
Shorewood
Brookfield
Elm Grove
Wauwatosa
West Milwaukee
West Allis
Milwaukee
Lake Michigan
TO MUSKEGON, MI (MAY TO OCT.)
Norfolk
Hampton
FT. MONROE NAT'L MON.
CHESAPEAKE BAY
HAMPTON ROADS
Newport News
Norfolk
Portsmouth
CHESAPEAKE BAY BRIDGE TUNNEL
MONITOR-MERRIMAC MEMORIAL BRIDGE-TUNNEL

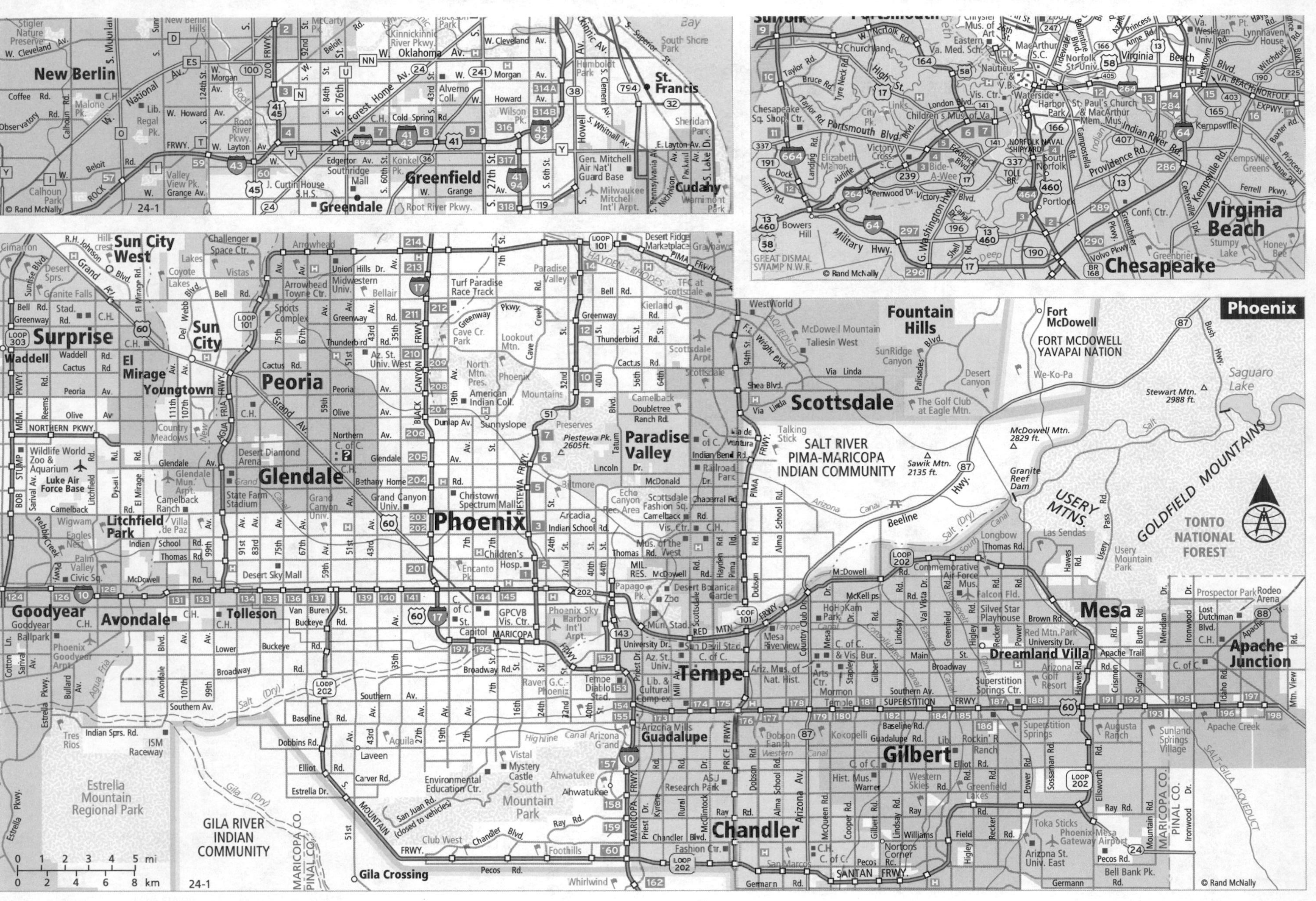
New Berlin
St. Francis
Greenfield
Greendale
Cudahy
Virginia Beach
Chesapeake
Phoenix
Sun City West
Sun City
Surprise
El Mirage
Youngtown
Peoria
Glendale
Litchfield Park
Goodyear
Avondale
Tolleson
Paradise Valley
Scottsdale
Fountain Hills
SALT RIVER PIMA-MARICOPA INDIAN COMMUNITY
FORT MCDOWELL YAVAPAI NATION
GOLDFIELD MOUNTAINS
TONTO NATIONAL FOREST
USERY MTNS.
Mesa
Apache Junction
Dreamland Villa
Tempe
Guadalupe
Gilbert
Chandler
South Mountain Park
Estrella Mountain Regional Park
GILA RIVER INDIAN COMMUNITY
Gila Crossing
© Rand McNally

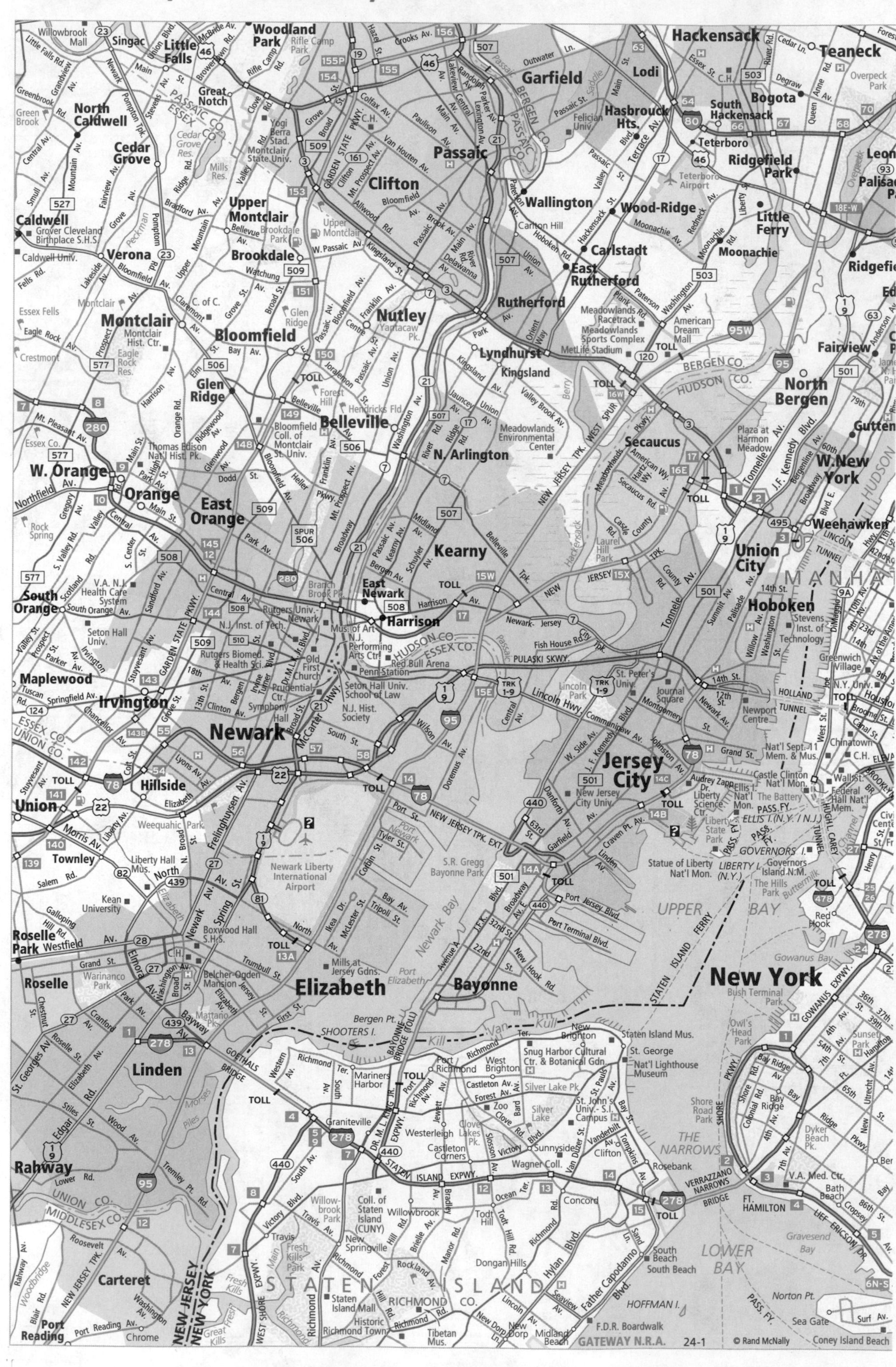

Willowbrook Mall
Singac
Little Falls
Woodland Park
Hackensack
Teaneck
Garfield
Lodi
Bogota
Hasbrouck Hts.
South Hackensack
Teterboro
Ridgefield Park
North Caldwell
Cedar Grove
Great Notch
Passaic
Clifton
Upper Montclair
Wallington
Wood-Ridge
Little Ferry
Moonachie
Caldwell
Verona
Brookdale
Carlstadt
East Rutherford
Rutherford
Montclair
Bloomfield
Nutley
Lyndhurst
Kingsland
Glen Ridge
Fairview
North Bergen
Belleville
N. Arlington
Secaucus
W. Orange
Orange
East Orange
Kearny
W. New York
Weehawken
Union City
Hoboken
South Orange
East Newark
Harrison
Maplewood
Irvington
Newark
Jersey City
Hillside
Union
Townley
Newark Liberty International Airport
Roselle Park
Roselle
Elizabeth
Bayonne
New York
Linden
Rahway
Carteret
Port Reading
Chrome
Staten Island
Upper Bay
Lower Bay
The Narrows
Statue of Liberty Nat'l Mon.
Ft. Hamilton
Coney Island Beach
Sea Gate
Gateway N.R.A.
New Jersey
New York
© Rand McNally
24-1

New York /
Newark
& Vicinity
Englewood
Englewood Cliffs
Fort Lee
Edgewater
Cliffside Park
BRONX
QUEENS
BROOKLYN
Sands Point
Manorhaven
Kings Point
Great Neck
Kensington
Great Neck Estates
Great Neck Plaza
Russell Gardens
Thomaston
University Gardens
Saddle Rock
Harbor Hills
Bellerose
Bellerose Terrace
Alden Manor
Valley Stream
Woodmere
Cedarhurst
Lawrence
Inwood
Atlantic Beach
HUNTERS ISLAND
HIGH I.
HART ISLAND
CITY ISLAND
DAVIDS I.
PEA I.
GLEN I.
Orchard Beach
Pelham Bay Park
Eastchester Bay
Manhasset Bay
Little Neck Bay
RIKERS I.
N. BROTHER I.
S. BROTHER I.
WARDS I.
Randall's Island Park
La Guardia Airport
Flushing Bay
Flushing Meadows Corona Pk.
Forest Park
Highland Park
Prospect Park
Jamaica Bay
Grassy Bay
John F. Kennedy International Airport
GATEWAY NATIONAL RECREATION AREA
Jamaica Bay Wildlife Refuge/ Vis. Ctr.
Floyd Bennett Field
U.S. MARINE CORPS RES. CENTER
Rockaway Beach
Rockaway Park
Arverne
Edgemere
Far Rockaway
Broad Channel
Howard Beach
Canarsie
Flatlands
Flatbush
Gravesend
Sheepshead Bay
Manhattan Beach
Brighton Beach
Coney Island
N.Y. Aquarium
Kensington
Brownsville
Bedford-Stuyvesant
Williamsburg
Greenpoint
Astoria
Long Island City
Sunnyside
Woodside
Jackson Heights
Elmhurst
Rego Park
Forest Hills
Middle Village
Maspeth
Ridgewood
Bushwick
Glendale
Kew Gardens
Richmond Hill
Woodhaven
Ozone Park
Jamaica
Hollis
St. Albans
Rochdale
Laurelton
Rosedale
Springfield Gardens
Cambria Heights
Queens Village
Flushing
Whitestone
College Point
Bayside
Douglaston
Little Neck
Glen Oaks
Throg's Neck
Unionport
Parkchester
Morris Park
Baychester
Williamsbridge
Mott Haven
Hunts Point
Soundview
Harlem
Washington Hts.
Inwood Hill Park
The Cloisters
Yankee Stadium
Citi Field
USTA Billie Jean King Nat'l Tennis Ctr.
Aqueduct Race Track
Barclays Center
The Brooklyn Museum
Botanical Garden
Brooklyn Coll. (CUNY)
Kings Plaza Shop Ctr. & Marina
UBS Arena
Belmont Pk. Race Track
Green Acres Mall
Lawrence Yacht & C.C.
Silver Point Beach Club
Prospect Pt.
Sands Pt.
Barker Pt.
Hewlett Pt.
Elm Pt.
Locust Pt.
Clason Pt.
Hunts Pt.
College Pt.
Pond Rd.
TOLL
ATLANTIC OCEAN
0 1 2 mi
0 1 2 3 km

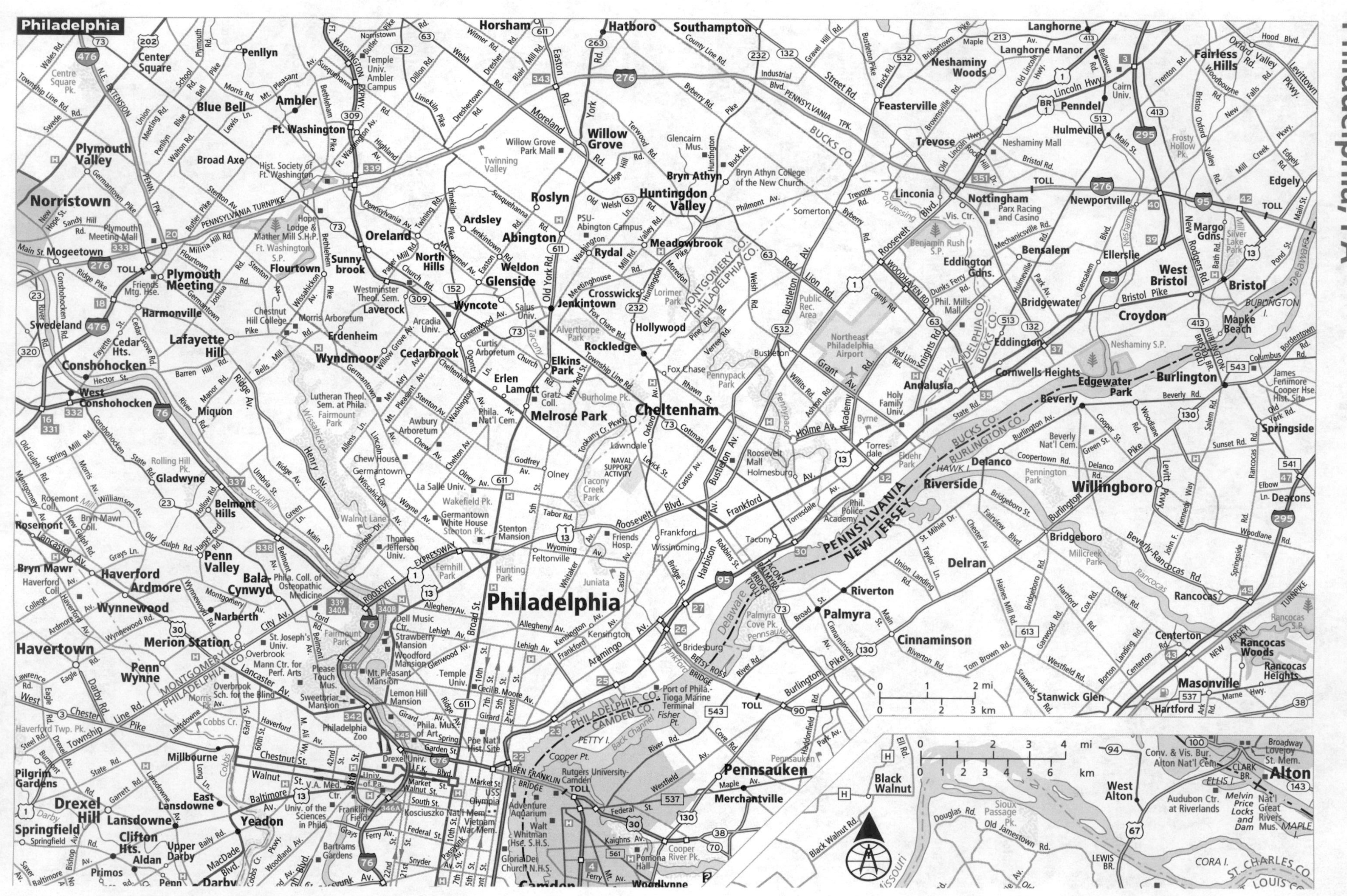
Philadelphia
Horsham
Hatboro
Southampton
Langhorne
Langhorne Manor
Fairless Hills
Levittown
Center Square
Penllyn
Blue Bell
Ambler
Ft. Washington
Plymouth Valley
Broad Axe
Norristown
Willow Grove
Roslyn
Huntingdon Valley
Bryn Athyn
Feasterville
Trevose
Neshaminy Woods
Penndel
Hulmeville
Linconia
Nottingham
Newportville
Edgely
Oreland
Ardsley
Abington
Rydal
Meadowbrook
Mogeetown
Plymouth Meeting
Flourtown
Sunny-brook
North Hills
Weldon
Glenside
Jenkintown
Crosswicks
Eddington Gdns.
Bensalem
Ellerslie
West Bristol
Bristol
Margo Gdns.
Harmonville
Laverock
Wyncote
Hollywood
Bridgewater
Croydon
Mapke Beach
Swedeland
Lafayette Hill
Erdenheim
Wyndmoor
Cedarbrook
Rockledge
Eddington
Conshohocken
West Conshohocken
Elkins Park
Erlen
Lamott
Cornwells Heights
Edgewater Park
Burlington
Andalusia
Beverly
Miquon
Melrose Park
Cheltenham
Springside
Gladwyne
Delanco
Riverside
Willingboro
Deacons
Belmont Hills
Rosemont
Penn Valley
Bryn Mawr
Haverford
Ardmore
Bala-Cynwyd
Wynnewood
Narberth
PENNSYLVANIA
NEW JERSEY
Bridgeboro
Delran
Riverton
Palmyra
Rancocas
Philadelphia
Merion Station
Havertown
Penn Wynne
Cinnaminson
Centerton
Rancocas Woods
Rancocas Heights
Masonville
Stanwick Glen
Hartford
Millbourne
Pilgrim Gardens
Drexel Hill
Springfield
Lansdowne
East Lansdowne
Yeadon
Clifton Hts.
Aldan
Upper Darby
Primos
Darby
Pennsauken
Merchantville
Black Walnut
West Alton
Alton
Northeast Philadelphia Airport
Delaware
Schuylkill
0 1 2 mi
0 1 2 3 km
0 1 2 3 4 mi
0 1 2 3 4 5 6 km

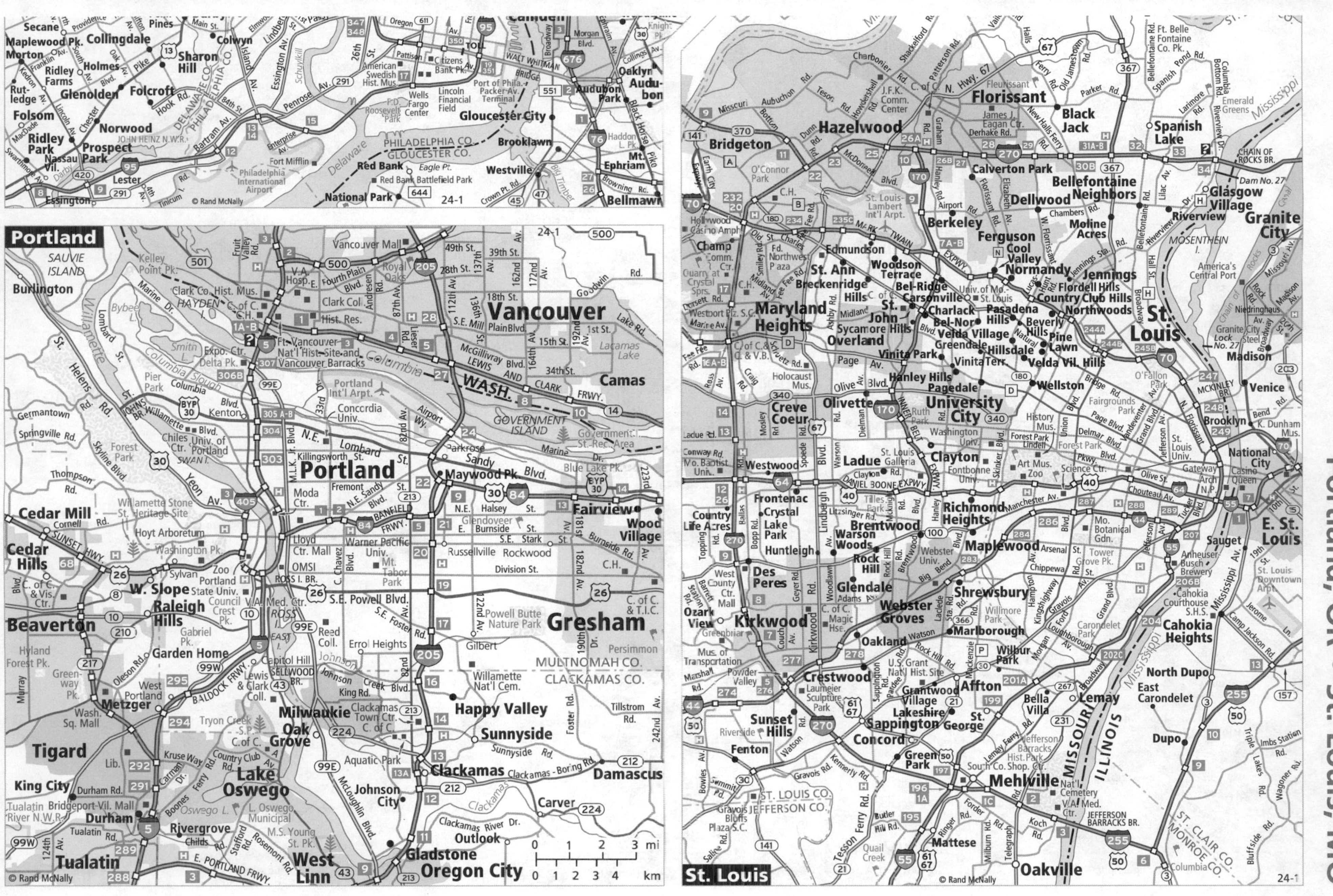
Portland
St. Louis
Vancouver
Camas
Gresham
Fairview
Wood Village
Beaverton
Tigard
Lake Oswego
Milwaukie
Oak Grove
Happy Valley
Sunnyside
Clackamas
Damascus
Oregon City
Gladstone
West Linn
Tualatin
Durham
King City
Cedar Mill
Cedar Hills
W. Slope
Raleigh Hills
Garden Home
Metzger
Rivergrove
Johnson City
MULTNOMAH CO.
CLACKAMAS CO.
Burlington
SAUVIE ISLAND
Florissant
Hazelwood
Bridgeton
Black Jack
Spanish Lake
Bellefontaine Neighbors
Calverton Park
Dellwood
Ferguson
Berkeley
Maryland Heights
Creve Coeur
Olivette
University City
Clayton
Ladue
Richmond Heights
Maplewood
Brentwood
Kirkwood
Webster Groves
Shrewsbury
Crestwood
Affton
Sunset Hills
Fenton
Mehlville
Oakville
Mattese
Granite City
Madison
Venice
Brooklyn
National City
E. St. Louis
Sauget
Cahokia Heights
North Dupo
East Carondelet
Dupo
Secane
Collingdale
Sharon Hill
Folcroft
Glenolden
Norwood
Ridley Park
Prospect Park
Gloucester City
Brooklawn
Westville
Red Bank
National Park
Bellmawr
Audubon
Mt. Ephriam
PHILADELPHIA CO.
GLOUCESTER CO.
© Rand McNally

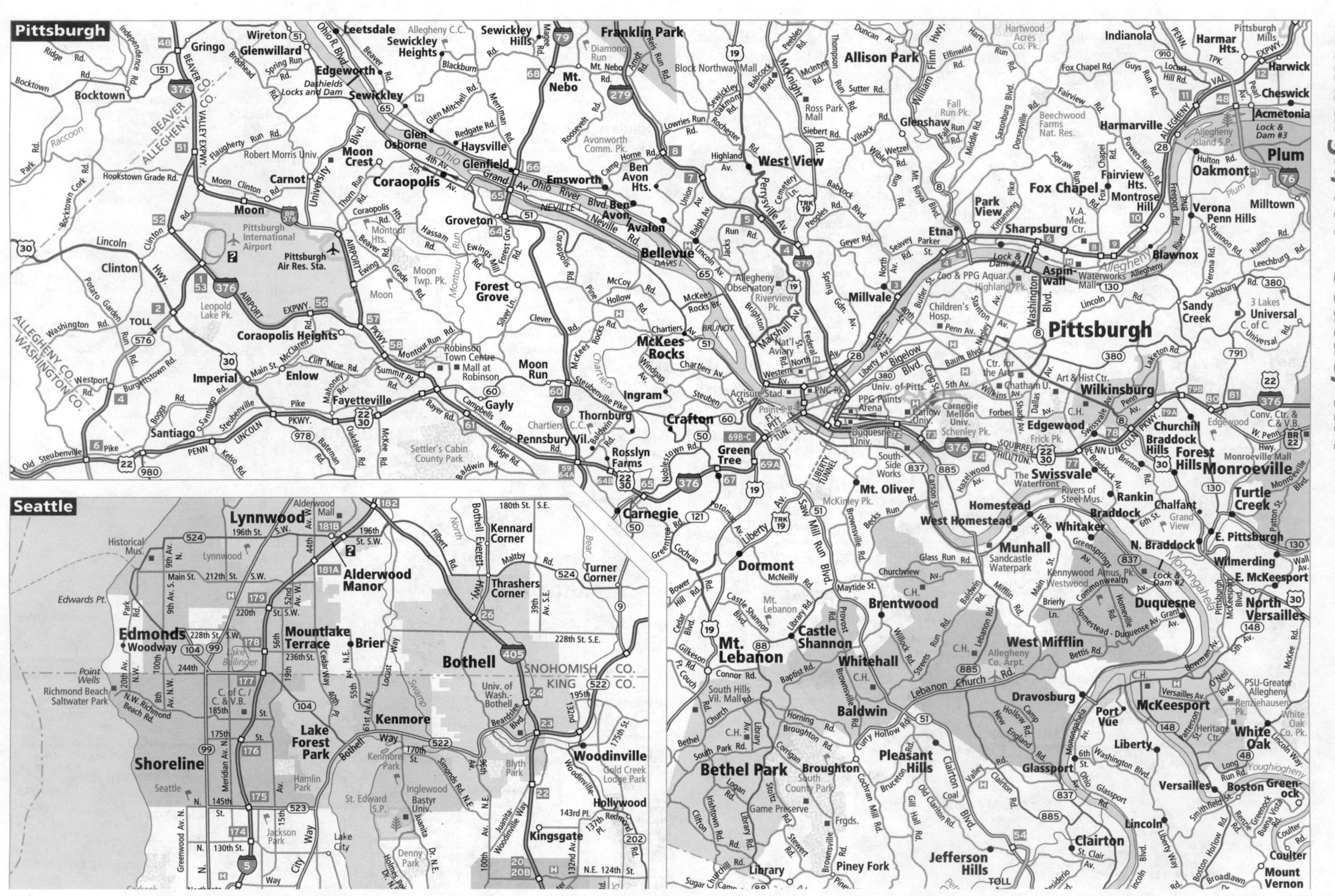

Pittsburgh
Seattle
Pittsburgh
Oakmont
Plum
Cheswick
Harwick
Harmar Hts.
Verona
Penn Hills
Milltown
Universal
Sandy Creek
Blawnox
Harmarville
Indianola
Fox Chapel
Sharpsburg
Aspinwall
Wilkinsburg
Churchill
Braddock Hills
Forest Hills
Monroeville
Turtle Creek
E. Pittsburgh
Wilmerding
E. McKeesport
North Versailles
White Oak
McKeesport
Versailles
Boston
Lincoln
Liberty
Port Vue
Clairton
Duquesne
Dravosburg
Glassport
West Mifflin
Homestead
West Homestead
Munhall
Whitaker
Rankin
Braddock
N. Braddock
Swissvale
Edgewood
Etna
Glenshaw
Allison Park
Millvale
Mt. Oliver
Brentwood
Whitehall
Baldwin
Pleasant Hills
Jefferson Hills
Piney Fork
Castle Shannon
Dormont
Mt. Lebanon
Bethel Park
Library
West View
Bellevue
Avalon
Ben Avon
Emsworth
McKees Rocks
Ingram
Crafton
Green Tree
Carnegie
Rosslyn Farms
Thornburg
Franklin Park
Mt. Nebo
Sewickley Hills
Haysville
Glenfield
Sewickley Heights
Leetsdale
Edgeworth
Sewickley
Glen Osborne
Coraopolis
Moon Crest
Groveton
Forest Grove
Moon Run
Gayly
Fayetteville
Coraopolis Heights
Enlow
Imperial
Santiago
Carnot
Moon
Glenwillard
Wireton
Gringo
Clinton
Bocktown
Pittsburgh International Airport
Pittsburgh Air Res. Sta.
ALLEGHENY CO.
WASHINGTON CO.
BEAVER CO.
Woodinville
Hollywood
Kingsgate
Bothell
Turner Corner
Thrashers Corner
Kennard Corner
Alderwood Manor
Brier
Kenmore
Mountlake Terrace
Lake Forest Park
Lynnwood
Edmonds
Woodway
Shoreline
SNOHOMISH CO.
KING CO.

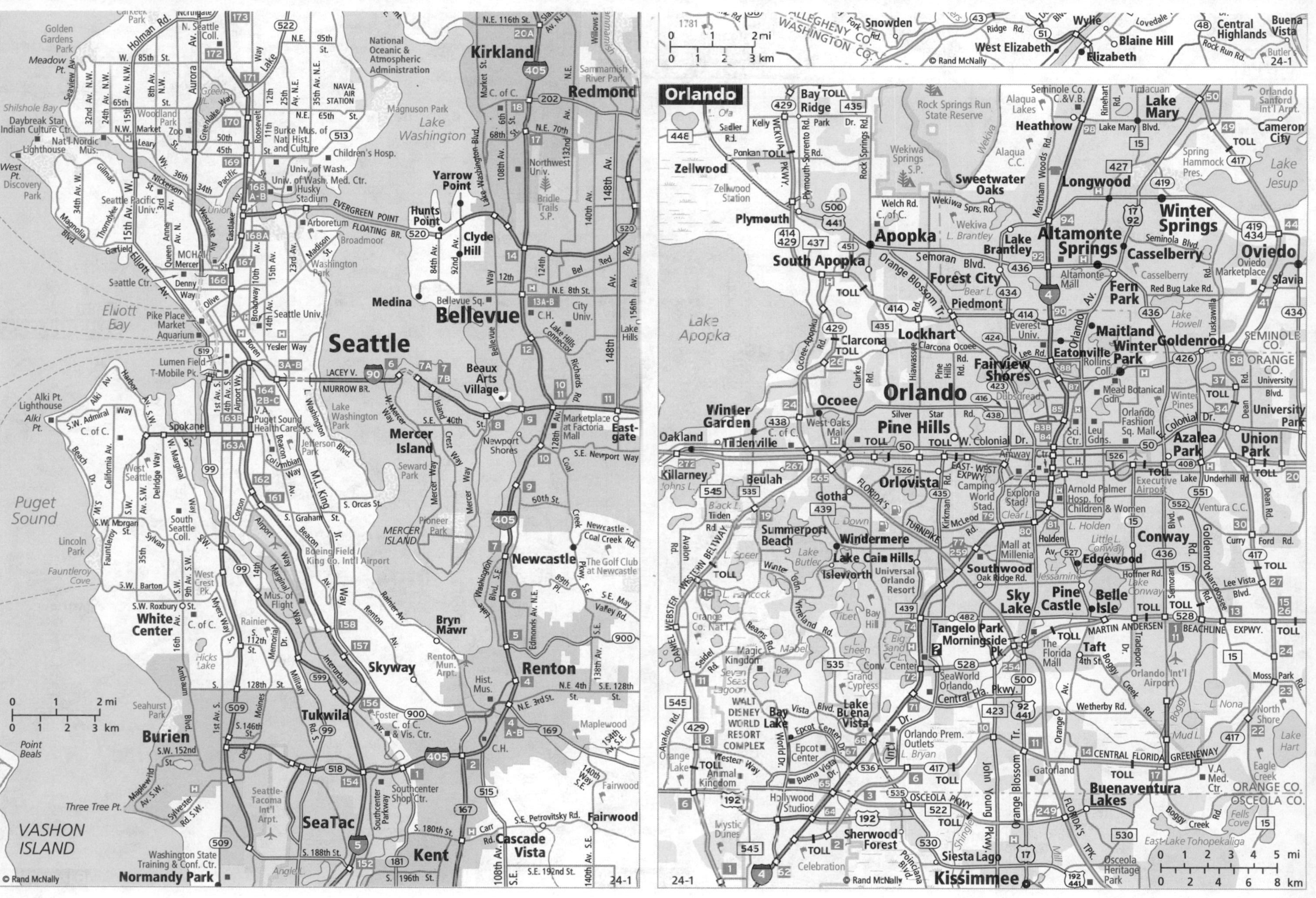
Seattle
Bellevue
Kirkland
Redmond
Renton
Newcastle
Mercer Island
Tukwila
SeaTac
Burien
Kent
White Center
Skyway
Medina
Lake Washington
Puget Sound
Elliott Bay
VASHON ISLAND
© Rand McNally
Orlando
Orlando
Apopka
Winter Park
Kissimmee
Oviedo
Winter Springs
Altamonte Springs
Lake Mary
Winter Garden
Ocoee
Pine Hills
Conway
Azalea Park
Union Park
Casselberry
Longwood
Maitland
Eatonville
Lockhart
Windermere
Buenaventura Lakes
Lake Apopka
© Rand McNally

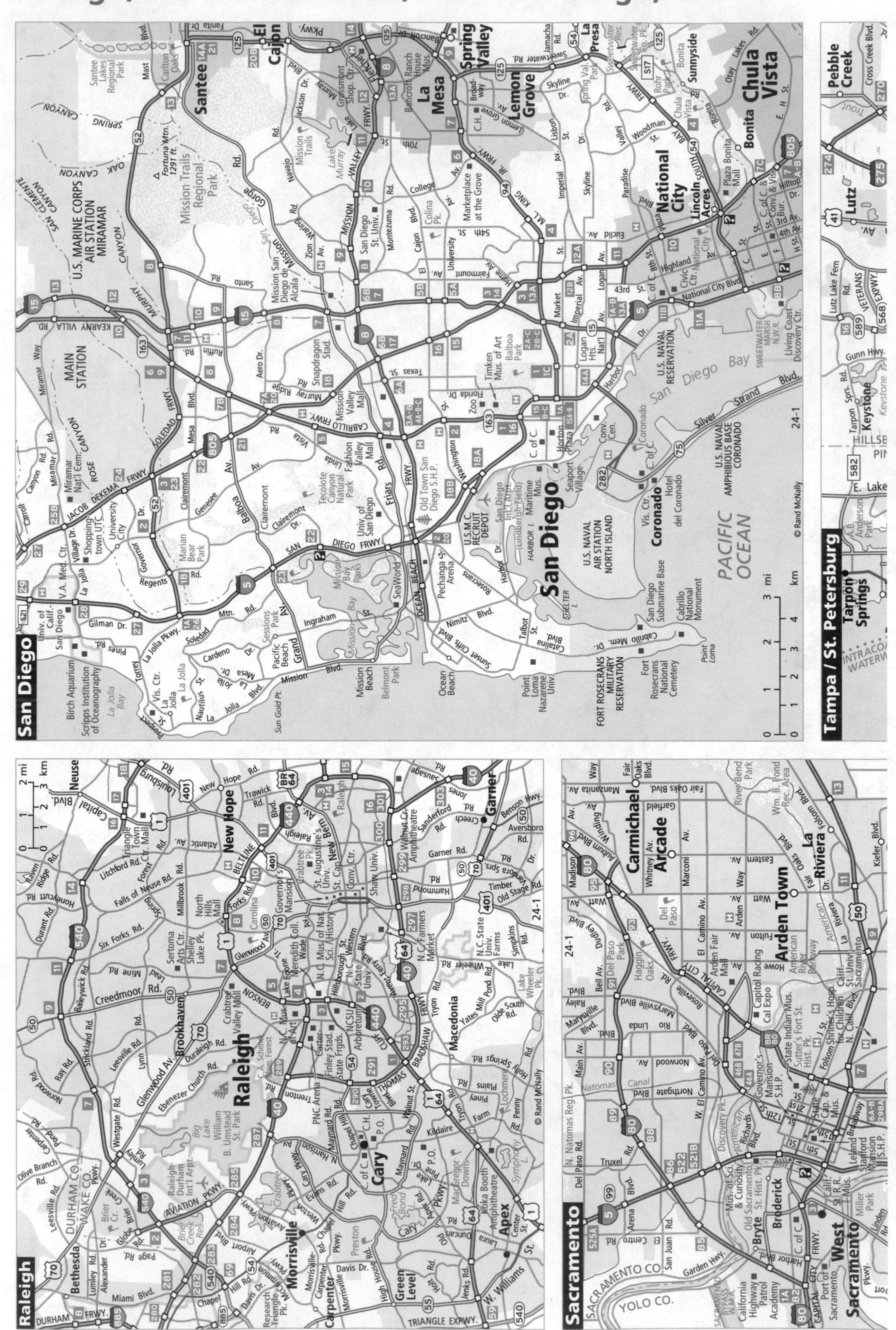

San Diego
Raleigh
Sacramento
Tampa / St. Petersburg
PACIFIC OCEAN
San Diego Bay
Chula Vista
National City
La Mesa
El Cajon
Spring Valley
Lemon Grove
Santee
Coronado
Cary
Garner
Apex
Morrisville
Carmichael
Arden Town
Arcade
West Sacramento
Broderick
© Rand McNally

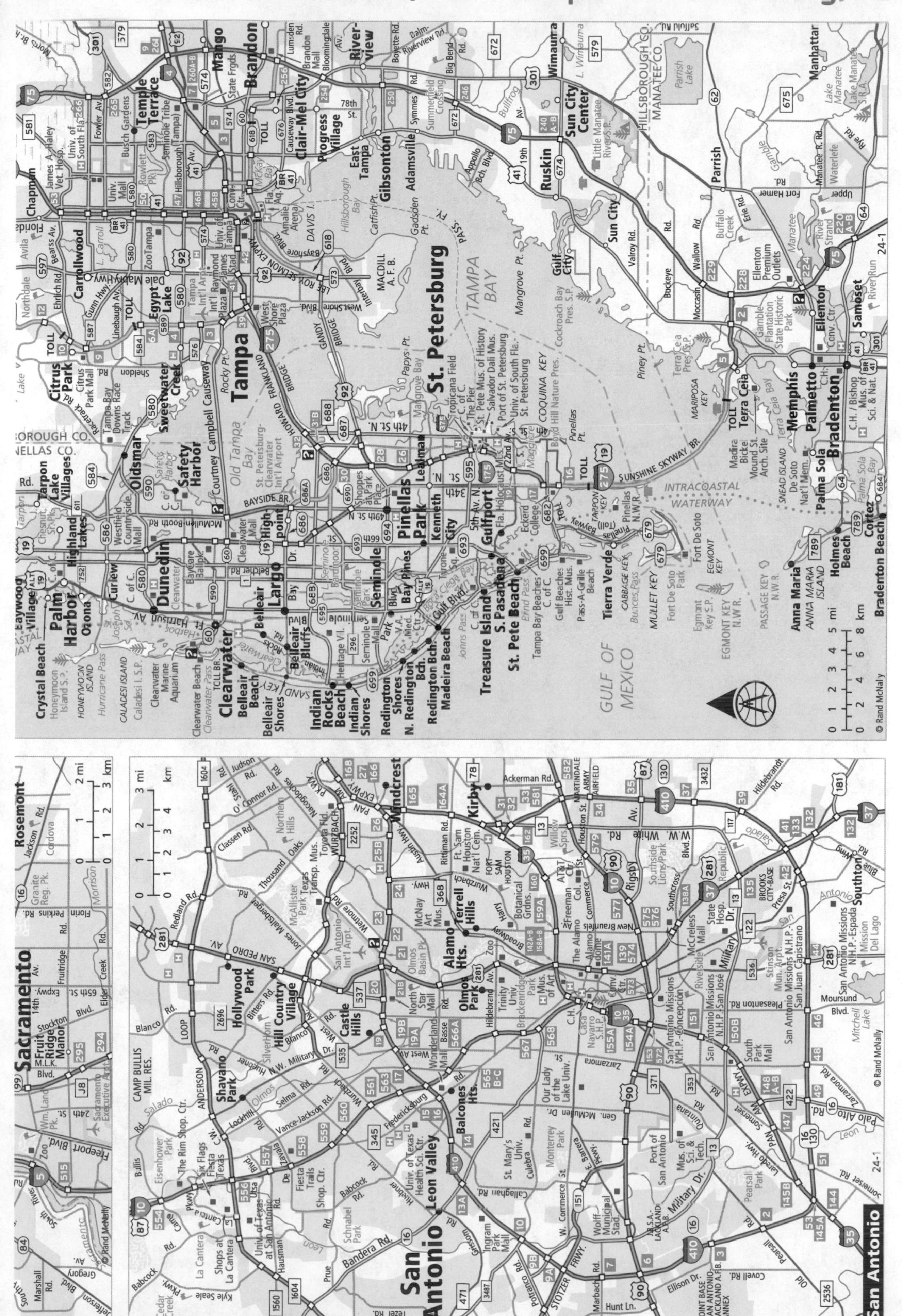
Tampa
St. Petersburg
Clearwater
Dunedin
Largo
Pinellas Park
Seminole
Gulfport
Oldsmar
Safety Harbor
Palm Harbor
Brandon
Temple Terrace
Ruskin
Sun City Center
Palmetto
Bradenton
Ellenton
Parrish
Apollo Bch. Blvd.
Tampa Bay
Gulf of Mexico
Sunshine Skyway Br.
Hillsborough Co.
Manatee Co.
Pinellas Co.
© Rand McNally
Sacramento
Rosemont
© Rand McNally
San Antonio
Alamo Hts.
Terrell Hills
Olmos Park
Castle Hills
Hollywood Park
Hill Country Village
Shavano Park
Balcones Hts.
Leon Valley
Windcrest
Kirby
Southton
© Rand McNally
San Antonio

Antioch
Pittsburg
Clayton
Concord
Clyde
Pacheco
Vine Hill
Martinez
Mountain View
Pleasant Hill
Walnut Creek
Lafayette
Saranap
Orinda
Moraga
Alamo
Danville
Diablo
Blackhawk
San Ramon
Dublin
Pleasanton
Castro Valley
Fairview
Cherryland
San Lorenzo
Ashland
San Leandro
Fairmont Terrace
Piedmont
Oakland
Alameda
Berkeley
Albany
Kensington
El Cerrito
Emeryville
Richmond
San Pablo
El Sobrante
Hercules
Pinole
Tara Hills
Rollingwood
North Richmond
San Francisco
South San Francisco
Brisbane
Daly City
Colma
Broadmoor
Pacifica
Sausalito
Tiburon
Belvedere
Strawberry
Mill Valley
Tamalpais Valley
Corte Madera
Larkspur
Kentfield
San Anselmo
San Rafael
Santa Venetia
Ross
Greenbrae
Marin City
SAN FRANCISCO BAY
PACIFIC OCEAN

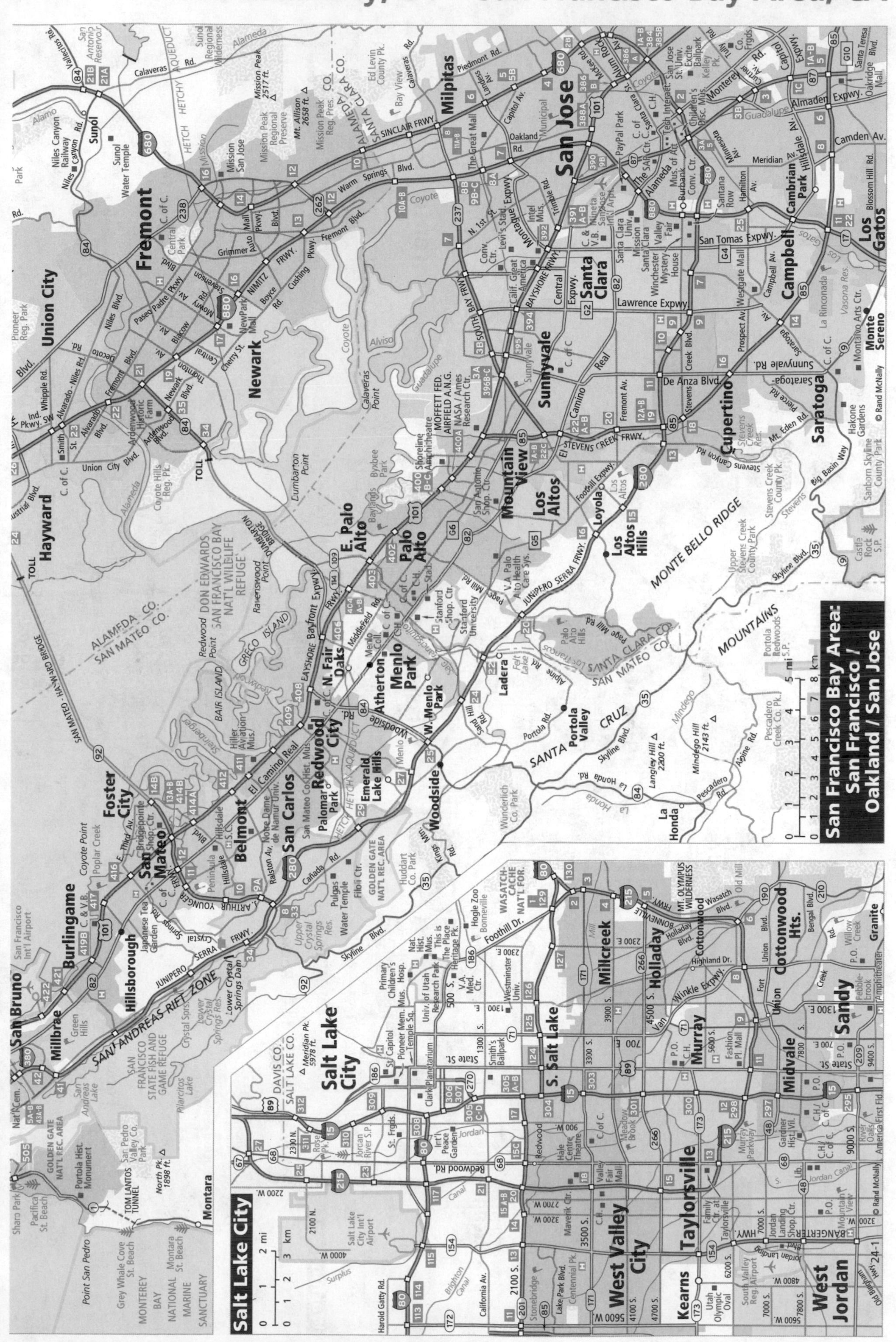
San Francisco Bay Area: San Francisco / Oakland / San Jose
Salt Lake City
© Rand McNally
San Jose
Fremont
Union City
Hayward
Newark
Milpitas
Santa Clara
Sunnyvale
Mountain View
Los Altos
Los Altos Hills
Palo Alto
E. Palo Alto
Menlo Park
Atherton
Redwood City
San Carlos
Belmont
Foster City
San Mateo
Burlingame
Hillsborough
Millbrae
San Bruno
Cupertino
Campbell
Los Gatos
Saratoga
Woodside
Portola Valley
La Honda
Montara
Salt Lake City
S. Salt Lake
Millcreek
Holladay
Murray
Cottonwood Hts.
Midvale
Sandy
West Valley City
Taylorsville
Kearns
West Jordan

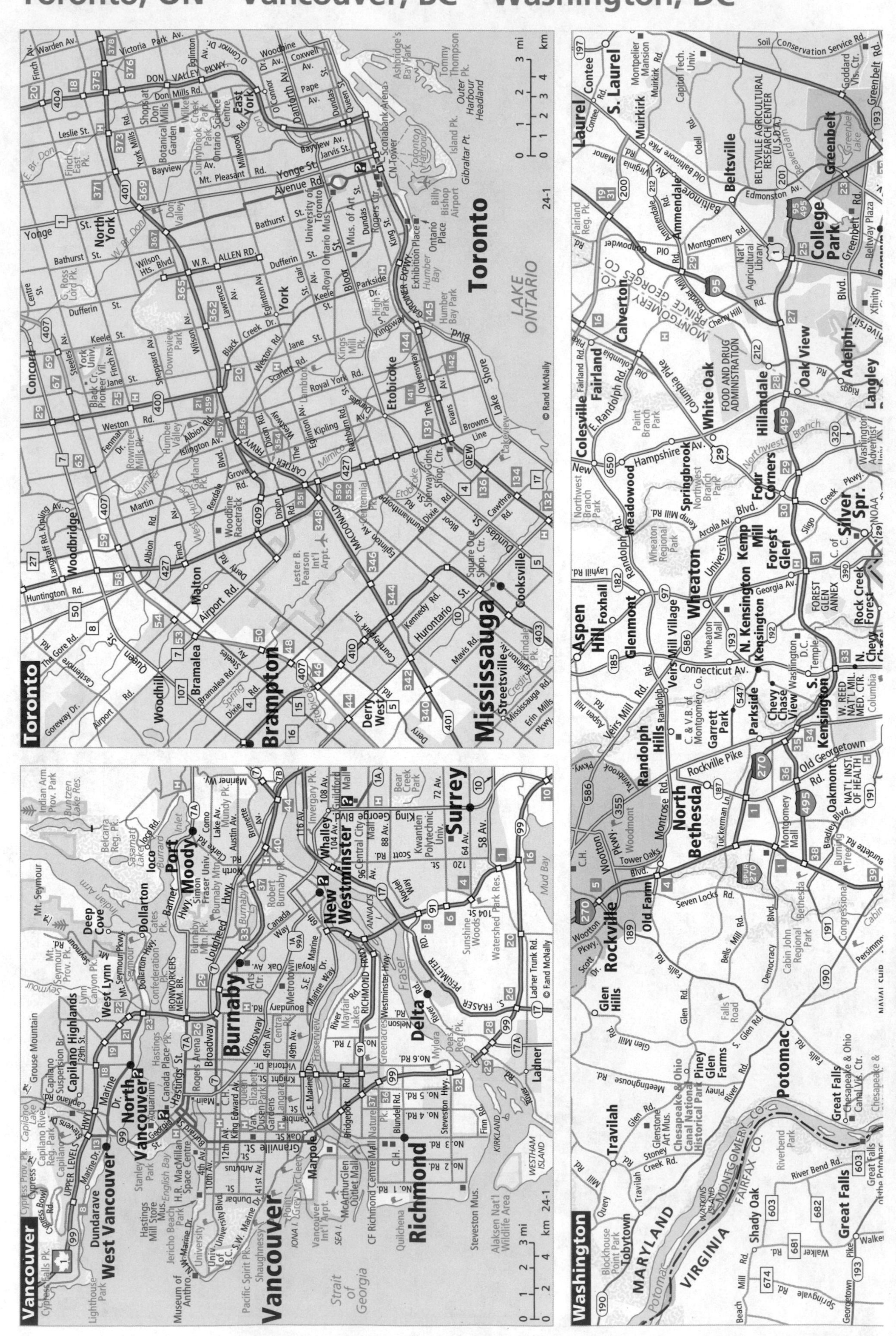
Toronto
Vancouver
Washington
© Rand McNally
LAKE ONTARIO
Mississauga
Brampton
Richmond
Surrey
Burnaby
North Vancouver
West Vancouver
Rockville
Potomac
College Park
MARYLAND
VIRGINIA

Washington
Arlington
Alexandria
Bethesda
Chevy Chase
Somerset
Friendship Vil.
Brookmont
Glen Echo
Cabin John
Cropley
McLean
Langley
Chesterbrook
Franklin Park
Lewinsville
Pimmit Hills
Tysons Corner
Dunn Loring
Vienna
Merrifield
Mantua
Fairfax
Oakton
Four Corners
Idylwood
Falls Church
Jefferson Vil.
Tyler Park
Broyhill Park
Holmes Run Acres
Seven Corners
Ravenwood
Culmore
Baileys Crossroads
Annalee Hts.
Masonville
Belvedere
Parklawn
Lincolnia Heights
Lincolnia
Weyanoke
Annandale
North Springfield
Ravensworth
Kings Park
Burke
Springfield
West Springfield
Barkers Crossroads
Chapel Acres
Franconia
Hayfield
Groveton
Virginia Hills
Wilton Woods
Huntington
Bucknell Manor
Hybla Valley
Belle Haven
New Alexandria
Wellington
Fort Foote Village
Friendly
Oxon Hill
Glassmanor
Forest Hts.
Barnaby Vil.
Hillcrest Hts.
Silver Hill
Suitland
Temple Hills
Camp Springs
Clinton
Oaklawn
Marlow Hts.
Morningside
District Heights
Forestville
Walker Mill
Coral Hills
Capitol Hts.
Seat Pleasant
Fairmount Heights
Cedar Hts.
Peppermill Village
Palmer Park
Kent Village
Columbia Pk.
Cheverly
Tuxedo
Landover
Landover Hills
Defense Hts.
Riverdale
Riverdale Park
University Park
Hyattsville
Edmonston
Bladensburg
Colmar Manor
Brentwood
Mt. Rainier
Cottage City
Chillum
Lewisdale
Takoma Park
New Carrollton
Lanham
Seabrook
Glenarden
Springdale
Ardmore
CAPITAL BELTWAY
George Washington Mem. Pkwy.
Potomac
Anacostia
JOINT BASE ANDREWS-NAVAL AIR FACILITY WASHINGTON
BOLLING A.F.B.
ANACOSTIA NAVAL STATION
FORT MYER
ARLINGTON NAT'L CEM.
The Pentagon
Ronald Reagan Wash. Nat'l Arpt.
White House
PRINCE GEORGES CO.
ARLINGTON CO.
FAIRFAX CO.
MD.
VA.
0 1 2 mi
0 1 2 3 km
© Rand McNally

Mexico

Population: 128,932,753
Land Area: 750,558 sq. mi.
Capital: Mexico City

Cities and Towns

Acaponeta D-4
Acapulco F-6
Acayucan E-8
Aguascalientes D-5
Arriaga F-8
Atlixco E-7
Autlán de Navarro E-5
Bahía Kino B-3
Bermejillo C-5
Buenaventura B-4
Campeche E-9
Cancún D-10
Champotón E-9
Chetumal E-10
Chihauhua B-4
Chilpancingo F-6
Choix C-4
Cintalapa F-8
Ciudad Camargo C-6
Ciudad del Carmen E-9
Ciudad de México E-6
Ciudad Juárez A-4
Ciudad Madero D-7
Ciudad Mante D-6
Ciudad Obregón B-3
Ciudad Valles D-6
Ciudad Victoria D-6
Coatzacoalcos E-8
Colima E-5
Cozumel D-10
Cuajinicuilapa F-7
Cuauhtémoc B-4
Cuernavaca E-6
Culiacán C-4
Durango D-5
El Fuerte C-4
El Sueco B-4
Ensenada A-2
Escárcega E-9
Fresnillo D-5
Gómez Palacio C-5
Guadalajara E-5
Guamúchil C-4
Guanajuato D-6
Guaymas B-3
Guerrero B-4
Guzmán E-5
Hermosillo B-3
Hidalgo del Parral C-4
Huajuapan de León E-7
Iguala E-6
Irapuato E-6
Jalpa D-5
Jiménez C-5
Juan Aldama C-5
La Paz C-3
La Pesca D-7
León D-6
Linares C-6
Loreto C-3
Los Mochis C-4
Manzanillo E-5
Matamoros C-7
Matehuala D-6
Mazatlán D-4
Mérida D-9
Mexicali A-2
Mexico City E-6
Monclova C-6
Monterrey C-6
Morelia E-6
Navojoa B-3
Nogales A-3
Nueva Rosita B-6
Nuevo Casas Grandes A-4
Nuevo Laredo B-6
Oaxaca F-7
Ojinaga B-5
Orizaba E-7
Pachuca E-6
Parras C-5
Piedras Negras B-6
Pitiquito A-3
Poza Rica E-7
Puebla E-7
Puerto Ángel F-7
Puerto Escondido F-7
Puerto Morelos D-10
Puerto Peñasco A-2
Puerto Vallarta E-5
Punta Prieta B-2
Querétaro E-6
Reynosa C-7
Río Lagartos D-10
Rosario A-2
Sabinas B-6
Sabinas Hidalgo C-6
Sahuaripa B-4
Salamanca E-6
Saltillo C-6
San Blas D-5
San Carlos C-3
San Felipe A-2
San Fernando C-7
San Francisco del Oro C-4
San José del Cabo D-3
San Luis Potosí D-6
Santa Ana A-3
Santa Bárbara C-4
Santa Rosalia B-3
Santo Domingo Tehuàntepec F-8
Tamazunchale D-6
Tampico D-7
Tapachula F-8
Taxco E-6
Tepehuanes C-4
Tepic D-5
Tijuana A-1
Tlaxcala E-7
Toluca E-6
Tónichi B-3
Topolobampo C-3
Torreón C-5
Tuxpan D-7
Tuxtla Gutiérrez F-8
Uruapan E-5
Veracruz E-7
Villahermosa E-8
Villagrán C-6
Xalapa E-7
Zacatecas D-5
Zihuatanejo F-6

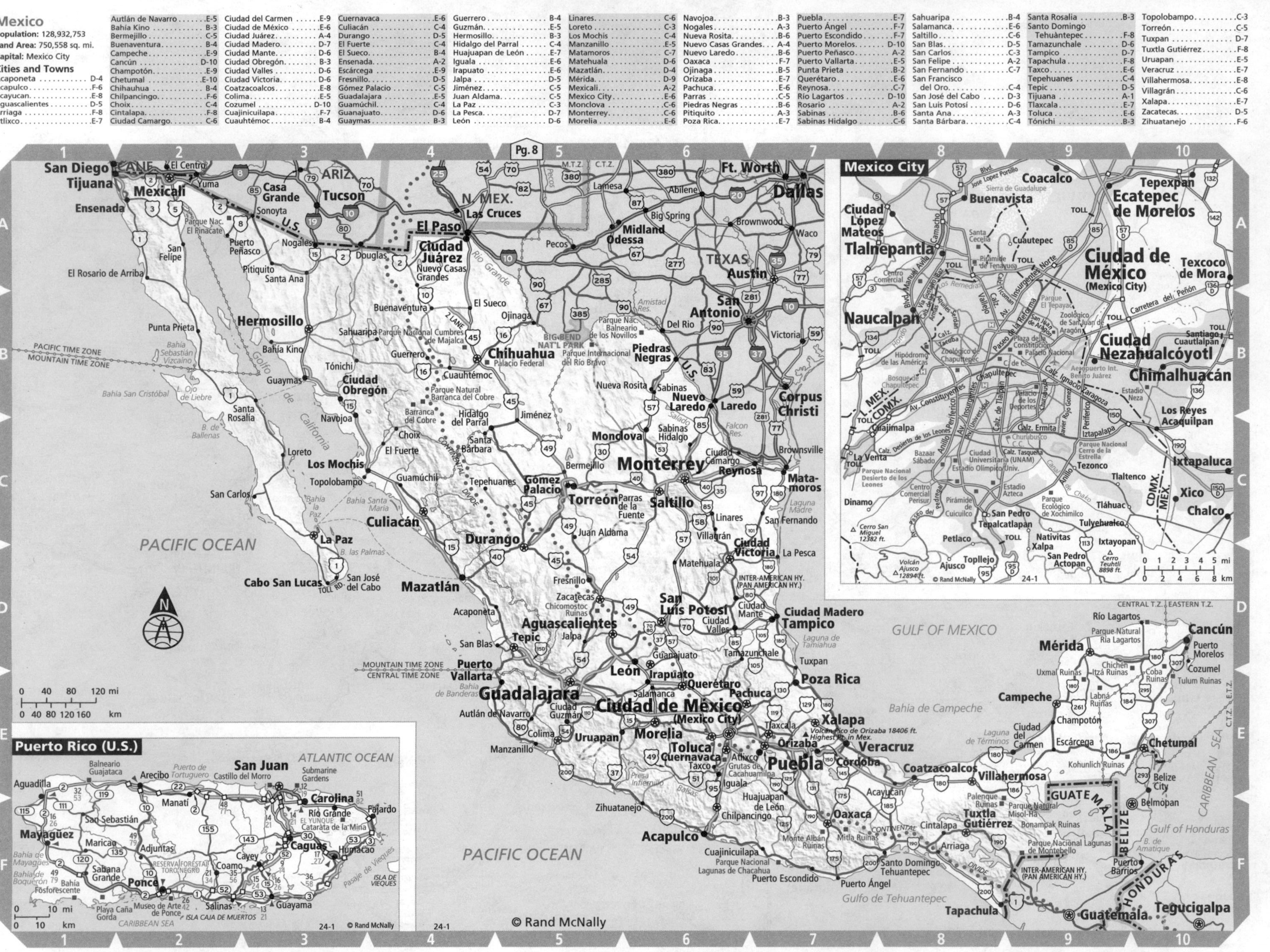